Look Smarter Than You Are with Essbase 11

An Administrator's Guide

Edward Roske
Tracy McMullen

1ˢᵗ Edition

interRel Press, Arlington, Texas

Look Smarter Than You Are with Essbase 11
An Administrator's Guide

Edward Roske
Tracy McMullen

Published by:

interRel Press
A Division of interRel Consulting Partners
Suite 304
1000 Ballpark Way
Arlington, TX 76011

Copyright © 2009-Present by Edward Roske and Tracy McMullen
1st edition
Printed in the United States of America

Library of Congress Cataloging-in-Publication Data
Roske, Edward and McMullen, Tracy
Look Smarter Than You Are with Essbase 11

Edward Roske, Tracy McMullen 1st ed.
p. 668 cm.
Includes index.
ISBN 978-0-557-06351-2

Trademarks
Various trademarked names appear throughout this book. Rather than list all the names and the companies/individuals that own those trademarks or try to insert a trademark symbol every time a trademarked name is mentioned, the author and publisher state that they are using the names only for editorial purposes and to the benefit of the trademark owner with no intention of trademark infringement.

To

Paulet Howard

who taught me that

"the strong take it from the weak,
but the wise take it from the strong."

Edward Roske

ABOUT THE AUTHORS

Edward Roske fell in love with Hyperion at first sight. In 1995, Edward was working for the Moore Business Forms printing facility in Mundelein, Illinois. While his official title was "Coordinator of Finance", his role focused on coordinating the linking of many, many Microsoft Excel sheets. When someone in his area would delete a row in a supporting workbook and #REF errors would show up in the summary workbook, Edward personally tracked them down cell-by-cell. When he saw his first demonstration of Arbor Essbase (as it was known at the time), he quit his job to become a full-time Essbase consultant (becoming in the process one of those rare individuals who quit a stable job to consult on a product for which he had absolutely no experience).

Edward is a pioneer. He was one of the first Essbase Certified consultants in the world. He was also one of the first people in the world to become certified in Hyperion Planning. While at Moore, he also obtained his first patent proving that there are still new ideas waiting to be discovered and exploited for financial gain.

In May of 1997, Edward left his senior consulting position with a Chicago-based firm to co-found interRel Consulting along with Eduardo Quiroz. Proving that being humble will get you nowhere, Edward helped write interRel's original motto: "Reaching for perfection, we deliver the impossible in record time." He has been the CEO of interRel Consulting since its inception growing them to be a multi-million dollar firm with offices from coast-to-coast.

Edward still keeps his Essbase skills sharp. He has overseen successful Hyperion implementations at over 100 companies. His optimizations have resulted in Essbase calculation improvements of more than 99.99%.

Continuing his quest to become the world's foremost Essbase-evangelist, Edward has been a regular speaker at annual Hyperion user conferences since 1995 and he is noted for his humorous slant to technically boring information. He is the Essbase Domain Lead for the Oracle Applications Users Group (OAUG) and chair of the Hyperion track for the Oracle Developer Users Group's (ODTUG) annual Kaleidoscope conference. Recently, Oracle awarded him the title of "Oracle ACE Director." Visit Edward's blog at **http://looksmarter.blogspot.com/**.

Though not especially relevant, he also likes puppies.

ABOUT THE AUTHORS

Tracy McMullen, Oracle ACE Director, has been leading the development of Enterprise Performance Management and Data Warehousing applications for over 10 years. Roles on projects have ranged from developer, to architect and project manager on technologies from Hyperion and Business Objects to Cognos and Oracle. She's seen all of the business intelligence tools and Hyperion is her favorite.

Tracy started her career at Arthur Andersen Business Consulting on a project programming in RPG (fun stuff!). Thankfully, her next project introduced her to the world of multi-dimensional databases with a Cognos PowerPlay implementation for an oil and gas client (many years ago Tracy was certified in Cognos PowerPlay and Impromptu). Next, she helped clients from various industries revolutionize their information delivery with Hyperion and other technologies. After years of successful business intelligence implementations, a few shredded documents changed her career path from future Partner to eliminating cancer.

Tracy next joined The University of Texas M.D. Anderson Cancer Center where she lead the charge in implementing budget and planning solutions utilizing Hyperion Planning. Fate stepped in once again with relocation to the South Texas Coast and Tracy found her new home with interRel Consulting as Director of Special Projects (which really means she does a million different things from consulting to training to project management to sales).

Tracy is a Hyperion Certified Consultant for Hyperion Essbase, Hyperion Certified Solutions Architect for Hyperion Planning and a Certified Project Management Professional (PMP). Tracy has been a regular instructor at interRel, Hyperion's user conferences and other professional seminars since 2000 on topics including information delivery, business intelligence, data warehousing, and Hyperion implementations. Visit Tracy's blog at **http://looksmarterthanyouare2.blogspot.com/.** Her strong technical background is complimented by comprehensive practical experience in project management, a skill important not only on the job but at home as well where she manages her kids on a daily basis (ok, she attempts to manage with moderate success).

ABOUT INTERREL CONSULTING

Integrated solutions are key to providing our clients the timely information they need to make critical business decisions. Our philosophy, experience, and methodologies are integral components of our application development, project management, optimization and training. As a result of our experience and commitment to excellence, interRel has become one of the premier providers of analytical solutions using Oracle BI and Hyperion solutions.

interRel solves business problems through utilizing Business Intelligence (BI) and Enterprise Performance Management (EPM) technologies. Our EPM Assessment is designed to identify an organization's current EPM current state relative to the corporate strategy.

interRel has been in business since 1997, and we take pride in delivering our solutions with small teams composed of members with an average of over eight years of Oracle Hyperion and BI related tools, application and consulting experience.

Exclusive EPM/BI consultancy

- 100% of revenue is Oracle EPM / BI-Derived
- 100% of Consultants specialize in Oracle EPM System/Hyperion
- 100% of Senior Consultants are Hyperion Certified
- Senior Consultants have 8+ years of experience
- Junior Consultants have 5+ years of experience

Oracle Hyperion Community - Training, Free Webcasts, and More

Through our various outlets, our focus is always to interact and help others in the Oracle Hyperion community.

If you like this book, join us in person for a hands-on training class. interRel Consulting offers classroom education on a full spectrum of EPM/BI solutions, including standard course offerings such as *Essbase and Planning Accelerated Fundamentals*, tailored for new Administrators as well as unique advanced courses like *Essbase Calc Scripts for Mere Mortals*. All classes are taught by knowledgeable, certified trainers whose experience combines to an average of 8+ years. This interactive environment allows attendees the opportunity to master the skill sets needed to implement, develop and manage EPM/BI solutions successfully. All classes are held at headquarters in Dallas and offer CPE accreditation. interRel Consulting also provides custom training to clients.

interRel Consulting proudly offers free weekly webcasts. These webcasts include the full scope of Oracle BI and EPM System (Hyperion) products, including Essbase, Planning & HFM. Webcasts are primarily held every non-holiday week and twice in most weeks. Topics include 'Tips, Tricks & Best Practices,' which gives you an insider's guide to optimize the usage of your solution. The 'Administration' series focuses on making your job easier and giving a snapshot of the Accelerated Fundamentals course outline while the 'Overview' webcasts discuss the highlights of a solution and how it can be used effectively. All webcasts include interactive examples and demonstrations to see how the products really work.

Awards & Recognitions

- 2008 Oracle Titan Award winner for "EPM Solution" of the year
- 2008 Oracle Excellence Award winner with Pearson Education
- One of the fastest growing companies in USA (Inc. Magazine, '08)
- The only company in the world *of any kind* with two Oracle ACE Directors and one Oracle ACE

interRel's commitment to providing our customers with unsurpassed customer service and unmatched expertise make interRel the partner of choice for a large number of companies across the world. To learn more, visit **www.interrel.com**.

ACKNOWLEDGEMENTS

If we were to thank all of those who assisted us in the creation of this book, we would have to not only personally mention hundreds of people but also several companies and one or two federal agencies (though we will give a special shout-out to those wacky guys over at the Internal Revenue Service: keep it real, yo!). Suffice to say, if this book stands tall, it is only by balancing on the heads of giants.

Those contributing significant content to this book include Eduardo "Short Stack" Quiroz and John "Grumpy Smurf" Scott, though most of their actual submissions were later removed due to incorrectness, decency laws and the unanimous decision by the authors that delivery of technical information in sonata verse, though revolutionary, would not be acceptable to the audience of this book. Thanks also to Kelli Stein, Lisa DeJohn, Christopher "CTI" Solomon, Debbie Riter, Josie Manzano, and Robin Banks.

Thank you to Laura Gregor, Jane Arrington, Donna Garner, and Steve Press for being long-time, strong supporters. We would like to thank some of the product folks at Oracle for their insight and advice: thanks to Shubhomoy Bhattacharya, Guillaume Arnaud, Shankar Viswanathan, Al Marciante, Aneel Shenker, John O'Rourke, Rich Clayton, and Mike Nader.

Our guest authors deserve a special acknowledgement for actually volunteering to submit content for our book. Thank you to: Troy Seguin–Sharing Data, Josie Manzano, Rob Donohue-LCM, Rick Sawa-Advanced Tuning for BSO, and Gary Crisci-Analytic Dimensions for ASO.

A special thank you is extended to John Kopcke for agreeing to write our foreword.

Edward also wants to say "thank you" to Melissa Vorhies Roske, Vanessa Roske, and Eliot Roske for giving up their time with him on evenings and weekends, so he could make his publishing deadline. On a related note, Edward would also like to thank in advance anyone who can figure out a way to get rid of publishing deadlines.

Tracy McMullen would like to thank Blanche and Randy McMullen Sr. for babysitting so that she could write a large portion of this book. Thanks to mom and dad, Dot and Bob Collins, for their never-ending support and Randy, Taylor and Reese for their patience and understanding.

We give our sincerest gratitude to all the people above, and we hope that they feel that this book is partly theirs as well (just without the fame, glory and most importantly, the royalties).

DISCLAIMER

This book is designed to provide supporting information about the related subject matter. It is being sold to you and/or your company with the understanding that the authors and the publisher are not engaged by you to provide legal, accounting, or any other professional services of any kind. If assistance is required (legal, expert, or otherwise), seek out the services of a competent professional such as a consultant.

It is not the purpose of this book to reprint all of the information that is already available on the subject at hand. The purpose of this book is to complement and supplement other texts already available to you. For more information (especially including technical reference information), please contact the software vendor directly or use your on-line help.

Great effort has been made to make this book as complete and accurate as possible. That said, there may be errors both typographic and in content. As such, use this book only as a general guide and not as the ultimate source for specific information on the software product. Further, this book contains information on the software that was generally available as of the publishing date.

The purpose of this book is to entertain while educating. The author and interRel Press shall have neither liability nor responsibility to any person living or dead or entity currently or previously in existence with respect to any loss or damage caused or alleged to be caused directly, indirectly, or otherwise by the information contained in this book.

If you do not wish to abide by all parts of the above disclaimer, please stop reading now and return this book to the publisher for a full refund.

TABLE OF CONTENTS

FOREWORD

When I was told that someone outside of Hyperion was finally going to write a book on Hyperion Essbase, I was neither surprised nor impressed. Not surprised because, with over three million Essbase users worldwide, it was actually an anomaly that there was no independent book on learning the leading multidimensional database analytics platform. Sure, there are plenty of training classes out there and Hyperion had always included the Database Administrator's Guide and the Essbase Excel Add-In manuals with the software, but you couldn't go out to Amazon.com and find a book on Essbase.

And so why I wasn't impressed? Over the years, I've heard at least a hundred people say, "As soon as I get the time, I'm going to write the first Essbase book." This is generally followed by a mighty rough estimate of the tens of thousands of copies that will be sold in just the first year, as well as the proposed title. I must have heard "Essbase for Fun and Profit" proposed at least ten times. Purely for my own amusement, I often ask those people months later how the Essbase book is going. The reply is something along the lines of, "Well, things have gotten really busy, what with the economy and all."

Now, I am impressed. Edward Roske and Tracy McMullen have finally written the Essbase book. While I don't expect that it will ever be a *New York Times* bestseller, it may well be remembered in the Hyperion world as our *Da Vinci Code*. End users will pick up a copy to help figure out better ways to use the Essbase Add-In. Administrators will buy it to help build a better application. Companies may one day give out copies to new Essbase users instead of leaving them to figure it out on their own.

I've been architecting decision support systems for over 25 years, and I've been involved with Essbase virtually since its inception. I'm proud that yet another avenue has been opened to bring this great product to even more people. Use the information in it to become the Essbase expert at your company.

John Kopcke
Senior Vice President of BI & EPM
Oracle Corporation
March 30, 2007

What is Essbase?

Chapter 1:
Worst Mistake Ever

It was a dark and stormy night on the streets of New Orleans. Actually, it was mid-afternoon and I was in an office building, but that's a lousy way to start a story. Outside, it was very stormy, though, and that did make it much darker than it should have been. The year was 1998, and Entergy Corporation, the largest power company in Louisiana and the primary provider of electricity to New Orleans sent out a summons for Edward Roske to report to their corporate headquarters in the Big Easy. The server room was more than twenty stories up in a building overlooking downtown.

Entergy had been trying to get Crystal Reports to talk to Essbase (version 3.2, if I recall correctly). That was back in the days when Crystal was its own company and Essbase was the primary product of a Sunnyvale, California startup named Arbor. I had a reputation at the time for being a troubleshooter and Entergy needed some trouble shot. While we hadn't gotten into the details yet, I did know that Essbase was shutting down whenever someone tried to connect to it with Crystal. Arbor tech support and Crystal tech support were blaming each other when they weren't trying to blame the hardware. Since I was one of the few consultants in the world with both a Crystal and an Essbase background, I was truly their last option. The pressure to solve the problem was intense and you could feel the electricity in the room. Of course, being in a server room of a power company, this made perfect sense.

There must have been twenty people crowded around the server to watch me begin by recreating the problem. Even with the windows looking out on to the city, my claustrophobia was kicking into high gear. I diligently followed the instructions of Entergy's Essbase administrator. I hesitated before clicking the button that would execute the query and, presumably, crash the Essbase server. I wanted to make sure that I observed precisely what happened in order to quickly solve the problem, save the day, and get on a Southwest flight back to Dallas where it wasn't nearly as stormy. "When I click here, everything will shut down, right?" Their administrator assured me that it would, so I pressed the button, and the monitor shut off.

For that matter, all the lights in the server room shut off... and the servers themselves shut off. We went over to the window since server rooms are quite spooky with the lights off. We looked down twenty-plus stories to the street below and were shocked to realize that power was off to the entire city. My heart stopped and everyone turned to me.

We stood speechless in the dark until the back-up generators kicked in. Power was eventually restored. That was the only day of consulting I've ever done at Entergy and considering what happened, I don't even think we billed them for my time. It turns out that the storm had knocked power out to greater New Orleans and my Essbase actions were nothing but proof that God has a very dry sense of humor. For a time, though, I *knew* that I had committed the worst Essbase blunder ever.

I'm writing this book so that *you* will not repeat my mistakes.

Edward Roske

Chapter 2:
Analyze Essbase Data

A traditional computer book would begin at the beginning, giving you the complete history of the topic at hand from when the product was a twinkle in the eye of its creator through all the various versions up to the current, cutting edge product. This book will do no such thing. While we will cover the history of Essbase, let's first grab a beverage and actually learn to do something (connect to Essbase, retrieve data, learn about dimensions and members, analyze data, set options and more).

Imagine a company that sells soft drinks. The Beverage Company sells products across the United States and they want to find out which products and markets are profitable and which are losing money faster than their poorly named drink from 2001, "Diet Enron with Lemon."

To help with their analysis, they bought a product from Oracle called Essbase. They followed the more than 400 pages of instructions to get Essbase installed. During installation, they chose to install the sample applications and were pleasantly surprised to find that one of those applications was dedicated to analyzing The Beverage Company proving that Carson Daly and Earl were right about Karma.

To follow along as a temporary employee of TBC (**The Beverage Company**, *do* try to keep up), make sure that whoever installed Essbase at your company installed the sample applications. Until she's prepared the sample applications, you can either stop reading or follow along in your own mind instead of on the computer. If you are the administrator, check out the Essbase Database Administrator Guide (DBAG) online for the steps to set up the sample applications:

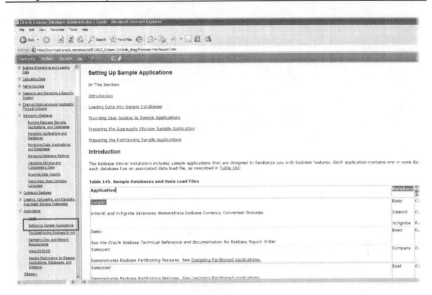

CONNECTING TO ESSBASE WITH SMART VIEW

Go ahead and launch Microsoft Excel. If you are in Excel 2007, you should see the *Hyperion* ribbon appear on your menu bar (in Excel 2003, you will find it under *Add-in* menu). At this point, temporary TBC employee, you're probably faced with a blank Excel workbook and you have no idea where to begin. Luckily, you have a book, so go up to the *Hyperion* menu and near the left side of the ribbon, you will see *Data Source Manager*:

Some of you will be saying "Wait, I don't see a ribbon. I'm on Office 2003." Never fear, you will find all of the same options under the Hyperion menu option. You'll use this menu for performing actions and should see all of the same commands like Zoom In and Refresh plus more. For those of you on Office 2007, you can also access the Hyperion menu for the full list of functions. This Hyperion menu is available under Add-ins ribbon:

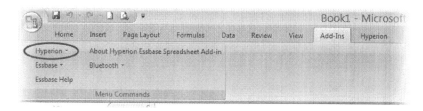

Note!

If you have read the end user companion guide to this book, *Look Smarter Than You Are with Smart View 11x and Essbase*, you may be experiencing a bit of déjà vu. We pulled the first two chapters of that book to help provide a basic introduction to the end user perspective for this Essbase administration book. If you haven't read the Smart View book, we encourage you to check that book out as well. We only see the tip of the ice berg in this book related to end user reporting and analysis capabilities.

Now where were we? Oh, yes, connecting to Essbase. Before you click *Data Source Manager*, though, notice some of the items in the *Hyperion* ribbon that we'll be using later. For instance, one menu option is *Refresh*. Presumably, we'll be using this to refresh data from Essbase. When we want to drill-down to detailed information, we'll be using *Zoom In*. When we need to send data back into Essbase (for budgeting, say), we'll use the *Submit Data* option. Before you begin to question whether or not you need this book if Essbase is going to be so darned easy to use, click *Data Source Manager*. From there click on the red text *Connect to Provider Services*:

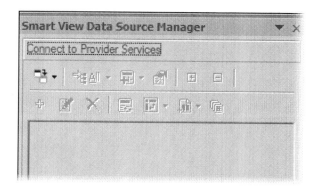

If this is the first time you've used the Smart View add-in, you may need to specify the URL to connect to the Hyperion Provider Services (don't worry, we'll come back to defining what in the heck the Provider Service is in a later section). You'll know this if the data source manager is empty or you are prompted.

Click the *Options* button on the far right section of the Hyperion ribbon:

Choose *Override Default* option and then type in the URL for the Hyperion Provider Services – something like http://*server*:13080/aps/SmartView (the resource who installed Smart View should be able to provide this to you):

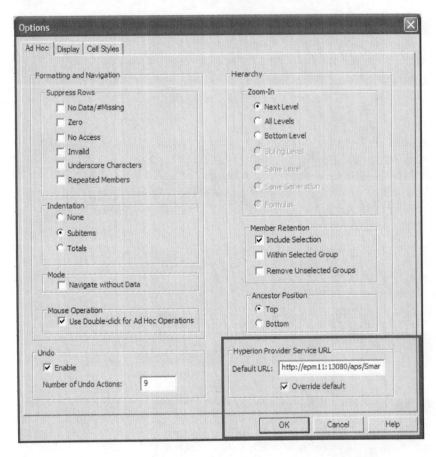

Click *OK*. Now you should see three folders: Oracle BI Server, Oracle Essbase, and Oracle Hyperion Planning. Click on the plus sign next to Oracle Essbase and you should see one or more Essbase servers.

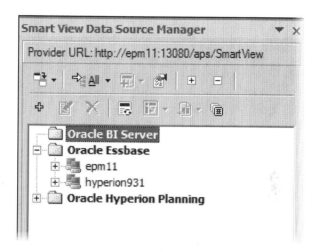

If you don't see the Essbase server, check and make sure you are viewing all connections:

So what exactly is an Essbase server? Somewhere off in the basement of your company (or more likely these days, in a server farm in Malaysia) is a really powerful machine that holds the Essbase software and all of the data for the Essbase databases we'll be using. The sample applications mentioned earlier are stored on this server.

Your computer (or in computer terms, the "client") talks to this server (through a networking protocol called TCP/IP, but you probably couldn't care less about that). While all the data is stored on the server, all of the analysis happens on your client. Once we connect to the server, we can pull data back to the client and look at it in Excel. If we change the data, we should send it back to the server so that everyone else in the company can look at the same set of numbers. You've probably heard the saying "everyone is looking at a single version of the truth."

Before you continue, you need to know the name of your server as well as your Username and Password. Your login information controls access to various parts of the Essbase server. Depending on your Username, you might have access to the entire Essbase server, specific databases on the server, or you might have no access at all (in which case, this book will be somewhat unhelpful to you).

For instance, at my company, I am an Essbase administrator. In this God-like state, I am master of all Essbase databases. For the servers that I supervise, there is not a database that I cannot see, not a setting that I cannot change, and not a user that I cannot delete. While this does make me feel really special, it also means that whenever anything goes wrong, I am probably going to get blamed.

Tip!

Only get Essbase access to what you need to do your regular job and avoid getting blamed for everything!

The Username and Password given to you by your Essbase Administrator (see "God-like administrator" above) will grant you access to only some of the databases. Double click your Essbase server (again, if you're not sure which one is the right server, give your handy Essbase admin a call).

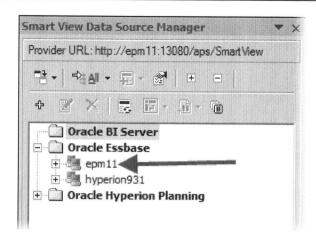

When prompted, enter your id and password. Click *Connect*:

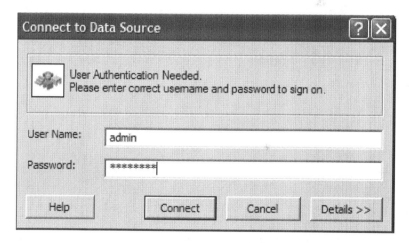

You will see a series of Applications appear in a list underneath the Essbase server (yellow cylinder icon denotes application). If you click the plus sign next to the application, you will see the databases (blue cube icon denotes Essbase databases or cubes).

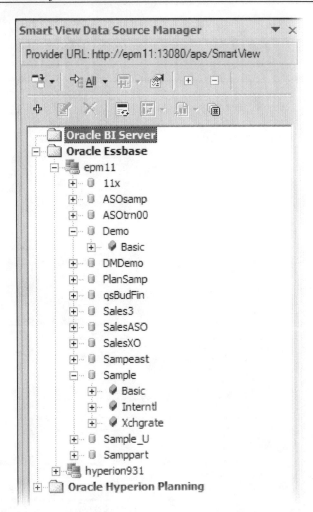

An Essbase application is a collection of one or more Essbase databases, but usually an application will contain only one database. In the image above, the Demo application has one database, Basic. The Sample application has three databases within it: Basic, Interntl, and Xchgrate.

Note!

If your company uses Hyperion Planning, the Essbase applications that support Planning often have more than one database and can have as many as five.

RETRIEVE ESSBASE DATA

The anticipation is overwhelming – you can't wait to start analyzing data. We'll be using the Basic database in the Sample application. We'll call it Sample.Basic, for short. Right click on the *Sample.Basic* database and choose *Ad-hoc Analysis*:

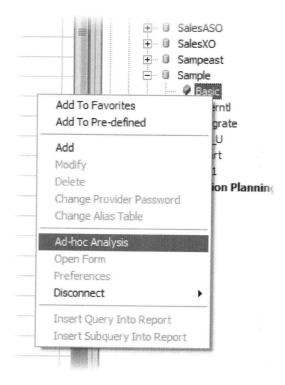

You are now connected to the database and ready to analyze data:

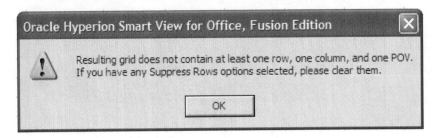

If you don't see the above grid, let's troubleshoot (and even if you do see the above grid, read along because at some point, you may see these issues). The first possible issue is that you might not see a number in cell B2. Instead of a number, there might be a dash or the word "#Missing" (more on that later). Or you also might see an error message:

Quite simply, the Sample.Basic database doesn't have any data. Nicely ask your Essbase Administrator to load the Sample.Basic database, right click on Sample.Basic and select *Adhoc Analysis* again, and you should see the spreadsheet grid shown above.

Before we start zooming and drilling (boy, Essbase sounds really exciting!), let's discuss connection information. The current spreadsheet tab in the current Excel workbook is the only one that's connected to Essbase. If you went from Sheet1 to Sheet2, Sheet2 wouldn't be connected. It is possible to click over to Sheet2 and connect it to Essbase, but at the moment, it's not.

This does bring up the interesting point that each sheet can be connected to a different Essbase database or no database at all. Sheet2 could be connected to Demo.Basic while Sheet1 is connected to Sample.Basic. All this can get a bit confusing and unfortunately in Smart View, there isn't a way to easily see the database you are connected to in the spreadsheet if you looking at all sources.

In the Data Source Manager, change your view from *All Sources* to *Favorites*:

From there you can select and choose your data source in the *Activate* drop down selection in the Hyperion ribbon:

Now you know the database you are connected to within a selected spreadsheet.

DIMENSIONALITY

Can we zoom now? Can we, can we? (My four year old just bounced into my head for a moment.) Not yet. First let's define "dimensions", something you need to know before zooming and drilling can commence. Remember our initial spreadsheet:

◢	A	B	C	D	E	F
1		Measures				
2	Year	105522		POV [Book1 ▼ ×		
3				Product ▼		
4				Market ▼		
5				Scenario ▼		
6				Refresh		
7						
8						
9						
10						

What is a Dimension?

Those two words at the top of the spreadsheet (Year, Measures) and three words in the POV (Product, Market, and Scenario) are the dimensions of Sample.Basic. To oversimplify, a *dimension* is something that can be put into the rows or columns of your report (or it applies to the whole page). Different databases have different dimensions, and Sample.Basic has the five just mentioned.

Let go of your mouse for a second, and have a look at this really simple Profit & Loss Statement:

	Actual	**Budget**
Sales	400,855	373,080
COGS	179,336	158,940
Margin	221,519	214,140
Total Expenses	115,997	84,760
Profit	**105,522**	**129,380**

It only has two dimensions. Down the rows, we have our "Measures" dimension (often called "Accounts"). Across the columns, we have our "Scenario" dimension. Some people like to call this dimension Category, Ledger, or Version. It is Essbase tradition to call the dimension that contains Actual, Budget, Forecast, and the like "Scenario," and we'll follow the tradition.

The only two dimensions so far are Scenario and Measures. The more detailed breakdowns of Measures (Sales, COGS, Margin, et al) are the members of the Measures dimension. Actual and Budget are members in the Scenario dimension. A *member* identifies a particular element within a dimension.

If we pivot the Measures up to the columns and the Scenario dimension over to the rows, our report will now look like this:

	Sales	COGS	**Margin**	Total Expenses	**Profit**
Actual	400,855	179,336	221,519	115,997	105,522
Budget	373,080	158,940	214,140	84,760	129,380

While it doesn't look very good, it does illustrate a couple of important points. First, a dimension can be placed into the rows, columns, or the page (as we'll see in a second). If it's really a dimension (as Scenario and Measures both are), there are no restrictions on which dimensions can be down the side or across the top. Second, notice that the values in the second report are the same as the values in the first report. Actual Sales are 400,855 in both reports. Likewise, Budgeted Profit is 129,380 in both reports. This is not magic.

A dimension cannot be in both the rows and columns.

Note!

Three Dimensions

A spreadsheet is inherently two dimensional (as are most printed reports). They have rows and columns. This is great if your company only produces a Profit & Loss Statement one time, but most companies will tend to have profit (be it positive or negative) in every month. To represent this in Excel, we use the spreadsheet tabs (one for each month):

	Actual	Budget
Sales	31,538	29,480
COGS	14,160	12,630
Margin	17,378	16,850
Total Expenses	9,354	6,910
Profit	8,024	9,940

All Products and Markets.xls

Tabs: **Jan** / Feb / Mar / Apr / May / Jun / Jul / Aug / Sep / Oct / Nov / Dec /

We've now introduced a third dimension. Most people call it "Time" but Sample.Basic calls it "Year" just to be contrary. It could be across the columns (if you wanted to see a nice trend of twelve months of data) or down the rows, but we've put in the pages (a new tab for each "page"). That is, if you click on the "Jan" tab, the whole report will be for January.

If you're looking for Actual Sales of 400,855, you won't find it now because that was the value for the whole year. We could get it by totaling the values of all twelve tabs onto a summary tab.

Four Dimensions and More

Right now, this spreadsheet is not broken down by product or market. Within Excel, it's problematic to represent more than three dimensions (since we've used the rows, columns, and tabs). One way is to have a separate file for each combination of product and market:

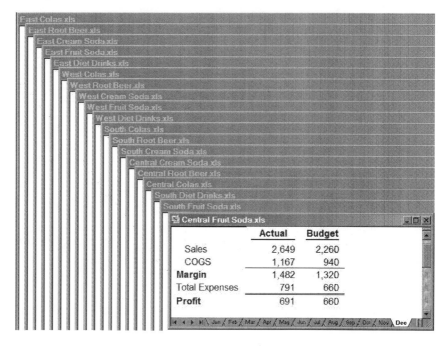

As you can see, this is getting ridiculous. What if we want to pivot our market dimension down to our columns so that we could compare profitability across different regions? To do this, we'd either have to have a series of linked spreadsheet formulas (which would break as soon as we added or deleted a new product or market) or we could hire a temporary employee to print out all the spreadsheets and type them in again with the markets now in the columns. While the latter method is obviously error-prone, the "rekeying" method is the one used by the majority of the companies in the world that do not own Essbase.

Since Market and Product are dimensions, it should be no more difficult to put them in the columns or rows than Scenario or Measures. As we'll learn about later, producing a report with markets down the side and products across the top is no more difficult than dragging-and-dropping:

		Actual	Profit	Year	
	Colas	Root Beer	Cream Soda	Fruit Soda	**Product**
East	12,656	2,534	2,627	6,344	**24,161**
West	3,549	9,727	10,731	5,854	**29,861**
South	4,773	6,115	2,350	–	**13,238**
Central	9,490	9,578	10,091	9,103	**38,262**
Market	**30,468**	**27,954**	**25,799**	**21,301**	**105,522**

In the bottom-right corner, you'll see our familiar actual profit for the year of 105,522. At the top of the report, you'll see that we have to specify the three dimensions in our application that are not in our rows or columns or Essbase wouldn't know which values to display. For instance, if we didn't specify "Profit", Essbase wouldn't know if we wanted Profit, Sales, Margin, or some random measure to be named later.

Tip!

Always specify a member from each dimension for each intersection. If Essbase doesn't know which member of a dimension to use for an intersection, it will use the topmost member of that dimension.

ANALYZING DATA

Now that we understand that a dimension is anything that can be placed in the rows, columns, or the page, let's get back to retrieving data and analyzing data.

Try It!

In case you weren't following along, go to a blank sheet in your workbook, connect to Essbase and then right click on Sample.Basic and select *Ad-hoc Analysis*.

Try It!

Go to another blank sheet in your workbook, connect to Essbase. Select Sample.Basic from the *Activate* drop down. Click *Refresh*.

You now have two spreadsheets that are connected to Essbase. Choose one and click on the cell that shows 105,522 and look at the formula bar just above the spreadsheet grid:

	A	B	C	D	
				fx	105522
1		Measures			
2	Year	105522		POV [Book1 ▼ ×	
3				Product ▼	
4				Market ▼	
5				Scenario ▼	
6				Refresh	
7					
8					
9					

105,522 represents the total of all the months, products, and markets in our application, but notice that the content of the cell is not an Excel formula summing up other values. The total is being calculated on the Essbase server and then returned back to us as a plain, old number. This is one of the main reasons that Essbase is far faster than, say, a pivot table: all of the detail stays on the Essbase server and only the value we care about is returned to us.

Tip!   Since there are no formulas linking this spreadsheet to Essbase (but only values), you can send this spreadsheet to people in your company who don't have access to the Essbase server.

Select the cell that contains *Measures* (cell B1 if you're following along). Measures tells us nothing, so go ahead and type the word "Profit" into that cell instead and press Enter. The numbers will not change, because you haven't told Essbase to re-retrieve your data yet. Choose *Refresh* from the ribbon:

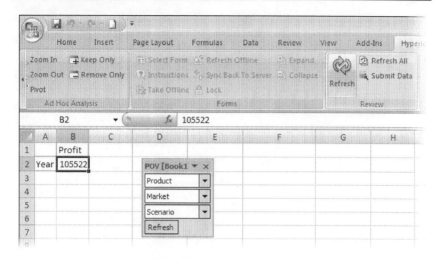

Now let's turn our attention to the POV. This floating window contains the other dimensions in the database that are not part of the spreadsheet. We can easily move these dimensions back and forth from the POV to the spreadsheet and back again. For example, select Scenario and drag it from the POV to the columns section of the spreadsheet, near Profit:

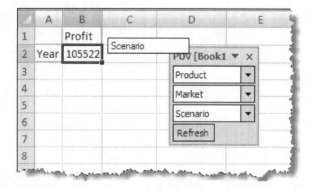

Scenario will be dropped into the grid either above or below profit depending on where you left your mouse:

⊿	A	B	C	D	E
1		Scenario			
2		Profit		POV [Book1 ▼ ×	
3	Year	105522		Product ▼	
4				Market ▼	
5				Refresh	
6					
7					

Next, let's update our analysis to focus on Budget. Type in "Budget" over Scenario and click *Refresh*:

⊿	A	B	C	D	E
1		Budget			
2		Profit		POV [Book1 ▼ ×	
3	Year	129380		Product ▼	
4				Market ▼	
5				Refresh	
6					
7					

If you spelled Profit or Budget wrong, Essbase will kindly put the dimension it thinks you didn't specify into the POV for you. Type "Budgets" over "Budget" in cell B1. Click *Refresh*:

⊿	A	B	C	D	E
1		Budgets			
2		Profit		POV [Book1 ▼ ×	
3	Year	105522		Product ▼	
4				Market ▼	
5				Scenario ▼	
6				Refresh	
7					
8					

Notice that cell B1 says "Budgets" so when we retrieved, Essbase put "Scenario" in the POV (thinking that we had forgotten a dimension). Essbase is very particular about spelling. It has no idea that "Budgets" and "Budget" means the same thing to you, so watch your spelling if you're going to be typing in the names of members.

Tip! While spelling is important, members are not case-sensitive (unless the person setting up an Essbase application specified that it should be case-sensitive). Type in "BuDgEt" and Essbase will retrieve the data and replace your funky capitalization with "Budget".

Let's go through one more scenario (bah ha ha ha ... get it? *Scenario*? Oh, you're right: not funny.). Let's perform another exercise. Follow along with me. Open a new spreadsheet and type in the following:

	A	B	C
1		Actual	Budget
2	East		
3			
4			

Notice that we don't have a floating POV window and that we are not connected to a database. Right click *Sample.Basic* and select *Ad-hoc Analysis*. You should be prompted with the following message (maybe slight different but you'll get the gist of the message):

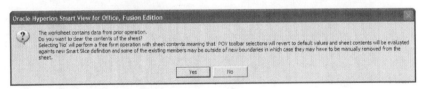

What Smart View is asking in easier terms: Do you want to remove the contents of your spreadsheet or do you want to keep them? The message also points out that if you are adhoc analyzing on a Smart Slice, certain things will happen (we'll cover smart slices later). We do not want to clear the contents of the sheet so we say no by clicking the *No* button. Now our spreadsheet is connected to the database and has retrieved values. The dimensions not specified in the spreadsheet were placed in the POV referencing the dimension member name.

	A	B	C	D	E	F
1		Actual	Budget			
2	East	24161	28390		POV Sheet3 ▼ ×	
3					Measures ▼	
4					Product ▼	
5					Year ▼	
6					Refresh	
7						
8						

Go ahead and close this spreadsheet for now. We'll use the original query going forward. Are you ready to zoom?

Zooming In and Out

Assuming that your spreadsheet looks something like the following:

	A	B	C	D	E
1		Budget			
2		Profit		POV [Book1 ▼ ×	
3	Year	129380		Product ▼	
4				Market ▼	
5				Refresh	
6					
7					

Select the cell that says Year (cell A3) and choose *Zoom In* from the Hyperion ribbon (you could also choose *Hyperion >> Ad-hoc Analysis >> Zoom in*):

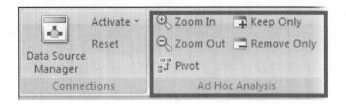

Though your report might not look exactly like this (depending on your current Essbase Options and Excel formatting), you should see the quarters that make up the total year:

	A	B	C	D
1		Budget		
2		Profit		POV [Book1 ▼ ✕
3	Qtr1	30580		Product ▼
4	Qtr2	32870		Market ▼
5	Qtr3	33980		Refresh
6	Qtr4	31950		
7	Year	129380		

Select the Qtr1 cell (cell A3) and again choose *Zoom In*. This will show you the three months that comprise Qtr1.

Tip!

There are also mouse shortcuts for zooming in and zooming out. To Zoom In using the mouse, double-click with the *left* mouse button on a member name. To Zoom Out, double-click with the *right* mouse button on a member name.

When we zoom in, we are navigating from the top of a dimension down the various levels, eventually getting to the bottom of the dimension. Zooming can also be known as drilling. In our example, we zoomed (or drilled) from Year to Quarter. Select Qtr1 and select *Zoom in* and we see the three months that make up quarter 1 – Jan, Feb, and Mar. We can zoom on any dimension in Essbase, quickly retrieving the data at various levels across the Essbase database (or for various member intersections within the database). For example, we've very quickly retrieved profit data for the three months that make up Qtr1 for all products and markets.

To go back up a dimension from bottom to top, you can either *Zoom Out*. Highlight any of those three months and choose *Zoom Out* from the *Hyperion* ribbon. Select a quarter and choose *Zoom Out* again and we're back to where we started.

If you are needing to "go back", Smart View provides Undo capabilities (that fortunately works great for undoing our actions in Smart View but unfortunately doesn't work anywhere else in our life).

Essbase Undo

To undo your last Essbase action, don't look under the *Edit* menu in Excel for Undo (and don't click the ![undo icon] button on the Excel toolbar). Simply click the *Undo* button on the Hyperion ribbon:

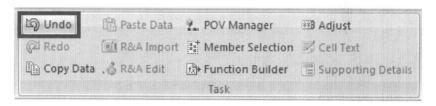

Note that you can also "Redo" which will reapply performed actions. How many times can you undo or redo? Well, it depends. Select the *Options* button from the Hyperion ribbon. On the Adhoc tab, you can define how many "undos" you would like Smart View to perform:

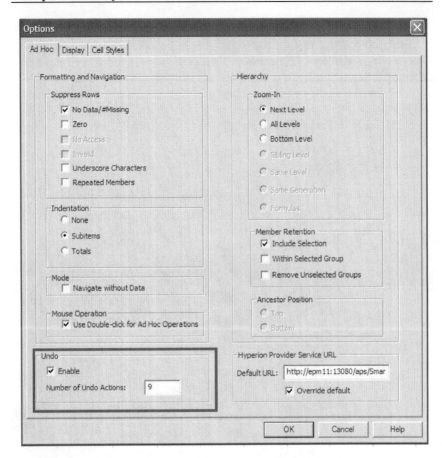

Tip!

If the Undo didn't work for you, make sure it is enabled under *Options >> Adhoc* tab.

You can type in the number of undo actions you want to allow. Should I set this number to 100? No, higher values can impact performance negatively so keep this number to just what you need.

Try It!

Assuming that your report is back to looking like the one above with only the quarters and the year showing, click on Qtr1 and choose *Zoom Out*. Either *Undo* or *Zoom In* to display the quarters again.

Keep Only / Remove Only

Let's say that you want to remove Year from the report. There are two ways to accomplish this. The first is by using the power of Excel: highlight row six and choose *Delete* from Excel's *Edit* menu. You can also use the power of Essbase by highlighting the Year cell and choosing *Remove Only* from the *Hyperion* menu. Try it – *Remove Only* the member Year. *Keep Only* is the opposite of *Remove Only*. It will keep the members you have selected in the spreadsheet.

Keep Only / Remove Only works on multiple cells as well. Select the Qtr1 cell, hold down the control key, and then click the Qtr2 cell. Now select *Keep Only*. Your report should be reduced to two quarters:

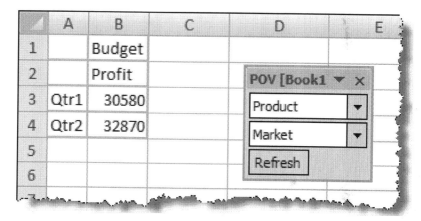

Drilling, Dragging and Pivoting

Since this report is fairly useless, click on Qtr1 and choose *Zoom Out* to return to the previous report. *Zoom In* again to display the quarters above the year. Let's drill down a second dimension: highlight the Profit cell and choose *Zoom In*:

	A	B	C	D	E	F
1		Budget	Budget	Budget		
2		Margin	Total Expenses	Profit		
3	Qtr1	51540	20960	30580		
4	Qtr2	54780	21910	32870		
5	Qtr3	56410	22430	33980		
6	Qtr4	51410	19460	31950		
7	Year	214140	84760	129380		
8						
9						
10						

POV [Book1 ▼ ✕
Product ▼
Market ▼
Refresh

Now select Margin and click *Pivot* from the Hyperion menu:

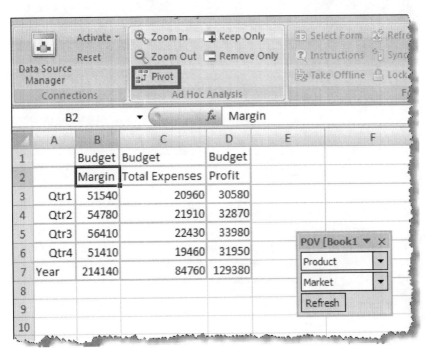

The result should look as follows:

	A	B	C	D	E	F
1			Budget			
2	Margin	Qtr1	51540			
3		Qtr2	54780			
4		Qtr3	56410			
5		Qtr4	51410			
6		Year	214140		POV [Book1 ▼ ×	
7	Total Expenses	Qtr1	20960		Product ▼	
8		Qtr2	21910		Market ▼	
9		Qtr3	22430		Refresh	
10		Qtr4	19460			
11		Year	84760			
12	Profit	Qtr1	30580			
13		Qtr2	32870			
14		Qtr3	33980			
15		Qtr4	31950			
16		Year	129380			
17						

Tip!

Did your retrieval look different, repeating the members Margin, Total Expenses and Profit for each time period? Select *Options >> Adhoc* tab and under the Suppression section, check Repeated Members. Click *Refresh* to update the spreadsheet.

We see how Smart View can show two dimensions on either the row or column axis at the same time. To get the quarters and years up to the columns, we could do that "hiring the temp to rekey method" we mentioned before, or we can do it the Essbase way. Highlight any of the member names in Year column, column B (Qtr1, say), and choose *Pivot*:

	A	B	C	D	E	F	G	H
1		Qtr1	Qtr2	Qtr3	Qtr4	Year		
2		Budget	Budget	Budget	Budget	Budget		
3	Margin	51540	54780	56410	51410	214140		
4	Total Expenses	20960	21910	22430	19460	84760		
5	Profit	30580	32870	33980	31950	129380		
6								
7							POV [Book1 ▼ ×	
8							Product ▼	
9							Market ▼	
10							Refresh	
11								

Admit it: you're impressed. There is also a mouse shortcut for pivoting dimensions: it's called a "right drag-and-drop." Select the Qtr1 cell using your left mouse button. Now, with the mouse cursor over that cell, hold down the right mouse button. After a little while, a row of white member names should appear showing you what you're about to pivot. Don't let go of the right mouse button yet:

	A	B	C	D	E	F	G
1		Qtr1	Qtr2	Qtr3	Qtr4	Year	
2		Budget	Budget	Budget	Budget	Budget	
3	Margin	51540	54780	56 Year 51420		214140	
4	Total Expenses	20960	21910	22430	19460	84760	
5	Profit	30580	32870	33980	31950	129380	
6							
7							POV [Bo

Move the white cells over to the cell where you want to pivot the dimension. In our case, drag the members over to cell A3. Okay, now let go of the right mouse button:

	A	B	C	D	E	F
1			Budget			
2	Qtr1	Margin	51540			
3		Total Expenses	20960			
4		Profit	30580			
5	Qtr2	Margin	54780			
6		Total Expenses	21910			
7		Profit	32870			
8	Qtr3	Margin	56410			
9		Total Expenses	22430			
10		Profit	33980			
11	Qtr4	Margin	51410			
12		Total Expenses	19460			
13		Profit	31950			
14	Year	Margin	214140			
15		Total Expenses	84760			
16		Profit	129380			
17						

POV [Book1 ▼ ✕

Product ▼

Market ▼

Refresh

While you're back to having two dimensions on the rows, you've changed the orientation of the two dimensions to show each measure by each time period. If all we wanted to show for each time period was Profit, we can use the *Keep Only* function. Select one of the Profit cells (cell B4, say), and choose *Keep Only*. This will remove all the instances of Margin and Total Expenses (alternatively, we could also have used *Remove Only* on the other two members).

	A	B	C	D	E	F
1			Budget			
2	Qtr1	Profit	30580			
3	Qtr2	Profit	32870			
4	Qtr3	Profit	33980			
5	Qtr4	Profit	31950			
6	Year	Profit	129380	POV [Book1 ▼ ×		
7				Product ▼		
8				Market ▼		
9				Refresh		
10						
11						

This method is much more efficient than simply adding and deleting rows in Excel.

To clean up the report (since it looks a bit silly showing the same member repeatedly in the rows), again select one of the Profit cells and choose *Pivot*. Since there is only one member to be pivoted, Essbase will assume that you want the member to be pivoted up to the page instead of the columns.

Try It!   At this point in time we're letting the reins go. Continue to play around with the features we've just illustrated. Try zooming in, zooming out, and pivoting the five dimensions of Sample.Basic. While you can make a very ugly report (no offense, but you *can*), you can't harm the data in any way: it's safely stored on the Essbase server.

Refresh the Data

You can refresh the data in a spreadsheet at any time. Let's say that you've stared at the same screen for three hours while you count down the number of seconds until your next vacation. Suddenly, your boss approaches and you're worried that she will see three hour old data and reward you with a permanent vacation. To refresh the data to the current values in Essbase, select the *Refresh* button:

You can also refresh the data by selecting *Hyperion* >> *Refresh* or *Refresh All*. Refresh All will refresh all worksheets in a workbook for the database connection. This is really helpful in instances when you've created a workbook of reports that you run on a regular basis. For example, you create and update your monthly reporting package each month. With one menu item, you can refresh the data for all reports within your workbook.

Aliases

Using your new Essbase knowledge, create the following query:

	A	B	C	D	E	F	G	H	I
1			Qtr1	Qtr2	Qtr3	Qtr4	Year		
2	Product	Margin	51540	54780	56410	51410	214140		
3		Total Expenses	20960	21910	22430	19460	84760		
4		Profit	30580	32870	33980	31950	129380		
5									
6								POV [Book1 ▼ ×	
7								Market ▼	
8								Budget ▼	
9								Refresh	
10									

Zoom in on Product:

	A	B	C	D	E	F	G	H	I
1			Qtr1	Qtr2	Qtr3	Qtr4	Year		
2	100	Margin	15670	16890	17770	15540	65870		
3		Total Expenses	5880	6230	6330	5490	23930		
4		Profit	9790	10660	11440	10050	41940		
5	200	Margin	14920	15390	15580	15450	61340	POV [Book1 ▼ ×	
6		Total Expenses	6440	6550	6750	5650	25390	Market ▼	
7		Profit	8480	8840	8830	9800	35950	Budget ▼	
8	300	Margin	11580	12620	12850	11650	48700		
9		Total Expenses	4610	4940	5140	4650	19340	Refresh	
10		Profit	6970	7680	7710	7000	29360		
11	400	Margin	9370	9880	10210	8770	38230		
12		Total Expenses	4030	4190	4210	3670	16100		
13		Profit	5340	5690	6000	5100	22130		
14	Diet	Margin	14340	14910	15180	14250	58680		
15		Total Expenses	5430	5690	5800	5040	21960		
16		Profit	8910	9220	9380	9210	36720		
17	Product	Margin	51540	54780	56410	51410	214140		
18		Total Expenses	20960	21910	22430	19460	84760		
19		Profit	30580	32870	33980	31950	129380		
20									
21									

Note! Product does not equal the sum of the products underneath this, but it does equal the sum of products 100, 200, 300, and 400. Diet Drinks is a custom total that includes select products from the other product groupings. This is called an alternate hierarchy (discussed in detail in a later section).

Product 100 is doing very well this year especially compared to product 400. "100" is the member name of a specific Product member. Member names are the short "computer-like" way of referencing things that is completely unintuitive to the average user. Essbase allows member names to have longer, more user-friendly descriptions for members called "Aliases." For instance, the alias for "100" is "Cola". So how do we change the display from member names to aliases? First let's make sure the alias table is defined. Select the Hyperion menu (not the ribbon), so if you are on Office 2007, select *Add-ins >> Hyperion >> Ad-hoc Analysis >> Change Alias table:*

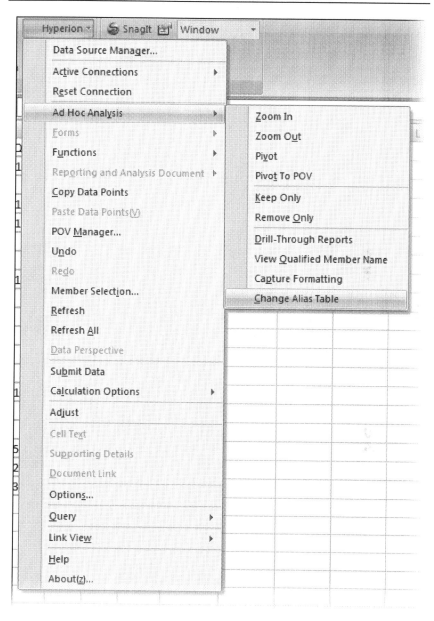

Note!

Not all Essbase features and functions are available on the ribbon. You will have to use the Hyperion menu as well.

Select the *Default* alias table and click OK:

The spreadsheet will refresh with the aliases:

	A	B	C	D	E	F	G
1			Qtr1	Qtr2	Qtr3	Qtr4	Year
2	Colas	Margin	15670	16890	17770	15540	65870
3		Total Expenses	5880	6230	6330	5490	23930
4		Profit	9790	10660	11440	10050	41940
5	Root Beer	Margin	14920	15390	15580	15450	61340
6		Total Expenses	6440	6550	6750	5650	25390
7		Profit	8480	8840	8830	9800	35950
8	Cream Soda	Margin	11580	12620	12850	11650	48700
9		Total Expenses	4610	4940	5140	4650	19340
10		Profit	6970	7680	7710	7000	29360
11	Fruit Soda	Margin	9370	9880	10210	8770	38230
12		Total Expenses	4030	4190	4210	3670	16100
13		Profit	5340	5690	6000	5100	22130
14	Diet Drinks	Margin	14340	14910	15180	14250	58680
15		Total Expenses	5430	5690	5800	5040	21960
16		Profit	8910	9220	9380	9210	36720
17	Product	Margin	51540	54780	56410	51410	214140
18		Total Expenses	20960	21910	22430	19460	84760
19		Profit	30580	32870	33980	31950	129380
20							

If you type in a member, you can type in either the member name or the alias, and Essbase will be able to find it. For instance, below the cell with Product, type in the word "100-20" (without the quotes). "100-20" is the actual product member name. Re-retrieve your data and you'll see that Essbase replaced "100-20" with "Diet Cola". "Diet Cola" is the alias name.

Tip! To type in a member name that Essbase could confuse with a number (like "100"), type in a single apostrophe before the member name. For "100", you would type in: '100. This tells Essbase (and Excel) that this is text and not a number.

Since some companies have multiple ways of referring to the same items (for instance, product 100 might be called "Cola" in the Northeast and "pop" in the Northwest), Essbase allows up to nine different aliases for each member. Right now, you're using the "Default" alias, but if your application has other descriptions for members beyond the defaults (called "alternate alias tables"), you can choose to use those in the drop-down box under Alias in the *Display* options.

Note! Sample.Basic comes with another alias table called Long Names in addition to Default.

Note! Select *Options >> Display* tab and note there is a section for displaying member names or descriptions. This is not available for Essbase connections. This section is used for Financial Management or Planning connections. A bit confusing, we agree.

OPTIONS

As mentioned before, your report might not look identical to the pictures in this book. The most common reason for this is that your Options have been changed. Options are tab-specific settings that control how Essbase operates. All of these settings are found by selecting the *Options* icon on the *Hyperion* ribbon.

Smart View options are used and remembered across spreadsheets. They are not saved with individual spreadsheets or workbooks. For example if you turn on suppression of Repeated Members and you refresh data, any repeated members will be suppressed even if in the original spreadsheet you did not suppress. If you go to a new tab or new workbook (one that's never had the Options set) and retrieve, Smart View will use the Options that were last assigned.

Indentation

Notice that in our retrieves to this point, the detail beneath each member (for example, the quarters underneath the Year member) is indented. For those who went to accounting school prior to 1990, it might seem better to indent the totals. On the "Indentation" section on the Adhoc tab, you can switch the indentation from *Subitems* to *Totals*.

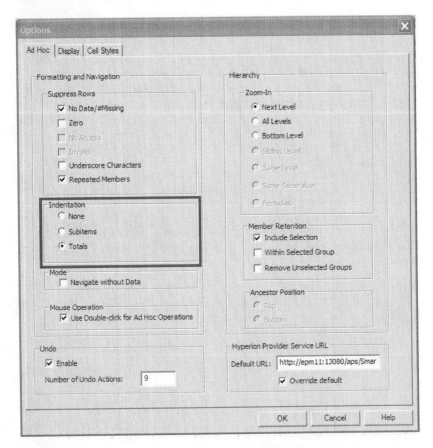

The next time you retrieve your data, each summary-level of totals will be further indented. See the example below where

Quarters are indented from months and Year is further indented from the quarters:

	A	B	C	D	E	F
1			Budget			
2	Margin	Jan	16850			
3		Feb	17330			
4		Mar	17360			
5		Qtr1	51540			
6		Qtr2	54780		POV [Book1 ▼ ×
7		Qtr3	56410		Market ▼
8		Qtr4	51410		Product ▼
9		Year	214140		Refresh
10	Total Expenses	Jan	6910			
11		Feb	6980			

To turn off indentation entirely, choose *None* under Indentation.

Zoom In Level

One of the other things that might have been changed under your options is the "Zoom In level." When you zoom in, you tend to want to see the members that comprise the current member. When you *Zoom In* on Year, you most likely want to see the quarters. Likewise, a *Zoom In* on Qtr1 should show the first three months of the year. Some impatient people don't like passing through the levels in the middle on the way to the bottom-level of a dimension. To control how far Essbase drills with each zoom, go to the Hierarchy section on the *Options >> Adhoc* tab:

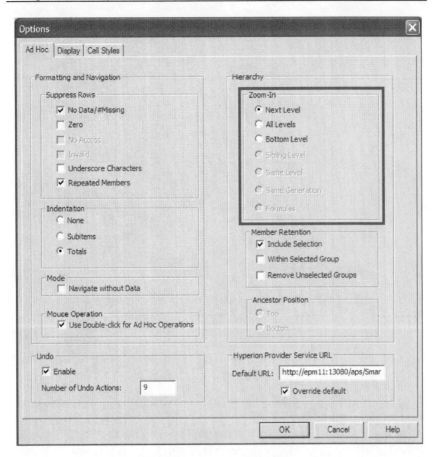

Right now, Zoom In is set to *Next Level*. This means that when you drill into Year, you see the quarters. If when you drill into Year, you want to see every single member in the Year dimension, set your Zoom In to *All Levels*. If you then drill on Year, you'd see every month and every quarter. If you want to jump from the Year down to showing all the months without showing any of the quarters, select *Bottom Level*.

Change your Zoom In level and then try zooming in and out on several dimensions. You can make a very large spreadsheet very quickly, and Essbase still remains extremely fast.

Try It!

Before you drill into a dimension that has thousands of members, make sure that your Zoom level is not set to *All Levels* or *Bottom Level*. Sample.Basic has no dimension

Tip!   with   more   than   25   members,   so   you're   safe   for   the
moment.

The Member retention allows you to define what happens to
the member that you drill on – do you want to keep it as part of the
grid or remove it? If *Include Selection* is checked and you zoom in
on Year, Year will still remain. If you uncheck this option, when
you zoom in on Year, you will only see the children of Year.

Missing Data

On   your   *Options*   >>   *Adhoc*   tab,   review   the   available
suppression alternatives: suppress no data/missing data, zeros,
underscore characters and repeated members. Uncheck the box for
No Data / #Missing.

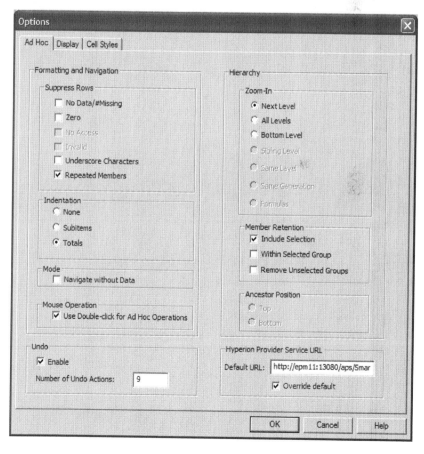

Select the Display tab and note the #Missing Label:

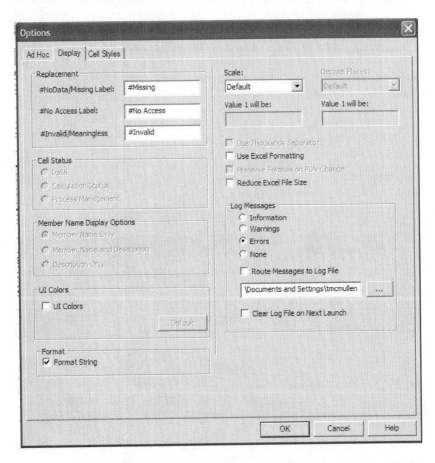

Click *OK* and go back to your report. *Keep Only* on Fruit Soda so that you only have data for the one product (one row). Now, drag Market into the report and click *Zoom In* on Market:

	A	B	C	D	E	F	G	H
1				Qtr1	Qtr2	Qtr3	Qtr4	Year
2	East	Fruit Soda	Margin	2450	2620	2740	2400	10210
3			Total Expenses	560	630	620	490	2300
4			Profit	1890	1990	2120	1910	7910
5	West	Fruit Soda	Margin	2910	3010	3130	2680	11730
6			Total Expenses	1490	1540	1550	1480	6060
7			Profit	1420	1470	1580	1200	5670
8	South	Fruit Soda	Margin	#Missing	#Missing	#Missing	#Missing	#Missing
9			Total Expenses	#Missing	#Missing	#Missing	#Missing	#Missing
10			Profit	#Missing	#Missing	#Missing	#Missing	#Missing
11	Central	Fruit Soda	Margin	4010	4250	4340	3690	16290
12			Total Expenses	1980	2020	2040	1700	7740
13			Profit	2030	2230	2300	1990	8550
14	Market	Fruit Soda	Margin	9370	9880	10210	8770	38230
15			Total Expenses	4030	4190	4210	3670	16100
16			Profit	5340	5690	6000	5100	22130
17								

Notice that the South is not a big fan of Fruit Soda. Budget Profit for the year is missing (denoted by Essbase with the term "#Missing"). A missing value to Essbase is very different from a value of zero. A profit of zero means that your sales were cancelled out exactly by your expenses. A profit of #Missing means that we have neither sales nor expenses at this particular combination. Data for Budgeted, South, Fruit Soda Profit for the year simply does not exist.

If you don't want to see #Missing on your reports, you can replace it with a label that makes more sense to you. Go to your Display options and in the box next to "#Missing Label", fill in something that makes sense to you:

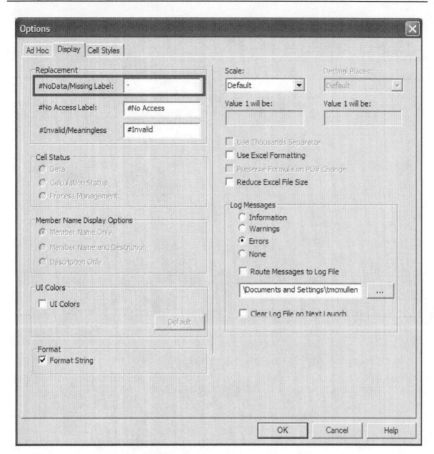

The most common #Missing labels are: N/A, 0, -, and a space.

Tip!

In general, there will be lots of intersections of data in your applications that don't exist, and retrieving them into a report takes unnecessary time. If you have 100,000 products and 5,000 stores, as few as 2,000 products might be sold each day at each store. Do you really want to see a report that's 98% empty? If you don't, check the box next to suppress *No Data / #Missing* on the Ad Hoc tab. This will suppress any rows where the data all the way across the row is #Missing. If a single column has a real number, the row will not be suppressed.

If you also don't want see intersections where all the values in the row are zero, check the box to suppress *Zero* as well.

Other Options

Navigate without data on the Adhoc tab allows you to set up your spreadsheet, defining the layout without the added time of retrieving data. This can speed up report creation time as you don't have to wait for Essbase to send the data. You can turn off mouse operations by unchecking *Use Double-click for Adhoc Operations.*

Now that you know some of the most used Smart View options, let's turn our attention to something really exciting – changing data in the Essbase databases.

CHANGING DATA

Submitting Data

So far, all of your work with the add-in has been for reporting and analysis. One of the major uses of Essbase is for budgeting (or planning or forecasting or whatever you call putting information back into Essbase instead of just taking it out).

Using the techniques you've learned to this point, create a new report that looks like the following:

	A	B	C	D	E	F
1		Actual	Budget			
2	New York	678	640		POV [Book1 ▼ ×	
3	Massachusetts	494	460		Sales ▼	
4	Florida	210	190		Cola ▼	
5	Connecticut	310	290		Jan ▼	
6	New Hampshire	120	110		Refresh	
7	East	1812	1690			
8						
9						

Tip!

To make a quick report, you can always type the member names into a blank spreadsheet. Put a zero where you want the numbers to appear, and refresh. Make sure that each intersection is represented by all dimensions.

The budget for cola sales in New York is looking a little light, so let's up it to 700. Type 700 into cell C2 (or wherever your report has the intersection of New York and Budget). Note the cell color changes to a yellow, highlighting an adjusted number. Choose *Submit*.

The data will automatically refresh showing you the saved 700 data value.

Now type in "Variance" next to Budget in cell D1. Click *Refresh*:

	A	B	C	D	E	F	G
1		Actual	Budget	Variance			
2	New York	678	700	-22			
3	Massachusetts	494	460	34		POV [Book1 ▼ ×
4	Florida	210	190	20		Sales ▼
5	Connecticut	310	290	20		Cola ▼
6	New Hampshire	120	110	10		Jan ▼
7	East	1812	1690	122		Refresh
8						

This isn't going to make any sense but we want to show you a possible scenario that you could run into in your application. Type 50 in cell D2 (you're saying "what in the ..." but trust us). The cell shading will change to yellow. Now select *Submit*:

	A	B	C	D	E	F	G
1		Actual	Budget	Variance			
2	New York	678	700	50			
3	Massachusetts	494	460	34		POV [Book1 ▼ ✕	
4	Florida	210	190	20		Sales ▼	
5	Connecticut	310	290	20		Cola ▼	
6	New Hampshire	120	110	10		Jan ▼	
7	East	1812	1690	122		Refresh	
8							
9							

Was the data saved to Essbase? Nope. Depending on the Essbase and security design, there will be some data points where you can't save data. In the case of Variance, this member is a dynamically calculated member and never stores any data. The other common causes are due to insufficient rights to edit those numbers and due to sending numbers into summary members (also called upper-level members).

Running Calculations

Now submit the data value 735 over 700 in the example above. Math wizards in the audience will immediately note that 735+460+190+290+110 does not equal 1,690. It's actually 95 short, because we haven't told the Essbase server to recalculate the totals. For the most part, this is not done automatically. The majority of the summary members in an Essbase application are "stored" meaning that Essbase stores the pre-calculated totals to speed retrieval. This follows the common Essbase belief that analysis tends to start at the top of the hierarchy and then drill down.

Note!   One of the major differences between Essbase and a relational database is that relational databases assume that you want to look at detail (so displaying totals is much slower) and Essbase assumes that you want to look at summaries (though detailed data is not any slower).

Other members are "dynamically calculated" (though the cool kids say "dynamic calc") meaning that Essbase calculates those members at the time the user requests them. While some members in Sample.Basic are dynamically calculated (the upper-level

Measures, for instance), it's always best to assume that you should recalculate the database after submitting data.

Assuming that you have access to recalculate the database, choose *Hyperion >> Calculation Options >> Calculate*:

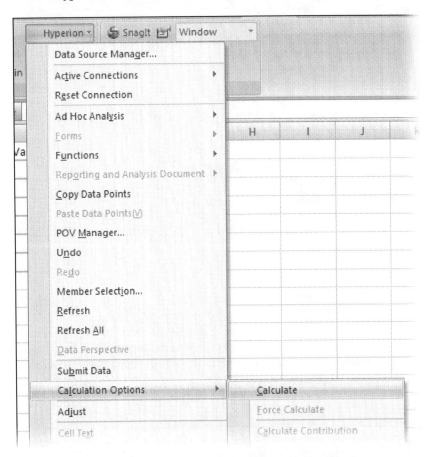

This will pull up a list of calc scripts for which you have access. You can filter this list by database. Select the calc script you wish to run and click *Launch*. In this example, choose Default for the Basic cube (basically means "calculate everything in the database that needs to be recalculated.")

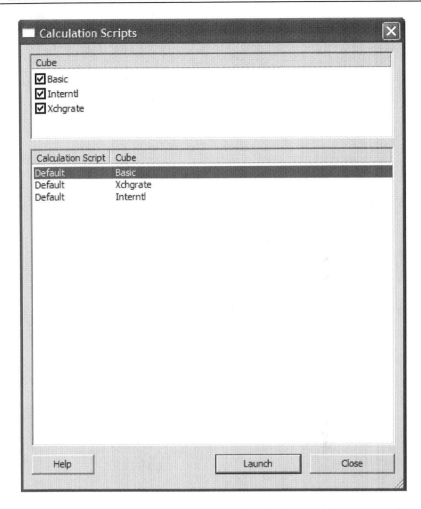

Smart View will check with the Essbase server every few seconds to see if the calculation has completed yet. You can always continue to work in Excel in the meantime, just don't work with this Essbase database unless you're okay with potentially erroneous results.

While the default calculation for Sample.Basic will always take just a few seconds, complex calculations against large databases can take several minutes or even hours. For instance, if your company had a multi-step allocation process that allocated corporate expenses by thousands of stores for thousands of products (to get a complete Income Statement by location by SKU), it would take a whole lot longer than five seconds. Be patient, and Smart View will let you know when the calculation is finished.

Once you get the calculation message, re-retrieve your data and you should see the correct value for East with the additional 95 in it:

	A	B	C	D	E	F	G
1		Actual	Budget	Variance			
2	New York	678	735	-57			
3	Massachusetts	494	460	34		POV [Book1 ▼ ×	
4	Florida	210	190	20		Sales ▼	
5	Connecticut	310	290	20		Cola ▼	
6	New Hampshire	120	110	10		Jan ▼	
7	East	1812	1785	27		Refresh	
8							
9							

Logging Off

You can disconnect from a spreadsheet if you choose. Simply right click on the Essbase database and select *Disconnect*. You can also just close the spreadsheet and this will end your connection to the active Essbase database for the spreadsheet.

MEMBER SELECTION

Up to this point, we've primarily been navigating our way to data by either zooming in or out, using keep/remove only, or just typing members into our spreadsheet. What if we wanted to make a fairly large report with all of the states down the rows and all of the months across the top of the page:

	A	B	C	D	E	F	G	H	I	J	K	L	M	N	O	P
1		Jan	Feb	Mar	Apr	May	Jun	Jul	Aug	Sep	Oct	Nov	Dec			
2	New York	512	601	543	731	720	912	857	570	516	766	721	753			
3	Massachusetts	519	498	515	534	548	668	688	685	563	477	499	518			
4	Florida	336	361	373	408	440	491	545	529	421	373	337	415			
5	Connecticut	321	309	290	272	253	212	198	175	231	260	310	262			
6	New Hampshire	44	74	84	86	99	125	139	136	93	81	75	89			
7	California	1034	1047	1048	1010	1093	1185	1202	1269	1122	1053	923	978			
8	Oregon	444	417	416	416	400	402	414	412	409	421	467	444			
9	Washington	405	412	395	368	378	372	372	392	394	397	385	371			
10	Utah	237	251	256	277	262	246	276	248	217	269	309	307			
11	Nevada	219	267	289	330	365	411	493	451	268	317	281	348			
12	Texas	504	547	531	507	547	556	556	595	552	531	497	502			
13	Oklahoma	241	234	243	277	279	306	335	338	292	284	309	353			
14	Louisiana	259	263	251	228	231	227	202	253	262	302	279	235			
15	New Mexico	-7	2	9	28	38	43	78	48	4	13	23	51			
16	Illinois	912	963	980	1036	1102	1160	1237	1191	1025	1017	915	1039			
17	Ohio	384	362	357	370	359	363	378	347	352	330	395	387			
18	Wisconsin	297	307	309	287	303	310	315	334	307	284	247	247			
19	Missouri	125	132	142	151	133	104	135	80	79	101	139	145			
20	Iowa	653	677	706	734	781	821	854	871	786	739	662	777			
21	Colorado	585	622	596	594	598	620	604	621	596	638	594	559			
22	New York	512	601	543	731	720	912	857	570	516	766	721	753			
23	Massachusetts	519	498	515	534	548	668	688	685	563	477	499	518			
24	Florida	336	361	373	408	440	491	545	529	421	373	337	415			
25	Connecticut	321	309	290	272	253	212	198	175	231	260	310	262			
26	New Hampshire	44	74	84	86	99	125	139	136	93	81	75	89			
27	California	1034	1047	1048	1010	1093	1185	1202	1269	1122	1053	923	978			
28	Oregon	444	417	416	416	400	402	414	412	409	421	467	444			

POV Sheet3 ▾ ×
Measures ▾
Product ▾
Scenario ▾
Refresh

You create this sheet by opening up a blank spreadsheet, typing Measures into cell B1, Product into C1, Scenario into D1, all the months into B2:B13, and all the states into the cells starting at A3. This, however, is silly since we all know that the correct method is not to type it yourself, but to hire a temp to type all this in for you.

Tip!

Consider getting an intern instead of hiring a temp. You don't have to pay interns!

As you might have guessed, Essbase has a better way: a previously ignored menu item called *Member Selection*.

Member Selection Basics

Member Selection is like your own personalized temp typist. Let's see how handy he can be at generating spreadsheets like the one above. First, we'll make Member Selection (often shortened to Member Select) type in our states for us.

In a blank worksheet, right click on *Sample*.Basic and select *Ad-hoc Analysis*. Drag the Market dimension to rows and the Year dimension to the column. Move Measures back to the POV. You spreadsheet should look something like this:

	A	B	C	D	E
1		Year			
2	Market	105522		POV [Book1 ▼ ×	
3				Product ▼	
4				Scenario ▼	
5				Measures ▼	
6					
7				Refresh	
8					
9					

On your default query, select cell A2 and then choose the *Member Selection* button:

The Member Selection window will display:

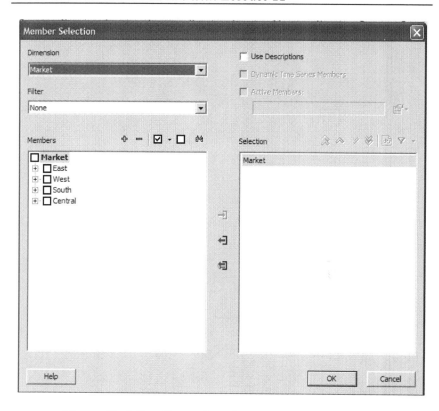

Notice that the dimension that comes up is Market. Smart View will retrieve dimension you want to use for picking members based on what's in the cell you currently have selected. Select a blank cell and try clicking *Member Selection*. What do you see?

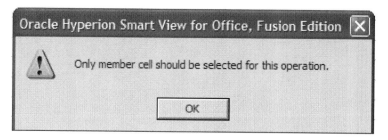

You could also see a Dimension Name Resolution screen which allows you to pick the desired dimension and the desired orientation for the spreadsheet (e.g. vertical position to list members down the page). As you can see, layout is very important when defining queries and using member selection.

Back to the task at hand, let us take a closer look at the Member Selection window:

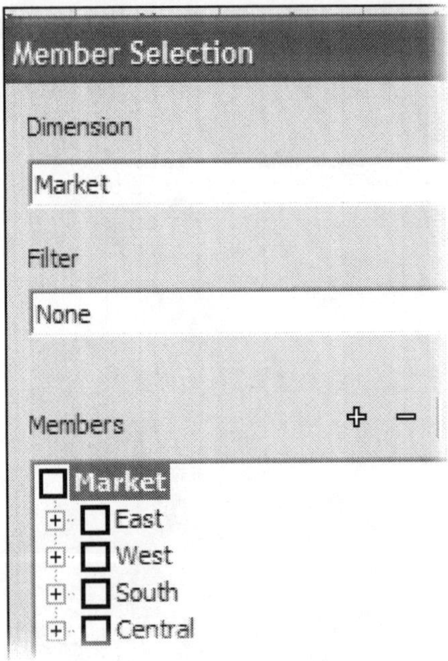

The members in the left box should change to show the Market dimension. Notice the Filter is set to "None" which means we can view the full Market hierarchy. Click the plus sign next to East and it will expand to show you the states in the East. As you would expect, the plus option expands the hierarchy and minus option collapses the hierarchy. Click the check box for the all of the East states:

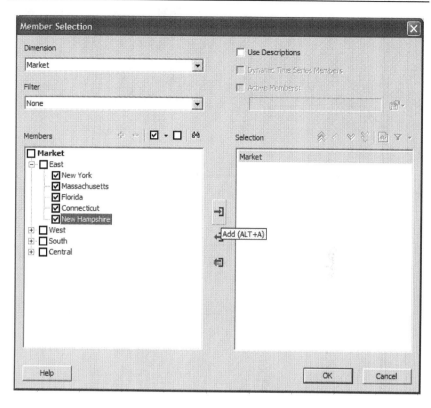

Now click the -> *arrow* button. You should now see five of the fifty most important states in the United States of America appear in the box to the right under Selection. Expand West, South and Central in the member selection window. Select the children of each and move them to the Selection box on the right. While this was a somewhat manual selection process, it certainly works. You should now be looking at the following:

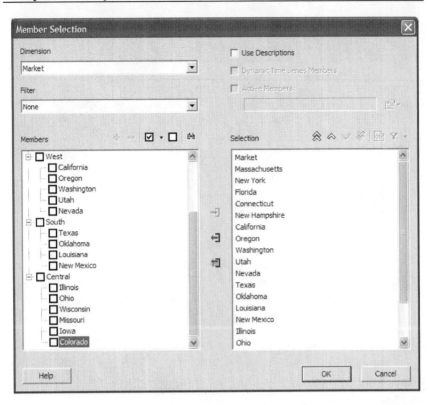

If you're an obsessive-compulsive type and want to manually alphabetize your state names before entering them into the sheet, highlight the state you want to rearrange in the list and then click either the *Move Item Up* or *Move Item Down* buttons:

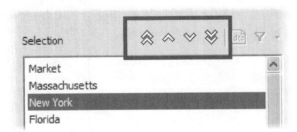

If you accidentally add any member more than once, highlight the member to remove and choose the *<- arrow* icon. To clear the whole list, click the double arrow icon:

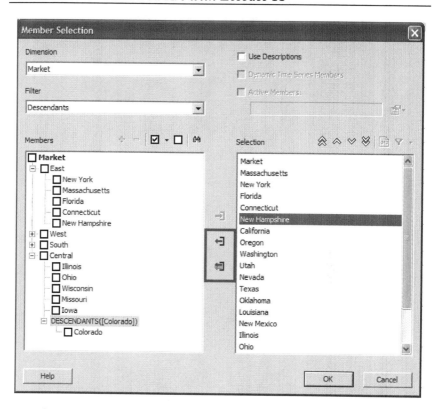

 Note! Try to shift+click or control+click to select multiple members. Unfortunately it doesn't work but don't worry, we'll show you more tips for selecting members.

Assuming your list is complete (and alphabetized if that's how you roll), click *OK* and you'll be able to watch while Essbase enters the states down the left side of your spreadsheet.

 Note! After you use Member Selection to type in your members, you will need to choose *Refresh* yourself. Member Selection does not do a retrieve on its own.

Let's use a slightly different method to type in the months. Select cell B1 and choose *Member Selection*. The Year dimension should appear. Under "Filter", choose *Level*:

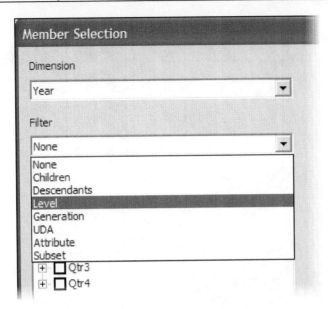

Remember that the months are level-0 since they don't have any children (through no lack of trying, mind you). Enter the level number in this case, 0:

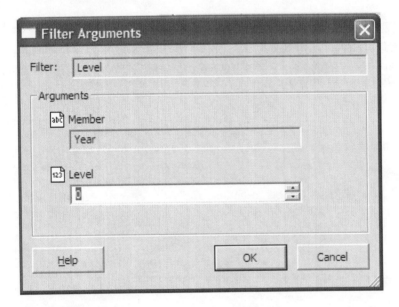

 You could also use the arrow keys to select the available levels for the selected dimension.

Tip!

Click *OK* and you will see the level zero months are available in the Members section. Note they haven't been selected yet. We've only filtered them in the Members section:

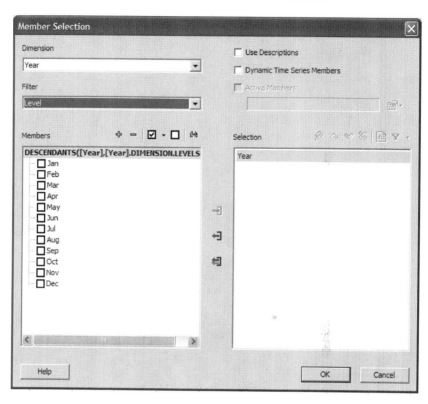

Click the *Check mark* icon (between the minus and blank square icons) to select all of the months (much easier than having to manually check month by month):

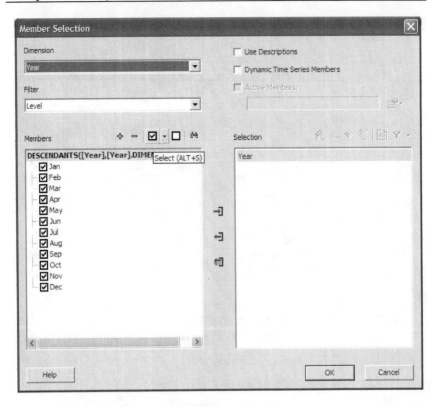

Now move the months over to the Selection section by clicking the right arrow icon. Click *OK* and the months are placed across the columns in your spreadsheet:

Note!

Smart View intuitively knows to place the months across the columns whereas in the old Excel Add-in, you had to manually check a box to place selections across the columns.

Remember to refresh to see the data.

More Member Selection Options

What about changing the members that are displayed in my POV? We'll follow a similar process but before we get there, let's do one thing – set the Alias table. By default the Alias table is set to none (we know, we know... Why isn't the Alias table set to Default by default? We haven't gotten a clear answer from Oracle development so for now it is just one of those things.) Go to *Hyperion>> Ad-hoc Analysis >> Change Alias Table* and select Default.

Tip!

You access the Hyperion menu through right click menu options.

Tip!

You have to set the alias table for each new connection to a spreadsheet. The default alias table for a connection is *None.*

Select the drop down arrow next to Product and choose the ellipses (...).

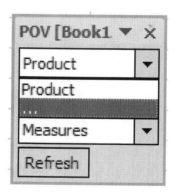

The Member Selection window is launched:

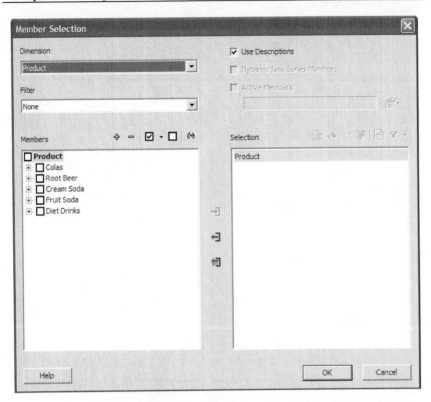

Notice the *Use Descriptions* check box is checked now that we have chosen an alias. Uncheck this box. Nothing changes, right? This check box is only applicable for Financial Management and Planning sources (another one of those things...).

Let's say we want to perform analysis on the Diet Drinks (in today's calorie conscious world, the diet business is booming). Check the Diet Drinks check box under the Members section. From the Select drop down box, choose Children:

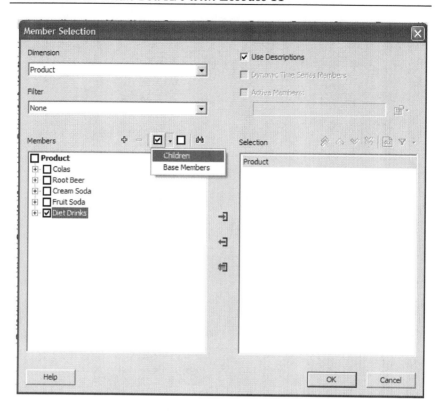

The children of Diet Drinks are automatically expanded and selected. If we had chosen Base Members, the level zero members would have been displayed and selected (in this case the same as children). Move the Diet Drinks members over to the Selection section and click *OK*.

Now in the Product drop down, all selected members are available:

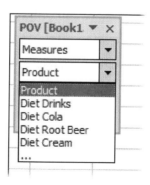

Change the selection from Product to Diet Drinks and click *Refresh* to see the new data.

Drag the Product dimension into the rows on the other side of Market. WOW! That was a really fast way to view diet drink performance across markets:

	A	B	C	D	E	F	G	H	I	J	K	L
1			Jan	Feb	Mar	Apr	May	Jun	Jul	Aug	Sep	Oct
2	Product	Market	8024	8346	8333	8644	8929	9534	9878	9545	8489	8653
3		Massachusetts	519	498	515	534	548	668	688	685	563	477
4		New York	512	601	543	731	720	912	857	570	516	766
5		Florida	336	361	373	408	440	491	545	579	421	373
6		Connecticut	321	309	290	272	253	212	19	231	231	260
7		New Hampshire	44	74	84	86	99	125	13	Measures	93	81
8		California	1034	1047	1048	1010	1093	1185	120	122	122	1053
9		Oregon	444	417	416	416	400	402	41	409	409	421
10		Washington	405	412	395	368	378	372	372	392	394	397
11		Utah	237	251	256	277	262	246	276	248	217	269
12		Nevada	219	267	289	330	365	411	493	451	268	317
13		Texas	504	547	531	507	547	556	556	595	552	531
14		Oklahoma	241	234	243	277	279	306	335	338	292	284
15		Louisiana	259	263	251	228	231	227	202	253	262	302
16		New Mexico	-7	2	9	28	38	43	78	48	4	13
17		Illinois	912	963	980	1036	1102	1160	1237	1191	1025	1017
18		Ohio	384	362	357	370	359	363	378	347	352	330
19		Wisconsin	297	307	309	287	303	310	315	334	307	284
20		Missouri	125	132	142	151	133	104	135	80	79	101
21		Iowa	653	677	706	734	781	821	854	871	786	739
22		Colorado	585	622	596	594	598	620	604	621	596	638
23	Diet Drinks	Market	2279	2362	2376	2396	2434	2506	2610	2595	2327	2379
24		Massachusetts	#Missing	#Missing	#Missing	#Missing	#Missing	#Missing	#Missing	#Missing	#Missing	#Missing
25		New York	#Missing	#Missing	#Missing	#Missing	#Missing	#Missing	#Missing	#Missing	#Missing	#Missing
26		Florida	151	156	163	187	197	203	236	193	160	146
27		Connecticut	30	29	26	24	22	19	16	16	23	21
28		New Hampshire	#Missing	#Missing	#Missing	#Missing	#Missing	#Missing	#Missing	#Missing	#Missing	#Missing
29		California	188	185	191	185	199	231	241	268	205	223
30		Oregon	174	165	161	152	126	125	123	119	132	137

Can you believe it? You're already pretty sufficient in retrieving and analyzing data in Essbase. You successfully connected to an Essbase data, zoomed and pivoted, and set a number of options for analysis. And that really is just the beginning when it comes to end user features and functionality. Unfortunately, that is as far as we will take it in this book (see Look Smarter Than You Are with Smart View and Essbase 11 for the complete end user guide). Now on to bigger and better topics... How do we build the underlying Essbase database? First, put down your mouse as we take a trip through history and also review some important fundamental concepts of Essbase.

Chapter 3:
What is Essbase?

Essbase is currently produced by a company named Oracle. Prior to the earthshaking acquisition by Oracle, Essbase was produced by a company named Hyperion Solutions Corporation. Although Hyperion was founded in 1981, the Essbase product came along in the early 1990's compliments of a company whose only product was Essbase: Arbor Software. Up until 1998 when Hyperion and Arbor "merged", the two companies were fierce competitors who were just as likely to spit on each other in waiting rooms as work together. (We are kidding, but only slightly.)

Arbor Software was founded in 1991 by Jim Dorrian and Bob Earle. They noticed at the time that companies were beginning to use spreadsheets not just for presentation of information but as a place to store data and business logic. Often, multiple sources of data were being consolidated together in spreadsheets and they were even seeing companies begin to release analysis to the public based on data in spreadsheets.

Jim and Bob wanted to build a database for spreadsheets. The original name for the solution was *eSSbase* which stands for Spread Sheet database (the e was added to help folks pronounce it correctly).

Check out the actual memo that was sent to the Arbor employees:

InterOffice Memo

To: All Arbor

From: Mike Florio

Date: March 12, 1992

Subject: Product Name

As you probably have heard by now, our product name is

eSSbase™

It stands for "Spread Sheet Database" (the "e" is there to help people pronounce it correctly.)

Our graphic designer thinks it looks better shown as above (bold, italic, serifed typeface.)

The Lawyers have provided us with the attached guidelines for useage, please take a few minutes to review the attached. If you have any questions, just contact me

Thanks,

Mike.

Thanks to some creativity and some venture capital (of course) from Hummer Winblad, they released the first version of Essbase in 1992. This original release of the product garnered three whole paragraphs of press coverage in Software Magazine on May 15, 1992. Here it is in all its "babe in the woods waiting to be eaten by bears" naiveté:

DATA SERVER "FEEDS" 1-2-3 OR EXCEL
Arbor Software Corp.'s Essbase data server
Software Magazine; May 15, 1992

Following a three-year development effort, start-up Arbor Software Corp., Santa Clara, Calif., has built a data server that "feeds" popular desktop offerings, including 1-2-3 from Lotus Development Corp., and Excel from Microsoft Corp., on client machines.

"We conceded the front end to [widely installed] spreadsheets," said James Dorrian, president and co-founder. "We built the product with two assumptions: that people knew their spreadsheets and that people knew their jobs."

According to Marketing Vice President Michael Florio, the OS/2-based $22,000 Essbase offers users in client/server environments simultaneous access to large volumes of multidimensional spreadsheet data.

Notice that it was originally developed to run on OS/2 and its claim to fame was that it fed spreadsheets. Also, notice that you could get a copy for only $22,000 which sort of goes to show you that technology doesn't always get cheaper over time.

The first version of the product wasn't nearly as user friendly as it is today. Ignoring the Herculean steps required to actually build an Essbase database, retrieving data into Excel (or Lotus, at the time) required writing requests to Essbase in a language known as "Essbase Report Scripting."

	A
1	<PAGE (Measures, Product, Market)
2	Profit
3	Product
4	Market
5	<COLUMN (Scenario)
6	<CHILD Scenario
7	<ROW (Year)
8	<ICHILD Year
9	!
10	

But with time we came to know and love the Essbase Spreadsheet Add-in for Excel. When you chose *Essbase >> Retrieve*, you'd see a much friendlier interface:

	A	B	C	D	E
1			Profit	Product	Market
2		Actual	Budget	Variance	Variance %
3	Qtr1	24703	30580	-5877	-19.21844343
4	Qtr2	27107	32870	-5763	-17.53270459
5	Qtr3	27912	33980	-6068	-17.85756327
6	Qtr4	25800	31950	-6150	-19.24882629
7	Year	105522	129380	-23858	-18.44025352
8					

The Essbase Add-in was everything we thought we needed for Essbase until Smart View came along.

INTRODUCTION TO SMART VIEW

What is Smart View? This may be a silly question because you used Smart View in the entire last chapter. But in case you missed it, Smart View is THE Office Add-in for all of the Oracle Enterprise Performance Management System products including Essbase, BI Server, Planning, Financial Management, Web Analysis, and Financial Reporting. It's Oracle's version of the Swiss army knife and that makes you MacGyver.

Many of you old Essbase users might think you're completely satisfied with the Essbase Spreadsheet Add-In for Excel (the old school add-in for analyzing Essbase data). Per Oracle, you are wrong. They do have a point: among other things, the Essbase Add-In only works in Excel. What if you want to pull some Essbase data into a Word document? What if you need to make PowerPoint presentations with tables that automatically update from Essbase? Well, your problems are solved by the Smart View Add-In.

When used in Excel, Smart View has similar functionality to the Essbase Add-In. Yes: two different tools to do the same thing. The navigation is a bit different in Smart View but you can drill down, swap rows and columns, etc. Why do we need two tools? Since there is a world-wide problem of starving computer programmers, one might speculate that Oracle is doing their part by keeping two development teams gainfully employed. But is there another reason?

Smart View takes Essbase reporting and analysis to another level above the Excel Add-in. With Smart View you can create reports in Word or PowerPoint with live data from Essbase sources. Features like Report Designer, Query Designer, and Cascade (report bursting) give end users powerful reporting capabilities in the tools they know and love: Excel, Word and PowerPoint (beat that, Excel Add-in).

Smart View also brings Add-In functionality for all of the Oracle EPM products that need an Add-In. Smart View provides a single Excel interface for Financial Management and Planning, replacing the Planning Spreadsheet Add-In and HFM Spreadsheet Add-In. You can import Reporting and Analysis documents as images into Microsoft Word or PowerPoint. You can import query ready or fully formatted grids into Microsoft Excel. Is there anyone at this point that doesn't want to toss the Essbase Add-In on the 8-track tape trash heap of obsolescence?

OLAP AND OTHER TERMS

When Essbase was first released, no one was quite sure what it was. Was it some sort of spreadsheet on steroids? Was it a temporary employee who was really good at typing? Was it a database? If so, why didn't it have records and fields and most importantly, why didn't it let IT geeks write SQL to access it?

Everyone was pretty sure what it wasn't: a typical relational database. The creators originally called it a "data server." Shortly after Essbase was created, they commissioned a study by the late Dr. E.F. Codd (the same Ph.D. who came up with the original rules for what constituted a true relational database) to determine what the heck Essbase was.

Dr. Codd was definitely impressed. He felt that this wasn't a relational database yet it was definitely a database and a very important new type to boot. He called it an "OLAP" database to separate it from every other database up to that point.

To put it simply, all databases prior to Essbase were built for the purpose of storing transactions. The goal for these systems was to get individual records into the database as quickly as possible and to get those same records back out again as quickly as possible. A side goal was to store that data in as small a space as possible, because those were the days when hard drive space cost as much as a good mule. Summarization of these types of databases was possible, but definitely not the objective of the database design. Dr. Codd classified traditional relational databases "OLTP" (On-Line Transaction Processing).

He knew that Essbase was the first database designed purely to support analysis. Knowing that this was going to be The Next Big Thing, he created a term to describe these databases: OLAP (On-Line Analytical Processing). There were several features that Essbase offered that no previous database could handle.

Multi-Dimensional Databases

First of all, Essbase was a multi-dimensional database (MDDB or MDB, for short). What did the good doctor mean when he said Essbase was multi-dimensional? Simply that any of the dimensions set up in a database could be put in the rows or the columns (or applied to the whole page/report).

All databases up to this point were two-dimensional: records and fields. Essbase had no theoretical dimension limit (though there was certainly a practical limit). The Sample.Basic database we were accessing above has five base dimensions: Year, Measures, Product, Market, and Scenario. (It actually has five more "attribute" dimensions that we haven't even seen yet: Caffeinated, Ounces, Pkg Type, Population, and Intro Date.) The ASOSamp.Basic database is a sample Aggregate Storage database with 14 dimensions. The largest database we've ever seen had over 100 dimensions, but we think they were just trying to show off. In general, Essbase databases have five to ten base dimensions. By base dimension, we mean dimensions that show up all the time (like the five mentioned above in Sample.Basic).

While any relational database can be set up to give the appearance of having multiple dimensions, it takes a lot of up front work by developers. Essbase and other OLAP databases have dimensionality built-in.

Optimized for Retrieval

Essbase databases were also optimized for retrieval at any level of the hierarchy, even the very topmost number that might represent every dollar the company has ever made in its history. OLTP databases (relational databases) were nicely optimized for retrieval of detailed records but definitely not hierarchical information. By pre-saving summarized information, Essbase allows analysis to happen from the top down with no decrease in performance.

For OLAP databases, the hierarchy is native to the database itself. This is far different from relational databases that store the data in one table and then have one or more other tables that can be joined in to view data in a rolled-up fashion. For Essbase, the hierarchy is the database. When you change the hierarchy logic in Essbase as to how a product is grouped or a market rolls-up, you actually change where the data is stored.

Because hierarchy is inherent to OLAP databases, drill-down (sometimes known as "slicing and dicing" but never known as "making julienne data") is inherent as well. Essbase is great at doing Ad hoc analysis (see Chapter 2) because it knows that when a user double-clicks on Qtr1, she wants to see Jan, Feb, and Mar. This is because the roll-up of months to quarters is pre-defined back on the server.

Dr. Codd came up with ten rules for defining OLAP databases. Some of them (such as the ability to write-back data) were more interesting than others. While some other databases at the time met one or more of the qualifications, the only OLAP database to meet all ten was Arbor Software's Essbase. (Remember that Arbor is the company that commissioned the study.)

DSS, EIS, BI, BPM, EPM...

For the first few years, everyone called Essbase (and its competitors like Cognos and Business Objects) either an MDDB or OLAP database. The problem was that this was very difficult to explain to a casual user. Since casual users (CEOs, COOs, CFOs, etc.) are the ones who tend to sign checks at most companies, this produced a marketing problem of the highest order. What is the actual purpose of these OLAP databases?

The overarching belief was that OLAP/MDDB databases "helped users make decisions and then provide them the information they needed to support those decisions." Since HUMDATPTTITNTSTD makes for a lousy acronym, the term DSS was created and thus the "Decision Support Systems" term was coined.

Since 1992 when Essbase was released, other terms have been bandied about at various times including EIS (either "Executive Information Systems" or "Enterprise Information Systems" depending on whom you ask) and BI (Business Intelligence). Business Intelligence is still used fairly frequently (thanks to a well funded marketing campaign by IBM in the late 90's), but its popularity is quickly being overtaken by BPM.

BPM (Business Performance Management) and more recently EPM (Enterprise Performance Management) is meant to include BI and expand it to also include any information a user needs to manage the performance of her company. Nowadays, this goes well beyond just a database and includes applications such as scorecarding, planning, and financial consolidation. If there is a number that needs to be manipulated, rolled-up, sliced, or diced, BPM should be able to handle it whether the original number is in an OLAP or OLTP database.

Historically, Essbase (and pretty much every other product Hyperion made) has been seen as a financial tool. The reason for this is two-fold. First, financial minds tend to understand Essbase really well. Financial analysis is inherently multi-dimensional. Income Statements tend to have accounts, time periods, scenarios, organizations, departments, companies and years on them. Since relational databases do a poor job at multi-dimensional data, finance types started using spreadsheets. Since Essbase was a database for spreadsheets, it made it really easy to explain the value to CFOs, Controllers, VPs of Planning, and the like.

The second reason for Essbase's traditional stereotyping as "something the bean counters use" has to do with sales and marketing. Since Essbase was so easy to explain to end users in accounting and finance, that's the group that the Essbase sales representatives tended to call on. The sad part about this is that the IT organization often felt left out and turned to inferior products from competing vendors because those vendors were seen as developing products that were more "IT-centric."

As for the current market, Oracle is generally accepted to be the market leader in the EPM space. They should be since they created the term in the first place in the early 21st century. EPM is quite the hot software niche these days thanks in no small part to Sarbanes-Oxley bringing compliance and management of data to the forefront. Simply put, Sarbanes-Oxley can put you in jail, and EPM can help keep you out.

Tip!

Putting Essbase, Hyperion, and EPM on your resume may very well get you a 10% boost in salary at your next job. Feel free to share half of that with the authors of this book.

ESSBASE TERMINOLOGY

We managed to make it all the way through the last chapter without learning a lot of Essbase terminology, but to truly succeed in the world of Essbase, there are some handy terms to pick up. Some of them we've already learned.

A "dimension" defines different categories for your data. A dimension can be located on the rows, columns, or pages of your queries. A "member name" is the short, computery name for the member of an Essbase dimension (like "100-10"). An "alias" is the longer, more descriptive name for a member (like "Cola"). All of the dimensions in a database make up the "outline."

Here is a portion of Sample.Basic outline:

```
Outline: Basic (Active Alias Table: Defau
⊟ Year
   ⊟ Qtr1 (+)
        Jan (+)
        Feb (+)
        Mar (+)
   ⊞ Qtr2 (+)
   ⊞ Qtr3 (+)
   ⊞ Qtr4 (+)
⊟ Measures
   ⊟ Profit (+)
        ⊟ Margin (+)
             Sales (+)
             COGS (-)
        ⊞ Total Expenses (-)
   ⊞ Inventory (~)
   ⊞ Ratios (~)
⊟ Product
   ⊞ 100 (+) (Alias: Colas)
   ⊞ 200 (+) (Alias: Root Beer)
   ⊞ 300 (+) (Alias: Cream Soda)
   ⊞ 400 (+) (Alias: Fruit Soda)
   ⊞ Diet (~) (Alias: Diet Drinks)
⊞ Market
⊞ Scenario
```

Family Tree Relationships

The most common way to refer to members in an outline relative to each other is by using "family tree" relationships. The members directly below a member are called its children. For instance, the Product dimension has five children: Colas, Root Beer, Cream Soda, Fruit Soda, and Diet Drinks. If we ever wanted to refer to those members on a report without hard coding them, we could say "give us all the children of Product."

The advantage to this aside from the saving in typing is that if a new product line was to be added (say, "Water"), we wouldn't have to modify our reports. Any report designed to display the children of Product would pick up the new "Water" product and add it to the list automatically.

If Colas, Root Beer, and the other rug rats are all the children of Product, what relation is Product to its children? Assuming you didn't fail "Birds and the Bees 101," you'll know that Product must be the *parent* of Colas, Root Beer, and the rest. In other words, the parent of any member is the one that the member rolls-up into. Qtr2 is the parent of May. Year is the parent of Qtr2.

Since Colas and Root Beer are both the children of Product, Colas and Root Beer are siblings. This is simple, but what relationship do January and May have? Well, their parents are siblings so that makes them... cousins. Correct, but "cousins" while technically correct isn't used that often. In general, people say that January and May are at the "same level."

What if you want to refer to all the members into which May rolls (not just the one right above)? Well, those are its ancestors which in this case would be Qtr2 and Year. Correspondingly, the descendants of Year would include all four quarters and all twelve months.

Note that there are members that don't have any children. In the picture above, May is childless. We refer to childless members as being "level-0". If you ever want all of the bottom, child-less members of a dimension, just ask for the level-0 members. For example, the level-0 members of the Year dimension are the months and the level-0 members of the Market dimension are the states.

Level-0 members are sometimes also referred to as "leaves," because they're at the edges of the family tree. Edward sometimes refers to level-0 members as "the ones who aren't allowed to sit at the main table on Thanksgiving," but we think he is the only one.

Make up your own name for level-0 members and try to get it to catch on at your company!

Try It!

All of the parents of the level-0 members are referred to as level-1. Since the level-0 members of the Year dimension are the months, then the level-1 members are the quarters. For the Market dimension, the level-1 members are the regions: East, West, South, and Central.

Just as the parents of the level-0 members are level-1 members, the parents of level-1 members are level-2 members. Their parents are level-3 members and so on up the hierarchy. There are many places in Essbase that you can specify, for example, "All the level-2 members of the Product dimension," so remember that levels count up from the bottom of a dimension starting at 0.

If you want to count down the hierarchy, use generations instead of levels. The dimension itself is considered generation-1 (or "gen1," for short). Its children are gen2. For the Year dimension, the gen2 members are the quarters.

Yes, the quarters are both level-2 and generation-2. Why do we need both levels and generations? Well, in some dimensions with many, many levels in the hierarchy, you'll want to count up from the bottom or down from the top depending on which you're closer to. We've seen a dimension with 17 levels in the hierarchy, and it definitely was nice to have both options available to me. The children of gen2 members are gen3 and so on down the hierarchy.

Note!

Why do generations start counting from 1 and levels from 0? It's because generation 0 is considered to be the outline itself making its children, the dimensions, generation 1.

While counting with generations is pretty straight-forward, levels can sometimes be a bit tricky. Look at this portion of the Measures dimension from Sample.Basic:

For this dimension, Gen1 is Measures. Gen2 is Profit and Inventory. Gen3 is Margin, Total Expenses, Opening Inventory, Additions, and Ending Inventory.

So far this is looking pretty easy, but let's switch our focus to the levels. The level-0 members are Sales, COGS, Marketing, Payroll, Misc, Opening Inventory, Additions, and Ending Inventory. The level-1 members are Margin, Total Expenses, and Inventory. What are the level-2 members? Profit (because it's the parent of level-1 members Margin and Total Expenses) and Measures (because it's the parent of level-1 member Inventory).

The trickiness is that Measures is *also* a level-3 member because it's the parent of Profit, a level-2 member. This means that if you ask Essbase for level-2 members, you'll get Measures, but you'll also get Measures if you ask for level-3 members. Notice that this counting oddity does not occur with generations.

 This instance of a dimension is also known as a ragged hierarchy.

Note!

Now that you can speak "Essbase", let us see this terminology applied in the different types of Essbase applications. Is Essbase just for finance? No! Let's see how Essbase can meet almost any type of reporting and analysis needs.

Chapter 4:
DIFFERENT APPLICATIONS

Everything we've done up to this point has been using the Sample.Basic database that comes with Essbase. While it's workable for exercises in this book, it's not terribly representative of databases in the real world. The goal for this chapter is to describe a few common types of databases in case you should ever run into them. For each application type, we'll review how the application is generally used and what the dimensions tend to be for that type of application. The most important take-away from this chapter: While Essbase is very good at financial analysis, it can support many, many different types of applications.

Note!

While an application can house one or more databases, most applications contain just one database. With that said, this chapter uses the terms "application" and "database" in the broader Information Technology sense.

COMMON DIMENSIONS

While every application will be different, most applications draw from a common set of dimension templates. The details within each dimension may change and the names of the dimensions may differ, but the same dimensions will keep appearing throughout many Essbase applications at your company. While we'll review later the differences for each specific application, it seems like a good idea to start with what we all have in common.

Time

All of us experience the constant effects of time and likewise (with very few exceptions), every Essbase database has one *or more* time dimensions. This is the dimension that contains the time periods for your database. Sample.Basic calls this dimension "Year":

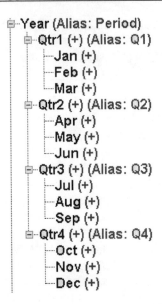

In addition to Year, other common names for this dimension include Periods, All Periods, Time (my personal favorite), Time Periods, Full Year, Year Total, and History. As you can tell from the plus signs above next to each member, this dimension generally aggregates from the bottom-up.

A Time dimension will usually have one or more of the following generations:

- Years
    - Seasons
        - Halves
            - Quarters
                - Months
                    - Weeks
                        - Days

While it is not unheard of to have an application that looks at hours or portions of hours, this is normally split off into its own dimension and called something like "Hours" or "Time of Day." Call center analysis applications and some retail sales applications analyze data by portions of a day.

It is quite common for an Essbase application to have two time dimensions. One dimension will house the quarters, months, days, and so forth. A separate dimension, generally called "Years" or "FY" (for Fiscal Year), will contain the calendar year. Here's an example of a Years dimension:

```
⊟ Years (Alias: Current Year)
    ├─ FY03 (~) (Alias: 2003)
    ├─ FY04 (~) (Alias: 2004)
    ├─ FY05 (~) (Alias: 2005)
    ├─ FY06 (+) (Alias: 2006)
    ├─ FY07 (~) (Alias: 2007)
    ├─ FY08 (~) (Alias: 2008)
    ├─ FY09 (~) (Alias: 2009)
    └─ FY10 (~) (Alias: 2010)
```

Unlike the Time dimensions that usually contain quarters and months, Years dimensions typically do not aggregate. Most often, the top member of a Years dimension is set to equal the data in the current year. In the above image, the tilde (~) signs (also called "no consolidate" tags) denote which years are not to be added into the total. As you can see, only FY06 has a plus next it, and therefore, is the only one to roll into Years. As such, Years equals FY06.

Some applications will combine a Time and Years dimension into one. This is often done when the Time dimension goes all the way down to the day-level and a company wants to do analysis by day of the week:

```
⊟ Time {Day of Week}
    ⊞ 2005 (+)
    ⊞ 2006 (+)
    ⊟ 2007 (+)
        ⊞ Jan, 2007 (+)
        ⊞ Feb, 2007 (+)
        ⊞ Mar, 2007 (+)
        ⊞ Apr, 2007 (+)
        ⊞ May, 2007 (+)
        ⊟ Jun, 2007 (+)
            ├─ Jun 1, 2007 (+) {Day of Week: Friday}
            ├─ Jun 2, 2007 (+) {Day of Week: Saturday}
            ├─ Jun 3, 2007 (+) {Day of Week: Sunday}
            ├─ Jun 4, 2007 (+) {Day of Week: Monday}
            ├─ Jun 5, 2007 (+) {Day of Week: Tuesday}
            ├─ Jun 6, 2007 (+) {Day of Week: Wednesday}
            ├─ Jun 7, 2007 (+) {Day of Week: Thursday}
            ├─ Jun 8, 2007 (+) {Day of Week: Friday}
            ├─ Jun 9, 2007 (+) {Day of Week: Saturday}
            ├─ Jun 10, 2007 (+) {Day of Week: Sunday}
            ├─ Jun 11, 2007 (+) {Day of Week: Monday}
            ├─ Jun 12, 2007 (+) {Day of Week: Tuesday}
            └─ Jun 13, 2007 (+) {Day of Week: Wednesday}
```

Each date in the dimension has a "Day of Week" user-defined attribute (UDA) assigned to it. "Jun 1, 2007," for instance, has a "Day of Week" attribute of Friday. If we had the years in a separate dimension, we would have to declare every June 1ˢᵗ to be a Friday. While the people born on June 1ˢᵗ would absolutely love this, the calendar makers would not. As such, we have to put the year in to specify a specific date as being a specific day of the week. Here is the "Day of Week" attribute dimension that is used in conjunction with the dimension above:

⊟·**Day of Week [Type: Text]**
 ├···**Sunday**
 ├···**Monday**
 ├···**Tuesday**
 ├···**Wednesday**
 ├···**Thursday**
 ├···**Friday**
 └···**Saturday**

While most Time dimensions use Essbase Dynamic Time Series functionality to calculate year-to-date and quarter-to-date members, it's not uncommon to come across an older Essbase outline that has actual YTD and QTD members. Usually, there will be a member called YTD (and/or QTD) in the Time dimension that will have a child for each month. For January, the member would be called either "Jan YTD" or "YTD Jan." Here's an example of a Time dimension with stored YTD members:

```
⊟ All Periods
  ⊟ MTD (+) (Alias: Full Year)
    ⊟ Qtr1 (+)
        Jan (+)
        Feb (+)
        Mar (+)
    ⊞ Qtr2 (+)
    ⊞ Qtr3 (+)
    ⊞ Qtr4 (+)
  ⊟ YTD (~)
      Jan YTD (~)
      Feb YTD (~)
      Mar YTD (~)
      Apr YTD (~)
      May YTD (~)
      Jun YTD (~)
      Jul YTD (~)
      Aug YTD (~)
      Sep YTD (~)
      Oct YTD (~)
      Nov YTD (~)
      Dec YTD (~)
```

Measures

Like Time, almost every Essbase application has a dimension that lists the metrics for the database. While common practice is to call this dimension Measures (as Sample.Basic does), other frequently used names include Accounts and Metrics.

In Sample.Basic, the Measures dimension contains some profit and loss accounts, inventory metrics, and three calculated ratios:

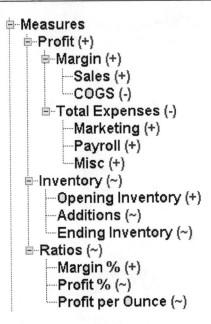

You'll notice that under "Profit," there are two members for "Margin" and "Total Expenses." Each one of these members has members below it. It's quite common for a Measures dimension to have many levels of hierarchy. A financial reporting application, for instance, might have hierarchy all the way down to a sub-account level.

While most every application will have a Measures dimension, what constitutes the Measures dimension will differ wildly:

- A financial reporting application will have accounts for income statement, balance sheet, and sometimes cash flow.
- An inventory analysis application will have measures for beginning inventory, ending inventory, additions, returns, adjustments, and so forth.
- A sales analysis application will have measures for sales dollars, units sold, and average sales price.
- A human capital analysis application will have metrics for payroll, FICA, FUTA, sick days, vacation days, years of employment, and so on.

The Measures dimension is the most important dimension in any application since it lets you define what metrics you're going to analyze, but you can safely expect every Measures dimension to be unique for every application.

It's worth pointing out that the Measures dimension in Sample.Basic is very odd. It's not normal to see inventory statistics along with profit and loss accounts in the same database. From what we can tell, this was only done to show in a sample database that Essbase can handle things beyond just financial metrics.

Scenario

This dimension is common to applications that in addition to actual data also have budget, forecast, or planning information. The "Scenario" dimension usually houses members such as Actual, Budget, Forecast, What-If, and several variances (differences between one scenario and another). While the most popular name for this dimension is Scenario (or Scenarios), other common names include Category, Ledger, Cases, and Versions.

As a general rule, we try to avoid calling my Scenario dimension "Versions," because Hyperion Planning also has a dimension called "Versions" in addition to a "Scenario" dimension. In Planning, the Versions dimension is used to differentiate between different drafts of budget and plan data. Members in a Versions dimension could be Initial, Draft 1, Draft 2, Draft 3, and Final. To avoid confusion in case you run across any lost Planning users at your company, don't name your Scenario dimension "Versions" when there are so many other good names from which to choose.

Here is Sample.Basic's Scenario dimension:

Most Scenario dimensions are non-aggregating (since it doesn't make a lot of sense to add Actual and Budget together). In Sample.Basic, the only

```
⊟ Scenario
   ├ Actual (+)
   ├ Budget (~)
   ├ Variance (~)
   └ Variance % (~)
```

child of Scenario to roll-up is Actual, in effect, setting Scenario equal to Actual.

Other Dimensions

Many applications have a dimension that differentiates between different organizational entities. Commonly, this dimension is called Entities (the name Hyperion Planning prefers), Organization (the name we prefer), Departments, Cost Centers, Companies, Locations, and other industry specific names (like Stores or Branches). The closest Sample.Basic has to an Organization dimension is the Market dimension.

Another common dimension that you might run across is Product which houses the relationships between products and their categories and families. This is one of the few dimensions where just about everyone calls it the same thing although the alias differs at the top of the dimension, containing something like "All Products" or "Total Products." The greatest difference in this dimension is the depth to which different applications go. Some Product dimensions stop at different classes of products while others will go all the way down to individual parts, items, or SKUs (Stock Keeping Units).

Other dimensions tend to be specific to different types of applications. For instance, a Customer dimension will tend to show up in Sales Analysis and Accounts Receivable applications. We'll cover some of the major applications you'll tend to see. This is by no means thorough, because every day, a company comes up with some new way to use Essbase that no one has ever tried before.

Please don't think that Essbase can only be used for financial applications. We once built an Essbase cube to track projects that families signed up for at our church Advent workshop. Okay, that's really geeky, but it goes to show you what you can do if you get out of the finance realm.

FINANCIAL REPORTING

Financial reporting (often called General Ledger, or GL analysis) databases are by far the most common type of Essbase application. This goes back to the early days of Essbase when the Arbor Software sales team used to sell pretty much exclusively into finance and accounting departments. Even today, the first Essbase database most companies build is to facilitate general ledger analysis.

In all fairness, Essbase is very good at doing GL analysis. Essbase has hundreds of built-in financial functions that make it a good fit for GL reporting. The Essbase outline provides a user friendly view of how accounts, departments, and other entities roll up within hierarchies and dimensions. It is also very easy for finance-minded personnel to manage those hierarchies. The most attractive thing about Essbase to accountants, though, is that accountants love Excel and as you just saw from the earlier chapters, Excel loves Essbase (or is that the other way around?).

Financial Reporting applications generally receive data from one or more GL Systems (including those that are part of a larger ERP solution). Generally, this data is loaded monthly right after a financial close, but it is sometimes loaded more frequently during the close process.

Typical Financial Reporting dimensions include those common dimensions just discussed: Time, Measures, Scenario, Organization and Years. Measures will contain your account hierarchies for income statement, balance sheet, metrics, and cash flow. You can have alternate hierarchies to support different reporting requirements (more on that later).

In addition to the common dimensions, you will have those dimensions for which you'd like to perform analysis – by Geography, Product, Channel, or any other imaginable dimension that makes sense for your company. That's the beauty of Essbase: dimensionality is flexible and 100% customizable.

SALES ANALYSIS

Sales Analysis applications are a natural fit for Essbase, because they require fast retrievals at detailed levels. We once built a Sales Analysis application (sometimes called Flash Sales) that had data by store (for over 5,000 stores) by SKU (for over 100,000 products) by day for three years. It was an obscene amount of detail, but Essbase handled it flawlessly with retrievals measured in seconds.

Typical dimensions for this class of application such as Product, Location, and Geography. You can also view sales data by demographics like age and income level of buyer, by store information like store manager, square footage, store type, or location, or by product information like promotion or introduction date:

```
⊟ Age
  ⊟ Teens (+)
    ├ 1 to 13 Years (+)
    └ 14 to 19 Years (+)
  ⊟ Adults (+)
    ├ 20 to 25 Years (+)
    ├ 26 to 30 Years (+)
    ├ 31 to 35 Years (+)
    ├ 36 to 45 Years (+)
    └ 46 to 54 Years (+)
  ⊞ Senior (+)
```

Time dimensions will often go to the day level (and be tracked across multiple years) and have attributes for day of week. Measures or accounts will often include units sold, cost of goods sold, price, revenue, and much more. Some sales applications have inventory data as well and include weeks of supply calculations.

With the introduction of Aggregate Storage Option (known in System 9 as "Enterprise Analytics"), the level of detail that can be loaded into Sales Analysis applications has grown exponentially. The advent of 64-bit Essbase has expanded the size of some of these databases even further since 64-bit Essbase allows far more RAM to be allocated to individual Essbase applications.

Unlike financial reporting applications which are generally fed from GLs or ERPs, Sales Analysis applications are generally fed from data warehouses, operational data stores, and legacy systems. It is not uncommon for Sales Analysis databases to be loaded every night with the prior day's sales data.

HUMAN CAPITAL ANALYSIS

Human Capital Analysis applications allow companies to analyze one of their most important assets: their people. (How important are certain people in your organization? Discuss.) Sometimes these applications are called Human Resources analysis, Employee analysis, or Salary analysis. We'll go with "Human Capital" analysis because it's trendy. "Human Resources" is *so* five minutes ago.

In addition to the ubiquitous Measures and Time, common dimensions for Human Capital applications include employee, employee status, job grade, and function.

⊟ 501000 (+) (Alias: Total Compensation)
  ⊟ 501100 (+) (Alias: Salaries and Wages)
    ⊞ 501110 (+) (Alias: Total Salary)
    ⊞ 501120 (+) (Alias: Overtime)
     501130 (+) (Alias: Bonus Expense)
     501150 (+) (Alias: Auto Allowance)
  ⊞ 501200 (+) (Alias: Taxes and Benefits)

Detailed applications could also include title, start dates, and other employee-level information. It's also not uncommon to have Equal Employment Opportunity Commission attributes such as race, gender, age, and veteran status.

The Measures dimension will have accounts that tend to map to the General Ledger (particularly, the payroll or compensation section of the income statement).

You can also use different drivers to budget and plan employee costs. Headcount, Start Month, Vacation Days, Sick Days, and many more can be used in calculations to complete accurate planning numbers.

These drivers can also provide invaluable insight into historical employee trends. We once knew a company that analyzed employee sick time patterns to find out which employees tended to be "sick" on Mondays more than any other day of the week. Apparently, the Monday morning flu was a big problem at their company.

CAPITAL EXPENDITURE ANALYSIS

Capital Expenditure applications (often abbreviated to "Cap Ex" and sometimes called Capital Equipment or Fixed Asset) are another frequent type of Essbase cube. Whether it is determining the rate of return on an investment or it is tracking capital equipment requests from your organization, you can implement a CapEx application to suit your company's needs. Dimensions include capital equipment item, equipment type, asset category, and asset life.

Here are some examples of capital equipment dimensions:

⊟ Equip Type
  ⊟ All Equip Types (+)
    — Building (+)
    — Leasehold Improv (+)
    — Mfg Machinery (+)
    — Office Furniture (+)
    — Computer Equip (+)
    — New Software (+)
    — Auto (+)
  — No Equip Type (+)

⊟ Category
  — Capacity (+)
  — Capability (+)
  — Cost Reduction (+)
  — Maintenance (+)
  — Market Opportunity (+)
  — Quality (+)
  — No Category (+)

⊟ Projects
  ⊟ All Projects (+)
    — Laser Weld (+)
    — Plasma R&D (+)
    — Networking (+)
    — BPM Implementation (+)
  — No Project (+)

The Account dimension for these applications usually contains a portion of your Balance Sheet:

⊟ BalanceSheet (~) (Alias: Balance Sheet)
  ⊟ 100000 (+) (Alias: Total Assets)
    ⊟ 150000 (+) (Alias: Fixed Assets)
      ⊟ 151000 (+) (Alias: Gross PPE)
        — 151100 (+) (Alias: Construction in Progress)
        — 151200 (+) (Alias: Land)
        — 151300 (+) (Alias: Buildings)
        — 151400 (+) (Alias: Leasehold Improvements)
        — 151500 (+) (Alias: Mfg Mach and Equip)
        — 151600 (+) (Alias: Office Furn and Fixtures)
        — 151700 (+) (Alias: Computer Equipment)
        — 151800 (+) (Alias: Computer Software)
        — 151900 (+) (Alias: Vehicles)
      — 152000 (+) (Alias: Accumulated Depreciation)

Other metrics that tend to show up in the Measures dimension include quantities, charges, months in service, asset life, and other drivers related to capital equipment.

Generally, CapEx applications are loaded from the Fixed Asset module from your ERP, but it is not uncommon for plan data for capital expenditures to be entered directly into Essbase (or via

Hyperion Planning's Capital Expenditure model available in System 9.3).

BUDGETING, PLANNING, AND FORECASTING

With highly sophisticated write back capabilities, Essbase provides an excellent solution for budgeting, planning, and forecasting systems. Hyperion Planning was built on top of Essbase specifically to take advantage of Essbase's sublime ability to not only be used for reporting of data, but also multi-user submission of data.

Back in the days before Hyperion Planning was invented, many companies built Essbase cubes for budgeting purposes. They sent their data in via the Essbase Add-In and they were happy. Essbase security limited the dimensions and members for which data could be entered by users and calc scripts were used to calculate data if necessary.

If Essbase is perfect for budgeting, why was Planning created? The answer is simply due to the needs of planners and budgeters expanding beyond the abilities of Essbase. Modern forecasters require things like audit trails, integrated workflow, web-based data entry, and more. While Essbase can meet straight-forward budget needs, it doesn't have the built-in functionality that you get when you pay for Hyperion Planning.

Budgeting and forecasting applications written in Essbase (or built in Essbase via Hyperion Planning) will tend to look very similar to your reporting and analysis applications. For example, you may have a budgeting application to capture budget for income statement items, another application for capital equipment planning, and another application for salary planning. Though these applications will be similar to your reporting and analysis applications, they often do not contain the same level of detail. In general, budget data is not as granular as actual data.

In the example below, budget is captured at the reporting line level of Market while actual data is captured by GL account:

So...can we just capture budget and forecast information in my reporting and analysis applications? Yes, but there are some

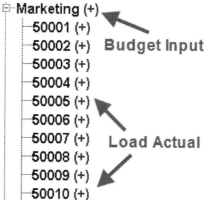

things to consider. First, understand the level of detail. If you are capturing budget at a higher level, you have to think carefully about how consolidations will take place in Essbase. If you enter data at an upper level and then run an aggregation, you could easily erase the data that was entered by users at the higher points in the dimension. There are ways to prevent this but the traditional work around is to use "dummy" members (see page below).

Second, we need to think about the dimensionality required for each purpose. In your reporting and analysis databases, you may want to analyze actual data by more dimensions or slices than you would for budget data. Too many dimensions can overly complicate the budgeting and planning process.

Third, you may also want to think about splitting reporting and budgeting for backup reasons. You'll want to backup your budgeting and planning applications more often as data changes far more frequently.

NOT JUST FINANCIAL

While Essbase is great at financial reporting and analysis, it is not limited to just the "financials". You can report and analyze on practically any subject area if it includes dimensions, hierarchies and numbers (and even text and dates in Essbase 11). You can easily manage performance with reporting key metrics and drivers across the organization, delivering actionable information to change the way you do business for the better. Customer analysis is possible, providing detailed information for millions of customers. Procurement analysis databases can track many products across many vendors. Logistics analysis delivers near real-time updates of product shipments and Market Basket analysis can show important correlations between product purchases. As long as your reporting and analysis requirements don't include detailed "columns and columns" type reports (think Human Resources report with the following columns: Name, Address, City, State, Zip, Position, Home Phone, Work Phone, Cell Phone, Emergency Contact), Essbase is likely a good solution.

Now that you understand some of the basics from an end user perspective and some concepts and terminology for Essbase, let's get to the part you care about: creating Essbase databases.

Become an Essbase Administrator

Chapter 5:
Create an Application

In the beginning there was spreadsheet craziness, linked formula nightmares, broken reference mania... and then we found Essbase. In order to use an Essbase database to analyze information and save your sanity, you must first create an Essbase database (sometimes called a cube).

In the next series of chapters we will create an Essbase database from start to finish. The primary interface for creating and managing Essbase databases is the Administration Services Console in versions 7x through 11x. In version 11, a new interface was added into the mix called Essbase Studio. This book focuses on the Administration Services Console but never fear. We have a chapter that will introduce Essbase Studio later in the book. Hold on to your hats, boys and girls, because we're about to build an Essbase database.

Tip!

Save yourself some time and email us at info@interrel.com, requesting the book workshop files. This book will walk you through the process to create Essbase objects step by step but in some cases, you may want to get your hands on the sample load files and validation worksheets versus creating them yourself.

ADMINISTRATION SERVICES

Administration Services (also known as *Essbase* Administration Services – EAS – or *Analytic* Administration Services – AAS – depending on your version) is a central administration tool for managing and maintaining all of Essbase. The goal of Administration Services is to make Essbase applications easier to maintain in a modernized interface that is fully cross-platform supported.

Administration Services replaced the Essbase Application Manager of Essbase 6x. For those of you who enjoy living in the Paleolithic era, Administration Services is leaps and bounds better than Application Manager (although the first few builds of EAS sucked eggs).

Administration Services consists of a client console (Administration Services Console). This is the graphical interface that Essbase administrators and designers use to build and manage Essbase applications. The Administration Services Console talks to a middle-tier application server (the "Administration Server").

The Administration Server is something that no one will see once it's working correctly. Administration Server serves as a centralized management point as it communicates directly with multiple Essbase servers, and allows multiple administrators to focus their work in a single shared environment.

Administration Server communicates directly with Essbase servers. One Administration Server can talk to multiple Essbase servers. All Administration Services components are J2EE-compliant. J2EE stands for Java 2 Enterprise Edition which in English-speak means that they're java-based. For those who believe a picture is worth a thousand words, here's a diagram to illustrate all those tiers:

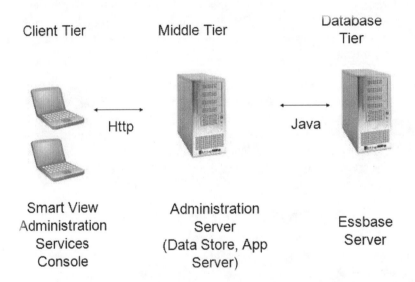

Client Tier	Middle Tier	Database Tier
Http		Java
Smart View Administration Services Console	Administration Server (Data Store, App Server)	Essbase Server

Administration Services Console is where you as the administrator or designer will build outlines, create dimensions, load data, calculate, assign security, define filters, manage all of your Essbase servers, and about 1.652 gazillion other things Essbase-related. This is *the* interface for all of your Essbase databases (well, it *was* the interface for all of your Essbase databases; Studio is a new alternative discussed later in the book).

So, go ahead, start the Administration Console. Feel the power coursing through your veins.

Starting the Console

1. Double-click on the Admincon.exe icon.

   or

   Select *Start >> Oracle EPM System>> Essbase >> Administration Services >> Start Administration Console.*

2. Type or select the Administration Services server (in our example our server is named epm111):

3. Type the user name and password and then click *OK*:

The Administration Services console will display:

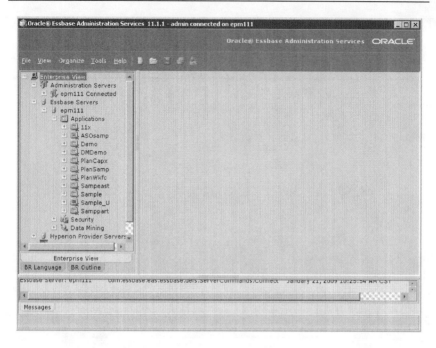

In the console, you can view and manage all Administration servers installed in your environment. In most cases, you have one Administration Server that manages all of your Essbase servers including development and production:

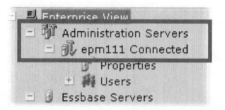

To view and manage all of the Essbase servers installed in your environment, expand the *Essbase Servers* section of the Enterprise View:

One of the big benefits of Administration Services is that you can manage development, QA, test, and production environments in one window. Copying objects across Essbase servers (even if they are different platforms like Unix and Windows) becomes child's play in Administration Services.

An Essbase administrator once deleted a production application, thinking he was connected to the development Essbase server. This same administrator also copied an unfinished development application from the development Essbase server to the production server, mixing up the 'to' and 'from' server during the copy. If you don't want to get fired, make sure you know which server you are connected to before you start performing potentially serious actions.

Navigate in Administration Services

There are three main ways to perform actions in the Administration Services console:

1. Menu items:

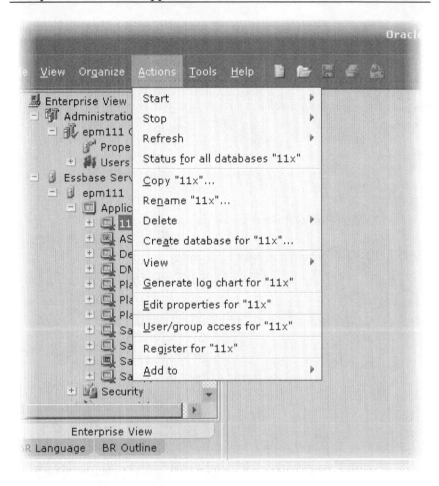

2. Icons:

3. Right click:

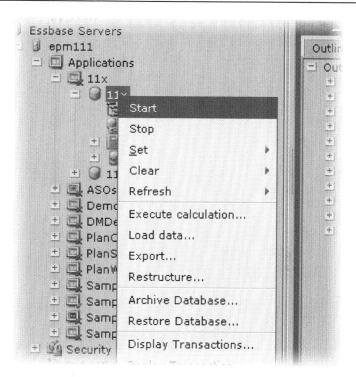

We personally prefer right clicking since it's an easy way not to have to remember which actions are available for a specific item. Right click on an object in the Enterprise View (the pane on the left) and you'll see all the relevant actions available to you.

Generally, when you open an item on the left (in the View pane), it will open in the pane to the right. There is another important pane in Administration Services: Messages. This section is found (unless you went to the *View* menu and turned it off) in the lower part of your window. Messages about whether actions are successful or not will be posted here:

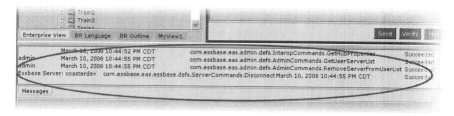

Administration Services may not send up a big, flashy error message so be mindful of the information communicated in this section. Although messages will almost always be displayed here, the messages displayed here will almost always be highly summarized, and in computer-speak.

Stare at the messages a while and at least you'll be able to tell if the message is informational or it's a major error. For example, if a message was displayed saying "It's currently sunny with a chance of rain late in the day," this would be informational. If the message "Fatal error occurred: self-destruct sequence initiated" appears, stare at it for a nanosecond and then run.

Note!

You are very unlikely to see a "self-destruct" message.

What Can You Do in Administration Services?

Helpful
Info

- Define the database outline.
- Create dimension build rules.
- Create data load rules.
- Create calculation scripts.
- Create report scripts.
- Partition databases.
- Review log reports and database / server information.
- Manage Essbase servers.

CREATE AN ESSBASE ASO APPLICATION

Creating new applications and databases using Administration Services is ridiculously simple. An application is a container of databases. A database is the actual Essbase "cube" that stores and organizes data for analysis and reporting. Essbase allows two database types: aggregate storage databases (ASO) and block storage databases (BSO). We won't go into the details yet on the differences between the two because honestly, your eyes will glaze over and it won't make sense any way. We'll get there after you get your feet wet creating your first Essbase database.

Create an Application and Database

1. Select *File >> New*
    or
    right click on Applications under the Essbase server and select *Create Application >> Using aggregate storage* or *Create Application >> Using block storage*.

2. Choose either *Block Storage Application* or *Aggregate Storage Application*. Select Aggregate Storage since we won't be covering Block Storage right now:

3. Select the Essbase Server and specify a new application name. For our example, call it "Juggle". (Do not check "Unicode mode". We'll cover this in a later section.):

4. Click *OK*. You now have an application with no databases within it. This is completely useless, so don't stop now.
5. Right click on the application you just created and select *Create Database*:

6. Your server and application should already be selected, so type in a new database name (for our example, use "Juggle").
7. Optional: Choose to *Allow duplicate member names*:

Beginning in System 9, Essbase allows you to create duplicate members. But should you use it? Only if you absolutely need to... In our example, we'll check this option so that we can show you how to set up duplicate members. More on this feature in a few pages.

Tip!

Name your Essbase applications and databases the same name if possible. This eliminates confusion.

Note!

Notice database type options *Normal* and *Currency* are grayed out as they are only applicable to Block Storage databases.

Note!

For Block Storage Databases, don't select Currency, because you shouldn't be using Essbase's Currency Conversion module *ever*.

8. Click *OK*.

That's it. Creating the application is the easy part. Now it gets a bit more complicated, but we'll be here for you (imagine the Bon Jovi song playing in the background – "I'll Be There For You").

Try It!

If you didn't follow along, create a new application (Aggregate Storage Option) database and Allow Duplicate Member Names. Name both of them Juggle. Why Juggle? Geez... you ask a lot of questions.

Essbase Outlines are *Very* Important

The single most important thing that you will work with in Essbase is the outline. Your Essbase outline contains *all* of the hierarchical information for your application and if you recall the earlier chapters on analyzing Essbase data you will know that hierarchies are EVERYTHING to an Essbase end-user. Unlike a relational database where the hierarchy is applied to data already stored in tables, in Essbase, the outline (and as such, the hierarchy) directly controls *how* data is stored and indexed. When you modify your outline, you restructure your database.

Note!   Essbase allows one and only one outline per database.

Building dimensions, ordering them, adding hierarchies, adding members with member attributes, and creating member formulas all drive the performance of your Essbase application. First and foremost, your outline needs to reflect your business requirements.

Do not commit the cardinal sin of looking at your source data first and then building an Essbase outline to hold it all. Do not turn every field in your relational table into a dimension in Essbase. This will result in a very flat **Tip!**   Essbase cube that's extremely difficult to use and your users will burn your image in effigy.

We strongly recommend beginning this process by analyzing the reports that need to be created. Your reports will help you identify the dimensions for your database. What's in the rows and columns will become dimensions in your outline. If you're looking at an income statement that has accounts down the side and months across the top, you have an outline with at least two dimensions: Measures and Time. Pay attention to what applies to the whole report. If multiple copies of income statements are generated, one for each department in the company, then your outline will need an Organization dimension.

Let's start with baby steps and review some key outline concepts.

Dimensions are the common groupings of data elements for which we analyze and report. Examples include Time, Account, Product, and Market.

Dimensions are made up of members. Members will have a member name and alias: two ways to view the member. In the example below, we see product number is the member name and the product description is the alias:

Note!

You can use either or both member name and alias when reporting against Essbase databases.

There are six dimension types that you will utilize in Essbase: Accounts, Time, Time Date, Country, Currency Partition, and Attribute. You could also have "None" or no dimension type assigned. Essbase provides some built in functionality associated with each one of these dimension types. The Accounts dimension type has special account attributes like time balance and expense reporting. Time allows dynamic time series. Country and Currency Partition are important when using the Essbase Currency Conversion module in BSO applications (although you should *never* use the Currency Conversion module).

Note!

Time Date dimensions were initially introduced for ASO Essbase applications and are now available for BSO Essbase applications.

Edit the Outline

Let's pretend for a second that you're starting your own business. No, it doesn't matter what type of company, but in the interest of simplicity, let's say your lifelong passion is to juggle wolverines (ah...so that's why we named our application and database Juggle). You run out and buy yourself some wolverines, a copy of Excel, and a copy of Essbase. Since you have a lot of venture capital (wolverine juggling is a growth industry), you pay to have a consultant come in and install the Essbase suite of products.

Since the Juggling Wolverine Company (JWC) isn't that complicated (for instance, your only GL accounts are revenue, operating expenses, and other expenses), you've decided to create a simple, four-dimensional outline. While most BSO outlines have five to nine dimensions and ASO outlines can have 20+, we're okay with four until the business starts to expand.

1. In Administration Services, navigate to the Database Outline beneath the database you've already created.
2. Right click and select *Edit*. The outline editor will open:

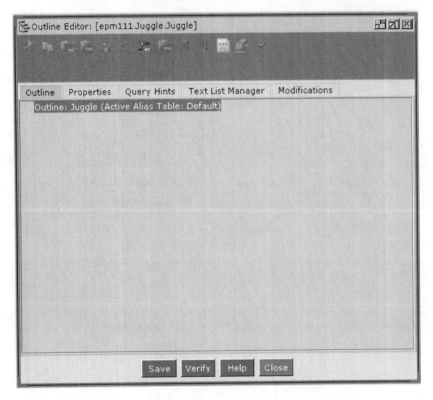

3. Right click and select *Add Child* or *Add Sibling*:

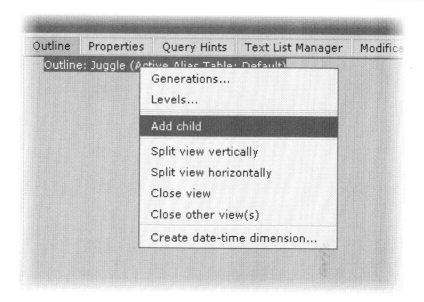

You can also click on the *Add Child* or *Add Sibling* icon in the Outline Editor Menu:

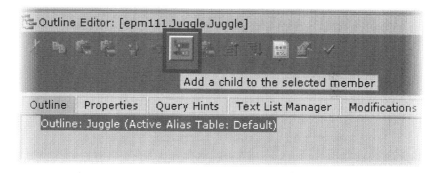

4. Begin adding dimensions and members.

For our cash cow company in the making, add Year, Period, Scenario, and Account dimensions to build an outline that looks like the following:

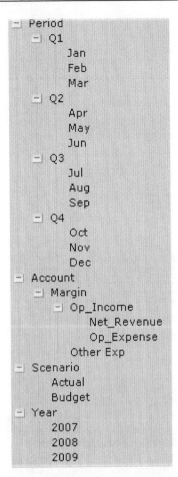

DEFINE MEMBER PROPERTIES AND DIMENSION TYPES

So you've built the basic structure of the outline with four dimensions and their hierarchies and members. Now let's discuss more member properties. There are common member properties that exist across all dimensions. We've already discussed two – member name and alias. Other common member properties include consolidation, UDAs, and member formulas. Some member properties are applicable to ASO databases while others are only applicable to BSO databases. Some member properties are specific to a dimension type like Expense Reporting and Time Balance.

Note!
In Essbase 11, ASO and BSO member properties are more closely aligned than in previous versions.

Consolidation Operators

Consolidation operators tell the outline how to consolidate the member (yes, a user friendly description that accurately describes the property. Imagine that!) Should the members Dallas and Houston add together to reach a total for Texas? Should units sold be multiplied by price to calculate revenue? You can use consolidation operators to define how a member rolls up in the database.

Valid consolidation operators include:

- Addition (+) – This is the default consolidation property.
- Subtraction (-)
- Multiplication (*)
- Division (/)
- Percent (%)
- No consolidate (~) (in the same dimension)
- Never consolidate (^) (for all dimensions)

Tip!
System 9.3 introduced a new consolidation type ^ - never consolidate for BSO databases. ^ is not available for ASO databases.

In most cases you will use the default Addition consolidation tag:

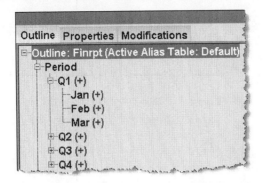

The second most common consolidation tag is "No consolidate". Use this in places where it doesn't make sense to add up members. Would we want to add Actual and Budget together for Scenario? No, so we would tag both Actual and Budget "no consolidate" or ~ in the outline.

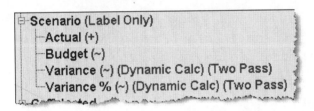

A new consolidation attribute was added to Essbase in System 9.3 – never consolidate or ^. This consolidation is similar to the ~ which will not consolidate a member up its assigned dimension. The never consolidate option will not consolidate data across ANY dimension in the Essbase database. Use this tag for stored members like price or index where it doesn't make sense to sum up together across dimensions like Customer or Product.

Data Storage Property

The Data Storage property tells Essbase how the member should be stored. Valid data storage options include:
- Store: Store the data value with the member.
- Never share: Do not allow members to be shared implicitly (don't worry, a good explanation for this confusing concept is just below).
- Label Only: Create members for navigation and grouping. These members usually won't make sense from a logical consolidation standpoint.
- Shared Member: Share data between two or more members.

- Dynamic Calc and Store: Do not calculate the data value until a user requests it, but store the data value immediately after the retrieval. (Applicable to BSO only)
- Dynamic Calc: Do not calculate the data value until a user requests it, and then discard the data value. (Applicable to BSO only)

When should you set a member to Store? In ASO databases, most of your members by default will be set to *Store Data*.

When should you use Never Share? When you have a parent that only has one child that rolls up to the parent. Essbase has a built in feature called Implicit Sharing, a mischievous function that can cause confusion in your Essbase databases. Essbase tries to be smart for us. When a parent only has one aggregating child, the values for both the parent and the child will always be the same, right? So Essbase decides to only store one value, the child value, which reduces your database size. But this causes issues at times so you may choose to use Never Share.

When should you use Label Only? Use Label Only for members like "Scenario", "Ratios", or "Drivers", members whose sole purpose in life is to organize the dimension and hierarchy: members for which it never makes sense to add their children together. A member marked as Label Only will automatically pull the value of its first child when referenced. Because of this, when we make a member Label Only, we will often make its first child have a plus and the other children have a tilde to designate that only the first child is rolling to the member. This is entirely to help indicate what's going on in Essbase to a user who might not know that a Label Only member pulls the value from its first child.

In this example below, it makes no sense to add Actual and Budget together, so we flag Scenario as Label Only:

```
⊟ Scenario (Label Only)
    ─ Actual (+)
    ─ Budget (~)
    ─ Variance (~) (Dynamic Calc) (Two Pass)
    └ Variance % (~) (Dynamic Calc) (Two Pass)
```

When should you use Shared Members? First, let's further define "Shared Members." Shared members have the same name as another member, belong to the same dimension and point to the same data values; however, shared members belong to different parents and participate in different roll-ups for alternate views of the same data. The original member contains the value and the Shared Member has a pointer to the original member. Members can be shared among many parents and can be shared with multiple generations.

Let's look at example from Sample.Basic, where products are organized by product category. An alternate hierarchy to obtain a total for all Diet drinks is present, utilizing Shared Members for all of the different diet products underneath the parent:

```
⊟ Product
    ⊟ 100 (+) (Alias: Colas)
        ─ 100-10 (+) (Alias: Cola)
        ─ 100-20 (+) (Alias: Diet Cola)
        └ 100-30 (+) (Alias: Caffeine Free Cola)
    ⊞ 200 (+) (Alias: Root Beer)
    ⊞ 300 (+) (Alias: Cream Soda)
    ⊞ 400 (+) (Alias: Fruit Soda)
    ⊟ Diet (~) (Alias: Diet Drinks)
        ─ 100-20 (+) (Alias: Diet Cola) (Shared Member)
        ─ 200-20 (+) (Alias: Diet Root Beer) (Shared Member)
        └ 300-30 (+) (Alias: Diet Cream) (Shared Member)
```

So back to the question at hand: when to use Shared Members? Use this feature when you'd like to create alternate rollups of data in the same dimension. For example, rolling up products both by Market and by Product Category, rolling up a department both by Manager and by Organization Structure, and rolling up revenue both by standard income statement hierarchy as well as a custom reporting hierarchy. Shared members provide powerful analysis capabilities by aggregating and analyzing values in many different ways, without creating a burden on either the end-user or the administrator.

User Defined Attributes (UDAs)

User defined attributes are tags assigned to outline members and are used to describe a member, to reference members for specific calculation purposes, or to isolate members for specialized reporting and analysis. A member can have more than one UDA associated with itself.

In the example below from Sample.Basic, a UDA describing each market's category has been assigned:

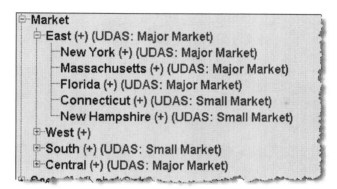

This UDA can now be used in calculations (e.g. estimating budgeted product sales based on market size). We can even create a market category specific report, only pulling states that are considered a "Major Market."

Other examples of UDA usage include reference flags like Flip_Sign or Expense_Report. The reference flag type UDAs can then be used in load rules (to flip a sign for data values being loaded into the database) or in a member formula (to help calculate valid positive / negative variances). UDAs can be used for almost anything that business requirements dictate, and do it without adding the storage requirements of extra dimensions or members.

User Defined Attributes are defined in the Member Properties window, when you click on the "UDA" tab.

Note!   Data cannot be summarized by UDA.

Member Types

We're happy to say that in Essbase 11, a member in the dimension tagged Accounts may be one of three types: numeric, text or date. In earlier versions, Essbase only stored numeric data ("numbers"). A new feature was introduced in 11.1 that allows the administrator to create and display text or date values to users. What is really happening is that behind the scenes, Essbase is still storing a numeric value, but a translation happens between the stored value and a look up list with the assigned text or date value.

Member Formulas

Member formulas allow you to define specific logic for calculating that member. This logic can range from very simple to highly complex. For most variance members, you will use a member formula for the variance calculation. Member formulas are utilized to calculate averages and ratios. The syntax for the formulas will vary depending on the type of Essbase database. ASO databases use MDX syntax while BSO databases leverage specific Essbase calc script syntax.

Formulas are defined in the Member Properties window, under the rightmost tab labeled "Formula":

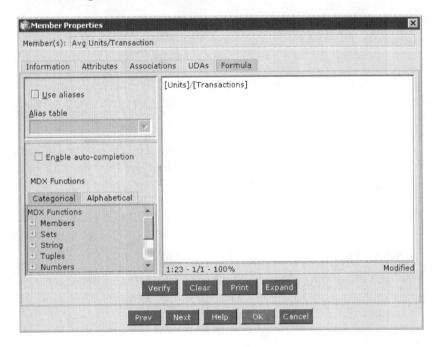

The different elements in a member formula could include mathematical operators, conditional operators, cross-dimensional operators, and functions.

The dimension reference area of the editor allows you to navigate the outline within the Formula window. You can search for a member and can insert a member name into the script area:

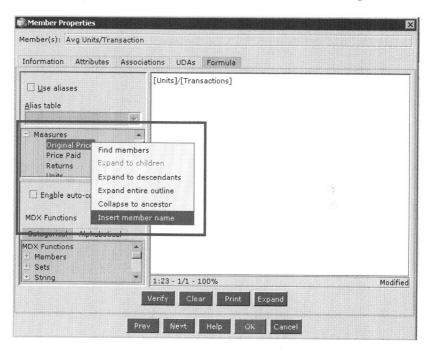

The functions section of the editor lists functions and operators available for member formulas. You can insert arguments into the script area (on BSO databases), assisting the administrator with the formula syntax (trust me... this is very helpful). Turning on auto-completion will speed up the development of formulas:

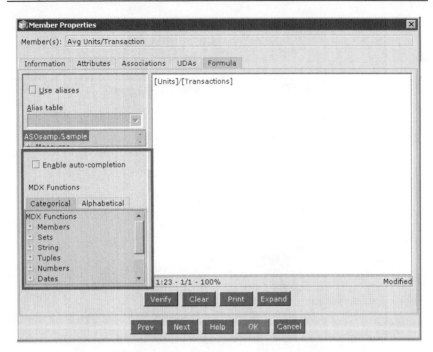

Here is a list of the available mathematical operators:
- Add, +
- Subtract, -
- Multiply, *
- Divide, /
- Evaluate a member as a percentage of another, %
- Control calculation order of nested equations, ()

For example, the member formula for the member "Avg Units/Transaction" is:

```
[Units]/[Transactions]
```

Note!

Note how the formula editor changes the formatting of keywords and operators to make the equation easier to read.

Time Balance Attributes

Time balance attributes are only available in the dimension tagged as Accounts, and are used to tell Essbase how a given member should be aggregated up the Time dimension. For example, should Headcount for January, February, and March be added together for Q1? This definitely wouldn't make sense.

	Actual	FY2007			
	Jan	Feb	Mar	Q1	Q2
Headcount	100	125	122	347	#Mi…

In most cases you want Qtr1 to equal the March headcount, or in other words the last headcount in the period. To get Essbase to do this, you tag Headcount with the Time Balance Last ("TB Last") so that it will take the last member's value when aggregating time:

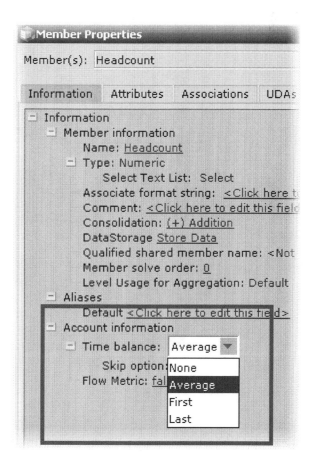

Depending on your requirements, you could also assign Time Balance First or Time Balance Average. Here is Q1's headcount now nicely equaling its last child, Mar:

	Actual	FY2007			
	Jan	Feb	Mar	Q1	Q:
Headcount	100	125	122	122	#M

What if we have just closed January? Then, showing the March headcount wouldn't be accurate because March is blank. A sub-property associated with Time Balance allows us to define how we handle missing and for BSO databases, zero data values. In this example, we would want to ignore any blanks (or #missing). So we set Headcount to TB Last, and then select Skip "Missing":

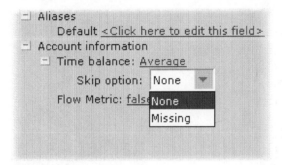

Now Qtr1 will correctly show the January value:

	Actual	FY2007			
	Jan	Feb	Mar	Q1	Q2
Headcount	100	#Missing	#Missing	100	#M

Tip!

Another example of Time Balance utilization is for inventory analysis members:

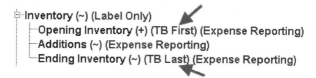

Inventory (~) (Label Only)
  Opening Inventory (+) (TB First) (Expense Reporting)
  Additions (~) (Expense Reporting)
  Ending Inventory (~) (TB Last) (Expense Reporting)

Solve Order

The solve order member property tells Essbase "here is the order to complete calculations" for ASO databases. Why is this important? You want to calculate the correct numbers in the correct order. Think order of operations for basic math. 4+5*2 does not equal (4+5)*2. Solve order is way you control the order of calculations in ASO databases.

Aggregate Storage Hierarchies

You know by now that a dimension contains a hierarchy or logical grouping of members. In ASO databases, there are two types of hierarchies: stored and dynamic:

Member solve order: 0
Hierarchy information
    Hierarchy: Hierarchies Enabled ▼
    Level Usage fo Stored
    Duplicate mem Dynamic   nension:
Aliases   Hierarchies Enabled
    Default < Click here to edit this field >

Notice in your Juggle outline that each hierarchy is by default set to stored. Let's learn the rules of stored vs. dynamic hierarchies.

Stored hierarchies will aggregate according to the structure of the outline. In our example, months will roll up to quarters up to a year total in the Period member. This aggregation is really fast (the nature of ASO databases). But stored hierarchies may only have the + for any member and ~ consolidation tags for members under a label only parent (other assigned consolidation tags are ignored). Also stored hierarchies cannot have member formulas and there are a few other restrictions on label only assignments.

Dynamic hierarchies are calculated by Essbase (vs. aggregated like in stored hierarchies) so all consolidation tags and member formulas are processed. The evaluation order for the calculation of members is dictated by the solve order as mentioned above. Dynamic hierarchies as expected do not calculate as fast as stored hierarchies.

You can also have multiple hierarchies within a single dimension. The hierarchies within a dimension can be stored, all dynamic or have one hierarchy stored and the other hierarchy dynamic. To enable multiple hierarchies within a dimension, choose *Hierarchies Enabled* under Member properties next to Hierarchy:

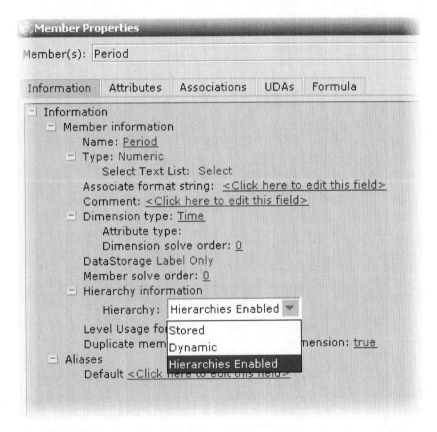

Multiple hierarchies can contain alternate hierarchies with Shared Members or completely different hierarchies.

Did you fully comprehend everything we just reviewed? Quick – name the 6 different dimension types? Didn't think so but don't worry, let's walk through the steps to set dimension types, hierarchy types, and member properties. Trust us, the fog of confusing terms, features and functions will begin to clear.

Define Dimension Types

You should be at this point in your Juggle ASO application:

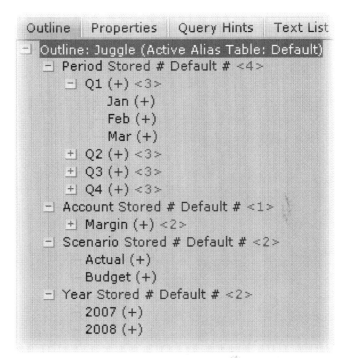

Note!

Note "Stored" next to the Period, Account, Scenario, and Year indicates these are stored dimensions.

1. Select the *Period* dimension.
2. Right click and select *Edit Member Properties*.
3. On the Information Tab, set Dimension type for Period to *Time*:

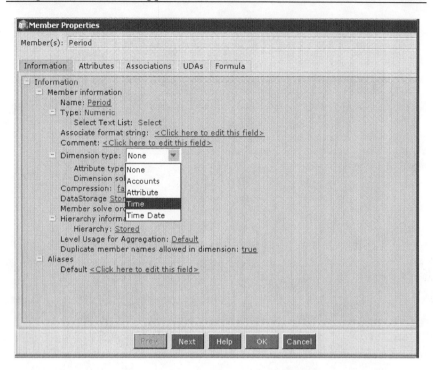

4. Click *OK*.
5. Select the *Account* dimension.
6. Right click and select *Edit Member Properties*.
7. On the Information Tab, set Dimension type for Account to *Accounts*:

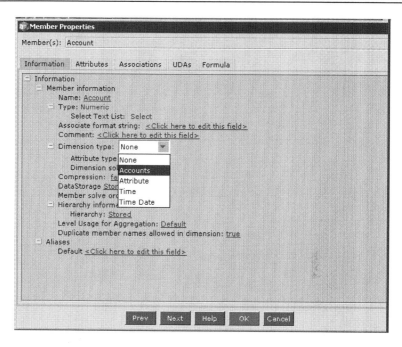

8. Click *OK*.

In the outline, you should see Period and Account with their new dimension type assignments. Notice anything interesting about the Account dimension? The Accounts dimension is no longer a Stored hierarchy:

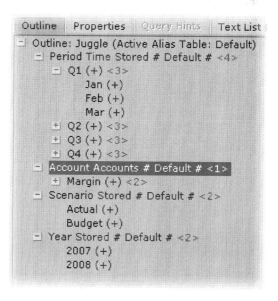

In ASO applications, the dimension tagged Accounts will automatically be a dynamic hierarchy. Can you think of another reason why you would have tagged this hierarchy dynamic even if Essbase hadn't done this for us? In this hierarchy, we want to use other consolidation tags besides the + tag. We don't want to add *Net_Revenue* to *Op_Expense*. We want to subtract *Op_Expense* from *Net_Revenue*. The same reasoning applies to *Other_Expense*. In order to use all consolidation tags, we must set the hierarchy to dynamic.

The dimension tagged Accounts is also the dimension that will be used for compression (more on this in the Tuning ASO section later in the book). The remaining dimensions still contain stored hierarchies (hierarchies that will aggregate up based on the + consolidation tag).

Next, let's set some member properties:

Edit Member Properties

To edit member properties,

1. Right click on the member, in this case *Op_Expense*.
2. Select *Edit Member Properties*.
3. The Member Properties window will display.
4. Select *(–) Subtraction* as the consolidation:

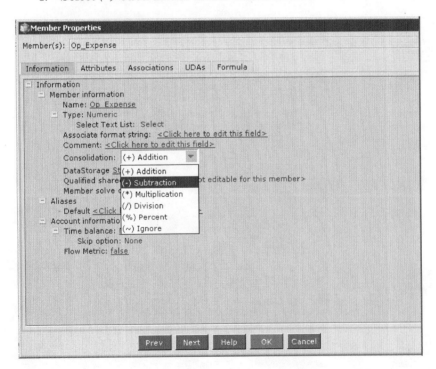

5. Click the *Next* button.
6. Set *Other Exp* to *(-) Subtraction* and click *OK:*

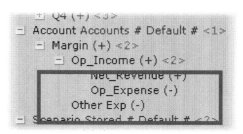

7. Select Scenario and click the *Label Only* icon at the top of the outline editor:

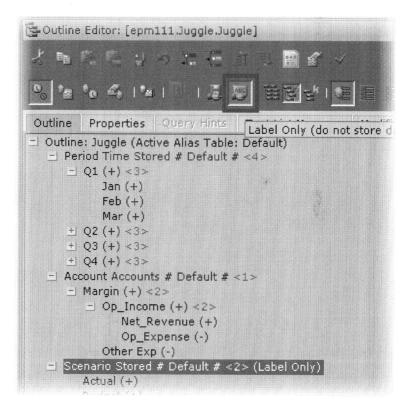

In many cases set the member properties using the icons at the top of the outline editor without having to open the Member Properties window.

8. Set Year to *Label Only* following the same steps as the Scenario dimension.

9. Select *Actual* and *Budget* (using Shift or Control click to select both members at the same time).

10. Select the ~ consolidation tag for the members Actual and Budget:

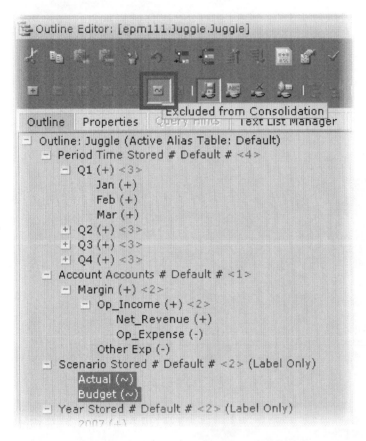

Would we ever want to total budget and actual data? Of course not, we tag this with the "~". Why didn't we choose the ^ consolidation tag (aside from the fact it isn't an option for ASO databases)? We do want to roll up Actual and Budget data across the other dimensions. If we had selected the ^ tag, Actual and Budget would remained wherever it was loaded and would not have totaled up the other dimensions like Time, Customer, or Product.

Note!

Did you notice that the ~ tag did not become available for selection until we defined Scenario as Label Only? In a stored hierarchy, the ~ tag is only allowed for children under a Label only member. In all other cases in a stored hierarchy, a + tag must be used.

Tip!

In many cases you can select multiple members with Control+Click or Shift+Click and assign the same properties at the same time via the icons at the top of the outline editor or by right-clicking and selecting *Edit Member Properties*.

Tip!

You can select the *Previous* or *Next* buttons within the member properties window to move up and down the hierarchy. This will save you a few clicks when updating member properties for several members.

Verify and Save Your Outline

You've now added dimensions, members and assigned member properties. As with anything that you are working on, we recommend you save often. So let's do that before we continue.

First, verify your outline and make sure you haven't broken any of the Essbase rules (those we discussed earlier and some others - see the next page). Click the *Verify* button to do this. Any errors or issues will display. In the example error message below, we have two members named "Jan":

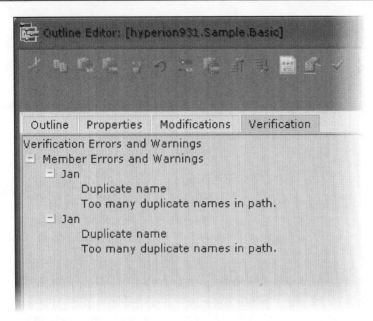

You can double-click on the issue, and you'll be taken directly to the place in the outline where the error occurs. Fix the issue and you are ready to verify once again. Once everything checks out ok, click the *Save* button to save the outline back to the server:

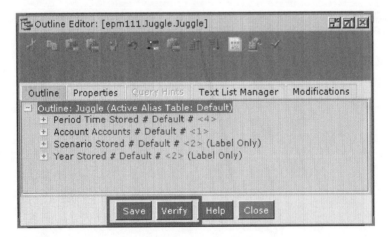

Essbase Outline Rules (Non-Unicode Applications*)

- Member name limit is 80 characters.
- Alias limit is 80 characters.
- Member names and alias names must be unique across all dimensions unless duplicate names have been enabled for the database.
- Names are not case-sensitive unless case-sensitivity is enabled.
- Do not use " (quotation marks) or tabs anywhere.
- Do not use the following special characters at the beginning of a member name or alias: @\{},- =<().+'_|
- Do not use a space at the beginning or end of member name or alias.
- Do not use any of the key words used in calc scripts, report scripts, or other functions (see Technical Reference).
- Do not use Essbase specific words like ALL, MEMBERNAME, DIM, DYNAMIC, #MI (see DBA Guide for full list).

Helpful Info

*Unicode applications are discussed in a later chapter.

Tip!

Some rules are specific to ASO databases (like stored vs. dynamic hierarchy rules) while others are specific to BSO databases.

Try It!

Verify and save your wolverine juggling outline.

Congratulations! You've created your very first Essbase outline, database and application.

Chapter 6:
UDAs, Alternate Hierarchies & Attributes

Until now our wolverine juggling application has been pretty simple and not really that helpful. We can see revenue and income across time but that's about it. We certainly haven't come close to testing the power of Essbase and analysis across many dimensions and attributes. We've decided to add a Customer dimension that lists the different customers or events that have paid for our juggling wolverine services:

```
Customer Stored # Default # <4>
   Corporate Events (+) <3>
      1001 (+) (Alias: interRel EPM Roadtrip User Group Meeting)
      1002 (+) (Alias: ODTUG Kaleidoscope)
      1003 (+) (Alias: OAUG IOUG Collaborate)
   Weddings (+) <2>
      2001 (+) (Alias: Hyperion-Oracle Happily Ever After Wedding)
      2002 (+) (Alias: Hyperion-Brio Happily Ever After Wedding (maybe))
   Birthday Parties (+) <2>
      3001 (+) (Alias: interRel 10th Birthday Party)
      3002 (+) (Alias: Essbase 15th Birthday Party)
   Street Peddling (+) <3>
      4001 (+) (Alias: Essbase 7th Street)
      4002 (+) (Alias: System 9th Ave)
      4003 (+) (Alias: Oracle EPM Fusion 11th Rd)
```

Try It!

Add the customer dimension to the juggling wolverine application using icons or right click menu options.

Tip!

You can add the full list of members and then use drag and drop features to move members around the outline.

We have eight wolverine juggling customers. OK, we can't track all of our street peddling customers individually so we'll track revenue and costs by street. And yes, Oracle and Hyperion has had a few weddings – we don't have the most monogamous of customers but they sure love wolverine juggling.

We can now perform analysis by Customer rolling up into event category. But what if we wanted to also roll up Customer a different way? Maybe by customer rating or customer size? What are the options available to us?

- Add another dimension.
- Assign a User Defined Attribute.
- Create an alternate hierarchy with shared members.
- Create an attribute dimension.

Excellent choices. In your real-life implementation, you will evaluate the best alternative that meets your analysis and reporting requirements.

The simplest way to add a grouping of data elements is to create another dimension called customer rating or customer size. It may look something like this:

```
Customer Multiple Hierarchies Enabled <2> (Label Only) {Customer Size}
   Total_Customer Stored # Default # (+) <4>
      Corporate Events (+) <3>
         1001 (+) (Alias: interRel EPM Roadtrip User Group Meeting) (UDAS: Large)
         1002 (+) (Alias: ODTUG Kaleidoscope) (UDAS: Large)
         1003 (+) (Alias: OAUG IOUG Collaborate) (UDAS: Large)
      Weddings (+) <2>
      Birthday Parties (+) <2>
      Street Peddling (+) <3>
   By Customer Rating Stored # Default # (~) <3>
      A Customers (+) <3>
         1001 (+) (Alias: interRel EPM Roadtrip User Group Meeting) (Shared Member)
         1002 (+) (Alias: ODTUG Kaleidoscope) (Shared Member)
         1003 (+) (Alias: OAUG IOUG Collaborate) (Shared Member)
      B Customers (+) <5>
         2001 (+) (Alias: Hyperion-Oracle Happily Ever After Wedding) (Shared Member)
         2002 (+) (Alias: Hyperion-Brio Happily Ever After Wedding (maybe)) (Shared Member)
         3001 (+) (Alias: interRel 10th Birthday Party) (Shared Member)
         3002 (+) (Alias: Essbase 15th Birthday Party) (Shared Member)
         4003 (+) (Alias: Oracle EPM Fusion 11th Rd) (Shared Member)
      C Customers (+) <2>
         4001 (+) (Alias: Essbase 7th Street) (Shared Member)
         4002 (+) (Alias: System 9th Ave) (Shared Member)
   Customer Size Attribute [Type: Text] # Default # <3>
```

While this option is fairly easy to create, it does pose some disadvantages. You will hear a recurrent theme when it comes to designing Essbase databases: reduce dimensionality whenever possible. More dimensions equal a bigger database which could mean performance issues. This is true for both ASO and BSO databases (especially BSO databases).

Our other alternatives allow us to add dimensionality or additional groupings to the Essbase database without increasing the database size. Let's review each.

DEFINE A UDA

We could easily create a UDA and assign it to the customer members.

1. Select member *1001* and right click.
2. Select *Edit Member Properties*.
3. Select the *UDAs* tab:

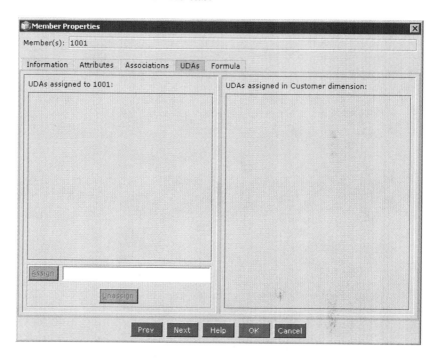

Notice the UDA listing is blank.

4. In the text box next to the disabled Assign button, type in "Large":

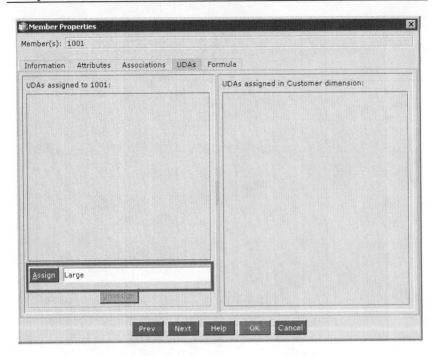

5. Click *Assign*.
6. Click the *Next* button.

The Next button will move one member down in the hierarchy (just as the Prev button moves one member up in the hierarchy).

7. Now that we've typed in Large once, we can reuse it again. Click *Assign* to assign the Large UDA to member 1002:

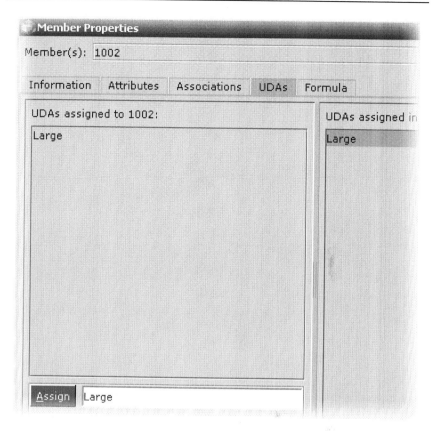

8. Click *Next*.
9. Assign the Large UDA to member 1003 and 2001.
10. For member 2002, type in a new UDA "Medium". Assign the "Medium" UDA to customer 2002.

To remove a UDA from a selected member, simply click the *Unassign* button on the UDAs tab.

Try It!

Follow the same process assigning the remainder of the UDAs:

- 3001-Medium
- 3002-Medium
- 4001-Small
- 4002-Small
- 4003-Small

You outline should look like the following:

```
Customer Multiple Hierarchies Enabled <5> (Label Only)
 - Corporate Events Stored # Default # (+) <3>
       1001 (+) (Alias: interRel EPM Roadtrip User Group Meeting) (UDAS: Large)
       1002 (+) (Alias: ODTUG Kaleidoscope) (UDAS: Large)
       1003 (+) (Alias: OAUG IOUG Collaborate) (UDAS: Large)
 - Weddings Stored # Default # (+) <2>
       2001 (+) (Alias: Hyperion-Oracle Happily Ever After Wedding) (UDAS: Large)
       2002 (+) (Alias: Hyperion-Brio Happily Ever After Wedding (maybe)) (UDAS: Medium)
 - Birthday Parties Stored # Default # (+) <2>
       3001 (+) (Alias: interRel 10th Birthday Party) (UDAS: Medium)
       3002 (+) (Alias: Essbase 15th Birthday Party) (UDAS: Medium)
 - Street Peddling Stored # Default # (+) <3>
       4001 (+) (Alias: Essbase 7th Street) (UDAS: Small)
       4002 (+) (Alias: System 9th Ave) (UDAS: Small)
       4003 (+) (Alias: Oracle EPM Fusion 11th Rd) (UDAS: Small)
```

UDAs allow us to easily describe a member and in analysis, we can say "Give me all of my Small customers" and Smart View will display the list of small customers. You can use the UDA in a calculation. For example, you can apply a certain discount for all of the small customers (those tagged with the "Small" UDA). But what it can't do is easily give me a subtotal for the small customers. So now what?

DEFINE AN ALTERNATE HIERARCHY

Another alternative is to define an alternate hierarchy that groups members by an alternate grouping. To be a bit clearer (and less funny...ok, it wasn't that funny), within a dimension, you can group the same set of members in different ways.

In an ASO database, we have one preliminary step to do before we can create an alternate hierarchy. Note the Customer dimension was created by default as a stored hierarchy and all consolidation tags are set to +. For ASO cubes, we need to enable the dimension for multiple hierarchies to build alternate hierarchies.

1. Right click on *Customer* and select *Edit Member Properties.*

2. On the Information tab, select *Hierarchies Enabled* for the Hierarchy Information:

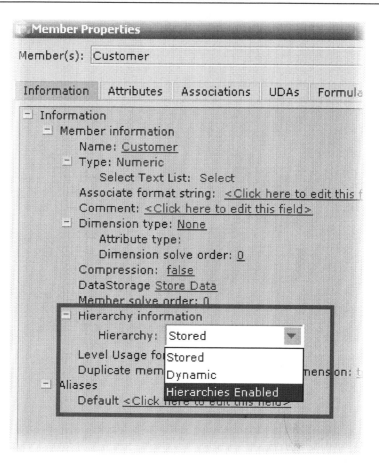

Next create the following two hierarchies under the Customer dimension: (Hierarchy) Total_Customer, grouping the Corporate Events, Weddings, Birthday Parties and Street Peddling and (Alternate Hierarchy) By Customer Rating, grouping customers by A, B, or C categories.

```
Customer Multiple Hierarchies Enabled <2> (Label Only) {Customer Size}
  Total_Customer Stored # Default # (+) <4>
    Corporate Events (+) <3>
        1001 (+) (Alias: interRel EPM Roadtrip User Group Meeting) (UDAS: Large)
        1002 (+) (Alias: ODTUG Kaleidoscope) (UDAS: Large)
        1003 (+) (Alias: OAUG IOUG Collaborate) (UDAS: Large)
    Weddings (+) <2>
    Birthday Parties (+) <2>
    Street Peddling (+) <3>
  By Customer Rating Stored # Default # (~) <3>
    A Customers (+) <3>
        1001 (+) (Alias: interRel EPM Roadtrip User Group Meeting) (Shared Member)
        1002 (+) (Alias: ODTUG Kaleidoscope) (Shared Member)
        1003 (+) (Alias: OAUG IOUG Collaborate) (Shared Member)
    B Customers (+) <5>
        2001 (+) (Alias: Hyperion-Oracle Happily Ever After Wedding) (Shared Member)
        2002 (+) (Alias: Hyperion-Brio Happily Ever After Wedding (maybe)) (Shared Member)
        3001 (+) (Alias: interRel 10th Birthday Party) (Shared Member)
        3002 (+) (Alias: Essbase 15th Birthday Party) (Shared Member)
        4003 (+) (Alias: Oracle EPM Fusion 11th Rd) (Shared Member)
    C Customers (+) <2>
        4001 (+) (Alias: Essbase 7th Street) (Shared Member)
        4002 (+) (Alias: System 9th Ave) (Shared Member)
  Customer Size Attribute [Type: Text] # Default # <3>
```

3. Add a new member "Total_Customer" under the Customer dimension.

4. Move the *Corporate Events, Weddings, Birthday Parties,* and *Street Peddling* under *Total_Customer.*

5. Add the new member "By Customer Rating" and set the member properties to ~ *consolidation* and *Store* data store.

6. Add members for customer ratings: A Customers, B Customers, C Customers.

To create the shared members, you could manually type in the values but a faster way is to copy and paste the desired members.

7. Select customers 1001, 1002, 1003 and right click.

8. Choose *Copy:*

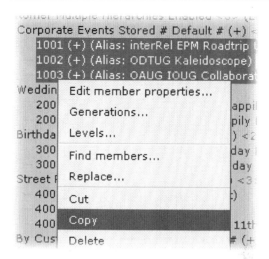

9. Select A Customers member and right click.
10. Choose *Paste Child:*

11. Repeat this process for the remaining customers until they've been added to the appropriate customer rating members.
12. Select all of the copied customer members and choose the *Shared Member* icon:

In a matter of a few seconds you've created another way to group, analyze and report on customers. You're resulting hierarchy should look as follows:

Note that the alternate hierarchy is a stored hierarchy which makes sense in this scenario. The aggregation is a straight roll up from customer to customer rating. No member formulas or additional consolidation tags are needed.

Alternate Hierarchy Rules for ASO Databases

Helpful Info

- Composed of shared members that refer to nonshared members of a previous hierarchy
- Non shared member must occur before a shared member
- First hierarchy in a dimension enabled for multiple hierarchies cannot contain a shared member
- Shared members can only reside in a dynamic hierarchy dimension or a multiple hierarchy dimension
- Stored hierarchy cannot contain multiple copies of the same shared member
- Nonshared members must be in the same dimension as the shared member
- Shared members automatically inherit any attributes associated with the nonshared member

Alternate Hierarchy Rules for BSO Databases

Helpful Info

- Shared members must be in the same dimension and must reside below the nonshared member
- Shared members cannot have children
- Unlimited number of shared members allowed
- Shared members cannot have UDAs, member formulas, attributes
- Shared members may have aliases

The alternate hierarchy allows us to easily create a subtotal by customer rating where our Small/Medium/Large UDA did not. But what you can't do with an alternative hierarchy (and UDA) is create a cross tab report of Rating by Customer or Size by Customer. What's an administrator to do?

DEFINE AN ATTRIBUTE DIMENSION

In early versions of Essbase, you were limited (by practicality, if nothing else) in the number of dimensions that you could have per database. Most databases were five to nine dimensions and anymore than that was seriously stretching the capabilities of Essbase Block Storage cubes. But users complained that they needed to be able to analyze data by more dimensions. For instance, if you had a product dimension, you might want to also have Product Start Date, Sales Manager, Packaging, Size, Weight, Target Group, and more as dimensions too. Since all these "dimensions" were really just alternate ways of divvying up the Product dimension (in our case), attribute dimensions were born.

Attribute dimensions are dimensions that can be placed in the rows or columns (as we discussed above) with some special considerations. Just like regular dimensions, they define characteristics about the data that is loaded to Essbase. They have hierarchies and members just like any other dimension.

One of the special qualities of attribute dimensions is that adding them to the outline does not impact the size of the Essbase database. You can add an virtually unlimited number of attribute dimensions (we've seen cubes with over 100 attribute dimensions).

Another big benefit with attributes is that they can be used to develop really nice cross tab reports. For example, we can create a report with flavors across the columns and package types down the side. You can't do this with shared members from the same dimension, but attribute dimensions give you a great way to do detailed product and customer analysis that isn't possible otherwise. You can even analyze sum totals, minimums, maximums, averages and counts of members in attribute dimensions which certainly isn't possible with UDAs.

But wait, before you get too excited, let's learn a bit more about attributes. There are four types of Attribute dimensions: Text, Numeric, Boolean, and Date.

Text attributes are the default type and are used to describe text characteristics.

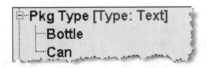

When *AND, OR NOT*, <, >, =, >=, <=, <>, !=, *IN*, and *NOT IN* operations are performed on text dimensions, Essbase makes logical comparisons for text attribute dimensions. Not always the most logical thing to do, but it's there all the same.

Numeric attribute dimensions contain numeric values at level 0. You can perform *AND, OR NOT, <, >, =, >=, <=, <>, !=, IN,* and *NOT IN* operations on numeric attribute dimensions. You can group numeric values into ranges (using the : symbol) and include these numeric values in calculations.

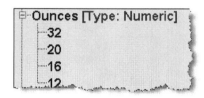

Boolean attribute dimensions contain exactly two members: True and False, Left and Right, or Yes and No. Once the two Boolean member names are defined, you must use same names for all Boolean attribute dimensions in the database. When you perform *AND, OR NOT, <, >, =, >=, <=, <>, !=, IN,* and *NOT IN* operations on Boolean attribute dimensions, Essbase translates true to 1 and false to 0.

Date attribute members must contain date members at level 0 that are formatted properly. Valid date formats are mm-dd-yyyy or dd-mm-yyyy. All dates must be after 01-01-1970 and before 01-01-2038.

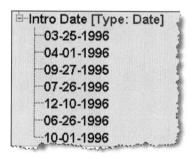

AND, OR NOT, <, >, =, >=, <=, <>, !=, IN, and *NOT IN* operations can be performed on Date attribute dimensions. Date values can be also included in calculations.

There are five ways to calculate attribute data: Sum, Count, Average, Minimum, and Maximum. Sum is the default when you don't specify which one to use, but you can use the other calculations as though it was yet another dimension:

	A	B	C		D		E		F
1			Year		Product		Market		Actual
2			Bottle		Can		Pkg Type		
3	Sales	Sum	$	270,593	$	130,262	$	400,855	
4		Min	$	11,750	$	30,469	$	11,750	
5		Max	$	46,956	$	62,824	$	62,824	
6		Avg	$	27,059	$	43,421	$	30,835	
7		Count		10		3		13	
8									
9									

Note! Attribute dimensions are always dynamically calculated which could mean slower performance any time an attribute is referenced in a retrieval.

Build an Attribute Dimension

There are 5 main steps to build an attribute dimension:

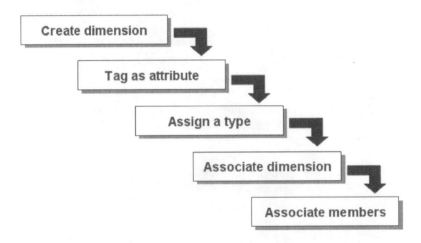

Create dimension → Tag as attribute → Assign a type → Associate dimension → Associate members

Let's build a Customer Size attribute dimension for our Juggle database,

1. Open the Juggle outline if necessary.
2. Right click on Outline and select *Add Child*.

   or

   Right click on an existing dimension and select *Add Sibling*.
3. Type in the new dimension name "Customer Size".
4. Right click on the new dimension and select *Edit Member Properties*.
5. Select *Attribute* for Dimension Type:

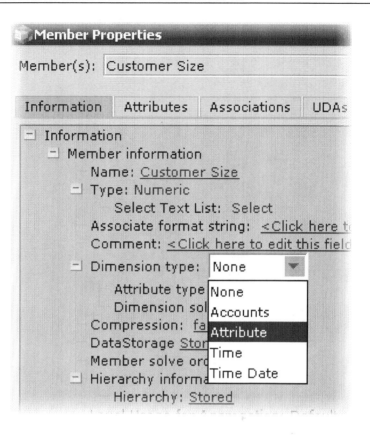

6. Select desired attribute type (Boolean, numeric, text, or date). In this case, choose *Text*:

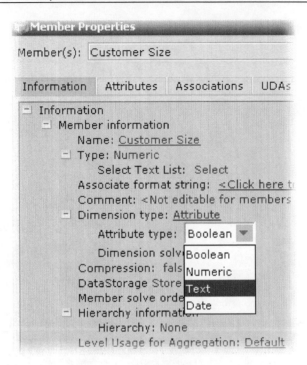

7. Click *OK*.
8. You may get a warning message - Click *Yes*.

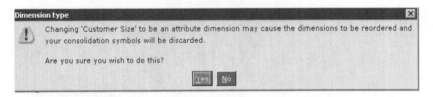

Attribute dimensions will always be placed last in the outline and consolidation tags cannot be assigned to attribute members – see Attribute Dimension rules just below.)

9. Next add members and hierarchies to the dimension as you normally would by selecting *Add Child* or *Add Sibling*. In our example, add members: "Small", "Medium", "Large":

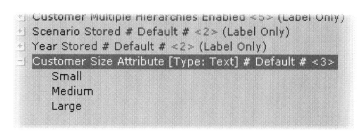

Next you need to associate a base dimension. All attribute dimensions are associated with one and only one base dimension.

Note! A base dimension can have one or more attribute dimensions.

10. On the base dimension Customer, right click and select *Edit Member Properties.*
11. Select the *Attributes* tab.
12. Select the attribute dimension *Customer Size* and click the *Assign* button to assign the base dimension *Customer*:

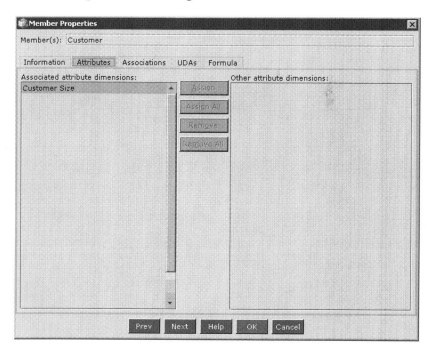

13. Click *OK.*

After associating the base dimension, you then need to associate the attribute members. We now need to assign "Small" to customer 4001, "Large" to customer 1001, etc.

14. On base member *1001*, right click and select *Edit Member Properties*.
15. Select the *Associations* tab.
16. Select the attribute member *Large* and click the *Assign* button to assign the associated member:

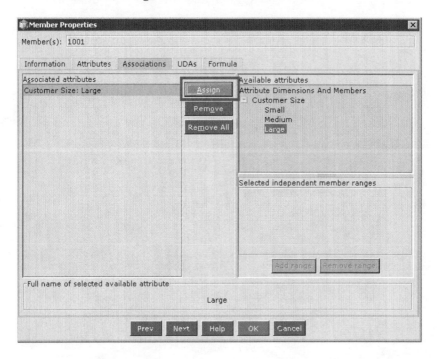

17. Click *OK*.
18. Repeat the same steps to assign the attribute associations to the base members:
    - 1002-Large
    - 1003-Large
    - 2001-Large
    - 2002-Medium
    - 3001-Medium
    - 3002-Medium
    - 4001-Small
    - 4002-Small

- 4003-Small

You resulting hierarchy should looks as follows:

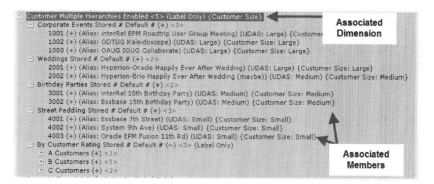

Save and verify your Juggle outline.

Tip!

You can define prefixes or suffixes for attribute members to ensure that all level 0 non-text member names are unique. A prefix is a value that Essbase attaches to the beginning of a member name while a suffix is a value that Essbase attaches to the end of a member name. Right click and select *Edit Member Properties* to assign a prefix or suffix to an attribute member.

Attribute Dimension Rules for ASO Databases

- Only the + consolidation operator is allowed
- All associations for an attribute dimension must be at the same level
- Attributes can be associated to any level 0 member of a dynamic or stored hierarchy that does not have a member formula

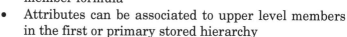

Helpful
Info

- Attributes can be associated to upper level members in the first or primary stored hierarchy
- Attribute dimensions do not have hierarchy types
- Essbase treats attribute dimensions as stored alternate hierarchies of the base dimension
- Can be used in query tracking

Attribute Dimension Rules for BSO Databases

Helpful Info

- Position attribute dimensions last in the outline
- Consider the implication of Dynamic Calculations as reporting on Attribute dimensions can be slow
- Define attribute dimensions on sparse dimensions only
- Cannot tag attribute members as a shared members
- Cannot tag attribute members to use two-pass calculation
- Cannot assign attribute members a UDA
- Cannot create alias combinations
- Cannot use consolidation symbols or formulas

Recap – Steps to Build an Attribute Dimension

Helpful Info

1. In Administration Services, open the outline.
2. Add a dimension in the Outline Editor.
3. Change the dimension type to attribute.
4. Set the Attribute type (Boolean, Number, Date, Text).
5. Add the Attribute members.
6. Associate the attribute dimension to a base dimension.
   a. Select the base dimension.
   b. Right click and select Edit Member Properties.
   c. Select on the Attributes Tab.
   d. Assign the attribute dimension.
7. Select the base members and associate the appropriate attribute members.
   a. Select the base dimension member.
   b. Right click and select Edit Member Properties.
   c. Select on the Associations Tab.
   d. Assign the attribute member.

Our new Customer Size attribute dimension adds dimensionality to my database without increasing the database size. What more could you ask for? Well, the thing about attribute dimensions is that they are tied to one base member and cannot vary over, say, time. In our Juggle database, we want to group our customers by Sales Manager but Sales Manager can vary over time (e.g. Larry manages customer 1001 from January through May and then Bob took over the account in June). A regular attribute wouldn't meet this requirement of varying sales managers over time. Pre-Essbase 11, if we had this requirement, we had to build Sales Manager as a regular dimension vs. an attribute dimension. And unfortunately, in Essbase 11 for ASO databases, we still have to do this. However, for our BSO databases, a new feature, Varying Attributes, is now supported (more on that in the BSO section).

Note!

Varying attributes are not supported for ASO databases in 11.1.1.

WHAT TO USE WHEN

In some cases, the design decisions are clear cut on when to use UDAs vs. alternate hierarchies vs. attribute dimensions. In other scenarios, the answer will be less obvious. The type of Essbase database (ASO or BSO) will factor into your decision. Let's review some design decision points.

When should you use Attributes?

Use attributes when you need to create crosstab reports (examples include Product in the rows and Product Start Date across the columns or Product Packaging Type in rows and Product Start Date in the columns). Also use attributes when you need to hide a level of detail in most reports but still want it available upon request (e.g. showing product revenue by packaging type vs. the entire list of products).

Attributes are very helpful when performing comparisons based on certain types of data or when you're performing calculations based on characteristics. Finally, use attributes when you need to add dimensionality to the database without increasing size of the database. Attributes are "available on request." By default they do not show up in end user Ad-hoc Analysis. In Smart View, attributes can be brought into the query using the Query Designer or Report Designer (as well as free form typing).

When should you NOT use Attributes?

Do not use attributes when you need to define characteristics that vary over time in ASO databases. For example, let's say we had "Employee Status" as an attribute dimension based on the "Employee" dimension. Shaquille O'Neal is fired in September and his employee status is changed from "Active" to "Terminated" (who would ever fire Shaq?). If we run reports for the month of January, it will look like Shaq was terminated for that month. However, Shaq was active for months January through October but Essbase has no way of knowing this because employee status is solely tied to the Employee dimension.

If you need to track how an attribute changes over time in an ASO database, you must make it a stored dimension. However, in BSO databases, you could define the attribute as a Varying Attribute dimension.

Do not use attributes when you need to calculate a value by placing a formula on a member (member formulas aren't allowed on attribute members). Watch out for attributes when you need to improve retrieval performance (attributes are dynamically calculated and can be slow at times).

Comparing UDAs, Alternate Hierarchies and Attributes

In the instances where we can't define attributes, UDAs and / or shared members may make sense. Alternate hierarchies / shared members allow security to be set where Attributes do not. UDAs and alternate hierarchies can be defined for dense dimensions where attributes cannot.

All the alternatives we've mentioned for providing additional ways of categorizing and summarizing data (UDAs, attributes, and alternate hierarchies) can be used in Essbase without increasing the database size.

Chapter 7:
Add Thousands of Members

You now know how to build an Essbase outline. Are you ready to manually build the product dimension with 7,000 products? How about a Customer dimension with 10,000 customers? No way! Even a temp would quit halfway through the job (though an intern find the experience rewarding). Fortunately, there is an easy way to automatically build dimensions using a text file, Excel spreadsheet, or relational database query. The secret is to use Essbase dimension build rules.

DIMENSION BUILD RULES FILES OVERVIEW

Dimension build rules files contain the instructions to build dimensions dynamically in Essbase databases. With these handy files, you can add new dimensions and members, remove or change existing dimensions and members, or modify attributes and calculations automatically. You can even create an outline from scratch. There are three different primary build methods for dimension rule files: generation builds, level builds, and parent/child builds. The build method you chose depends upon the format of your source system and determines the algorithm that Essbase uses to modify the outline.

A generation build data file looks like this:

```
Gen2      Gen3        Gen4
500       500-10      500-10-10
500       500-10      500-10-20
500       500-20      500-20-12
500       500-20      500-20-15
500       500-20      500-20-20
```

A generation build rules file will translate the data file above into this hierarchy:

```
⊟ Product {Caffeinated, Intro Date, Ounces, Pkg Type}
  ⊞ 100 (+) (Alias: Colas)
  ⊞ 200 (+) (Alias: Root Beer)
  ⊞ 300 (+) (Alias: Cream Soda)
  ⊞ 400 (+) (Alias: Fruit Soda)
  ⊟ 500 (+) ◄───────────── Generation 2
    ⊟ 500-10 (+)
       ─ 500-10-10 (+)
       ─ 500-10-20 (+)
    ⊟ 500-20 (+) ◄───────── Generation 3
       ─ 500-20-12 (+)
       ─ 500-20-15 (+) ◄─── Generation 4
       ─ 500-20-20 (+)
```

A file suitable for a level build looks like this:

```
Level0          Level1   Level2
600-10-11       600-10   600
600-20-10       600-20   600
600-20-18       600-20   600
```

A level build rules file will translate the data file above into
this hierarchy:

```
⊟ Product {Caffeinated, Intro Date, Ounces, Pkg Type}
  ⊞ 100 (+) (Alias: Colas)
  ⊞ 200 (+) (Alias: Root Beer)
  ⊞ 300 (+) (Alias: Cream Soda)
  ⊞ 400 (+) (Alias: Fruit Soda)
  ⊞ 500 (+)
  ⊟ 600 (+) ◄───────────── Level 2
    ⊟ 600-10 (+) ◄───────── Level 1
       └ 600-10-11 (+)
    ⊟ 600-20 (+)
       ─ 600-20-10 (+)
       ─ 600-20-18 (+) ◄─── Level 0
```

A parent/child build data file looks like this:

```
Parent    Child      Alias
200       200-10     Old Fashioned
200       200-20     Diet Root Beer
200       200-30     Sasparilla
200       200-40     Birch Beer
200       200-50     With Caffeine
```

A parent/child rules file will translate the data file above into this hierarchy:

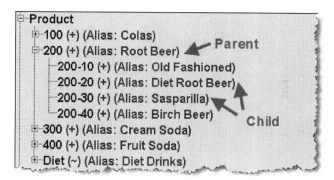

There are five steps in building a dimension build rules file:

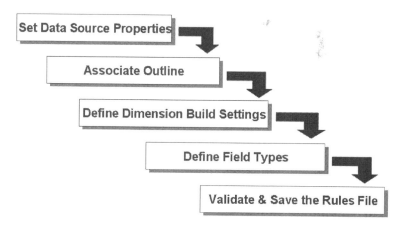

The Data Prep Editor is where you build all rules files:

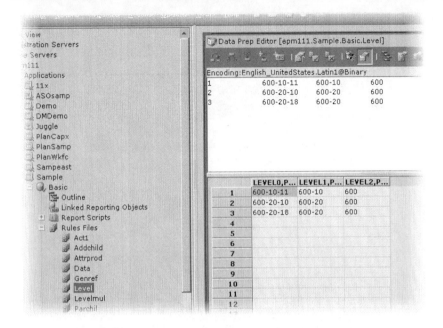

So now that you understand the basics, let's jump into the details and walk through the steps to create a dimension build rules file.

Note!

The process to build a load rules file is the same for both ASO and BSO databases.

CREATE A DIMENSION BUILD RULES FILE

In this example of creating a dimension build rules file (and other Essbase tasks), we are going to use some objects that are available with your Essbase install. Be sure to install the Sample applications that are delivered with Essbase. We'll use them now.

1. In the Administration Services Enterprise View panel, navigate to the *Rules Files* section under the Sample.Basic database.

2. Right click on the Rules Files and select *Create Rules File* (or if the Rules File section doesn't exist, right-click on the database to create your first rule file for that database):

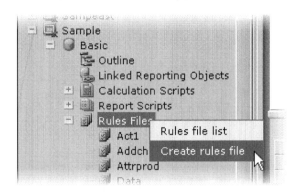

3. Select *File >> Open Data File*.
4. Browse to and open the dimension data source file. For this example, open the genref.txt file from the Sample.Basic database:

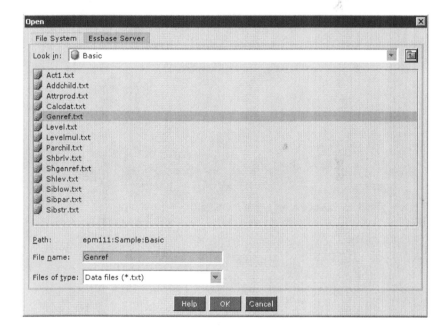

5. Click *OK*.
6. Select *Options >> Data Source Properties*.
7. The Data Source properties window will open.

Data source properties will tell Essbase the source file delimiters, what field edits have been made in the rules file, and what header rows may exist. On the Delimiter tab, specify Comma,

Tab, Spaces, Custom, or Column Width delimiter for the dimension build data source file:

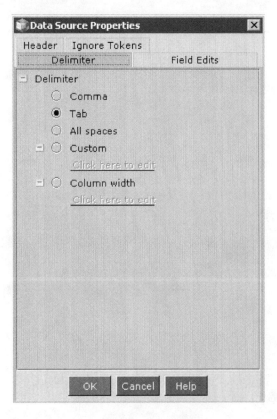

On the Header tab, you can specify how many lines to skip or define any records that may have header information and field information:

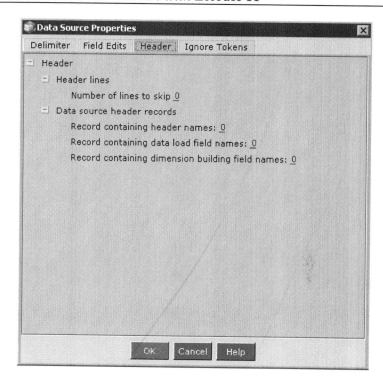

Next, let's associate the outline:

8. Select the *Associate Outline* button in the toolbar or if you prefer menus, choose *Options >> Associate Outline*.
9. The Associate Outline window will open.
10. Select the desired database:

There are two modes for rules files: dimension building and data loading (we'll talk about data loading soon enough). When working on a dimension build rules file, select the Dimension Building mode:

Note!

Note!

When working on a data load rules file, select the Data Load mode:

Next, to define the dimension build settings,
11. Select *Options >> Dimension Build Settings*.
12. The Dimension Build Settings window will open.

The Global tab of the Dimension Build Settings window allows you to define which alias table to update, autoconfiguration for sparse/dense, and exactly how the rules for selecting or rejecting should behave. Here you can specify which alias table to update from this source file (we'll cover alias tables in an upcoming section). In most cases, you'll want to leave the defaults alone for this tab:

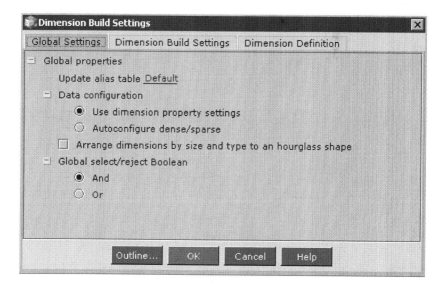

Tip!

Don't use "Autoconfigure dense/sparse", as it's almost always the surest way to de-optimize your database (meaning it's not even a good starting point!) We'll provide some good tips on how to set dense and sparse settings in a later chapter.

Next select the Dimension Build Settings tab to (drum roll, please) define the dimension build settings. Select the dimension that will be updated in the rules file. In this example, double-click on Product to select Product (so that Product displays next to Dimension):

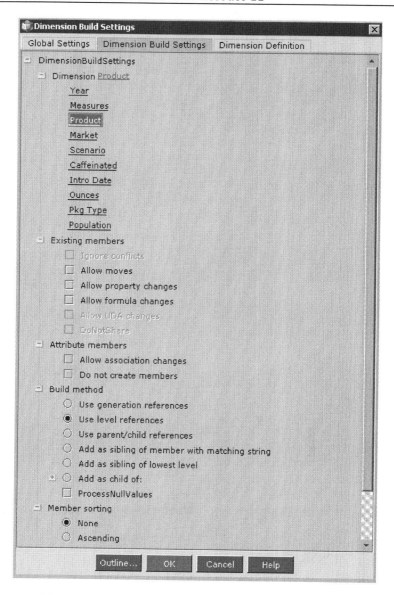

After selecting the dimension, you will define how existing members in that dimension should be handled: Allow moves, Allow property changes, Allow formula changes, Allow UDA changes, and Do not share.

"Allow moves" enables children to be moved from one parent to another. An example where you might use this: you want to reorganize your market dimension via a dimension build rules file, splitting Southwest into South and West.

This is what the dimension looks like before:

```
⊟ Southwest (+)
    ┈ Texas (+) (UDAS: Major Market) {Population: 21000000}
    ┈ Oklahoma (+) (UDAS: Small Market) {Population: 6000000}
    ┈ Louisiana (+) (UDAS: Small Market, New Market) {Population: 6000000}
    ┈ New Mexico (+) (UDAS: Small Market) {Population: 3000000}
    ┈ California (+) (UDAS: Major Market) {Population: 33000000}
    ┈ Oregon (+) (UDAS: Small Market) {Population: 6000000}
    ┈ Washington (+) (UDAS: Small Market) {Population: 6000000}
    ┈ Utah (+) (UDAS: Small Market) {Population: 3000000}
    ┈ Nevada (+) (UDAS: Small Market, New Market) {Population: 3000000}
```

After the dimension build rule (with "Allow Moves"):

```
⊟ West (+)
    ┈ California (+) (UDAS: Major Market) {Population: 33000000}
    ┈ Oregon (+) (UDAS: Small Market) {Population: 6000000}
    ┈ Washington (+) (UDAS: Small Market) {Population: 6000000}
    ┈ Utah (+) (UDAS: Small Market) {Population: 3000000}
    ┈ Nevada (+) (UDAS: Small Market, New Market) {Population: 3000000}
⊟ South (+) (UDAS: Small Market)
    ┈ Texas (+) (UDAS: Major Market) {Population: 21000000}
    ┈ Oklahoma (+) (UDAS: Small Market) {Population: 6000000}
    ┈ Louisiana (+) (UDAS: Small Market, New Market) {Population: 6000000}
    ┈ New Mexico (+) (UDAS: Small Market) {Population: 3000000}
⊞ Central (+) (UDAS: Major Market)
```

"Allow property changes" enables Essbase to update member properties based on the source file. For example, if you build your Accounts dimension from the GL and an account description changes, you will want to make sure the account alias is updated so that it is consistent with the description in the GL. Without this option selected, Essbase will not allow any alias changes.

Selecting the build method is a critical item – don't forget to do this, even though it's hidden at the bottom. You must specify the appropriate build method for the dimension selected that matches the dimension data file. Build options include:

The three core build methods (generation, level and parent/child) were discussed earlier, but there is also the flexibility to add a list of members as:

- A sibling of a member with a matching string
- A sibling of the lowest level
- A child of a specific member that you choose

For example, you may have a list of new cost centers that have not yet been mapped to a correct parent. You can add these cost centers to a specific parent called "New Cost Centers" so your aggregated data will be up-to-date even though the outline may not be.

The next step in the process is to define the properties of each of the data columns. Every column in the source file must either be explicitly ignored by the rules file, or assigned a specific generation, level, parent, child, or member property.

To define the field properties:

13. Select the first column in the data file.
14. Select *Field >> Properties*.
15. The Field Properties window will open.

The Global Properties tab allows you to translate text to upper / lower case, add prefixes and suffixes, convert spaces to underscores, and perform a find and replace:

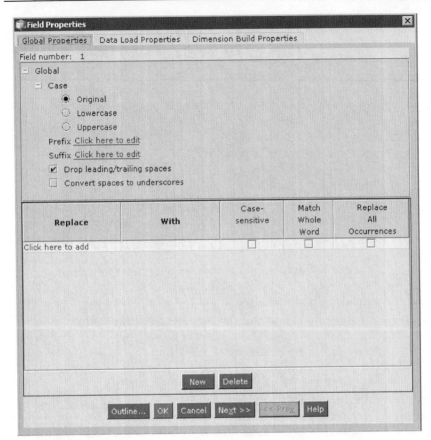

For example, let's say your Account number structure and Product number structure could have the exact same number. Unless you enable duplicate member names, Essbase won't allow you to have a member with the same name. You can add the prefix "Product_" to the Product dimension build so that the members will be unique.

Next we will select the Dimension Build Properties tab. (Ignore the Data Load Properties tab for now since we are focusing on dimension building).

Since we are looking at the first column of the genref.txt file for Sample.Basic, we will define the following field properties:

16. Select the dimension that maps to the field. Choose *Product*.

17. Select the dimension build type for the field. Choose *Generation*.

18. Enter the reference number which is 2 in this case (we want this value being added as generation 2).

19. Click *Next* to move to the next column in the data file.
20. Select the dimension that maps to the second field, in this case it is still Product.
21. Select the dimension build type for the field. Choose Generation.
22. Enter the reference number, in this case 3.
23. Click *Next*.
24. Select the dimension that maps to the field. Still Product,
25. Select the dimension build type for the field. Choose Generation.
26. Enter the reference number, in this case 4.

Tip! When navigating in the field property window, to select, you can Double-click a particular item. Make sure the item shows up in blue next to Dimension or Type. If you single click, the item may not be selected.

27. Click *OK* once all of the fields have been defined.

Here is a completed example of a generation build rules file:

	Data Prep Editor [epm111.Sample.Basic.Genref]		
Encoding:English_UnitedStates.Latin1@Binary			
1	500	500-10	500-10-10
2	500	500-10	500-10-20
3	500	500-20	500-20-12
4	500	500-20	500-20-15
5	500	500-20	500-20-20

	GEN2,Pro...	GEN3,Pro...	GEN4,Pro...
1	500	500-10	500-10-10
2	500	500-10	500-10-20
3	500	500-20	500-20-12
4	500	500-20	500-20-15
5	500	500-20	500-20-20
6			
7			
8			

Note how generations must be listed from highest generation to lowest– Gen2,Product; Gen3,Product; Gen4,Product.

Here is a completed example of a level build rules file:

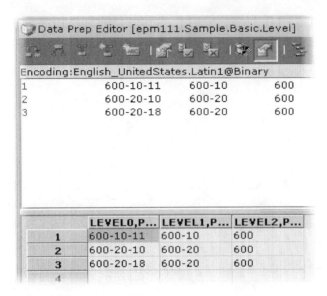

Note how levels must be listed from level zero to upper levels in sequential order – Level0,Product; Level1,Product; Level2,Product.

Here is a completed example of a parent/child rules file:

Data Prep Editor [epm111.Sample.Basic.Parchil]

Encoding:English_UnitedStates.Latin1@Binary

1	200	200-10	Old Fashioned
2	200	200-20	Diet Root Beer
3	200	200-30	Sasparilla
4	200	200-40	Birch Beer
5	200	200-50	With Caffeine

	PARENT0,...	CHILD0,P...	ALIAS0,P...
1	200	200-10	Old Fashio...
2	200	200-20	Diet Root ...
3	200	200-30	Sasparilla
4	200	200-40	Birch Beer
5	200	200-50	With Caffe...
6			
7			

The parent column must always precede the child column.

Note! You can choose to "Ignore a field during dimension building". This checkbox can be found at the bottom of the Dimension Build Properties tab under *Field >> Properties*.

The last steps are to validate and save the rules file. Rules files are validated to ensure member and dimension mappings line up with the associated outline. Validation also does things like checking to make sure the build method is appropriate for the field properties.

28. Select the *Validate* icon (or select *Options >> Validate*).

My Rules File won't Validate – What Should You Check?

Helpful
Info

- Is every field name valid?
- Are the reference numbers sequential?
- Are there repeated generations?
- Is the field type valid for the build method?
- Are the fields in correct order?
- Does the child field have a parent field?
- Do all dimension names exist in the outline?
- Are all dimensions referenced in the rules file?

29. Select the Save icon (or select *File >> Save*).
30. Specify the rules file name (must be 8 characters or fewer).

Like all things Essbase and in life, there is more than one path to get to a desired result. It's really about the journey, isn't it? Our journey now takes us to the ways to perform dimension build and outline updates for our Essbase database. Not the most exciting of journeys but this is one of those stops that we must learn.

PERFORM DIMENSION BUILD

The basic way to perform a dimension build for both ASO and BSO databases is as follows:

1. Right click on the database select *Load Data* (yes, Load Data is the correct choice):

2. The Data Load window will appear. Choose *Build Only* from the Mode drop down box:

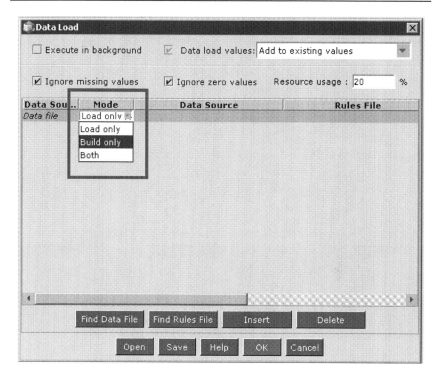

You can perform a dimension build only, data load only, or both build and load together in Essbase with a single rules file. One handy tip is to build in any new members that come through from the data source but may not exist in the outline. This way data is always fully loaded with no "fallout". New members can be added to a "Needs To Be Mapped" or "Unknown" parent member.

Often times Essbase administrators like to create separate rules for dimension building and data loading. While the number of objects to manage increase, the process and components may be more easily understood. This option is also dependent on whether the source file contains both dimension build elements and data.

3. Specify SQL if loading directly from a relational source or Data files if loading from a file.
4. Select *Find Data File* and navigate to the dimension data file.
5. Select *Find Rules File* and navigate to the dimension build rules file.
6. Specify the error file location and name.

7. Optionally, you can check the option to "Overwrite". This will overwrite any error file that may already exist.

8. Optionally, check *Deferred-restructure dimension build* for ASO databases.

The Deferred-restructure dimension build option is applicable when you are loading multiple sources. Essbase will wait to restructure the ASO database until all sources have been processed (which is faster than read source 1, restructure, read source 2, restructure, read source 3, restructure, etc.).

9. Click *OK* and the members will be added to the outline.

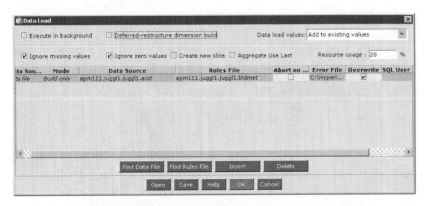

This dimension build method updated the outline and saved all changes. What stinks is that we didn't get a chance to preview the changes before they were saved to the database. Unfortunately for ASO databases, we're stuck with this method. (So if you are making some big changes to the database, make sure to back up the outline file and export the data before running the dimension updates. Just in case.)

For block storage databases, we have another alternative that does allow us to preview dimension build changes before saving them. Let's review this option now.

PERFORM DIMENSION BUILD IN OUTLINE EDITOR - BSO

For BSO applications, you can update the outline directly in the outline editor, previewing the dimension changes before saving and restructuring the database.

Tip!

Updating the outline in the outline editor is only available for BSO databases.

1. Open the outline in the Outline Editor.
2. Select *Outline >> Update outline*.
3. The Update Outline window will open:

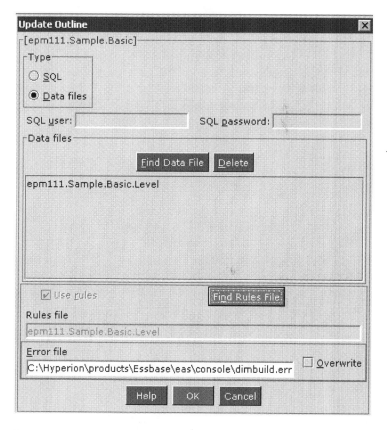

4. Specify SQL if loading directly from a relational source or Data files if loading from a file.
5. Select *Find Data File* and navigate to the dimension data file.
6. Select *Find Rules File* and navigate to the dimension build rules file.
7. Specify the error file location and name.
8. Optionally, you can check the option to "Overwrite". This will overwrite any error file that may already exist.

Note!

You're saying "I don't see the option to Update Outline". That is probably because either you are in an ASO outline or you've opened the BSO outline in view mode. Updating the outline in the outline editor is only available in edit mode for BSO outlines.

9. Click *OK* to update the outline.

DYAMICALLY BUILD ALTERNATE HIERARCHIES

The examples we've seen so far have been pretty straightforward. Now let's look at how you can build alternate hierarchies with shared members.

A generation build data file with a column for adding an alternate hierarchy looks like the following:

```
Gen2      Dupgen2  Gen3
100       Diet     100-20
200       Diet     200-20
300       Diet     300-30
```

The DUPGEN, "duplicate generation", column must follow the generation at which members are shared. The rules file will translate this data file into the following dimension hierarchy:

```
Product
  100 (+) (Alias: Colas)
    100-10 (+) (Alias: Cola)
    100-20 (+) (Alias: Diet Cola)
    100-30 (+) (Alias: Caffeine Free Cola)
  200 (+) (Alias: Root Beer)
    200-10 (+) (Alias: Old Fashioned)
    200-20 (+) (Alias: Diet Root Beer)
    200-30 (+) (Alias: Sasparilla)
    200-40 (+) (Alias: Birch Beer)
  300 (+) (Alias: Cream Soda)
  400 (+) (Alias: Fruit Soda)
  Diet (~) (Alias: Diet Drinks)
    100-20 (+) (Alias: Diet Cola)
    200-20 (+) (Alias: Diet Root Beer)
    300-30 (+) (Alias: Diet Cream)
```

A different way to build the same hierarchy with shared members would be to use a level dimension build method. The level build data file with a column for adding an alternative hierarchy looks like the following:

```
Level0          Level1   Level1
100-20          100      Diet
200-20          200      Diet
300-20          300      Diet
```

You could also use a parent/child build method to build alternate hierarchies. The parent/child dimension build data file looks like the following (make sure to uncheck "Allow Moves"):

```
Parent          Child
100             100-20
200             200-20
300             300-20
Diet            100-20
Diet            200-20
Diet            300-20
```

DYNAMICALLY ASSIGN MEMBER PROPERTIES

Under Field properties, you can update aliases, member properties, member formulas, and UDAs. If your dimension source file contains valid values, then the rules file can update any of these properties.

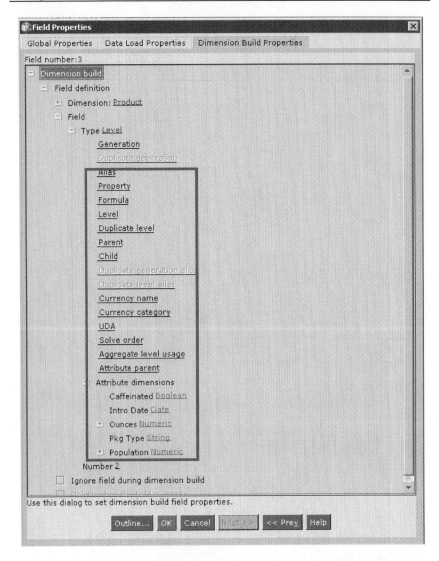

Here is a list of valid codes for assigning Essbase member properties for aggregate storage databases:

%	Set consolidation to express as a percentage of current total.
*	Set consolidation to multiply by the current total.
+	Set consolidation to add to the current total.
-	Set consolidation to subtract from the current total.
/	Set consolidation to divide by the current total.
~	Set to no consolidation.

A	Set to Time Balance Average (applies to accounts dimensions).
E	Assign expense reporting tag (applies to accounts dimensions).
F	Set to Time Balance First (applies to accounts dimensions).
L	Set to Time Balance Last (applies to accounts dimensions).
M	Exclude data values of #MISSING from the time balance.
N	Set data storage to Never Share.
O	Set data storage to Label Only (store no data).
C	Set member as top of a stored hierarchy (applies to dimension member or generation 2 member)
D	Set member as top of a dynamic hierarchy (applies to dimension member or generation 2 member)
H	Set dimension member as multiple hierarchies enabled (applies to dimension member only)

Here is a list of valid codes for assigning Essbase member properties for block storage databases:

%	Set consolidation to express as a percentage of current total.
*	Set consolidation to multiply by the current total.
+	Set consolidation to add to the current total.
-	Set consolidation to subtract from the current total.
/	Set consolidation to divide by the current total.
~	Set to no consolidation.
^	Set to no aggregation.
A	Set to Time Balance Average (applies to accounts dimensions).
B	Exclude data values of zero or #MISSING in time balance.
E	Assign expense reporting tag (applies to accounts dimensions).
F	Set to Time Balance First (applies to accounts dimensions).
L	Set to Time Balance Last (applies to accounts dimensions).
M	Exclude data values of #MISSING from the time balance.
N	Set data storage to Never Share.
O	Set data storage to Label Only (store no data).
S	Set data storage to Store (non-Dynamic Calc and not label).
T	Assign two-pass calculation (applies to accounts dimensions).
V	Set data storage to Dynamic Calc and Store (BSO databases only).
X	Set data storage to Dynamic Calc (BSO databases only).

Z	Exclude data values of zero from the time balance.

Tip! Remember your ASO and BSO rules when assigning member properties through a rules files (e.g. in ASO, level zero members cannot be set to Label Only). If you run into an error, check to make sure your data file isn't conflicting with an Essbase rule.

As an example, the following file will build an accounts dimension using a source file set up in Parent/Child format for a BSO outline. Member properties are also assigned in the source file. The rules file has defined the following field properties:

- Parent, Account
- Child, Account
- Alias, Account
- and Property, Account for the remaining property fields.

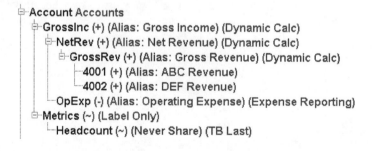

The resulting hierarchy will look like this:

```
⊟ Account Accounts
   ⊟ GrossInc (+) (Alias: Gross Income) (Dynamic Calc)
      ⊟ NetRev (+) (Alias: Net Revenue) (Dynamic Calc)
         ⊟ GrossRev (+) (Alias: Gross Revenue) (Dynamic Calc)
            ─ 4001 (+) (Alias: ABC Revenue)
            └ 4002 (+) (Alias: DEF Revenue)
      └ OpExp (-) (Alias: Operating Expense) (Expense Reporting)
   ⊟ Metrics (~) (Label Only)
      └ Headcount (~) (Never Share) (TB Last)
```

Note! If a member property is not specified in the source file, Essbase will assume the default value.

A new option introduced in Essbase System 9, "Delete when field is empty" option, allows you to leave a field blank in a data file and the mapped property will be reset to default or the UDA, formula, or associated attribute will be removed.

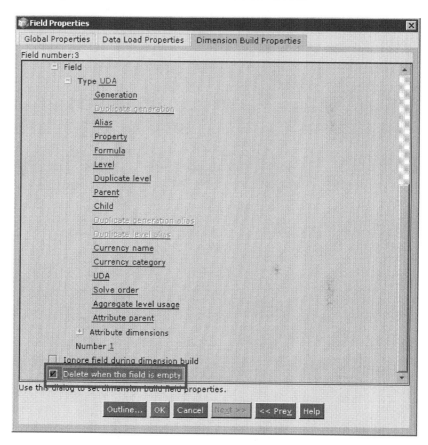

We've decided to add members to the Accounts dimension in our wolverine juggling application to track key metrics and drivers. We've been supplied the following file (you can easily create this file using notepad) for the new metrics (yes, there are only a few but let's pretend we have a long list of metrics):

```
Account, Metrics, , O,~,
Metrics, Avg_Wolverines_Juggled, Average Wolverines Juggled, S, ~, A
Metrics, Avg_Wolverines_Dropped, Average Wolverines Dropped, S, ~, A
Metrics, Headcount, , S,~, L
```

Next we build the following rules file to update the outline:

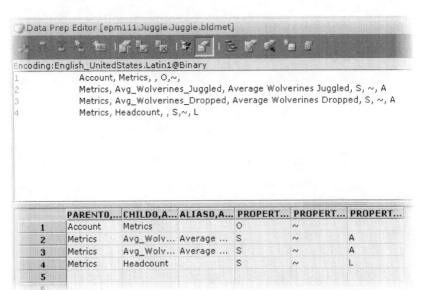

 Build a rules file to update the Accounts dimension in the juggling wolverine application. Try this on your own but just in case, we've provided the steps below.

Try It!

1. Create the acct.txt file above and move this file to your Hyperion install folder under EssbaseServer\app\juggle\juggle:

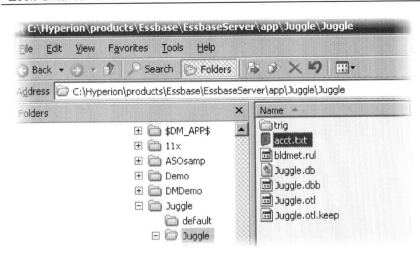

2. In Administration Services, right click on the Juggle database and select *Create >> Rules file:*

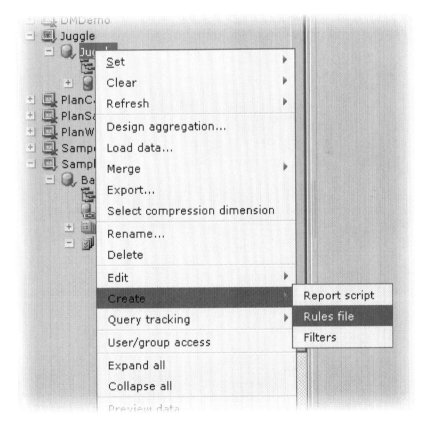

3. Select *File >> Open Data File* and navigate to and select the acct.txt file in the Juggle folder.

4. Select *Options >> Data Source Properties* and set the delimiter to Comma:

5. Click *OK.*

6. Select *Options >> Dimension Build Settings.*

7. On the Dimension Build Settings tab, select the Account dimension.

8. Define the build method as parent/child and allow moves and property updates:

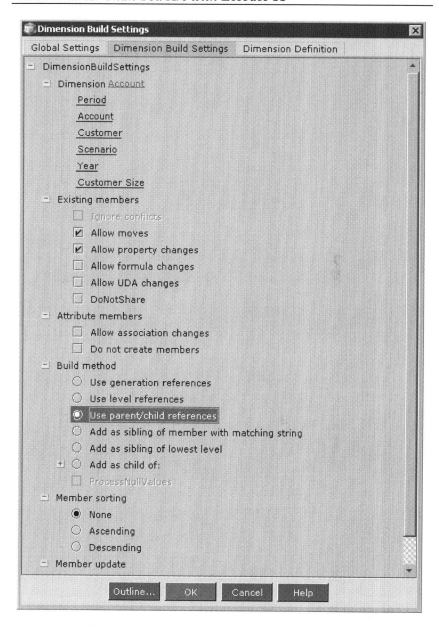

9. Click *OK*.
10. Select the first column and choose *Field >> Properties*.
11. On the Dimension Build Properties tab, choose the Account dimension and set the field to *Parent*:

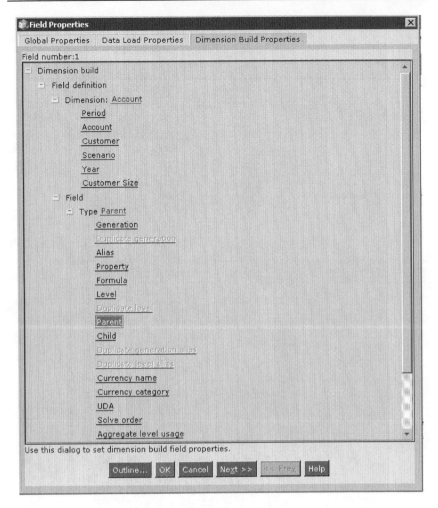

12. Click *Next*.
13. Set the field2 to the dimension *Account* and the field *Child*.
14. Click *Next*.
15. Set the field3 to the dimension *Account* and the field *Alias*.
16. Click *Next*.
17. Set the field4 to the dimension *Account* and the field *Property*.
18. For the remaining columns, set the dimensions to *Account* and field *Property*.
19. Verify and save the rules file.

20. Right click on the juggle database and select *Load Data.*
21. Choose *Build Only* mode.
22. Select the data file and rules file.
23. Click OK to run the dimension build process.

Open the outline and view the newly added metrics with the appropriate member properties:

```
Period Time Stored # Default # <14>
Account Accounts Dynamic Compression <2>
  + Margin (+) <2>
  - Metrics (~) <3> (Label Only)
        Avg_Wolverines_Juggled (~) (Alias: Average Wolverines Juggled) (TB Average)
        Avg_Wolverines_Dropped (~) (Alias: Average Wolverines Dropped) (TB Average)
        Headcount (~) (TB Last)
  Customer Multiple Hierarchies Enabled <5> (Label Only) {Customer Size}
  Scenario Stored # Default # <2> (Label Only)
  Year Stored # Default # <2> (Label Only)
  Customer Size Attribute [Type: Text] # Default # <3>
```

Tip!

The sample applications that are installed with Essbase have some great examples of different types of dimension build rules files. Use these as you create your own dimension build rules.

Note!

Would it have made sense to tag our new average members with the ^ vs. the ~? The ^ consolidation would prohibit consolidation across all dimensions in the Essbase database so in the case of the average members, yes, this makes more sense. BUT the ^ is not available for ASO applications in Essbase 11.1.1. Darn!

RULES FILES FOR ATTRIBUTE DIMENSIONS

You can use rules files to build attribute dimensions and associate base members. Let's see how.

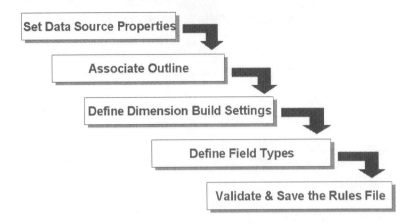

Does this process look familiar? It should. The process to build an attribute dimension is the same process for building a regular dimension.

Now what if you want to associate members in the base dimension with the attribute member? Here's an example: assigning packaging or size to a product member. To do this, you just need to accurately map the field definition.

See in the example below, columns three and four have been mapped to the correct attribute member. Notice the generation number of the attribute members matches the generation of the product member that is the associated base member:

Data Prep Editor [epm111.Sample.Basic.Attrprod]

Encoding:English_UnitedStates.Latin1@Binary

1	500	500-10	64	True
2	500	500-20	64	False

	GEN2,Pro...	GEN3,Product	Ounces3,Product	Caffeinated3,Product
1	500	500-10	64	True
2	500	500-20	64	False
3				

To assign the field properties to associate base dimension members,

1. Select *Field >> Properties*.
2. Click *Next* until you get to column 3.

3. For dimension, double click to select Product (if not already done).
4. Under Field Type, select the attribute dimension for column 3 (in this case Ounces).
5. Click *Next* to assign the next field property:

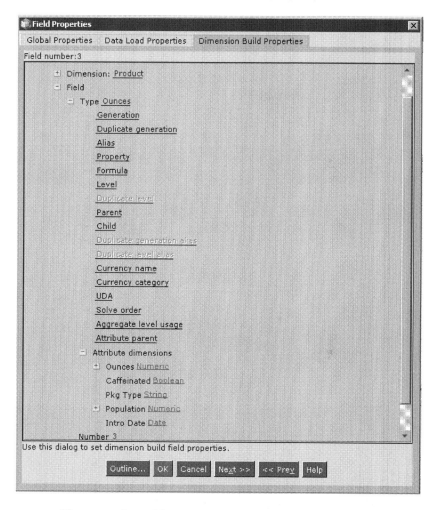

You can also add ranges to an attribute dimension. Ranges functionality allows you to use a model where numeric attribute members represent a range of values. Here is an attribute dimension with the numeric range:

⊟··**Ounces Attribute [Type: Numeric]**
   ├···**0** (Alias: 0-9 oz)
   ├···**10** (Alias: 10-19 oz)
   ├···**20** (Alias: 20-29 oz)
   ├···**30** (Alias: 30-39 oz)
   ├···**40** (Alias: 40-49 oz)
   ├···**50** (Alias: 50-59 oz)
   └···**60** (Alias: 60-69 oz)

Note!

Query processing, calculation and data load have no notion about a range model.

SELECT / REJECT RECORDS

Say your dimension data file has every possible account, but you have special hierarchy logic to apply to the revenue accounts. This requires a filter using wildcards to only load the revenue account range. Using Sample.Basic as an example, we want to update the level.rul to only build products that begin with 600-20.

To add a filter to your load rule,
1. Select *Record >> Select* or *Reject*:

2. Define the type: *String* or *Number*.
3. Type in the value.
4. Select the condition: equals, does not equal, greater than, greater than or equal to, less than, less than or equal to, contains, or does not contain.
5. Check whether the filter should be case sensitive:

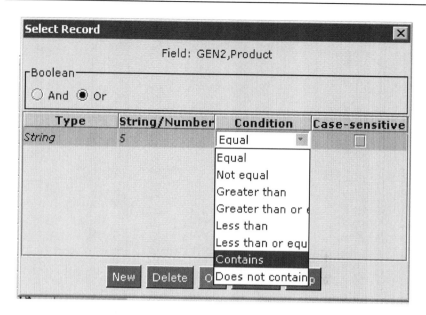

6. Click *OK*. The list of records shown in the data prep editor will not change even though you've added criteria, because Select/Reject is only processed when the rule is actually executed.

Try It!

Make a copy of gen.rul in Sample.Basic. Update the copied rules file to reject all records containing the value "500-10-10". This product has been discontinued but the source that provides the dimension hierarchy keeps sending the complete dimension list (those pesky IT administrators).

Note!

You can add multiple lines of criteria for Select or Reject records in a rules file.

CREATE COLUMNS USING TEXT OR JOIN

Often times we need to do some manipulation with the dimension build source file (or even the data load file). The file may be missing some information or you may need to join columns to create the desired member names.

For example, we have the following requirements for our product dimension. We want the alias value set to product number joined with the product description. And for level 1, we want to add on the words "Product Category" to the category number.

Here is the data file that we are provided:

```
600-10-11        600-10   600     Mountain Dew
600-20-10        600-20   600     Sprite
600-20-18        600-20   600     Seven up
```

Note this file doesn't meet our dimension build requirements so we are going to need to do some further manipulation in the rules file. There are lots of changes, so let's get started. First we want to move the level zero alias field to directly behind the level zero product number.

1. Select *Field >> Move.*
2. Select the desired field to move and click the *Up* or *Down* buttons to order the columns appropriately:

3. Click *OK.*
4. Select *Field >> Create Using Text:*

5. Type in the text " – " because we would like to have a hyphen between product number and alias:

6. Click *OK*.
7. Select *Field >> Create Using Join*:

8. Select the desired columns to join:

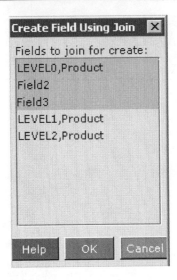

9. Click *OK*.

Note!

The fields will be joined in the order they are listed in the "Create Field Using Joins" window.

10. Notice the new field created with the three concatenated columns. We now need to move this new column to just after the product number. Select *Field >> Move* and move the column down.
11. Next assign the field property alias to the new column.
12. Assign "Ignore during dimension build" to the two extra columns.

Tip!

Select *Field >> Properties* to find the "Ignore during dimension build" option.

	Data Prep Editor [epm111.Sample.Basic.Level]			

Encoding:English_UnitedStates.Latin1@Binary

1	600-10-11	600-10	600	Mountain Dew
2	600-20-10	600-20	600	Sprite
3	600-20-18	600-20	600	Seven Up

	LEVEL0,Product	Product	Field3	Field4	LEVEL1,P...	LEVEL2,P
1	600-10-11	600-10-11-Mountain Dew	mountain		600-10	600
2	600-20-10	600-20-10-Sprite	sprite		600-20	600
3	600-20-18	600-20-18-Seven Up	seven up		600-20	600
4						

You can view and undo these field edits. Select *Options >> Data Source Properties.* Select the Field Edits tab to view field edits.

Try It! Make a copy of the parchil rules file in Sample.Basic. In the copy, update the rules file using "Create using Text/Join" functionality to assign product number concatenated with a hyphen concatenated with product description (e.g. 200-10-10 – Old Fashioned) as the alias.

PRINT A RULES FILE

You can print a rules file via Administration Services. This is helpful for documentation purposes or if you are just trying to understand what the rules file does (vs. opening all of the various windows to view the rules settings).

To print a rules file,
1. Select *File >> Print.*
2. Define what should be printed:

3. Click *OK*.

Recap – Steps to Building Dimensions via Rules File

1. In Administration Services, navigate to the Rules Files section under the application or database.
2. Right click and *Create Rules File*.
3. Once the data prep editor is open, select *File >> Open Data File*.
4. Navigate to the appropriate folder on the Essbase Analytic server. Find the dimension data file.
5. Make sure you've selected Dimension Build mode (dimension build icon).
6. Select *Options >> Data Source Properties*. Update any of the data source properties for the applicable file (e.g. skip first line).
7. Select *Options >> Dimension Build Settings*.
8. Update the Field Properties for each column (Select *Field >> Properties*).
9. Validate the rules file.
10. Save the rules file.
11. Use the *Load Data* option with Build mode for ASO and BSO databases, or for BSO databases, open the outline in the outline editor and select *Outline >> Update Outline*.

Helpful
Info

Now that your outline is complete, let's load some data!

Chapter 8:
Load Data

Thinking that you're going to have to learn a whole new interface for loading data? Not so... you will load data via ...wait for it... wait for it... a rules file that you create in the data prep editor. The last chapter covered dimension build rules files and thankfully creating data load rules files are very similar.

Before we get into the data load rules files, let's take a step back for a moment. There are many different ways to load data to Essbase:

- Smart View Submit
- Spreadsheet lock and send (via the antiquated Essbase Excel Add-in)
- Free-form data loading
- Data load rules against flat files
- Data load rules using SQL interface
- Essbase Studio
- Essbase Integration Services

We covered submitting data via Smart View in an earlier chapter. In this chapter, we'll recap submitting data via Smart View and then focus on free form data loading and data load rules.

LOAD DATA VIA SMART VIEW

Our end users will be submitting the information for our juggling wolverine metrics. Set up the following spreadsheet for them to submit the information:

Click *Submit* on the ribbon to send data back to the database. That's it for Smart View (pretty easy, right?).

Note! For ASO databases, data can only be input or loaded to level zero members (members at the bottom of every dimension).

FREE FORM DATA LOADING

Free-form data loading is a simple process to load data to Essbase. The data file can be loaded as is without any explicit description of its contents (i.e. no load rule), but the data <u>must</u> be in the natural order for Essbase. So what is the natural order for Essbase? Essbase must encounter a member from every dimension before a data value. Any valid dimension/member/alias name combination is acceptable. Data is read according to the member names Essbase finds.

Free Form Data Load Example 1:

Markets	Products	Scenario	Year	Measures	
East	Cola	Actual	Jan	Sales	$10
East	Cola	Actual	Feb	Sales	$21
East	Cola	Actual	Mar	Sales	$30
East	Cola	Actual	Apr	Sales	$35
East	Cola	Actual	May	Sales	$40
East	Cola	Actual	Jun	Sales	$45
East	Cola	Actual	Jan	Marketing	$8
East	Cola	Actual	Feb	Marketing	$16
East	Cola	Actual	Mar	Marketing	$20

Free Form Data Load Example 2:

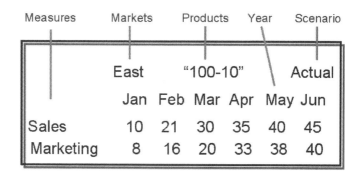

To load a free form data file,

1. Select the database and choose *Actions >> Load data for "dbname"* from the menu.
2. The Load Data window will open.
3. Under Data Source, specify Data files (default option).
4. Select *Find Data File* and navigate to the data file.
5. DO NOT select *Find Rules File*. A rules file is not necessary for a free form load:

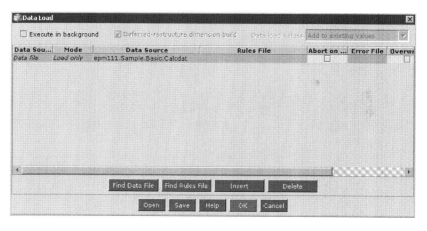

6. Click *OK*.

For Sample.Basic, load the free form file named calcdat.txt.

Try It!

That's it for Free Form Data loading. If all your input files are formatted that nicely, then your job as an Essbase Administrator is going to be very easy indeed.

DATA LOAD RULES OVERVIEW

Just as we used dimension build rules, we can use data load rules to perform transformations and define information in a text file for Essbase, but in this case to load data. We have to define what columns map to what dimensions, which columns contain data, and any necessary header information.

So when should you use a data load rule?
- You need to ignore fields or strings in data file.
- You need to change the order of fields by moving, joining, splitting or creating.
- You need to map the data in the data source to the database by changing strings.
- You need to change the data values in the data source by scaling data values or adding them to existing values in the data source.
- You need to set header records for missing values.
- You need to reject an invalid record and continue loading data.
- You want to add new dimensions and members in the database along with the data load.
- You want to change existing dimensions and members in the database along with the data load.

So what we are really saying is that in most cases you will use a data load rule to load data to Essbase.

Here is what a data load rule will look like in the Data Prep Editor:

```
Data Prep Editor [epm111.Sample.Basic.Act1]
Encoding:English_UnitedStates.Latin1@Binary
1       California,Caffeine Free Cola, Sales, 145,132,125,110,106,96,87,87,109,109,116,102
2       California,Caffeine Free Cola, COGS, 95,104,109,123,127,141,154,154,122,122,113,127
3       California,Caffeine Free Cola, Marketing, 30,33,34,39,40,45,49,49,39,39,36,40
4       California,Caffeine Free Cola, Payroll, 22,22,22,23,23,23,22,22,22,22,22,22
5       California,Caffeine Free Cola, Misc, 0,0,1,1,0,0,0,1,0,0,1,1
```

	Market	Product	Measures	Jan	Feb	Mar	Apr	May	Jun	Jul	
1	California	Caffeine F...	Sales	145	132	125	110	106	96	87	8
2	California	Caffeine F...	COGS	95	104	109	123	127	141	154	1
3	California	Caffeine F...	Marketing	30	33	34	39	40	45	49	4
4	California	Caffeine F...	Payroll	22	22	22	23	23	23	22	2
5	California	Caffeine F...	Misc	0	0	1	1	0	0	0	1
6											
7											
8											
9											
10											
11											
12											
13											
14											
15											
16											
17											

Look familiar? Yes. The same interface as dimension build rules files. So let's create a data load rules file.

CREATE A DATA LOAD RULES FILE

1. In Administration Services, navigate to the *Rules Files* option under the application or database.
2. Right click and select *Create Rules File*:

3. Select *File >> Open Data File*.
4. Browse to and open the data file. For this example, open the act1.txt from the Sample.Basic application
5. Once the data file is open, select *Options >> Data Source Properties*.
6. The Data Source properties window will open.

Data source properties will tell Essbase the data source delimiters, what field edits have been made in the rules file, and what header rows may exist.

On the Delimiter tab, specify Comma, Tab, Spaces, Custom, or Column Width delimiter for the data file (if someone with a perverse sense of humor gave you a data file with ! or ~ as the delimiter, Essbase can handle this with the custom option):

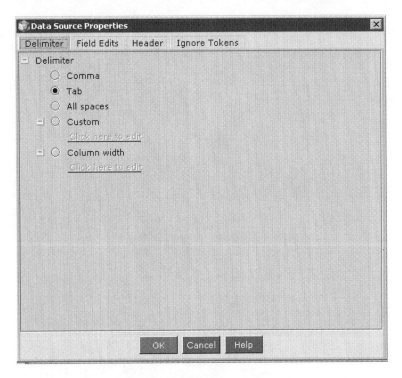

Specify how many lines to skip or define any records that may have header information and field information on the header tab:

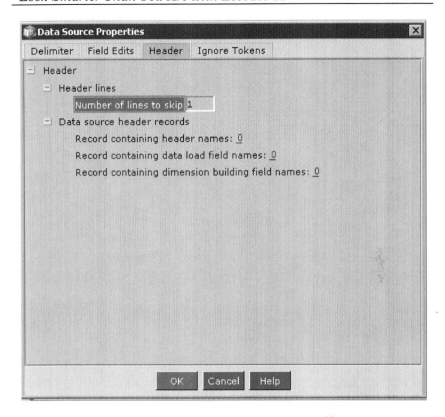

Next, associate the outline,

7. Select Associate Outline icon or *Options >> Associate Outline.*
8. The Associate Outline window will open.
9. Select the desired database.

To define the data load settings,

10. Select *Options >> Data Load Settings.*
11. The Data Load Settings window will open:

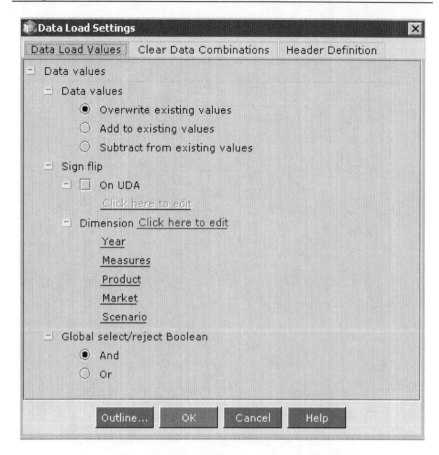

On the Data Load Values tab, define whether this rules file should overwrite, add to, or subtract from existing values. In most cases, you want to overwrite, but there are some exceptions.

Here's one: the source file you load to Essbase contains daily transaction data but your Essbase database contains aggregated monthly data. You would want to specify "Add To Existing Values" for the following text file to get Essbase to calculate the total for the month (and make sure not to load the same file twice)`. If the data load rule is set to overwrite, then only the final value in the file will be stored:

```
01/01/2007, Jan, California,Caffeine Free Cola, Sales, 145
01/02/2007, Jan, California,Caffeine Free Cola, Sales, 123
01/03/2007, Jan, California,Caffeine Free Cola, Sales, 132
01/04/2007, Jan, California,Caffeine Free Cola, Sales, 145
01/05/2007, Jan, California,Caffeine Free Cola, Sales, 102
01/06/2007, Jan, California,Caffeine Free Cola, Sales, 116|
```

You can also specify whether to flip a sign based on an assigned User Defined Attribute on the Data Load Values tab. If your source file contains debits and credits, you will want to load only positive values because you will be handling the sign flipping in Essbase using Unary Operators. To do this, you can assign a UDA of "Flip Input" (or something else descriptive of the task) to all of your accounts that will be arriving as negative values. Check the "Sign Flip on UDA" check box and select the "Flip Input" UDA. The sign will be flipped for all records in the data file for the accounts tagged "Flip Input".

To clear data for a specific intersection before loading the data file, utilize the Clear Data Combinations tab. This is helpful if you load actual data on a daily basis and want to automatically clear out the month being loaded before loading the daily data. In the example below, the rules file will clear all January Actual data before loading the new data file:

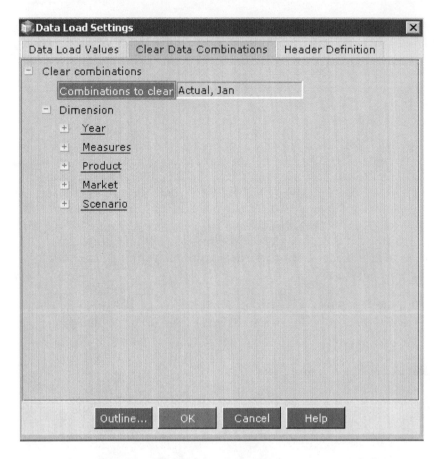

The Header Definition tab allows you to define any dimension not represented in the data file. In the example below, we've defined a header of 'Actual' because there isn't a column in the file that identifies the scenario. Essbase needs to know exactly where you want to load data for every dimension. Should it load data to Actual, or Budget, or both?

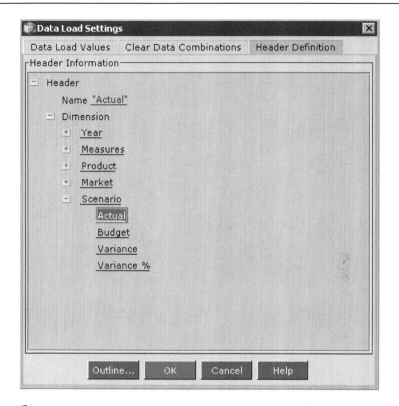

 A data load rules file must reference every dimension, either
in the fields section or in the header section.

Note!

Next, define the Field properties, mapping the columns to dimensions or members and identifying data values.

12. Select *Field >> Properties*.
13. The Field Properties window will open.

The Global Properties tab allows you to translate text to upper / lower case, add prefix and suffixes, convert spaces to underscores, and perform a find and replace. This is used to make sure that the values specified in the data load match what is in the outline, especially if you've used a dimension build file to add prefixes or suffixes to member names.

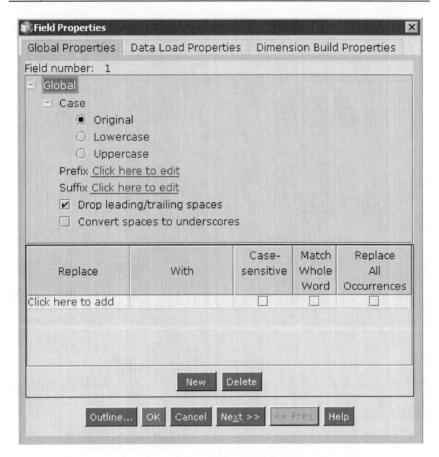

For example, let's say your Account number structure and Product number structure could have the exact same number. Essbase won't allow you to have a member with the same name so you built your Product dimension to include a prefix "Product_". Now your source file only has the product number. You need add the prefix "Product_" to the Product column so that data will load to the correct product member.

Tip!

Members in the data file must match the members in your outline exactly! If the Objects_Juggled dimension in our juggling wolverine application has the member "Super-sonic silver wolverine" but our data file has "Super sonic silver wolverine" with no hyphen, data will not be loaded for those records. But (whine) its close enough. Can't Essbase figure it out? Nope. Members in the data file must match member names in the outline.

Next we will select the Data Load Properties tab. (Ignore the Dimension Build Properties tab since we are focusing on data loading).

14. Select the dimension that maps to the field
    or select a specific member
    or select "Data Field"
    or select "Ignore field during a data load":

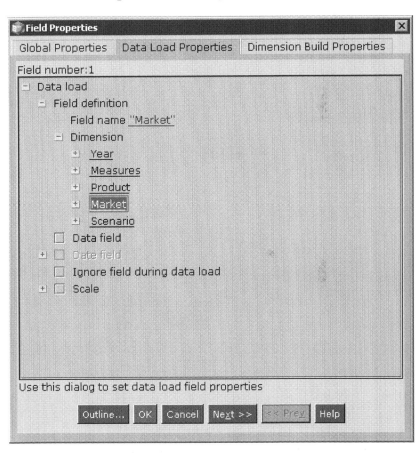

Tip!

When navigating in the field property window, double-click to select a particular item. Make sure the item shows up in blue next to Field Name. If you single click, the item will not be selected. This can be an annoying little feature that will test your memory and patience... "but I know I set that property" and you probably did but you single clicked instead of double clicked.

Note!

You can only have one column assigned "Data Field" within a data load rules file.

15. Click *Next* to move to next field.
16. Click *OK* once all of the fields have been defined.

Note!

There are two modes for rules files: dimension building and data loading. When working on a dimension build rules file, select the Dimension Building mode:

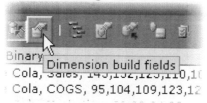

When working on a data load rules file, select the Data Load mode:

Here is an example of a data load rules file where the first three columns map to a dimension and the remaining columns map to a specific member in the Period dimension:

Encoding:English_UnitedStates.Latin1@Binary

Map Column to Dimension   Map Column to Specific Member

	Market	Product	Measur...	Jan	Feb	Mar	Apr	May	Jun	Jul
1										
2										
3										
4										
5										
6										
7										
8										
9										
10										
11										
12										
13										
14										

The last step before saving is to validate the rules file. Rules files are validated to ensure the member and dimension mapping defined in the rules file maps to the associated outline. Validation cannot ensure that the data source will load properly. For example, you've defined the rules file, setting source file and data load properties, assigned field columns, and everything validates successfully. But what if your source file contains the member "Forecast" but "Forecast" doesn't exist in the outline. Any records containing members that do not exist in the outline will not be loaded to Essbase. These invalid or "fallout" records are sent to an exception file that you can review after the load has finished.

17. Select the Validate icon (or select *Options >> Validate*).

My Data Load Rules File won't Validate – What Should You Check?

Helpful Info

- Is the field name valid?
- Are the file delimiters correctly placed?
- Is there a member in the field name?
- Is the dimension name used in another field name or the header?
- Are you using a member as member combination in one place and a single member in another?
- Is more than one field defined as the data field?
- Is the dimension used for sign flipping in the associated outline?
- Is the rules file associated with the correct outline?

18. Select the *Save* icon (or select *File >> Save*).

Within a rules file you can filter records from a source file using either Select or Reject. Say your data file had all accounts but you only wanted to load data for revenue accounts. You could define a filter using wildcards to only load data for the revenue account range.

To add a filter to your load rule,
1. Select *Record >> Select* or *Reject*.
2. Define the type: *String* or *Number*.
3. Type in the value.
4. Select the criterion: equals, does not equal, greater than, greater than or equal to, less than, less than or equal to, contains, or does not contain.
5. Check whether it is case sensitive.
6. Click *OK*.

Don't forget that starting in Essbase 9.3, you have the ability to use substitution variables in rules file. Say you receive a current month file every month but the file doesn't actually specify the month. Historically, you've updated the header of the rules file for each new month. Now you can use your &Curmo substitution variable in the header definition (no updates required each month).

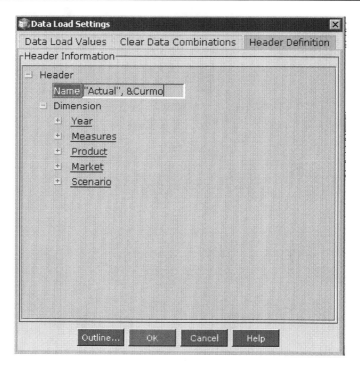

Now that we've covered the data loading basics, let's get ready load data to our juggling wolverine application. We've been supplied the following data file. (You can easily create this file in Excel, saving as tab delimited text named jugact.txt.)

			Jan	Feb	Mar	Apr	May	Jun	Jul	Aug	Sep	Oct	Nov	Dec	
2008	1001	Net_Revenue	1000	100	100	100	100	100	100	100	100	100	100	100	100
2008	1001	Op_Expense	200	200	200	200	200	200	200	200	200	200	200	200	200
2008	1001	Other Exp	100	100	100	100	100	100	100	100	100	100	100	100	100
2008	4001	Net_Revenue	2500	2500	2500	2500	2500	2500	2500	2500	2500	2500	2500	2500	2500
2008	4001	Op_Expense	500	500	500	500	500	500	500	500	500	500	500	500	500
2008	4001	Other Exp	250	250	250	250	250	250	250	250	250	250	250	250	250
2008	4002	Net_Revenue	2500	2500	2500	2500	2500	2500	2500	2500	2500	2500	2500	2500	2500
2008	4002	Op_Expense	500	500	500	500	500	500	500	500	500	500	500	500	500
2008	4002	Other Exp	250	250	250	250	250	250	250	250	250	250	250	250	250
2008	4003	Net_Revenue	3500	3500	3500	3500	3500	3500	3500	3500	3500	3500	3500	3500	3500
2008	4003	Op_Expense	500	500	500	500	500	500	500	500	500	500	500	500	500
2008	4003	Other Exp	250	250	250	250	250	250	250	250	250	250	250	250	250

What dimension is missing from this data file and where do you define them in the load rule? If you guessed the Scenario dimension was missing and "Header Definition" was where you specified this, you are correct (proving that your 4th grade teacher was right when she said you'd one day amount to something). If you guessed something else, well you couldn't exactly expect your 4th grade teacher to be psychic now, could you?

Try It!

Create a data load rule named ldact.rul to load the data file above to the juggling wolverine application. (No helpful hints this time – rules file building should be old hat by now.)*

*If you would like to obtain a copy of all of the wolverine juggle objects, please email info@interrel.com.

Your rules file should look similar to the following example:

				Jan	Feb	Mar	Apr	May	Jun
1				Jan	Feb	Mar	Apr	May	Jun
2	2008	1001	Net_Revenue	1000	100	100	100	100	100
3	2008	1001	Op_Expense	200	200	200	200	200	200
4	2008	1001	Other Exp	100	100	100	100	100	100
5	2008	4001	Net_Revenue	2500	2500	2500	2500	2500	2500
6	2008	4001	Op_Expense	500	500	500	500	500	500
7	2008	4001	Other Exp	250	250	250	250	250	250
8	2008	4002	Net_Revenue	2500	2500	2500	2500	2500	2500

Data Prep Editor [epm111.Juggle.Juggle.ldact]

Encoding:English_UnitedStates.Latin1@Binary

	"Year"	"Customer"	"Account"	"Jan"	"Feb"	"Mar"	"Apr"	"May"	"Jun"	"Jul"
1				Jan	Feb	Mar	Apr	May	Jun	Jul
2	2008	1001	Net_Rev...	1000	100	100	100	100	100	100
3	2008	1001	Op_Expe...	200	200	200	200	200	200	200
4	2008	1001	Other Exp	100	100	100	100	100	100	100
5	2008	4001	Net_Rev...	2500	2500	2500	2500	2500	2500	2500
6	2008	4001	Op_Expe...	500	500	500	500	500	500	500
7	2008	4001	Other Exp	250	250	250	250	250	250	250
8	2008	4002	Net_Rev...	2500	2500	2500	2500	2500	2500	2500
9	2008	4002	Op_Expe...	500	500	500	500	500	500	500
10	2008	4002	Other Exp	250	250	250	250	250	250	250
11	2008	4003	Net_Rev...	3500	3500	3500	3500	3500	3500	3500
12	2008	4003	Op_Expe...	500	500	500	500	500	500	500
13	2008	4003	Other Exp	250	250	250	250	250	250	250

LOAD DATA

We have the data file, we have the data load rules file. Let's load some data! (Is it sad that we are really excited about getting to this step? Ok, yes, we are complete geeks.)

To load data using a rules file,

1. Within Administration Services, select the database and choose *Actions >> Load data for "dbname"* from the menu (or right click on the database and select *Load Data*).

2. The Load Data window will open:

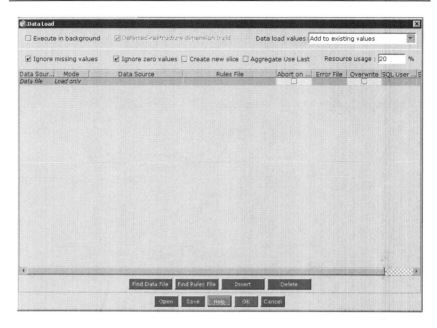

If you are loading data to an ASO database, you will see the following options across the top of the screen:

Data load values	Choose between: Add to existing values, Subtract from existing values, replace existing values, Replace All Data in the database
Ignore missing values	Ignore missing values in the source data files
Ignore zero values	Ignore zero values in the source data files
Create new slice	Creates a new slice when committing data to the database
Aggregate Use Last	Turns on the MaxL option AGGREGATE_USE_LAST which combines duplicate cells by using the value of the cell that was loaded last into the load buffer
Resource Usage	Set resource usage when using data load buffers

We'll return to these options in a later chapter when we discuss incremental loads and tuning for large volume data files.

3. Choose to *Overwrite Existing values* and leave the other options to their default values.

4. Select *Find Data File* and navigate to the dimension data file (the jugact file you just created).

5. Select *Find Rules File* and navigate to the data load rules file (the rules file you just created):

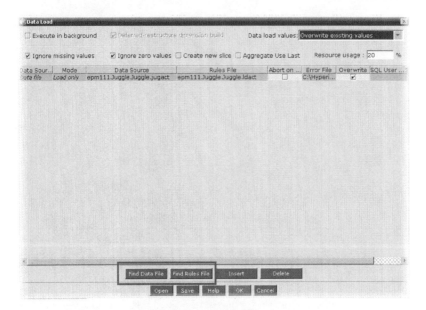

6. Specify the error file location and name.

7. Check the "Overwrite" check box if you want the error file replace an error file that may already exist.

8. If we were loading directly from a relational source instead of a text file, we would need to specify the SQL connection information.

9. Click *OK* to load data.

Tip!   You can load more than one load file with the same rules file if needed. Click the *Insert* button to insert a new record for specifying load information.

Abort on error during data load will stop the data load process if an error is found with the data file. If this is not selected, Essbase will load the valid records and send the invalid records to the error file.

Execute in the background will run the process in the background on your desktop, freeing up Administration Services to perform other tasks. If this is not selected and your data load takes

3 hours, you can't do anything else in Administration Services until the data load is complete (while the break would really do you some good, this will most likely frustrate the heck out of you).

Recap – Steps to Load Data via Rules File

1. In Administration Services, navigate to the Rules Files section under the application or database.
2. Right click and *Create Rules File*.
3. Once the data prep editor is open, select *File >> Open Data File*.
4. Navigate to find the data file
5. Make sure you've selected Data Load mode (use the data load icon to do this).
6. Select *Options >> Data Source Properties*. Update any of the data source properties for the applicable file (e.g. skip first line).
7. Select *Options >> Data Load Settings*.
8. Update the Field Properties for each column (Select *Field >> Properties*).
9. Validate the rules file.
10. Save the rules file.
11. Select the Database.
12. Right click and select *Load Data*.
13. Navigate to the data file and select.
14. Select the new rules file you just created.
15. Click *OK* to load data.

Helpful Info

Try It!

Just for practice, load the Act1.txt file using the Act1 rules file for Sample.Basic.

Once you've loaded your juggle database, perform analysis until your heart is thoroughly content. But wait, you ask... we haven't calculated anything, so how can we see anything above level-0? Because for ASO databases, no further calculation is required (though it can help performance to do so). See for yourself and connect to your juggle application and get started adhoc analyzing.

Try It!

Retrieve data from the juggling application.

Chapter 9:
Extending Your Database

Yes, you've created and loaded your first Essbase database but we've only seen the tip of the iceberg when it comes to Essbase functionality. Let's explore some additional features that further support Essbase as one of the top 10 innovations of the decade (Information Age Magazine).

TEXT AND DATE LISTS

In Essbase 11, Essbase can now store text and date information (which is just freaking awesome). Prior to 11, Essbase was limited to storing only numeric information in the data cells of a cube. The marketing types at Oracle call the ability to store texts "text lists" (and they are different than "smart lists" in Hyperion Planning). You can now perform analysis on text and dates in both ASO and BSO databases as you can see in the examples below:

	Sales	Package Type
Cola	40013.2	Bottle
Diet Cola	12640.6	Can
Caffeine Free Cola	6281.6	Can
Colas	58935.4	Bottle
		Can
		Invalid

	Sales Program Intro Date	Sales Program Term Date	Deviation from Average Life Span
All Merchandise	October 22, 2004	December 16, 2004	-22
Digital Cameras	April 6, 2004	July 25, 2004	-77
Camcorders	October 18, 2004	December 31, 2004	-41
Photo Printers	September 6, 2004	September 24, 2005	-18
Handhelds	June 17, 2005	November 6, 2005	-174
Memory	April 6, 2004	November 24, 2005	-27
Other Accessories	May 13, 2005	February 24, 2006	-174
Boomboxes	May 2, 2006	March 23, 2006	-23
Radios	June 24, 2006	May 12, 2006	28
		June 4, 2006	
		August 1, 2006	
Direct View	December 23, 2005	March 5, 2006	-38

Members in the dimension tagged "Accounts" can have a type of text or date:

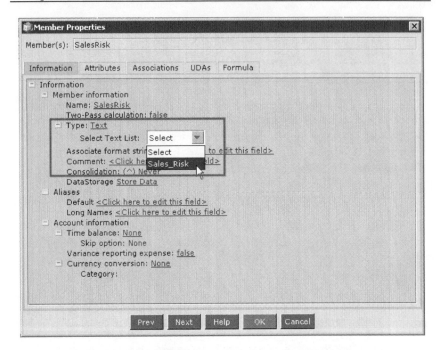

Behind the scenes Essbase is still storing numeric data and uses a lookup file to reference the text or date value. So if you wanted to return the numeric value, it is possible using the function @ENUMVALUE.

Text lists are defined at the database level and can be created in either Administration Services Console or the Essbase Studio. You can store 1024 unique values within a single text list plus a missing data value and out-of-range value.

Text lists can be imported into Essbase (free form text or date entry is not permitted). Intersections of data can be loaded via a load rule just like numeric data. Write back from Smart View is also permitted for users with the appropriate write access.

Let's add a new metric called Customer Satisfaction Rating to the Accounts dimension.

1. In Administration Services, edit the outline for the Juggle database in the Outline Editor.
2. Select the *Properties* tab.
3. Set Typed Measures to *true* (enabling text and date lists):

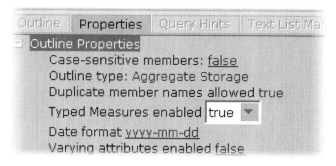

4. Click *OK* when prompted to convert the outline to support text lists:

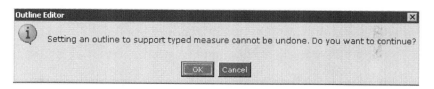

5. Optionally set the date format for any date measures that you will use in the application. Only one date format can be defined for an application and that same format will be applied for all date lists:

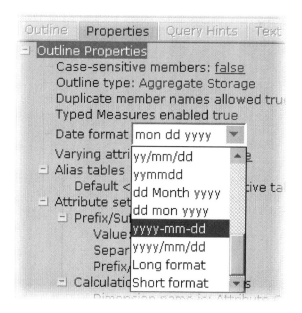

6. Save the outline.
7. Select the Outline tab.
8. Add a new member in the Measures dimension under Metrics called "Customer_Satisfaction_Rating":

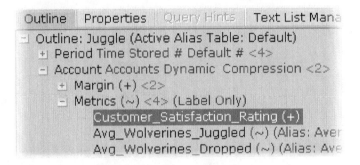

9. Select the Text List Manager tab.
10. Click the *New* button:

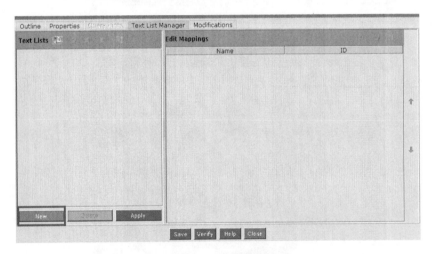

11. Double click in the highlighted space and type in the name for the new text list (*Double click here to create Text Lists*). Type in the name Customer_Satisfaction_Rating_TL:

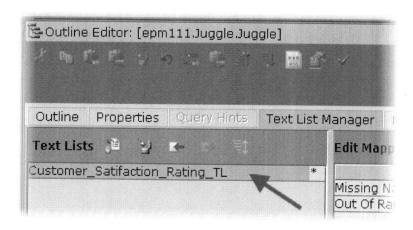

12. Click *Apply*.

Every text list will have 2 mappings by default: Missing Name (#missing) and Out Of Range Name (#Outofrange). #Missing allows unassigned text lists for values with no data. #outofrange will address any errors in loading for values that do not exist in the text list.

13. Click the plus icon in Edit Mappings to add new values to the text list:

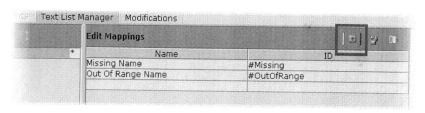

14. Add the following values to the text list:

Name	ID
Missing Name	#Missing
Out Of Range Name	#OutOfRange
Best Juggling in the World	1
Mildly Entertaining	2
Rather Eat Dog Food	3

15. Click *Save.*
16. If prompted, restructure the outline, retaining data.
17. Select the Outline tab and navigate to the new Customer_Satisfaction_Rating.
18. Right click on the member and select *Edit member properties.*
19. Choose Type as *Text:*

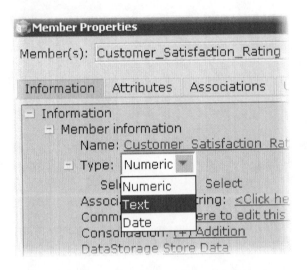

20. Choose *Customer_Satisfaction_Rating_TL* as the Text List:

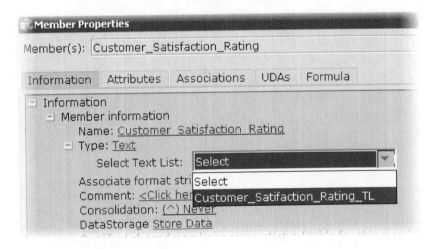

21. Save the outline.

Tip!

Click the Export Text List icon to export the listing in a .slt file format.

An exported text list looks like the following:

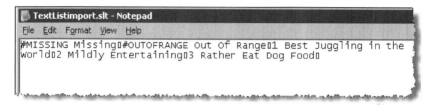

Let's create a new text list for Customer Risk Rating and import the customer dates. Create the following text file, listing three dates to import:

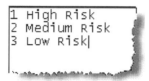

Note the file format is a simple listing with the ID *space* name *carriage return*. Save test list import files with extension *.slt*.

1. Create a new text list called Customer_Risk_TL but don't click Apply yet.
2. Select the *Import Text List* icon:

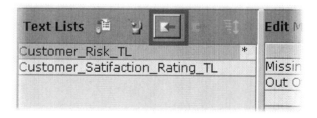

3. Navigate to and select the import file:

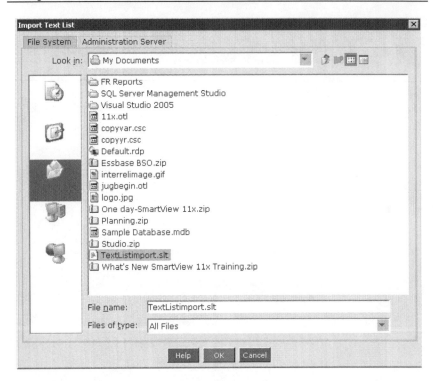

4. Click *OK* and the values should be imported into the text list:

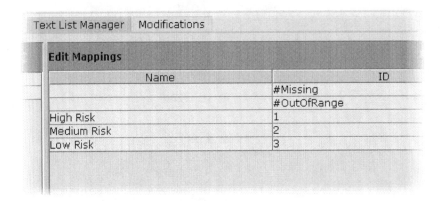

Note!

In version 11.1.1, the Import feature for text lists is finicky (finicky = buggy). In some cases, we found that you can only import the text list once when you initially create the text list. If you need to re-import, you have to delete the text list and re-create it.

Now that we've built the text list, we need to assign it to the new member, Customer_Risk.

5. In the outline editor, create a member named *Customer_Risk* and select *Edit member properties*.
6. Choose a type of *Text* and the Customer_Risk_TL as the selected text list:

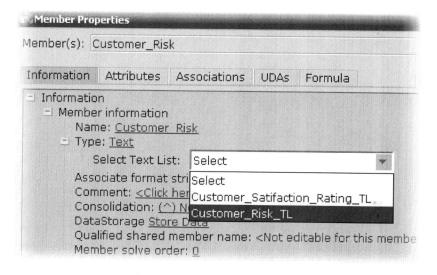

7. Click *OK* and save the outline, retaining all data if prompted.

Note!

Measures tagged with a type of text or date are automatically assigned the ^ tag. But ASO databases do not support the ^ tag? We'll call this a bug for right now:

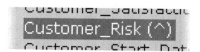

Just as you should do in your own Essbase environment, we need to brainstorm. How else can we take advantage of this new 11x feature? We want to analyze customers based on their start date and were originally considering an attribute dimension. Maybe a date member makes more sense?

1. Create a new member under Metrics called Customer_Start_Date.
2. In the outline editor, right click on Customer_Start_Date and select *Edit member properties.*
3. Select a type of *Date:*

4. Click *OK* and save the outline, retaining all of the data if prompted.

So what does this look like from an end user perspective? Let's check it out in Smart View. Here is a view of the Customer_Satisfaction_Rating (let's pretend like we've already loaded the data).

Users can view the assigned text list and if they have write back capabilities, they can also make changes to the assigned text lists:

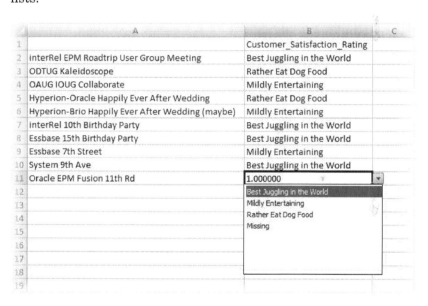

What is that 1.000000 that you are seeing in the cell? That's the numeric assignment from our Text List. Essbase is still storing the numeric value within the database but is using a look up reference to pull in and display the text value.

As the juggling company grows into thousands and thousands of customers, we can't manually input all of the ratings. Can you load text list values from rules file? Yes, you can.

 Create a text file and rules file to load Customer_Satisfaction_Rating data (see below for some hints).

Try It!

Your data file should look something like the following (in this case, tab delimited):

```
                    2008
1001    Customer_Satisfaction_Rating    Best Juggling in the World
1002    Customer_Satisfaction_Rating    Rather Eat Dog Food
1003    Customer_Satisfaction_Rating    Mildly Entertaining
2001    Customer_Satisfaction_Rating    Rather Eat Dog Food
2002    Customer_Satisfaction_Rating    Mildly Entertaining
3001    Customer_Satisfaction_Rating    Best Juggling in the World
3002    Customer_Satisfaction_Rating    Best Juggling in the World
4001    Customer_Satisfaction_Rating    Mildly Entertaining
4002    Customer_Satisfaction_Rating    Best Juggling in the World
4003    Customer_Satisfaction_Rating    Best Juggling in the World
```

Next, create a load rule to load it. Do you have to do anything special for the text list values? Nope. We'll assume that we distribute and collect customer satisfaction ratings once a year in December. Remember to reference all of the dimensions in the rules file, including header dimensions:

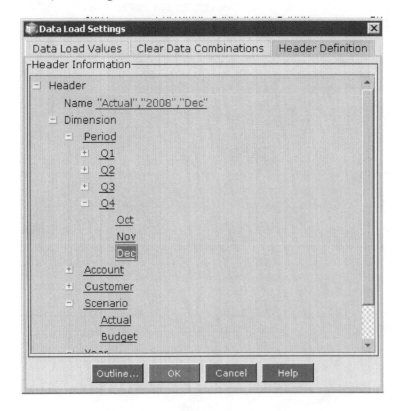

Your rules file should look like the following:

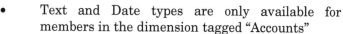

Data Prep Editor [epm111.Juggle.Juggle.ldcstsat]

Encoding:English_UnitedStates.Latin1@Binary

		2008	
1		2008	
2	1001	Customer_Satisfaction_Rating	Best Juggling in the World
3	1002	Customer_Satisfaction_Rating	Rather Eat Dog Food
4	1003	Customer_Satisfaction_Rating	Mildly Entertaining
5	2001	Customer_Satisfaction_Rating	Rather Eat Dog Food
6	2002	Customer_Satisfaction_Rating	Mildly Entertaining
7	3001	Customer_Satisfaction_Rating	Best Juggling in the World
8	3002	Customer_Satisfaction_Rating	Best Juggling in the World
9	4001	Customer_Satisfaction_Rating	Mildly Entertaining

	"Customer"	"Account"	*Data*
1			2008
2	1001	Custome...	Best Jug...
3	1002	Custome...	Rather E...
4	1003	Custome...	Mildly Ent...
5	2001	Custome...	Rather E...
6	2002	Custome...	Mildly Ent...
7	3001	Custome...	Best Jug...
8	3002	Custome...	Best Jug...
9	4001	Custome...	Mildly Ent...
10	4002	Custome...	Best Jug...
11	4003	Custome...	Best Jug...

Finally load the customer satisfaction ratings to the database. Right click on the database and select *Load Data*. Select the rules file and text file, and make sure to select Overwrite existing values.

Load the customer satisfaction ratings with your new load rule.

Try It!

Rules for Text Lists and Dates:

Helpful Info

- Maximum length 255 characters
- No free form allowed by end users
- Dimension tagged Accounts must be enabled for text lists
- Text and Date types are only available for members in the dimension tagged "Accounts"
- 1024 unique values in a single text list plus #missing and #outofrange
- Valid dates are from 1970 to January 19, 2038

[Tracy: don't ask why you can't go past 2038. Edward knows but everyone's eyes glaze over when he tries to explain it, so don't get him started.] [Edward: actually, it's pretty simple. It has to do with the way Essbase stores dates as seconds since January 1, 1970 in a long integer – AKA 2^31 or roughly 2.1 billion – and 2.1 billion seconds after the start of 1970 is 2038...] [Tracy's eyes glaze over.]

FORMATSTRING

Another new feature introduced in 11x called Formatstring provides text display and other formatting options for account members based on loaded numeric data. Formatstring is an alternative to a text list. Formatstring is a property of a member in the dimension tagged Accounts where you can specify an MDX expression that will be evaluated upon retrieval. The MDX expression can translate into a string or add prefixes and suffixes to existing data values:

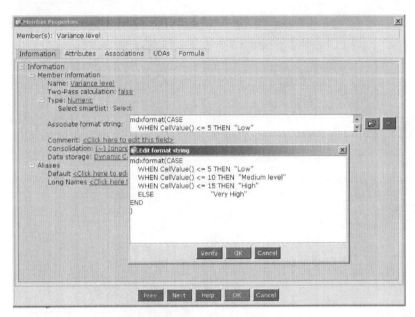

The resulting end user view would display:

	A	B	C	D	E	F	G
1					Market		
2					Sales		
3			Actual	Budget	Variance	Variance %	Variance level
4	100-10	Year	62824	67190	-4366	-6.50	Low
5	100-20	Year	30469	33520	-3051	-9.10	Low
6	100-30	Year	12841	13600	-759	-5.58	Low
7	100	Year	106134	114310	-8176	-7.15	Low
8	200-10	Year	41537	42300	-763	-1.80	Low
9	200-20	Year	38240	37860	380	1.00	Low
10	200-30	Year	17559	15270	2289	14.99	High
11	200-40	Year	11750	11310	440	3.89	Low
12	200	Year	109086	106740	2346	2.20	Low
13	300-10	Year	46956	39150	7806	19.94	Very High
14	300-20	Year	17480	14160	3320	23.45	Very High
15	300-30	Year	36969	31920	5049	15.82	Very High
16	300	Year	101405	85230	16175	18.98	Very High
17	400	Year	84230	66800	17430	26.09	Very High
18	Diet	Year	105678	103300	2378	2.30	Low
19	Product	Year	400855	373080	27775	7.44	Medium level

Other examples of formatstring MDX statements include sign flipping based on a UDA or formatting the display of a negative number:

```
/* Display negative values if current Account is an
      Expense type account */
IIF(IsUda(AccountTypes.CurrentMember, "Expense"),
    numtostr(-CellValue()),
    numtostr(CellValue()))
```

```
/* Enclose negative values in "(", ")" */
IIF(CellValue() < 0,
    Concat(Concat("(", numtostr(-CellValue())), ")"
    numtostr(CellValue()))
```

Let's walk through an example. In the juggle outline, create a new member under Metrics in the Accounts dimension called "Wolverines_Juggled_Classification".

1. Right click on the new member and select *Edit member properties*.
2. Select the Type as *Numeric*.
3. In the Associate format string, type the following:

```
mdxformat (CASE
WHEN CellValue() <= 50 THEN "Few Wolverines"
WHEN CellValue() <= 100 THEN "Many Wolverines"
ELSE "Too Many Wolverines to Count"
END
)
```

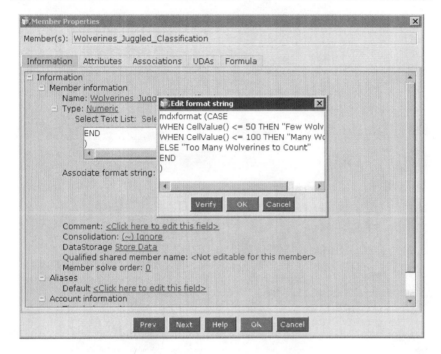

4. Click *Verify* to verify the MDX syntax.
5. Click *OK* and *OK*.
6. Save the outline.
7. If prompted to restructure the data, say *Yes*.

In order for the format string to work, we have to populate the member with data. In this example, we need to copy the values from the Avg_Wolverines_Juggled into the new Wolverines_Juggled_Classification member. We simply used our input sheet for the Avg_Wolverines_Juggled and modified it to input the same data for Wolverines_Juggled_Classification:

		Jan	Feb	Mar	Apr	May	Jun	Jul	Aug	Sep	Oct	Nov	Dec
1001	Avg_Wolverines_Juggled	100	100	100	100	100	100	100	100	100	100	100	100
	Wolverines_Juggled_Classification	100	100	100	100	100	100	100	100	100	100	100	100
1002	Avg_Wolverines_Juggled	-	-	-	-	-	200	-	-	-	-	-	-
	Wolverines_Juggled_Classification	-	-	-	-	-	200	-	-	-	-	-	-
1003	Avg_Wolverines_Juggled	-	-	-	-	200	-	-	-	-	-	-	-
	Wolverines_Juggled_Classification	-	-	-	-	200	-	-	-	-	-	-	-
2001	Avg_Wolverines_Juggled	-	-	-	150	-	-	-	-	-	-	-	-
	Wolverines_Juggled_Classification	-	-	-	150	-	-	-	-	-	-	-	-
2002	Avg_Wolverines_Juggled	-	-	-	-	100	-	-	-	-	-	-	-
	Wolverines_Juggled_Classification	-	-	-	-	100	-	-	-	-	-	-	-
3001	Avg_Wolverines_Juggled	-	-	-	-	200	-	-	-	-	-	-	-
	Wolverines_Juggled_Classification	-	-	-	-	200	-	-	-	-	-	-	-
3002	Avg_Wolverines_Juggled	100	-	-	-	-	-	-	-	-	-	-	-
	Wolverines_Juggled_Classification	100	-	-	-	-	-	-	-	-	-	-	-
4001	Avg_Wolverines_Juggled	100	100	100	100	100	100	100	100	100	100	100	100
	Wolverines_Juggled_Classification	100	100	100	100	100	100	100	100	100	100	100	100
4002	Avg_Wolverines_Juggled	100	100	100	100	100	100	100	100	100	100	100	100
	Wolverines_Juggled_Classification	100	100	100	100	100	100	100	100	100	100	100	100
4003	Avg_Wolverines_Juggled	200	200	200	200	200	200	200	200	200	200	200	200
	Wolverines_Juggled_Classification	200	200	200	200	200	200	200	200	200	200	200	200

POV Format: Actual / 2008 / Refresh

Once you have the template and values ready in Smart View, click *Submit Data* to submit the values back to the database. Note you could also use load rules to load this data as well. You'll notice as the data is refreshed, the formatstring logic is applied to the data values:

As you perform your analysis, do you see any issues with the formatstring? How does the formatstring value display at the quarters and period? While the juggle members are averaging, the translated formatstring is totaling.

Ideally we would tag this member ^ so that it would only display for the level 0. But the ^ is not available for ASO applications so be careful in how you define the MDX for the formatstring and make sure that it makes sense for all levels in the database. Formatstring is available for ASO but a bit more manageable in BSO because you can assign the never consolidate ^ tag.

DUPLICATE MEMBER NAMES

Essbase 9 and later supports outlines with duplicate member names. Should you ever really use this option? Only if you absolutely must have this functionality, because it makes referencing members very tricky.

Let's say we add a Market dimension to our juggling application and we have customers in both Paris, Texas and Paris, France. We may want to leverage duplicate member names in this case. Allowing Duplicate member names is an option specified during database creation:

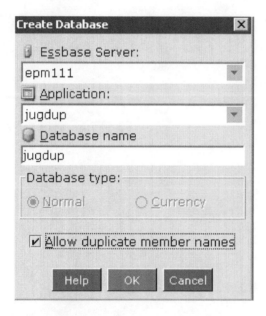

You then enable the dimension to allow duplicate names. Under Member Properties for the dimension, set *Duplicate member names allowed in dimension* to true:

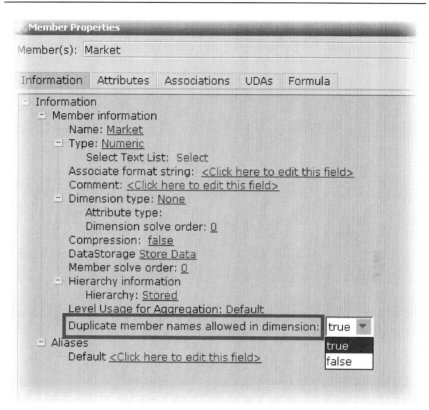

Once the dimension is enabled you can build duplicate members into the outline:

Essbase uses a qualified path to identify the duplicate members – [Texas].[Paris] and [France].[Paris]. View the qualified member names in outline view mode (vs. edit). You can use shortened forms of member-name qualification to uniquely reference members in duplicate member outline.

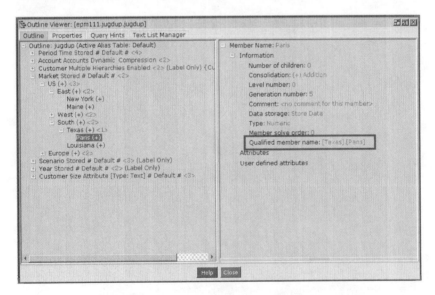

Duplicate members do introduce some complexity in your data loads and dimension builds so be careful there.

Tip!

Should you actually use duplicate member names? While technically it is possible, the complexity of your database increases from a maintenance standpoint and from an adhoc retrieval standpoint.

SUBSTITUTION VARIABLES

Substitution variables are one of the best tools for Essbase administrators and report designers who live in a world where the clock advances (which is all of us, to the best of my knowledge). Let's say you have 20 different current month reports across your Essbase applications. Do you want to modify all 20 reports each month to change the selected month? Do you want to modify all of your calc scripts that calculate current month each month? At year end, things are somewhat slow, so it won't be a problem to update all of your calc scripts and reports to reflect the new year, right? Trust me: you will be busy enough without adding those tasks to your plate.

Substitution variables are variables that serve as a placeholder for specific members. They are defined at the server, application, or database level. Originally, these variables could only be utilized in calc scripts and reporting and analysis tools (the Smart View Add-In, Financial Reporting, Web Analysis, and Smart View).

Nowadays, you can use substitution variables in outline formulas, security filters, areas and mapping definitions for partitions, MDX statements, rules file specifications for DSN definitions associated with using the SQL interface, and rules file specifications for dimension/member names in the data load header and in field specification for data load columns. (We haven't covered all of the items just listed but after the next few chapters you will have better understanding of the various components.)

Common substitution variables include curmth (current month), clsmth (closed month), CY (current year), and PY (prior year). You define the substitution variable name: just remember you are limited to eight characters.

To define a substitution variable,

1.   Under the Essbase Server name, right click and select *Create>>Variable:*

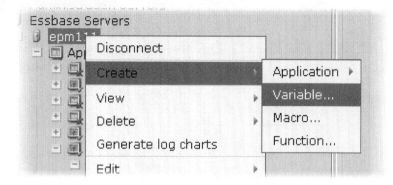

2. Specify the application and database for the substitution variable.

Tip!

Define substitution variables for all applications and all databases when possible. For example, define 'curmth' current month substitution variable once for use in all applications and databases.

3. Specify the variable name.
4. Specify the variable value:

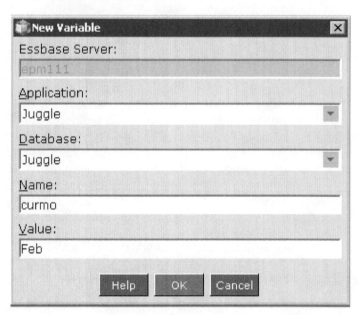

5. Click *OK* to save the variable.

We plan to build 3 different current month reports to help us analyze revenue and expense for our wolverine juggling business. Because we want to spend our time on value added analysis versus time spent updating reports, create a substitution variable for current month called "curmo" (not to be confused with the long lost brother of that lovable monster Elmo).

Try It!

To edit variables, right click on the server and select *Edit>>Variables*.

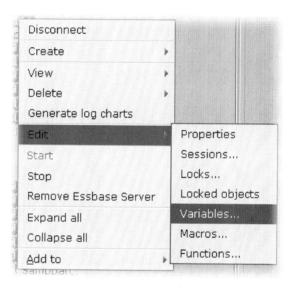

The Substitution variables window will display with the listing of all variables for the server. You can update the values for the variables by placing your cursor in the values cell and typing the new value. Click *Set* once you are finished. You can also copy and delete substitution variables from this window.

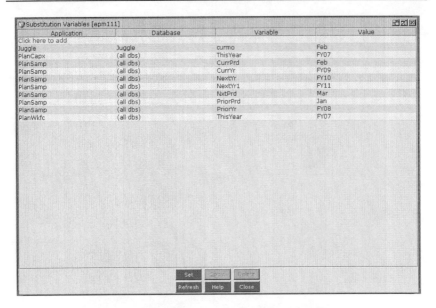

ALTERNATE ALIAS TABLES

Outlines will always have the default alias table to store aliases, but you may have a requirement for different descriptions within your application. For your human capital analysis application, you might need a few more ways to report on a single employee:

- Last name, first name, title
- First name last name
- Employee id, last name, first name

In order to meet all of these requirements, you will need to create some new alias tables. Jumping back to Sample.Basic, let's create an alternate alias table that will combine product number and name into the alias.

1. Open the Sample.Basic outline.
2. Select the Properties tab.
3. Right click on Alias table and select *Create alias table*:

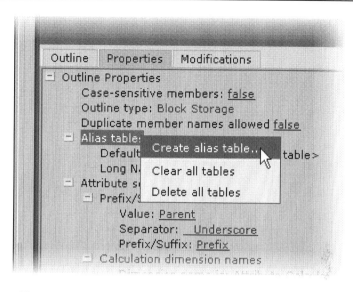

4. Type in a name for the alias table that best describes the alias and click *OK*:

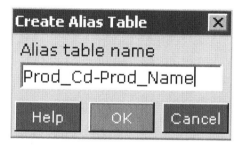

5. Right click on the new alias table and set the Prod_Cd-Prod_Name table as active:

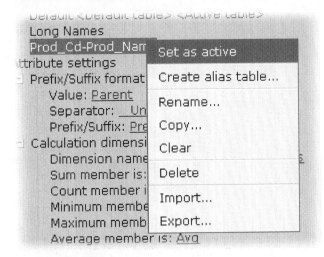

Long Names
Prod_Cd-Prod_Nam   Set as active
ttribute settings
Prefix/Suffix format   Create alias table...
  Value: Parent
  Separator: Un   Rename...
  Prefix/Suffix: Pre   Copy...
Calculation dimensi   Clear
  Dimension name
  Sum member is: Delete
  Count member i
  Minimum membe   Import...
  Maximum memb   Export...
  Average member is: Avg

Note!

You can rename, copy, clear and delete alias tables. You can also import and export alias tables from and to other applications.

6. Select the Outline tab.
7. Right click on a product member and select *Edit Member Properties*.
8. Assign the alias for the new alias table:

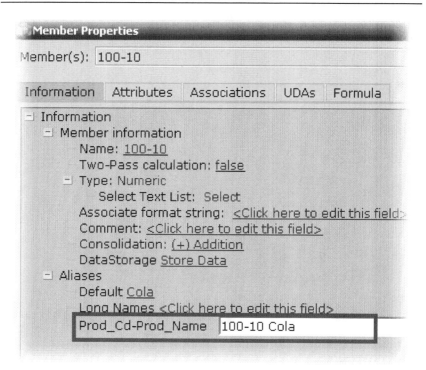

Once the aliases have been assigned, the alias is ready for use in reporting and analysis.

Add a new alternate alias table "Long Names" and manually populate the alias values for the juggling wolverine application.

Try It!

If your end users want to display both the member name and alias together in Smart View, simply create an alternate alias table that combines both.

Try It!

We've extended our database with text lists, dates, substitution variables, and more. Let's now learn how we can build calculated members into our Essbase database.

Chapter 10:
ASO Calculations

CALCUATIONS IN ESSBASE

So far we've only created input level zero members and aggregated members within the hierarchy. Essbase is known for its powerful calculation engine in block storage databases but what about ASO databases (our current focus)? While calculations are not ASO database's strong suit, you can use MDX to create some very helpful member calculations.

Why store calculations in Essbase database, even aggregate storage databases instead of just replicating the formula logic in all your reports? Essbase serves as a central place for all of your business rules. Calculation logic can be created and stored on the Essbase server in member formulas and users simply select the members in reports (versus trying to build calculations repeatedly across reports by users across the enterprise). We'll see in the case of our Juggle application that we can build in many types of calculations into our ASO database. This chapter will introduce you to several different calculations that you can leverage for your own applications.

If there is something you want to do calculation-wise but it doesn't seem possible in an ASO database, that will be your first clue that a block storage option database may be required (you can do anything calc related in BSO databases).

INTRODUCTION TO MDX

The syntax that we will use for calculated members in ASO databases is MDX based. MDX, short for Multidimensional Expressions, is supported by Essbase, Microsoft, SAS, and others as part of the XML for Analysis specification. At first glance, MDX queries look a lot like SQL with SELECTs, FROMs, and WHEREs. The result of an MDX query has no formatting, simply a raw data specification.

At its core, MDX is not like SQL at all. MDX is completely axis and hierarchy driven (tables and records nowhere to be found). MDX is the Data Manipulation Language for Essbase and is used in a number of ways in addition to calculated members in ASO databases.

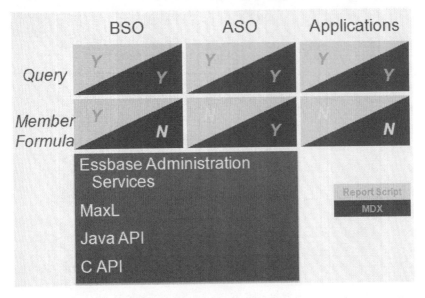

MDX provides the ability to perform advanced data queries against Essbase databases (an alternative to using Essbase report scripts). The MaxL Shell (essmsh) or MDX Editor in Administration Services executes MDX queries. While we don't cover MDX queries for Essbase in this book, we will show you how to add calculations to your Essbase database.

Note!

Documentation on the MDX query format can be found in the Technical Reference Guide under MDX.

Tip!

To create MDX queries, you can open the MDX Script Editor located under *File>>Editors>>MDX Script Editor*.

So how exactly do we use MDX to create calculated members in ASO databases? Always keep some basic rules in mind when using MDX. The first and most important rule to keep in mind is that all MDX calculations in ASO are dynamic. This means that if your outline has a dimension or two with a million plus members, it's probably not a good idea to apply an MDX query that works on level-0 members. Second, remember that formulas can only be applied to dynamic hierarchies.

MDX formula must always be an MDX numeric value expression that is any combination of functions, operators, and member names that:

- Calculates a value
- Tests for a condition
- Performs a mathematical operation

Rules for MDX:

- MDX is not case sensitive (ASOSamp.Sample is the same as asosamp.sample)
- MDX does not care about line breaks, tabs, or spaces
- Semicolons are not required at the end of MDX statements
- They are required at the end of MaxL statements, though

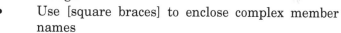

Helpful
Info

- Use [square braces] to enclose complex member names
- Use {curly braces} to enclose sets or Tuples
- Use (parentheses) for functions, Tuples, and to enclose the list of members in the WHERE statement
- Referencing members - [Jan] will work just fine as will [Time].[Jan]
- Use the standard /* Comment */ for multi-line comments
- Use -- for same-line comments

Here are some examples of MDX member formulas. Notice the use of brackets around member names with spaces.

```
[Units]/[Total Transactions]
```

```
[Curr Year]-[Prev Year]
```

```
([Curr Year]-[Prev Year])/[Prev Year]*100
```

```
Transactions/(Transactions,Time,
               [Transaction Type],[Payment Type],
               Promotions,Age,[Income Level],
               Products,Stores,Geography)
```

MEMBER FORMULA EDITOR

Simple Math

To expand our juggling database, let's add some calculated members, starting with some basic math. The juggling CFO office would like to include a metric calculating margin as a percentage of net revenue.

MDX provides the standard mathematical, logical and Boolean operators that you would expect.

Mathematical Operators:

+	-	*
/	%	

Logical Operators:

>	<	=
<>	>=	<=
In	Is	

Boolean Operators (used mostly with IIF and Case statements):

And	Or	Not

Comments can be added to MDX syntax by placing /* at the beginning of a comment and */ at the end of a comment. You can also use – to comment out a single line.

```
/*comment is ignored until the end you place the
     star-slash at the end*/
```

```
--comment is ignored until the end of the line
```

Now that we understand some of the basics, let's add our Margin_Pct metric.

1. Add a new member under Accounts called *Margin_Pct*.
2. Right click on Margin_Pct and select *Edit member properties*.
3. On the Information tab, set the consolidation tag to ~.
4. Select the Formula tab (and optionally resize the window to make it a bit bigger).

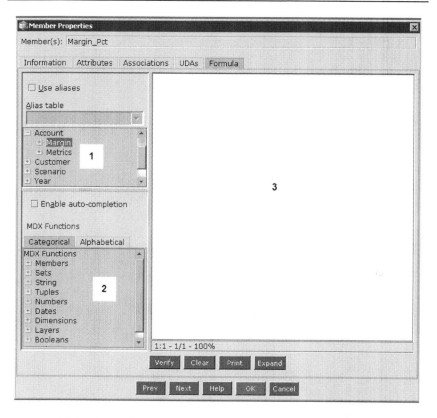

This Formula editor has three main panes:

1) Outline. This pane helps you to select members from the outline and add them automatically to the calc script being edited.

2) Functions. This pane lets you select functions and commands and add them to the calc script being edited. The check boxes above this pane determine if arguments to the functions and commands will be inserted as well.

3) Data entry. This is where you actually type your member formula. While you could live without panes one and two (though it would be a royal pain), all of the power of calc scripts is entered into pane three.

5. In the Dimension outline section of the formula editor, expand Account the account dimension until the member Margin is listed.

6. Select Margin and right click, choosing *Insert Member Name:*

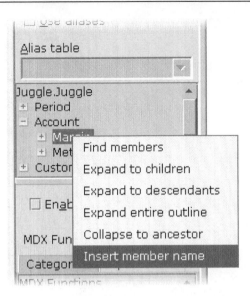

Tip!

The outline section of the member formula editor helps those of you out there with fat fingers. Remember, when you reference a member name the wording must match exactly.

7. You can also simply type in the formula if you know the member names. Type the remaining formula syntax:

```
Margin/[Net_Revenue]*100
```

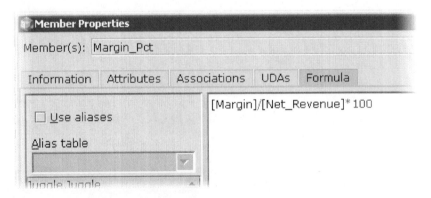

8. Click *Verify* to verify the formula.
9. Click *OK* to save the member formula.
10. Save the outline, choosing to retain data.

The member is updated with the storage tag and formula. Notice the 0 next to the member formula. This is the solve order for when the member formula should be calculated:

```
Other Exp (-)
Metrics (~) <8> (Label Only)
    Margin_Pct (~) [0: [Margin]/[Net_Revenue]* 100]
    Customer_Satisfaction_Rating (^)
    Customer_Risk (^)
```

As you begin to add calculations that are dependent on other calculations, you will need to update the solve order accordingly (more on solve order in just a bit).

Don't make the mistake of not fully unit testing each one of your member formulas. You need to test the calculation logic across dimensions, members, hierarchies and levels in the database to ensure data is presented as expected to the user. Let's perform a quick check of the calculations we've created and see if we have any issues. Create a spreadsheet in Smart View similar to the following and check the *Margin_Pct* calculation:

	Jan			Feb			Mar			Q1			Period	
	Net_Revenue	Margin	Margin_Pct	Net_Revenue	Margin	Margin_Pct	Net_Revenue	Margin	Margin_Pct	Net_Revenue	Margin	Margin_Pct		
1001	1,000	700	70	100	(200)	(200)	100	(200)	(200)	1,200	300	25		
Corporate Events	1,000	700	70	100	(200)	(200)	100	(200)	(200)	1,200	300	25		
4001	2,500	1,750	70	2,500	1,750	70	2,500	1,750	70	7,500	5,250	70		
4002	2,500	1,750	70	2,500	1,750	70	2,500	1,750	70	7,500	5,250	70		
4003	3,500	2,750	79	3,500	2,750	79	3,500	2,750	79	10,500	8,250	79		
Street Peddling	8,500	6,250	74	8,500	6,250	74	8,500	6,250	74	25,500	18,750	74	42,000	33,000
Total_Customer	9,500	6,950	73	8,600	6,050	70	8,600	6,050	70	26,700	19,050	71	104,100	73,500

Before we continue in our formula building efforts, let's review some new MDX functions that make our job a bit easier in creating calculations. First we'll introduce you to our friend CurrentMember and other functions that return a member or member set.

CURRENTMEMBER AND MEMBER FUNCTIONS

In MDX member formulas, we can hardcode members as we saw in our simple math example, referencing a specific member like "Q1" or "Net_Revenue". But in many cases we want to be more dynamic about the calculations we apply. If you had to hardcode logic for ever single member, you would have pages and pages of member formulas.

MDX provides a number of functions for identifying a member or list of members. In technical terms, they return a member or member value. CurrentMember is the one you'll use most often in your MDX member formulas. This function will return the "current" member that is selected in a dimension from the active query. Essentially you use this as your way to say, do this operation for the current member in the query. If you run a query for Q1 and a member formula references the current member for Period, Q1 will be evaluated. Syntax is as follows:

```
[Dimension].CurrentMember
```

Other single member referencing functions include (for the full list, see the Technical Reference Guide):

Function	Description	Example
Lag	Using the default order of the outline, returns a member that is *n* steps before the specified member	`[Jan].lag (3) /*returns Apr*/`
Lead	Using the default order of the outline, returns a member that is *n* steps past the specified member	`[Apr].lead (3) /*returns Jan*/`
NextMember	Returns the member in the same level that is one past the specified member	`[Jan].nextmember /*returns Feb*/`
PrevMember	Returns the member in the same level that is one before the specified member	`[Feb].Prevmember /*returns Jan*/`
Parent	Returns the parent of the specified member	`[Jan].Parent /*returns Qtr1*/`

Note! The functions above return a single member. To identify a list of members, you will use member set functions, discussed below.

You will typically use CurrentMember with other functions as we will see during the course of this chapter.

Let's next review some functions that return a list of members (vs. a single member). Multiple member referencing functions include (for the full list, see the Technical Reference Guide):

Function	Description	Example
Children	Returns all children of the specified member	`(Qtr1.Children)` `/*returns Jan, Feb, Mar*/`
Descendants	Returns all descendants of the specified member; can further define the number of layers to return	`(Year.Descendants)` `/*returns Qtr1, Qtr2, Qtr3, Qtr4, and all of the months*/`
Ancestors	Returns all ancestors of the specified member	`(Jan.Ancestors)/*returns Qtr1 and Year*/`
Attribute	Returns all base members assigned to the specified attribute member	`Attribute(Caffeinated)` `/*returns all of the caffeinated products*/`
Uda	Returns all base members assigned to the specified UDA	`Uda(Accounts, "Expense")` `/*returns the account members with the uda Expense*/`
MemberRange	Returns a range of members that exist between to specified members at the same generation or level	`MemberRange` `(Year.Jan:Year.Jun)` `/*returns all the months between Jan and Jun*/`
RelMemberRange	Returns a set based on the relative position of the specified member; first argument is the specified member, second argument is how many positions back in the outline at the same generation, third argument is how many positions forward in the outline at the same generation	`RelMemberRange(Apr, 5, 2) /*returns Jan, Feb, Mar, Apr, May, Jun*/`
Leaves	Returns the level 0 (AKA leaf) members under the specified member; doesn't return	`Leaves (Qtr1)`

> members that have
> #missing values and
> doesn't pre-expand prior
> to retrieval (which
> means smaller sets and
> faster performance)

As your head begins to swim with member referencing possibilities, we have another MDX member definition to cover: Tuples.

TUPLES

A tuple is a collection of members from a database, representing a single data cell. In our examples above, we were referencing a member or list of members from a single dimension. In many cases, we need to reference a specific intersection like actual margin for the current quarter or budgeted sales for level zero products. Examples of tuples include:

```
( [Qtr1])
```

```
( [Qtr1], [Sales])
```

```
( [Qtr1], [Sales], [Cola], [Florida], [Actual] )
```

This is not a valid tuple because the syntax includes two members from the same dimension:

```
( [Qtr1], [Sales], [Actual], [Budget])
```

Tip!

For those experienced Essbase administrators out there, this is similar to the cross dimensional operator in Block Storage databases (e.g. Qtr1->Sales->Cola->Actual).

Let's put these MDX member functions to work and use CurrentMember and Parent functions with tuples to create a dynamic percent of total calculation.

Pct of Total

1. Create a new member in the Account dimension under the Metrics parent called Pct_Total.

2. Assign the ~ consolidation tag.
3. Select the member formula tag and type in (or use the formula editor options) to insert the following formula:

```
(Customer.CurrentMember, [Net_Revenue]) /
    (Customer.CurrentMember.Parent, [Net_Revenue])
```

UDAs | Formula

(Customer.CurrentMember, [Net_Revenue]) / (Customer.CurrentMember.Parent, [Net_Revenue])

Note we are defining tuple 1 as the current member for Customer for net revenue divided by the parent of the current Customer member for net revenue. We've built a dynamic calculation that will calculate a percent of total for any level in the customer dimension.

4. Verify and save the formula.
5. Save the outline.

A	B	C	D
	Actual	Actual	Actual
	2008	2008	2008
	Period	Period	Period
	Net_Revenue	Margin	Pct_Total
1001	2100	-1500	100%
1002	-	-	-
1003	-	-	-
Corporate Events	2100	-1500	2%
Weddings	-	-	-
Birthday Parties	-	-	-
4001	30000	21000	29%
4002	30000	21000	29%
4003	42000	33000	41%
Street Peddling	102000	75000	98%
Total_Customer	104100	73500	100%

Tip!

Always try to create dynamic calculations that will calculate correctly across dimensions and levels / generations within dimensions.

Here are some other functions that use tuples to perform operations.

Function	Description	Example
Sum	Sum values based on the outline	`Sum()`
Aggregate	Aggregate based on Time Balance behavior (TB First, Last, Avg with skipping options)	`Aggregate()`
CellValue	Returns the numeric value of a cell	`Used in format strings`
Abs	Return the absolute value	`Abs(Scenario.Actual  -` `Scenario.Budget)`

SETS

Now that you are pretty comfortable with tuples, let's move on to sets. A set is a collection of tuples. Some rules for sets: No two members can be from the same dimension. If a dimension is not referenced or member not specified, all members of the dimension are assumed. For example, the following set contains four tuples, one for each quarter:

```
{ [Year].[Qtr1], [Year].[Qtr2], [Year].[Qtr3],
     [Year].[Qtr4]  }
```

The next set contains Actual Sales and Budget expenses.

```
{(Actual, Sales), (Budget, Expenses)}
```

Within a set, each tuple must list the same dimensions in the same order. So why do you care? You may need to use sets in some of your calculations within your Essbase database. Here are some functions that utilize sets:

Function	Description	Example

Avg	Averages the values of the tuples in a set; by default, missing values are not included. To include, use IncludeEmpty keyword	`Avg (`
		`[Year].[Jan]:[Year].[Jun`
		`[Measures].[Sales],`
		`INCLUDEEMPTY)`

CrossJoin	Joins the members identified in set1 and set2	`CrossJoin({[Qtr1],`
		`[Qtr2]}, {[New York],`
		`[California]})/*returns`
		`Qtr1, New York; Qtr2,`
		`New York, Qtr1,`
		`California, Qtr2,`
		`California*/`

Count	Returns the count of the number of tuples in a set (list of members)	`Count(Crossjoin (`
		`{[Measures].[Sales]},`
		`{[Product].children}`
		`)/*returns the count of`
		`product categories that`
		`have sales*/`

Max	Returns the maximum value found in the tuples of a set (list of members)	`Max([Year].CurrentMember`
		`.Children,`
		`[Measures].[Sales])`
		`/*returns the minimum`
		`value for children of`
		`the Current Year member`
		`for Sales*/`

Min	Returns the minimum value found in the tuples of a set (list of members)	`Min`
		`([Year].CurrentMember.Ch`
		`ildren,`
		`[Measures].[Sales])`
		`/*returns the minimum`
		`value for children of`
		`the Current Year member`
		`for Sales*/`

Average

We've covered functions that reference members. Now let's review functions that perform operations like counts or averages. Some of these numeric value and mathematical functions include (for the full list, see the Technical Reference Guide):

Instead of loading in average wolverines juggled, we would like to load in the total wolverines juggled and calculate the average in a dynamic member.

1. In the Juggle application Accounts dimension under Metrics, create a member called "Wolverines_Juggled".
2. Add a second new member called "Avg_Wolverines_Juggled_Calc".
3. Assign ~ to both new members.

4. For the *Average_Wolverines_Juggled_Calc* member,
   enter the following member formula:

```
Avg(Customer.CurrentMember.Children,
    [Wolverines_Juggled])
```

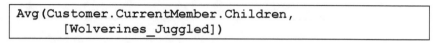

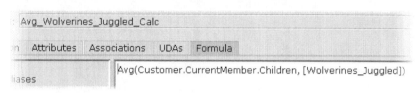

In this formula, we are simply averaging Wolverines
Juggled for the children of the current member of the Customer
dimension. So if your query requests *Total_Customer*, the values of
the children will be averaged and displayed. If your query requests
Corporate Events, the values of the children will be averaged and
displayed.

5. Verify and save the formula.
6. Save the outline.

To verify the formula, we'll need to load data into the new
Wolverines_Juggled member (we used the same input as the load
for the original *Average_Wolverines_Juggled* and simply submitted
via Smart View):

		Jan	Feb	Mar	Apr	May	Jun	Jul	Aug	Sep	Oct	Nov	Dec
1001	Wolverines_Juggled	100	100	100	100	100	100	100	100	100	100	100	100
1002	Wolverines_Juggled	-	-	-	-	-	200	-	-	-	-	-	-
1003	Wolverines_Juggled	-	-	-	-	200	-	-	-	-	-	-	-
2001	Wolverines_Juggled	-	-	-	150	-	-	-	-	-	-	-	-
2002	Wolverines_Juggled	-	-	-	-	100	-	-	-	-	-	-	-
3001	Wolverines_Juggled	-	-	-	-	200	-	-	-	-	-	-	-
3002	Wolverines_Juggled	100	-	-	-	-	-	-	-	-	-	-	-
4001	Wolverines_Juggled	100	100	100	100	100	100	100	100	100	100	100	100
4002	Wolverines_Juggled	100	100	100	100	100	100	100	100	100	100	100	100
4003	Wolverines_Juggled	200	200	200	200	200	200	200	200	200	200	200	200

POV [Metric ▾ ✕
Actual ▾
2008 ▾
Refresh

Once the data is loaded, create a spreadsheet that looks
similar to the one below and refresh the data. How does everything
look?

		Jan	Feb	Mar	Q1	Period
Corporate Events	Wolverines_Juggled	100	100	100	300	1,600
	Avg_Wolverines_Juggled_Calc	100	100	100	-	-
Weddings	Wolverines_Juggled	-	-	-	-	250
	Avg_Wolverines_Juggled_Calc	-	-	-	-	-
Birthday Parties	Wolverines_Juggled	100	-	-	100	300
	Avg_Wolverines_Juggled_Calc	100	-	-	-	-
4001	Wolverines_Juggled	100	100	100	300	1,200
	Avg_Wolverines_Juggled_Calc	-	-	-	-	-
4002	Wolverines_Juggled	100	100	100	300	1,200
	Avg_Wolverines_Juggled_Calc	-	-	-	-	-
4003	Wolverines_Juggled	200	200	200	600	2,400
	Avg_Wolverines_Juggled_Calc	-	-	-	-	-
Street Peddling	Wolverines_Juggled	400	400	400	1,200	4,800
	Avg_Wolverines_Juggled_Calc	133	133	133	-	-
Total_Customer	Wolverines_Juggled	600	500	500	1,600	6,950
	Avg_Wolverines_Juggled_Calc	200	250	250	-	-

POV [Metric ▼ ✕]
Actual ▼
2008 ▼
Refresh

The average calculation appears to work for the months but
not for the quarters. What is happening here? At the quarter and
period level, *Avg_Wolverines_Juggled_Calc* is not calculated. This is
because we've specifically said how to calculate for the Customer
dimension but not the period dimension. Additional logic needs to
be built in to handle the average calculation for Customer.

Count

Let's create a metric that calculates the count of customers
with revenue.

1. Add a new member to the Accounts dimension under
   Metrics called "CustomerCount".
2. Assign the ~ consolidation tag to the new member.
3. For the new member, enter the following member
   formula:

```
NonEmptyCount(CrossJoin({[Net_Revenue]},{Leaves(Cust
    omer)}))
```

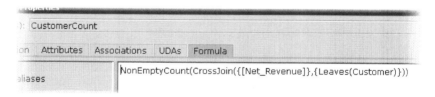

```
): CustomerCount
on   Attributes   Associations   UDAs   Formula
aliases          NonEmptyCount(CrossJoin({[Net_Revenue]},{Leaves(Customer)}))
```

4. Verify and save the formula.
5. Save the outline.

Create a spreadsheet similar to the following and verify the
member formula:

		Actual 2008	Actual 2008
		CustomerCount	Net_Revenue
1001	Period	4	$ 2,100
1002	Period	4	-
1003	Period	4	-
Corporate Events	Period	4	$ 2,100
2001	Period	4	-
2002	Period	4	-
Weddings	Period	4	-
3001	Period	4	-
3002	Period	4	-
Birthday Parties	Period	4	-
4001	Period	4	$ 30,000
4002	Period	4	$ 30,000
4003	Period	4	$ 42,000
Street Peddling	Period	4	$ 102,000
Total_Customer	Period	4	$ 104,100
By Customer Rating	Period	4	$ 2,100
Customer	Period	4	$ 104,100

Variance Calculations

Next, we want to add a series of variance calculations like "Actual vs. Budget Var" or "Current year vs. Prior year Variance" calculation to the database. Should we create this in the Year dimension or the Scenario dimension? Logically it makes sense to create Actual vs. Budget in the Scenario dimension and Current Year vs. Prior Year in the Year dimension.

```
   Customer multiple merarenics C
 - Scenario Dynamic <3> (Label O
       Actual (~)
       Budget (~)
       Act-Bud Variance (~) [0: IIF (
 - Year Dynamic <4> (Label Only)
       2007 (+)
       2008 (+)
       2009 (+)
       CY-PY (~) [0: &CY - &PY]
 +  Customer Size Attribute [Type: ]
```

This design will certainly work and may be necessary depending on your reporting requirements. The only "but" is that this design would require making both dimensions dynamic or enabling the dimensions for multiple hierarchies with a new dynamic hierarchy. Why? Remember dynamic hierarchies will process member formulas where stored hierarchies will only aggregate. For a number of different reasons, you may want to make one of these dimensions dynamic instead of both.

 There is no right or wrong answer for identifying stored vs. dynamic hierarchies. Simply weigh the reporting requirements vs. performance and determine the best Tip!   approach.

For our juggle application, we decide to follow the approach of adding all scenario and year type variances to the Scenario dimension. So in order to do this, we need to make the Scenario dimension a dynamic dimension.

1. Right click on Scenario and select *Edit member properties*.
2. Change the hierarchy from *Stored* to *Dynamic*:

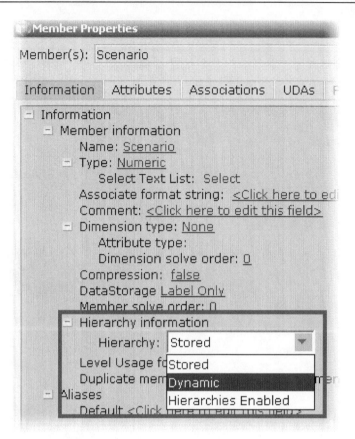

3. Click *OK*.

We'll start with the Current Year vs. Prior Year variance first.

1. Next, add a new member to the Scenario dimension called "CY-PY Actual Variance".
2. Set the consolidation tag to ~.

Because we are building this formula in the Scenario dimension, we can't simply specify 2008 – 2007. We need to further specify whether this should use actual data or budget data in the calculation. We'll use a tuple to do that. We could enter the following formula, hard coding in the years:

```
([2008],[Actual]) - ([2007], [Actual])
```

This works but now we've created something we need to update every year. As we add years of data into the database, we've also limited this calculation between two specific years. You would need to add in more members to handle variance calculations for the other years. Is there a way to make this more dynamic so that I don't have to update it every year and also be applicable for calculating current year – prior year variances for any selected year in the database? Of course there is, using some of the member functions we discussed earlier.

3. Right-click the new member *CY-PY Actual Variance* (if you're not already there) and select the member formula tab.
4. Enter the following member formula:

```
([Year].CurrentMember, [Actual]) -
    ([Year].CurrentMember.Lag(1), [Actual])
```

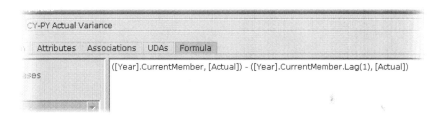

We've now created a formula that will subtract the current Year member being queried minus the member just above the current Year member. So let's say the user picks 2009, the variance will calculate 2009 Actual data – 2008 Actual data. If the user picks, 2008, the variance will calculate 2008 – 2007. This formula assumes the members are ordered: 2007, 2008, 2009. Using functions like Lag and Lead, you can create one dynamic formula versus many hardcoded formulas (e.g. one for each year). Note this formula assumes the years are listed in ascending order in the outline.

5. Verify and click *OK* to save the formula.
6. Save the Juggle outline.

To verify this member formula, we need to load in 2007 data. Create the following text file and load it into the juggle application with the ldact.rul file. We copied the 2008 data file and replaced "2008" with "2007" and updated a few of the numbers:

```
              Jan    Feb    Mar    Apr    May    Jun    Jul    Aug    Sep    Oct    Nov    Dec
2007  1001  Net_Revenue  950   950   950   950   950   950   950   950   950   950   950   950   950
2007  1001  Op_Expense   180   180   180   180   180   180   180   180   180   180   180   180   180
2007  1001  Other Exp     95    95    95    95    95    95    95    95    95    95    95    95    95
2007  4001  Net_Revenue  2200  2200  2200  2200  2200  2200  2200  2200  2200  2200  2200  2200  2200
2007  4001  Op_Expense   500   500   500   500   500   500   500   500   500   500   500   500   500
2007  4001  Other Exp    250   250   250   250   250   250   250   250   250   250   250   250   250
2007  4002  Net_Revenue  2200  2200  2200  2200  2200  2200  2200  2200  2200  2200  2200  2200  2200
2007  4002  Op_Expense   500   500   500   500   500   500   500   500   500   500   500   500   500
2007  4002  Other Exp    250   250   250   250   250   250   250   250   250   250   250   250   250
2007  4003  Net_Revenue  3000  3000  3000  3000  3000  3000  3000  3000  3000  3000  3000  3000  3000
2007  4003  Op_Expense   500   500   500   500   500   500   500   500   500   500   500   500   500
2007  4003  Other Exp    250   250   250   250   250   250   250   250   250   250   250   250   250
```

We then loaded the new 2007 file using our ldact.rul:

Once the data is loaded successfully, create a spreadsheet similar to the following and make sure the variance is calculating as expected:

IIF STATEMENTS

Next we will address conditional statements in MDX. Often times the calculation logic for a member may vary depending on a set of criteria or other test. To do this, you will use an "if" statement in MDX. The syntax is `IIF (condition, action if true, action if false):`

```
IIF (condition, true_part, false_part)
```

So what is the condition that we want to apply? In most cases, we want check for a certain list of members. A number of functions are available to return a Boolean - true or false (for the full list, see the Technical Reference Guide):

Function	Description	Example
Is	Returns true if two	IS([Year].CurrentMember.Pa rent, [Qtr1]) /*returns

	members match	true when the current member is Q1 – so Jan, Feb, Mar*/
IsAccType	Returns true if the current member has the associated account tag	`IsAccType([Measures].CurrentMember, First) /* returns true when the current member is assigned Time Balance tag First*/`
IsAncestor	Returns true if the first member is an ancestor of the second member specified	`IsAncestor([Year].CurrentMember, [Jan]) /*returns true when the current member is Qtr1 and Year*/`
IsChild	Returns true if the first member is a child of the second member specified	`IsChild([Year].CurrentMember, [Qtr1])) /*returns true when current member is Jan, Feb, Mar*/`
IsEmpty	Returns true if the value of an input is #missing (no data)	`Not IsEmpty(Sum(LastPeriods(3), Transactions)) /*returns true if the sum of the last 3 periods are not empty for Transactions*/`
IsGeneration	Returns true if the member is in a specified generation	`IsGeneration([Year].CurrentMember, 2) /*returns true when the current member is Qtr1, Qtr2, Qtr3, Qtr4 */`
IsLeaf	Returns true if a member is a level zero member	`IsLeaf([Year].CurrentMember) /* returns true for level zero members of the Year dimension – Jan, Feb, etc.*/`
IsLevel	Returns true if the member is in a specified level	`IsLevel([Year].CurrentMember, 1) /*returns true if current member is level 1 – Qtr1, Qtr2, Qtr3, Qtr4*/`
IsUda	Returns true if the member is assigned the specified UDA	`IsUDA([Measures].CurrentMember, "Expense") /* returns true if the current member is assigned the Expense UDA*/`

You will use these functions in conjunction with CurrentMember to perform tests on lists of members. For our next example, IsUDA is the perfect function for what we need.

Actual – Budget Variance Calculation

Let's now add in our variance calculation for Actual and Budget. For our variance, we want actual revenue to be larger than budget revenue; a positive variance is good. However, for expense accounts, it is generally not good when our actual expenses exceed our budgeted expenses: a positive variance is bad. In our variance formula, we need to apply Boolean logic: if the member is an expense account, subtract Actual from Budget, and for the remaining accounts, subtract Budget from Actual. Before we add the formula, let's add a UDA to the expense account members so that we can identify them in the member formula and calculate the good/bad variance accordingly.

1. In the outline editor for our Juggle outline, expand the outline and right click on *Op_Expense*.
2. Select the UDA tab.
3. Type in new UDA "Expense" and click *Assign:*

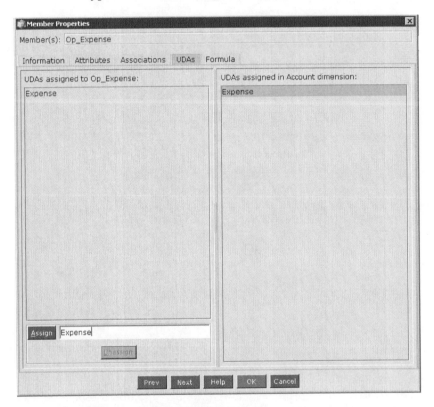

4. Click *Next* until you reach *Other Exp*.
5. Assign the "Expense" UDA to the *Other Exp* member.
6. Click *OK* to save the changes.
7. Save the outline, choosing to retain all data:

```
⊣ Account Accounts Dynamic Compression <2>
   ⊣ Margin (+) <2>
      ⊣ Op_Income (+) <2>
         Net_Revenue (+)
         Op_Expense (-) (UDAS: Expense)
         Other Exp (-) (UDAS: Expense)
   ⊣ Metrics (~) <8> (Label Only)
```

8. Under the Scenario dimension, add a new member called "Act-Bud Variance".
9. Assign the ~ consolidation tag.
10. For the new member, enter the following formula:

```
IIF (IsUDA ([Account].CurrentMember, "Expense"),
     [Budget] - [Actual], [Actual] - [Budget] )
```

Member Properties

Member(s): Act-Bud Variance

| Information | Attributes | Associations | UDAs | Formula |

☐ Use aliases   IIF (IsUDA ([Account].CurrentMember, "Expense"), [Budget] - [Actual], [Actual] - [Budget])

Essentially we are saying, if the current account member being retrieved is assigned the Expense UDA tag, then calculate Budget – Actual. Else calculate Actual – Budget.

11. Verify and save the formula.
12. Save the outline.

Try It! Review the juggle outline. Do you see any other members that may need the "Expense" UDA? How about wolverines dropped? If we drop less wolverines than budgeted, that is a good thing so add the "Expense" UDA to Avg_Wolverines_Dropped.

To verify the calculation, create a budget load file (we simply used the 2007 data file and updated the year).

			Jan	Feb	Mar	Apr	May	Jun	Jul	Aug	Sep	Oct	Nov	Dec	
2008	1001	Net_Revenue	950	950	950	950	950	950	950	950	950	950	950	950	950
2008	1001	Op_Expense	180	180	180	180	180	180	180	180	180	180	180	180	180
2008	1001	Other Exp	95	95	95	95	95	95	95	95	95	95	95	95	95
2008	4001	Net_Revenue	2200	2200	2200	2200	2200	2200	2200	2200	2200	2200	2200	2200	2200
2008	4001	Op_Expense	500	500	500	500	500	500	500	500	500	500	500	500	500
2008	4001	Other Exp	250	250	250	250	250	250	250	250	250	250	250	250	250
2008	4002	Net_Revenue	2200	2200	2200	2200	2200	2200	2200	2200	2200	2200	2200	2200	2200
2008	4002	Op_Expense	500	500	500	500	500	500	500	500	500	500	500	500	500
2008	4002	Other Exp	250	250	250	250	250	250	250	250	250	250	250	250	250
2008	4003	Net_Revenue	3000	3000	3000	3000	3000	3000	3000	3000	3000	3000	3000	3000	3000
2008	4003	Op_Expense	500	500	500	500	500	500	500	500	500	500	500	500	500
2008	4003	Other Exp	250	250	250	250	250	250	250	250	250	250	250	250	250

Next walk with us through the process of copying the ldact.rul and updating it to load budget.

13. In the Administration Services console, right click on ldact.rul and select *Copy:*

14. Paste to the same application and database, naming the rules file ldbud.rul:

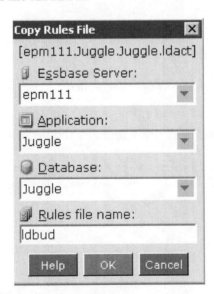

15. Click *OK.*

16. Edit the ldbud.rul, updating the header to reference "Budget":

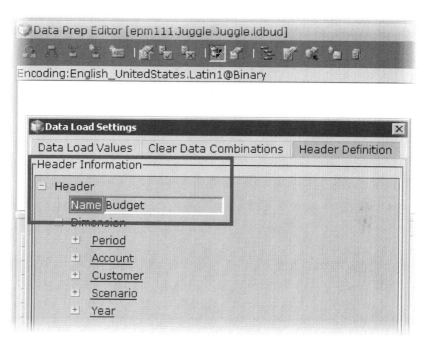

17. Click *OK* and save the rules file.
18. Right click on the Juggle database and select *Load Data*.
19. Choose the new budget data file and the ldbud.rules file:

Data Load			
☐ Execute in background	☑ Deferred-restructure dimension build		Data load
☑ Ignore missing values	☑ Ignore zero values ☐ Create new slice ☐ Aggregate

Data Sour..	Mode	Data Source	Rules File	Abo
Data file	Load only	epm111.Juggle.Juggle.jugbu...	epm111.Juggle.Juggle.ldbud	

20. Click *OK*.

Once the budget data is successfully loaded, create a spreadsheet similar to the one below and verify the Actual – Budget variance calculation (did the positive negative variances show up correctly?):

		Actual		Budget		Act-Bud Variance	
Net_Revenue	Period	$	104,100	$	100,200	$	3,900
Op_Expense	Period	$	20,400	$	20,160	$	(240)
Other Exp	Period	$	10,200	$	10,140	$	(60)
Margin_Pct	Period		70.61		69.76		0.84

POV Act: Buc ▾ ✕
Customer ▾
2008 ▾
Refresh

CASE STATEMENTS

In our Actual-Budget Variance example above, we needed to perform a simple if statement but what if our logic required multiple tests or conditions. We could insert nested if statements but an easier way may be to use the Case statement. The syntax for Case statements is as follows:

```
CASE
      WHEN Condition THEN Result_if_true
      WHEN Condition THEN Result_if_true
      ELSE result
END
```

Here is an MDX example using a Case statement for our juggle application where we wanted to create projection scenario that combines Actual data for closed months and budget data for remaining months. While this isn't the most optimal MDX, we wanted to keep this simple so you could see how to use a Case statement.

```
CASE
        WHEN IS ([Period].CurrentMember, Jan) THEN
                (Jan, Actual)
        WHEN IS ([Period].CurrentMember, Feb) THEN
                (Feb, Actual)
        WHEN IS ([Period].CurrentMember, Mar) THEN
                (Mar, Budget)
        WHEN IS ([Period].CurrentMember, Apr) THEN
                (Apr, Budget)
        WHEN IS ([Period].CurrentMember, May) THEN
                (May, Budget)
        WHEN IS ([Period].CurrentMember, Jun) THEN
                (Jun, Budget)
        WHEN IS ([Period].CurrentMember, Jul) THEN
                (Jul, Budget)
        WHEN IS ([Period].CurrentMember, Aug) THEN
                (Aug, Budget)
        WHEN IS ([Period].CurrentMember, Sep) THEN
                (Sep, Budget)
        WHEN IS ([Period].CurrentMember, Oct) THEN
                (Oct, Budget)
        WHEN IS ([Period].CurrentMember, Nov) THEN
                (Nov, Budget)
        WHEN IS ([Period].CurrentMember, Dec) THEN
                (Dec, Budget)
END
```

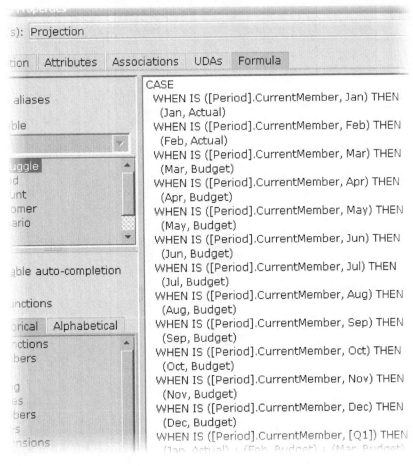

In this formula, we simply check to see if the current member requested is Jan, then pull in Actuals for January. If the current member requested is Feb, then pull in Actuals for February. If the current member is Mar, then pull in Budget for March, and so on. This member formula assumes the closed months are January and February where we want to show actual data and for the other months listed, we want to show budget.

We could even nest the Case statement within an If statement. Do we want this projection calculation to take place for all of the years? No, only the current year so we added some logic so this calculation will only take place for the current year.

```
IIF(
  IS(Year.CurrentMember, [2008]),
(CASE … END), 0
)
```

The new if statement will further filter how the Case statement is applied, only to the current year. We've still hardcoded the year in a member that we will have to update next year. Is there a way to make this more dynamic (one less thing…)? Did someone say "substitution variable"? Ding, ding, ding. Yes!

Substitution Variables [epm111]			
Application	**Database**	**Variable**	**Value**
(all apps)	(all dbs)	CY	2008

The new formula with the substitution variable reference would look something like:

```
IIF(
  IS(Year.CurrentMember, [&CY]),
(CASE … END), 0
)
```

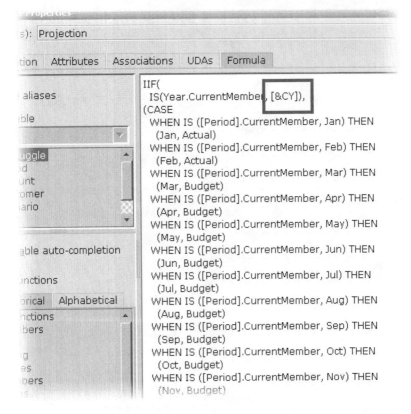

Before we conclude the section on calculation functions, we want to spotlight a special set of functions. They return a member set based on data within the Essbase database (these are the functions that sit at the cool kids' table at lunch).

Function	Description	Example
BottomCount	Returns *n* elements ordered from smallest to largest	`Bottomcount([Product].le vels(0).members, 10,( [Sales], [Actual] )) /* returns the 10 products with the smallest sales for Actuals */`
BottomPercent	Returns a list of members from smallest to largest that meet specified bottom percentage evaluation	`BottomPercent ({ [Product].members },5, ([Measures].[Sales], [Year].[Qtr2])) /*returns the products that make up 5 percent of the lowest sales for Qtr2*/`
BottomSum	Returns a list of members from smallest	`BottomSum( [Product].Members,`

	to largest that meet specified bottom sum evaluation	`10000, [Year].[Qtr1]`
		`) /*returns the`
		`products with sales less`
		`than 10,000 for Qtr1*/`

TopCount	Returns *n* elements ordered from largest to smallest	`Topcount([Product].level`
		`s(0).members, 10, (`
		`[Sales], [Actual] )) /*`
		`returns the 10 products`
		`with the largest sales`
		`for Actuals */`

TopPercen t	Returns a list of members from largest to that smallest meet specified top percentage evaluation	`TopPercent ({`
		`[Product].members },5,`
		`([Measures].[Sales],`
		`[Year].[Qtr2]))`
		`/*returns the products`
		`that make up 5 percent`
		`of the highest sales for`
		`Qtr2*/`

TopSum	Returns a list of members from largest to that smallest meet specified top sum evaluation	`TopSum(`
		`   [Product].Members,`
		`10000, [Year].[Qtr1]`
		`   ) /*returns the`
		`products with sales over`
		`than 10,000 for Qtr1*/`

We've built in some basic calculations and performed some quick validations. Before we leave the calculation chapter, we need to discuss the calculation order and solve order for aggregate storage databases so that your calculations will be valid across all intersections of the database. We've seen in our initial checks that the calculations appear to work correctly. But what happens as we add in calculations that are dependent upon other calculations? If two calculations are on the report, what is the order of the calculations?

CALCULATION ORDER AND SOLVE ORDER PROPERTY

As we've learned so far, aggregate storage databases will calculate following the outline structure, rolling up members to upper levels of the hierarchy (e.g. months roll up to quarters, quarters roll up to Period). Stored hierarchies will simply roll up or "sum" the hierarchy while dynamic hierarchies can process additional consolidation tags like minus and multiply. In this chapter, we learned that we can also add member formulas to members of a dynamic hierarchy.

When data is loaded to an aggregate storage database, no additional calculation is required. The Essbase server calculates values upon request, consolidating level 0 members and calculating member formulas.

Aggregate storage databases will first aggregate members in the stored hierarchies and attribute dimensions. What is the recommended order of dimensions for ASO (maybe you've heard something about an hourglass on a stick)? Dimension order in the ASO outline doesn't matter. The order in which the dimensions will be calculated is determined internally. Stored dimensions are simply aggregations or totals so aggregation order isn't important.

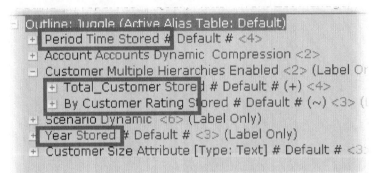

Not so for the dynamically calculated dimensions and members. Often times we need to define the calculation order for dimensions and/or members so that calculations will display the information properly. We control the calculation order of dynamic dimensions and members via the solve order property.

The solve order property identifies the order of calculations for dimensions or members. For example, if we have two members: a ratio like Margin_Pct and a Variance. What should be calculated first?

As the Essbase administrator, you can assign a solve order so that the Essbase Server knows the calculation order. Simply right click on the member, selecting *Edit Member Properties* and assign a solve order, a number between 1 and 127. The default sort order is 0.

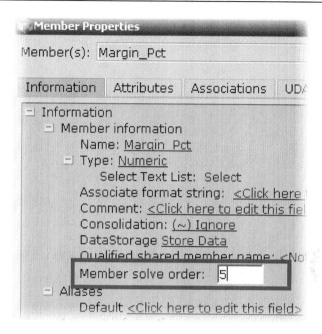

Solve order is best defined at the dimension level but this doesn't always meet calculation requirements. You can override dimension solve order with a specific member solve order.

As you assign solve orders for members and dimensions, Essbase uses the following sequence when calculating dynamic dimensions

1. Member solve order
2. Dimension solve order
3. If two or more members have the same solve order, the members are calculated in the reverse order of the dimensions in the database outline

Tip! Make room, make room! Use 10, 20, 30 that way if you need to insert in additional dependent calculations, you can without having to update solve order properties for all of your members.

The validations of our calculations that we performed so far were fairly limited to the individual member and initial input data sets. Let's review some queries that retrieve multiple calculated members and see if the calculation order is handled properly.

Let's check another intersection of calculated members: Margin_Pct and the Act_Bud_Variance. Create the following spreadsheet:

	Actual		Budget		Act-Bud Varia			
	Margin	Margin_Pct	Margin	Margin_Pct	Margin	Margin_Pct	POV SolveOi ▼ x	
Jan	$ 6,950.00	73.16	$ 5,825.00	69.76	$ 1,125.00	3.40	Customer	▼
Feb	$ 6,050.00	70.35	$ 5,825.00	69.76	$ 225.00	0.59	2008	▼
Mar	$ 6,050.00	70.35	$ 5,825.00	69.76	$ 225.00	0.59	Refresh	
Apr	$ 6,050.00	70.35	$ 5,825.00	69.76	$ 225.00	0.59		
May	$ 6,050.00	70.35	$ 5,825.00	69.76	$ 225.00	0.59		
Jun	$ 6,050.00	70.35	$ 5,825.00	69.76	$ 225.00	0.59		
Jul	$ 6,050.00	70.35	$ 5,825.00	69.76	$ 225.00	0.59		
Aug	$ 6,050.00	70.35	$ 5,825.00	69.76	$ 225.00	0.59		
Sep	$ 6,050.00	70.35	$ 5,825.00	69.76	$ 225.00	0.59		
Oct	$ 6,050.00	70.35	$ 5,825.00	69.76	$ 225.00	0.59		
Nov	$ 6,050.00	70.35	$ 5,825.00	69.76	$ 225.00	0.59		
Dec	$ 6,050.00	70.35	$ 5,825.00	69.76	$ 225.00	0.59		
Q1	$ 19,050.00	71.35	$ 17,475.00	69.76	$ 1,575.00	1.59		
Q2	$ 18,150.00	70.35	$ 17,475.00	69.76	$ 675.00	0.59		
Q3	$ 18,150.00	70.35	$ 17,475.00	69.76	$ 675.00	0.59		
Q4	$ 18,150.00	70.35	$ 17,475.00	69.76	$ 675.00	0.59		
Period	$ 73,500.00	70.61	$ 69,900.00	69.76	$ 3,600.00	0.84		

Well, that doesn't look right. The logic for the variance member seems to be calculating after the Margin_Pct logic, subtracting the Budget Margin_Pct from Actual Margin_Pct.

So what dimension should be calculated first? For the income statement accounts, we want to calculate those first before the variance calculations in the Scenario dimension. But for the Metrics calculations like Margin_Pct, we want to calculate those after variances. If we were in a BSO world, we'd be using a feature called two pass but two pass is unavailable for ASO databases. So to meet this requirement, let's assign the following:

- Account dimension solve order: 10
- Scenario dimension solve order: 30
- Margin_Pct member solve order: 50

1. In the Juggle outline, right click on the *Account* dimension member.
2. Select *Edit Member Properties*.
3. Type in the number "10" for the dimension solve order:

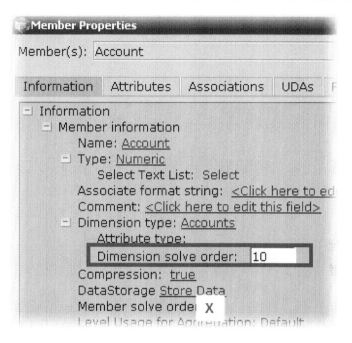

4. Click *OK*.
5. Right click on the *Scenario* dimension member.
6. Select *Edit Member Properties*.
7. Type in the number "30" for the dimension solve order.
8. Click *OK*.
9. Right click on the *Margin_Pct* dimension member.
10. Select *Edit Member Properties*.
11. Type in the number "50" for the dimension solve order:

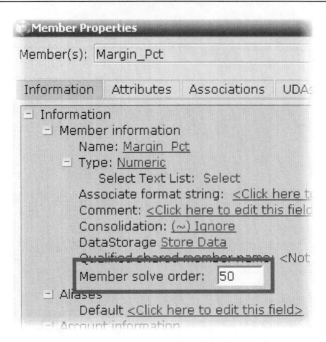

12. Click *OK*.
13. Save the outline, choosing to retain all data.

Now refresh your validation spreadsheets and note that the order of calculations has changed and so has your results:

	Actual Margin	Margin_Pct	Budget Margin	Margin_Pct	Act-Bud Varia Margin	Net_Revenue	Margin_Pct
Jan	$ 6,950.00	73.16	$ 5,825.00	69.76	$ 1,125.00	1150	97.83
Feb	$ 6,050.00	70.35	$ 5,825.00	69.76	$ 225.00	250	90.00
Mar	$ 6,050.00	70.35	$ 5,825.00	69.76	$ 225.00	250	90.00
Apr	$ 6,050.00	70.35	$ 5,825.00	69.76	$ 225.00	250	90.00
May	$ 6,050.00	70.35	$ 5,825.00	69.76	$ 225.00	250	90.00
Jun	$ 6,050.00	70.35	$ 5,825.00	69.76	$ 225.00	250	90.00
Jul	$ 6,050.00	70.35	$ 5,825.00	69.76	$ 225.00	250	90.00
Aug	$ 6,050.00	70.35	$ 5,825.00	69.76	$ 225.00	250	90.00
Sep	$ 6,050.00	70.35	$ 5,825.00	69.76	$ 225.00	250	90.00
Oct	$ 6,050.00	70.35	$ 5,825.00	69.76	$ 225.00	250	90.00
Nov	$ 6,050.00	70.35	$ 5,825.00	69.76	$ 225.00	250	90.00
Dec	$ 6,050.00	70.35	$ 5,825.00	69.76	$ 225.00	250	90.00
Q1	$ 19,050.00	71.35	$ 17,475.00	69.76	$ 1,575.00	1650	95.45
Q2	$ 18,150.00	70.35	$ 17,475.00	69.76	$ 675.00	750	90.00
Q3	$ 18,150.00	70.35	$ 17,475.00	69.76	$ 675.00	750	90.00
Q4	$ 18,150.00	70.35	$ 17,475.00	69.76	$ 675.00	750	90.00
Period	$ 73,500.00	70.61	$ 69,900.00	69.76	$ 3,600.00	3900	92.31

Try It!

Should we add solve orders for any other metrics? You bet. Add solve orders to the remaining metrics properties. Should you assign a solve order of "50" to all of the metrics? In our example, most of the metrics can have the same solve order because they are not dependent on one another. But if we did have a case where one calculated member is dependent on another calculated member, you will want to assign sequential solve order numbers accordingly.

Tip!

Your data validation plans should include several different views of the database with multiple intersections of members. It's easy to find the right numbers. It takes more testing to find the resulting intersections of data that may not make sense. You'll want to clean this up before rolling out to the end users.

Analytic dimensions are another way to build in views of the data using member formulas. Don't miss our appendix where our friend and Essbase expert, Gary Crisci, delves into using analytic dimensions in aggregate storage databases.

Now that your head is swimming with calculation possibilities and calculation intelligence, let's turn our attention to the Time intelligent features within Essbase.

Chapter 11:
Time Intelligence

Part of why you bought Essbase is that it is intelligent. We've just seen some of the calculation intelligence available for aggregate storage databases and we'll see even more when we get to block storage databases. Essbase is also Time intelligent: it has a number of built-in features to help analyze information along one or more time dimensions.

Time balance tags help Essbase understand how account or measures members should roll up across the Time or Period dimensions, whether it is averaging across the periods, taking the first period or taking the last period as it goes to summary members in the Time dimension. Dynamic Time Series is another Time intelligence feature that is available for block storage databases (we'll cover this in the BSO section of the book).

You've already used some of these features when we created the Period dimension and tagged it as the Time dimension type. This enabled us to utilize time balance tags for accounts and in BSO databases, Dynamic Time Series. In this chapter, we'll introduce you to Date-Time dimensions, a different type of dimension that allows you to build powerful structures for analyzing data across dates and time and space (well, not the space part). It is date analysis on steroids (the legal kind, of course).

INTRODUCTION TO DATE-TIME DIMENSIONS

A Date-Time dimension is a different dimension type available for ASO databases (and BSO databases starting in version 11). A Date-Time dimension is a wizard-created dimension based on complex calendar requirements.

The Date-Time wizard also builds a series of Linked Value Attributes based on the Date-Time dimension that allow you to perform cross tab reporting across time. Time is understood as a continuum and you can even load data based on time stamps. Time balance tags can be used with Date-Time dimensions. There are also about a zillion MDX functions for calculations and analysis.

Rules for Date-Time Dimensions in ASO

Helpful
Info

- The dimension will be tagged "Date-Time"
- Once created, a Date-Time dimension is not easily changed
- One Date-Time dimension per database
- Stored dimension with a single hierarchy
- Balanced hierarchy (no ragged structures)
- + consolidation tag for all members
- Avoid changing comments placed in the member properties

The best way to understand a Date-Time dimension is to build one. As the Juggling Wolverine CFO, you would like more visibility into the street peddling business. What days of the week generate the most revenue? What times of the day? Do weekends have higher revenue than weekdays? Answers to these questions will help JWC plan juggling resources, discover opportunities to increase revenue in low performing days or times, and maximize revenue in peak times.

Before we add in the Date-Time dimension, let's make a copy of our current Juggle application, keeping the current version intact.

1. Close the Juggle outline if necessary.
2. Right click on the Juggle application and select *Copy:*

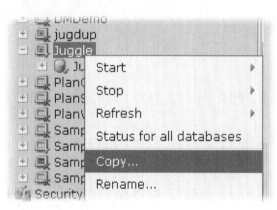

3. Type in a new application name: *JugglDT*:

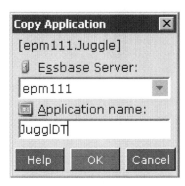

2. Click *OK*. The application should be created:

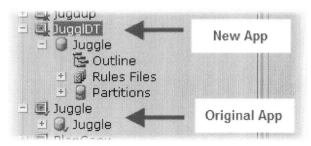

3. Next right click on the JugglDT.Juggle database and select *Clear >> All Data:*

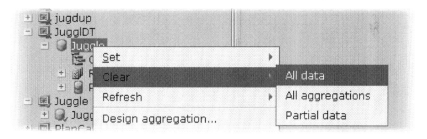

We will load new data based on the new Date-Time dimension that we are going to create.

4. Click *OK*.

CREATE A DATE-TIME DIMENSION

Let's get down to the business of date time dimensions and serious street peddling analysis over time.

1. Open the Juggle outline for the JugglDT application.
2. Delete the Period dimension (select the dimension and hit the *Delete* button or right click on Period and select *Delete)*.
3. Delete the Year dimension.
4. Delete the CY-PY Variance member (since the member formula references the dimension above).
5. Right click on *Outline* and select *Create date-time dimension:*

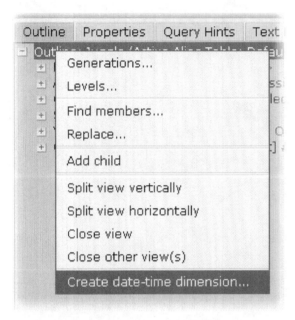

6. Type in the name "Date-Time" as the dimension name.
7. Specify the first day of the week: *Sunday*
8. Define the modeling period – start and end date: *January 1, 2008 to December 31, 2010:*

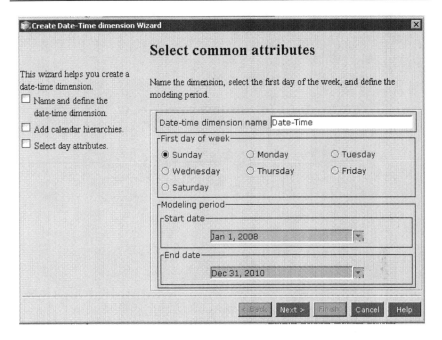

9. Click *Next.*
10. Click on the *Add* button to add hierarchies.

You can define one of the following calendar types for the date-time dimension:

Calendar Type	Description
Gregorian	Standard 12 month calendar: Jan. 1- Dec 31; Can add time depths for year, semester, trimester, quarter, month, week, day
Fiscal	Custom calendar based on an company's requirements; Can start on any date; Two months of 4 weeks and one month of 5 weeks repeated each quarter in either 4-4-5, 4-5-4, or 5-4-4 weeks)
Retail	Based on the National Retail Federation and is designed to analyze week-over-week data across years. Start date falls in early February. Available time depths are year, semester, quarter, month, week and day
Manufacturing	13 Period calendar made up of seven day weeks. Three quarters have three periods and one quarter has 4 periods: each period has 4 weeks

ISO8601	Calendar containing 7 day weeks and is based on ISO calendars. Year, week, day and time depths are required for the ISO calendar with no other options

Depending on the calendar type chosen, you may see different options. Gregorian options are as follows:

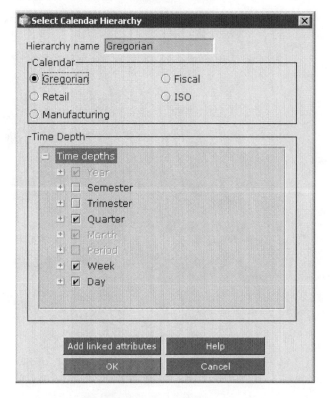

Fiscal calendar options are as follows:

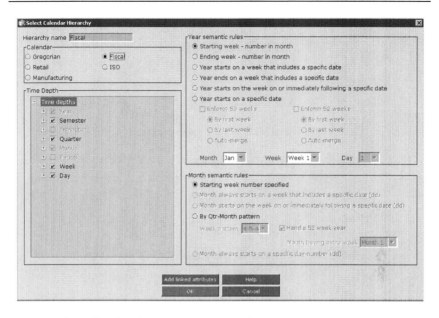

Retail calendar options are as follows:

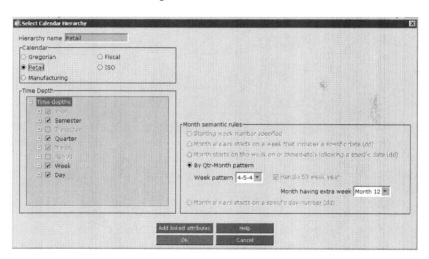

ISO calendar options are as follows:

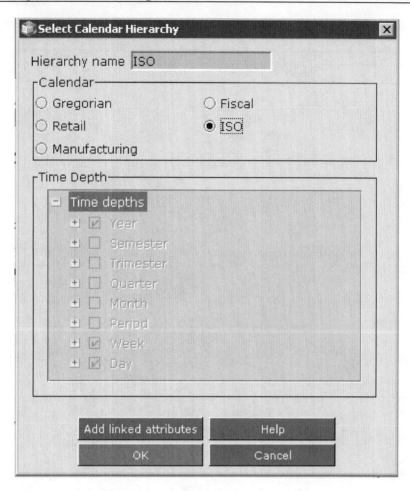

Manufacturing calendar options are as follows:

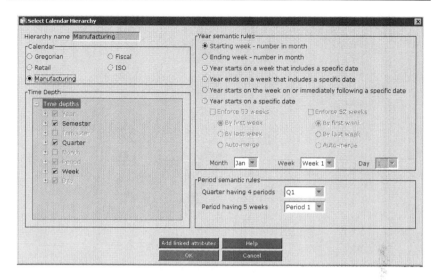

11. Choose *Gregorian* calendar option.

Our requirements dictate street peddling analysis by date. Can you imagine manually building 365 days for two or three years? Thankfully we have our handy date-time wizard.

12. Check *Quarter, Week, Day* options:

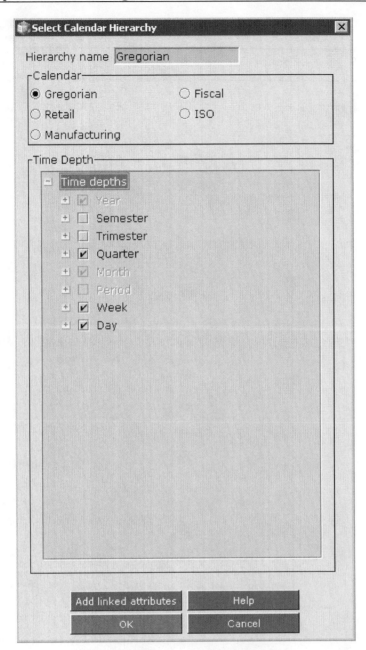

13. Click on the *Add linked attributes* button.

The Linked Attributes window will display. There is where you define how you want to analyze the Date-Time dimension. For example, JWC wants to analyze revenue by Day by Month, by Day by Week and more. Linked attribute dimensions are associated to the base Date-Time dimension and build in these analysis capabilities for us. Linked attributes capture periodicity and allow for cross-tab analysis of date elements. As with everything we have a few rules: linked attributes have 2 generations and ragged hierarchies are not allowed.

14. Click the check mark to *Select all linked attributes*.

15. Optionally, change the dimension names and aliases for the linked value attributes:

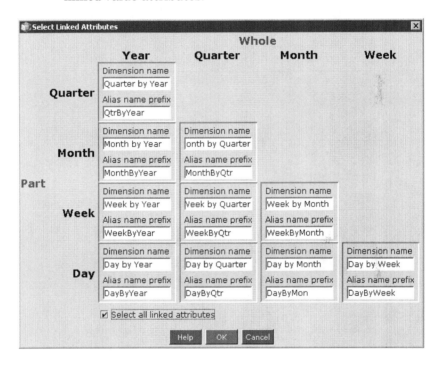

16. Click *OK*.

17. Click *OK* to finish adding the calendar hierarchies for the Date-Time dimension:

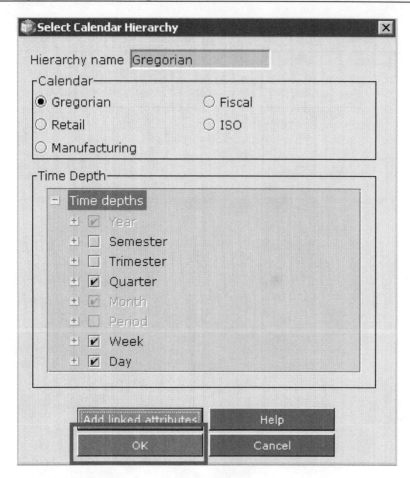

18. Click *Next*.

In this last portion of the wizard, you will define the day attributes like weekdays or weekends, holidays, and day modeling capabilities. Checking the day modeling feature will create a text attribute dimension for each day of the week and associate the values to the date-time dimension.

19. Complete the day attribute options so that your selections look like the following:

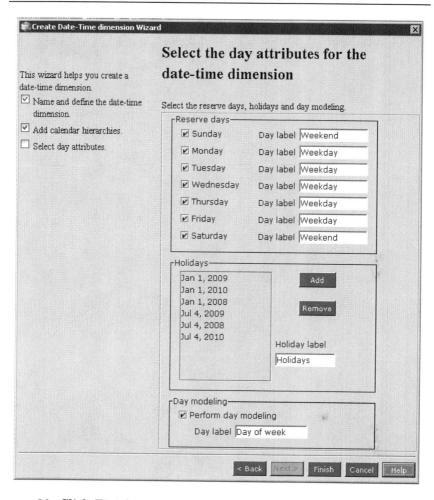

20. Click *Finish*.

Our outline just got a lot bigger – Juggle supersized – with detailed dimensionality for all kinds of time analysis.

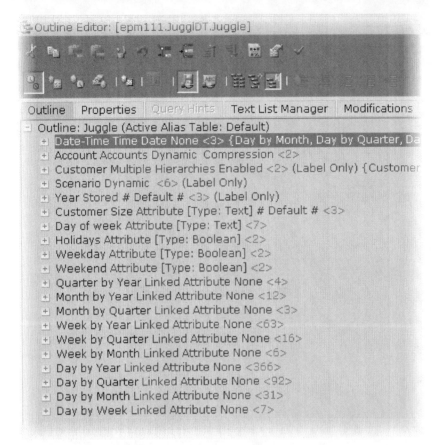

21. Save the outline.
22. If you are prompted with the following message, click *OK* (this means you skipped the clear step earlier)*:*

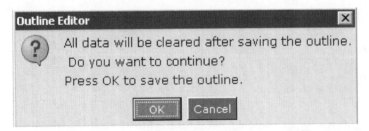

Let's get to know our new supersized Date-Time dimension, its Linked Attributes and Attributes in more detail. First note a stored dimension was created with all of the specified levels for year, quarter, month, week and day. Each member is tagged Never

Share. All members use the + consolidator. The date ranges are in a continuous order, increasing dates and time periods in ascending order, with consistent increments as defined in the wizard with no time gaps.

```
Date-Time Time Date Stored # Default # <3> (Day by Month, Day by Quarter, Day by Wee
  -  Gregorian Year 2008 (+) <4> (Never Share) /* TI-MBR,TSPAN[1-1-2008,12-31-2008]! */
     -  Quarter 1 of Gregorian Year 2008 (+) <3> (Never Share) {Quarter by Year: [Quarter
        -  Month 1 of Gregorian Year 2008 (+) <5> (Never Share) {Month by Quarter: [Mont
           -  Week 1 of Gregorian Year 2008 (+) <5> (Never Share) {Week by Month: [Wee
              Jan 01 2008 (+) (Never Share) {Day by Month: [Day by Month].[1]; Day by
              Jan 02 2008 (+) (Never Share) {Day by Month: [Day by Month].[2]; Day by
              Jan 03 2008 (+) (Never Share) {Day by Month: [Day by Month].[3]; Day by
              Jan 04 2008 (+) (Never Share) {Day by Month: [Day by Month].[4]; Day by
              Jan 05 2008 (+) (Never Share) {Day by Month: [Day by Month].[5]; Day by
           +  Week 2 of Gregorian Year 2008 (+) <7> (Never Share) {Week by Month: [Wee
           +  Week 3 of Gregorian Year 2008 (+) <7> (Never Share) {Week by Month: [Wee
           +  Week 4 of Gregorian Year 2008 (+) <7> (Never Share) {Week by Month: [Wee
           +  Week 5 of Gregorian Year 2008 (+) <5> (Never Share) {Week by Month: [Wee
        +  Month 2 of Gregorian Year 2008 (+) <5> (Never Share) {Month by Quarter: [Mont
        +  Month 3 of Gregorian Year 2008 (+) <6> (Never Share) {Month by Quarter: [Mont
     +  Quarter 2 of Gregorian Year 2008 (+) <3> (Never Share) {Quarter by Year: [Quarter
     +  Quarter 3 of Gregorian Year 2008 (+) <3> (Never Share) {Quarter by Year: [Quarter
     +  Quarter 4 of Gregorian Year 2008 (+) <3> (Never Share) {Quarter by Year: [Quarter
  +  Gregorian Year 2009 (+) <4> (Never Share) /* TI-MBR,TSPAN[1-1-2009,12-31-2009]! */
  +  Gregorian Year 2010 (+) <4> (Never Share) /* TI-MBR,TSPAN[1-1-2010,12-31-2010]! */
```

Right click on Jan 01 2008 and check out the associated attributes that were built for each member:

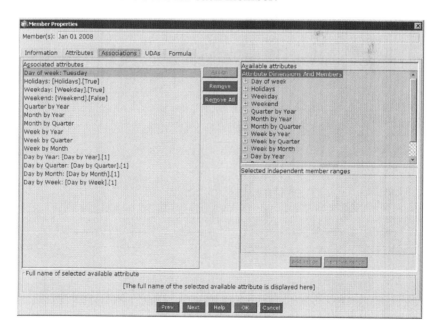

We see that January 1, 2008 is a Tuesday, a holiday, a weekday, not a weekend, is the first day of a year, the first day of a quarter, is the first day of a month, and the first day of a week.

Click *Next* to move to January 2 2008 and see the associated attributes for this member:

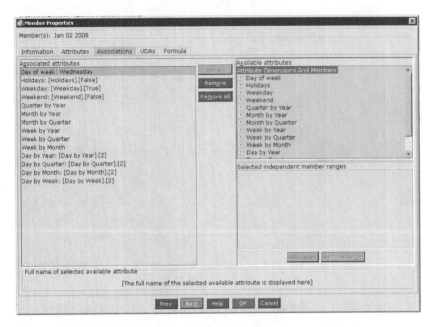

Click on the *Information* tab. Notice that a comment was also added for each member (looks fairly Star-Trekky in nature):

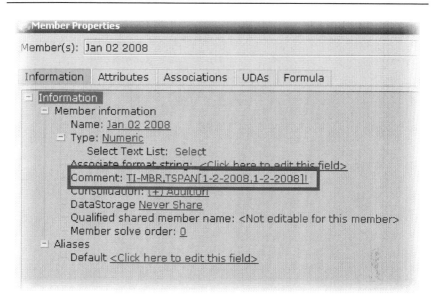

Essbase uses this comment for date time processing. While technically you can edit this comment, we recommend you leave this alone. If you need to add comments to the member, add them at the end after the exclamation point (!).

```
TI-MBR,TSPAN[1-1-2006,1-31-2006]! This is the First
    Month
```

Tip!

While it is possible to modify a Date-Time dimension manually, be careful in doing so. It may be easier to delete the Date-Time dimension and recreate a new dimension with the required changes.

Note!

It is not possible to go back and launch the Date-Time wizard for an existing Date-Time dimension.

Date-Time Dimension Rules

Helpful Info

- Created by the Date-Time Wizard
- Tagged Date-Time
- Stored dimension with a single hierarchy with no ragged structures (the hierarchy is balanced)
- + Consolidation tag
- Member comments created by the wizard must remain (TI-HIER, TP[] and TI-MBR,TSPAN[]
- Date ranges must be contiguous
- Dates must increase in ascending order
- No time gaps are allowed
- Time span of the parent must equal the time span of the children

Now let's look more closely at the day modeling attributes and the linked attributes.

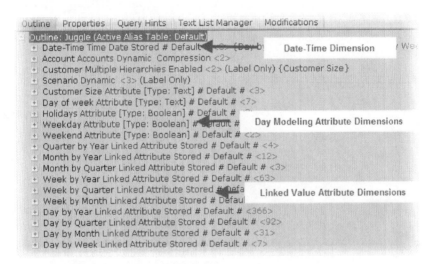

Four day modeling attributes were created based on our selections from the wizard: Day of Week, Holidays, Weekday, Weekend. Day of Week is a text attribute dimension listing each day of the week while the remaining day modeling attributes are Boolean:

```
⊐ Day of week Attribute [Type: Text] # Default # <7>
     Sunday
     Monday
     Tuesday
     Wednesday
     Thursday
     Friday
     Saturday
⊐ Holidays Attribute [Type: Boolean] # Default # <2>
     True
     False
⊐ Weekday Attribute [Type: Boolean] # Default # <2>
     True
     False
⊐ Weekend Attribute [Type: Boolean] # Default # <2>
     True
     False
```

Notice the Linked Value Attributes contain 2 generations and are basically a series of sequential numbers grouped by time analysis category (Month by Year, Quarter by Year, Month by Quarter, Day by Year, Day by Month, and so on):

⊟ Quarter by Year Linked Attribute Stored # Default # <4>
    1 (~) (Alias: QtrByYear 1)
    2 (~) (Alias: QtrByYear 2)
    3 (~) (Alias: QtrByYear 3)
    4 (~) (Alias: QtrByYear 4)
⊟ Month by Year Linked Attribute Stored # Default # <12>
    1 (~) (Alias: MonthByYear 1)
    2 (~) (Alias: MonthByYear 2)
    3 (~) (Alias: MonthByYear 3)
    4 (~) (Alias: MonthByYear 4)
    5 (~) (Alias: MonthByYear 5)
    6 (~) (Alias: MonthByYear 6)
    7 (~) (Alias: MonthByYear 7)
    8 (~) (Alias: MonthByYear 8)
    9 (~) (Alias: MonthByYear 9)
    10 (~) (Alias: MonthByYear 10)
    11 (~) (Alias: MonthByYear 11)
    12 (~) (Alias: MonthByYear 12)
⊟ Month by Quarter Linked Attribute Stored # Default # <3>
    1 (~) (Alias: MonthByQtr 1)
    2 (~) (Alias: MonthByQtr 2)
    3 (~) (Alias: MonthByQtr 3)
⊞ Week by Year Linked Attribute Stored # Default # <63>
⊞ Week by Quarter Linked Attribute Stored # Default # <16>
⊞ Week by Month Linked Attribute Stored # Default # <6>
⊞ Day by Year Linked Attribute Stored # Default # <366>
⊞ Day by Quarter Linked Attribute Stored # Default # <92>

Linked Attribute Dimension Rules

Helpful Info

- Created by the Date-Time Wizard
- Tagged Linked Attribute
- Associated with Date-Time dimension
- Limited to two levels only
- Member names are sequential numbers, starting with 1

Can you imagine if you had to build all of this manually – the detailed dimension and all of the associated attributes? No way. The Date-Time wizard is a definite "time" saver.

TIME BASED LOADS

Next let's load some data using Time based loading. Time based loading is loading a date field instead of a member name. Remember, in all other cases we must specifically reference a member name for each dimension in a column or header. Time based loading is the exception, allowing us to load to our Date-Time dimension using a specific date. But what if your Date-Time dimension goes down to the month or week level and your data file has specific dates? Can you still load using time based loading? Yes, Essbase intelligently knows to sum up the values and load into the specific week or month based on the individual date by selecting the option *Add to existing cells*.

Create and load / submit your own file so that it looks like the following (or email us for a copy of our data file):

	4001	4002	4003
01/01/08	400	700	1000
01/02/08	100	200	300
01/03/08	125	225	325
01/04/08	125	225	325
01/05/08	400	600	700
01/06/08	300	400	500
01/07/08	100	200	300
01/08/08	100	200	300
01/09/08	100	200	300
01/10/08	125	225	325
01/11/08	125	225	325
01/12/08	400	600	700
01/13/08	300	400	500
01/14/08	100	200	300
01/15/08	100	200	300
01/16/08	100	200	300
01/17/08	125	225	325
01/18/08	125	225	325
01/19/08	400	600	700
01/20/08	300	400	500
01/21/08	100	200	300
01/22/08	100	200	300
01/23/08	100	200	300
01/24/08	125	225	325
01/25/08	125	225	325
01/26/08	400	600	700
01/27/08	300	400	500
01/28/08	100	200	300
01/29/08	100	200	300
01/30/08	100	200	300
01/31/08	125	225	325
02/01/08	125	225	325

We're following the example where the data file contains a column with a specific date. Varying date formats can be used:

- "mon dd yyyy",   /* mon-short dd yyyy */
- "Mon dd yyyy",   /* mon-full dd yyyy */
- "mm/dd/yy",   /* mm/dd/yy */
- "yy.mm.dd",   /* yy.mm.dd */
- "dd/mm/yy",   /* dd/mm/yy */
- "dd.mm.yy",   /* dd.mm.yy */
- "dd-mm-yy",   /* dd-mm-yy */
- "dd Mon yy",   /* dd mon-full yy */
- "dd mon yy",   /* dd mon-short yy */
- "Mon dd yy",   /* mon-full dd yy */
- "mon dd yy",   /* mon-short dd yy */
- "mm-dd-yy",   /* mm-dd-yy */
- "yy/mm/dd",   /* yy/mm/dd */
- "yymmdd",   /* yymmdd */
- "dd Mon yyyy",   /* dd mon-full yyyy */
- "dd mon yyyy",   /* dd mon-short yyyy */
- "yyyy-mm-dd",   /* yyyy-mm-dd */
- "yyyy/mm/dd",   /* yyyy/mm/dd */
- "Long Name",   /* Long date format: Tuesday, March 14, 1995 */

Create a load rule just as you have in the previous chapters:

Data Prep Editor [epm111.JugglDT.Juggle.ldDTdat]

Encoding:English_UnitedStates.Latin1@Binary

		4001	4002	4003
1		4001	4002	4003
2	01/01/08	400	700	1000
3	01/02/08	100	200	300
4	01/03/08	125	225	325
5	01/04/08	125	225	325
6	01/05/08	400	600	700
7	01/06/08	300	400	500
8	01/07/08	100	200	300
9	01/08/08	100	200	300

	"Date-Tim...	"4001"	"4002"	"4003"
1		4001	4002	4003
2	01/01/08	400	700	1000
3	01/02/08	100	200	300
4	01/03/08	125	225	325
5	01/04/08	125	225	325
6	01/05/08	400	600	700
7	01/06/08	300	400	500

On the column that has the date field, specify the field properties as Date with the appropriate format:

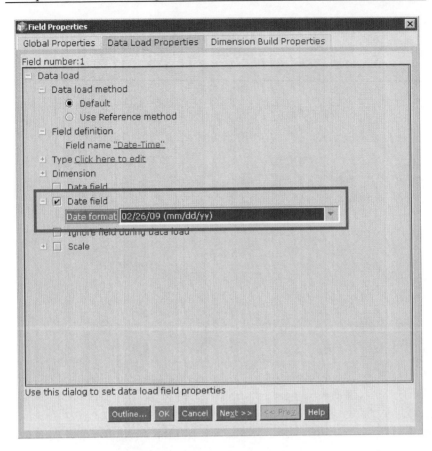

Then load the data file using the rules file and select the option to *Add to existing values:*

 Create a load rule to load a date field to your JuggleDT.Juggle database. Make sure to specify the headers Net_Revenue and Actual.

Try It! Load the data file using your new load rule.

ANALYZE WITH DATE-TIME DIMENSIONS

Out of the date-time box, you get powerful analysis capabilities with the new dimension and attributes. First let's see what days of the week generate the highest revenue:

Looks like the weekends is where we really see high revenue. What days of the month generate the most revenue? Is there something unique about these days and how can we learn from it to apply to lower performing days?

	A	B	C	D	E	F	G
1		4001	4002	4003	Street Peddling		
2	Day by Month	$ 65,775	$ 107,975	$ 144,975	$ 318,725		
3	[Day by Month].[1]	$ 2,375	$ 3,975	$ 5,375	$ 11,725		
4	[Day by Month].[6]	$ 2,475	$ 3,875	$ 5,075	$ 11,425		
5	[Day by Month].[13]	$ 2,475	$ 3,875	$ 5,075	$ 11,425		
6	[Day by Month].[20]	$ 2,475	$ 3,875	$ 5,075	$ 11,425		
7	[Day by Month].[27]	$ 2,475	$ 3,875	$ 5,075	$ 11,425		
8	[Day by Month].[5]	$ 2,375	$ 3,875	$ 5,075	$ 11,325		
9	[Day by Month].[12]	$ 2,375	$ 3,875	$ 5,075	$ 11,325		
10	[Day by Month].[19]	$ 2,375	$ 3,875	$ 5,075	$ 11,325		
11	[Day by Month].[26]	$ 2,375	$ 3,875	$ 5,075	$ 11,325		
12	[Day by Month].[2]	$ 2,250	$ 3,650	$ 4,850	$ 10,750		
13	[Day by Month].[9]	$ 2,250	$ 3,650	$ 4,850	$ 10,750		
14	[Day by Month].[16]	$ 2,250	$ 3,650	$ 4,850	$ 10,750		
15	[Day by Month].[23]	$ 2,250	$ 3,650	$ 4,850	$ 10,750		
16	[Day by Month].[4]	$ 2,100	$ 3,600	$ 5,000	$ 10,700		

POV Day of ! ▼ ×
Net_Revenue ▼
Date-Time ▼
Actual ▼
Refresh

Other questions we can now ask ourselves: How does the juggling business perform on holidays vs. non-holidays? Year over year, what months generate the most revenue? Understanding this information can help us make better decisions to improve overall performance. Now expand this thinking to other types of applications like logistics and shipping type applications with our Date-Time dimension built out to the time level. Wow! That about says it all.

And if that wasn't enough, there are still further things we can do with analyzing date time dimensions. A number of MDX functions are available to create calculated members for further analysis and insight.

Function	Description	Example
GetFirstD	Returns the start date	`(GetFirstDate([Apr`

ate	for a date hierarchy member	2009]) returns the start date for April 2009
GetLastDa te	Returns the end date for a date hierarchy member	GetLastDate ([Apr 2004]) returns the last date for April 2009
Today	Returns a number representing the current date	Today() returns
DateDiff	Returns the difference between 2 input dates	Datediff(GetFirstDate([D ate-Time].CurrentMember),Tod ay(),DP_MONTH) will return the difference between the months of the first date in the dimension Date-Time and today's date
DatePart	Returns the date part (Year, Qtr, Mth, Day, DayofYear) as a number	DatePart (Today(), DP_YEAR) returns the year for today's date e.g. 2009
DateRoll	For the specified date, adds or subtracts an interval, returning another date	DateRoll(GetFirstDate ([Jan 2009]),DP_MONTH,6) will return the date that is 6 months past the first date in January 2009
DateToMe mber	Returns the date-time member identified by the specified date and optionally layer	DateToMember(GetLastDate ([Apr 2009]), [Date-Time].Dimension, [Time dimension].[Weeks]) returns the last week of April 2009
FormatDat e	Formats a date by specified format	FormatDate("mm/dd/yy", Product.CurrentMember.[I ntro Date]) - e.g. 01/30/2009

The table above assumes an outline has a Date-Time dimension called "Date-Time".

You can use these functions in MDX queries as well as calculated members. Let's create a few examples. First let's create a member that identifies the current day of the year. You might need current date in another future calculation (you powers of foresight are amazing).

1. In the JuggleDT.Juggle outline, add a new member under Metrics called *Current_Day_of_Year*.
2. Change the consolidation tag to ~.
3. Assign a solve order of 50.
4. Add the following member formula:

```
DatePart (Today(), DP_DAYOFYEAR)
```

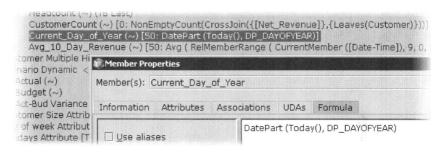

5. Verify and save the member formula.
6. Save the outline, choosing to retain the data.
7. Run a quick retrieve in Smart View to verify the calculation:

	Current_Day_of_Year
Jan 01 2008	57
Jan 02 2008	57
Jan 03 2008	57
Jan 04 2008	57
Jan 05 2008	57
Week 1 of Gregorian Year 2008	57

(This screenshot was taken February 26, 2009.)

Ring, ring! The juggling CFO just called with a request. He needs a report displaying 10 day average rolling revenue across the different markets for JWC. Let's create a member to add the 10 day average calculation in our Juggle outline (remember it is always better to build the calc into the database so that it stored centrally for use across multiple reports and for all users).

8. In the JuggleDT.Juggle outline, add a new member under Metrics called *Avg_10_Day_Revenue*.
9. Change the consolidation tag to ~.

10. Assign a solve order of 50.
11. Add the following member formula:

```
Avg ( RelMemberRange ( CurrentMember ([Date-Time]),
        9, 0, Level),
[Account].[Net_Revenue], INCLUDEEMPTY)
```

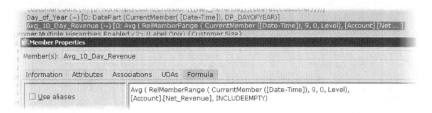

12. Verify and save the member formula.
13. Save the outline, choosing to retain the data.
14. Check that the calculation is performing as expected:

	Net_Revenue	Avg_10_Day_Revenue	Check	
Jan 01 2008	$ 2,100	$ 2,100	$ 2,100	POV Date-Ti ▼ ×
Jan 02 2008	$ 600	$ 1,350	$ 1,350	Customer ▼
Jan 03 2008	$ 675	$ 1,125	$ 1,125	Actual ▼
Jan 04 2008	$ 675	$ 1,013	$ 1,013	Refresh
Jan 05 2008	$ 1,700	$ 1,150	$ 1,150	
Jan 06 2008	$ 1,200	$ 1,158	$ 1,158	
Jan 07 2008	$ 600	$ 1,079	$ 1,079	
Jan 08 2008	$ 600	$ 1,019	$ 1,019	
Jan 09 2008	$ 600	$ 972	$ 972	
Jan 10 2008	$ 675	$ 943	$ 943	
Jan 11 2008	$ 675	$ 800	$ 800	
Jan 12 2008	$ 1,700	$ 910	$ 910	
Jan 13 2008	$ 1,200	$ 963	$ 963	
Jan 14 2008	$ 600	$ 955	$ 955	
Jan 15 2008	$ 600	$ 845	$ 845	

We've created applications, built dimensions, and loaded data. We've added calculated member formulas and date time dimensions to our Essbase database. We've focused on building an ASO database but the concepts we've covered so far are mostly applicable to both ASO and BSO types of databases. We're now going to reach a fork in the road where ASO and BSO databases split.

Let's first review the key differences between the two types of databases. We'll then cover more advanced topics for aggregate storage databases. The second main section of the book will be dedicated to creating block storage databases. While you have learned a lot so far, we still have a ways to go before we can deem you master Essbase administrator (there is a reason why Essbase administrators get paid big bucks).

Chapter 12:
ASO vs. BSO

This may seem a bit late in the discussion but what in the heck is an ASO database or cube really? And how does that differ from a BSO database? We felt it would be better to have you create a database and gain some fundamental knowledge before we dissected the anatomy of Essbase cubes. Up until now, most of the concepts that we have covered are applicable to ASO and BSO databases. Before we go any further, let's address at a high level ASO and BSO databases so you can understand the strengths and capabilities of each database type.

INTRODUCTION TO BSO

Block storage option (BSO) databases were the *original* Essbase databases or cubes. Data is stored in a way that business users intuitively understood and could perform analysis really, really fast. Administrators build BSO databases via an outline with members rolling up into hierarchies and dimensions. BSO databases come with a powerful calculation engine - so powerful that it can perform complex allocations and other business rules. Users can write data back to any point in the hierarchy. BSO databases utilize things like member formulas, calc scripts, blocks, dense and sparse dimensions, and page and index files (all to be covered in much more detail in the BSO section of the book).

Who could ask for anything more? We could, of course. While our BSO databases are awesome in many ways, there are a number of challenges. Unfortunately the block storage architecture that allows us to create complex business models starts to have performance issues as dimensionality and outline sizes grow. BSO databases can only get so big. We are typically constrained to 7-10 dimensions and as we add in thousands and thousands of members, calculation and/or retrieval performance can be negatively impacted. No matter how powerful computers have become in the past 15+ years since Essbase was created, you just can't have it all.

INTRODUCTION TO ASO

Aggregate storage option databases were introduced in Essbase 7.1 as a new alternative to BSO databases although we now feel they should be your default option unless you have a valid reason for creating a specific BSO database. Originally, ASO was created specifically to deal with requirements for very large sparse data sets with a high number of dimensions and potentially millions of members (any one of these requirements would make a BSO database hide under the bed and whimper for its mommy). ASO utilizes a new kind of storage mechanism that allows improved calculation times from ten to one hundred times faster than BSO databases – the calculations just aren't as complex. ASO can also store up to 2^{52} dimension-level combinations. If you aren't that great at math, just know this is a really, really big number.

New types of Essbase databases are now possible (imagine background music coming in as you read. It's the theme from Aladdin, "A Whole New World"). This includes Customer analysis on potentially millions of customers, logistics analysis where we can analyze near real-time updates of product shipments, and market basket analysis where we can analyze what products are purchased along with other products.

Let's take a look at the ASOSamp.Sample outline:

```
⊟ Outline: Sample (Active Alias Table: Default)
    ⊞ Measures Accounts <6> (Label Only)
    ⊞ Years Dynamic <4> (Label Only)
    ⊞ Time Time Multiple Hierarchies Enabled <3> (Label Only)
    ⊞ Transaction Type Stored <3>
    ⊞ Payment Type Stored <4>
    ⊞ Promotions Stored <5>
    ⊞ Age Stored <3>
    ⊞ Income Level Stored <6>
    ⊞ Products Multiple Hierarchies Enabled <2> (Label Only)
    ⊞ Stores Stored <2> {Square Footage, Store Manager}
    ⊞ Geography Stored <6> {Area Code}
    ⊞ Store Manager Attribute [Type: Text] <200>
    ⊞ Square Footage Attribute [Type: Numeric] <7>
    ⊞ Area Code Attribute [Type: Text] <9>
```

Yes, you are seeing correctly. No blurry vision. We have an outline that has 13 dimensions. We've already seen that we can also have attribute dimensions in ASO databases as well.

You can easily spot an ASO database in the Administration Services Console by the red star beside the application name:

Tip!

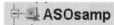

You may be saying "Yes, yes, I'm sold. ASO is so awesome that I'm wondering why we even need BSO databases anymore?" The answer, dear reader, lies just below...

THE COMPARISON

First, a quick disclaimer: this chapter was written mainly for Essbase 11.1.1.1. The hard working developers have constantly enhanced the ASO engine in System 9 and Essbase 11 so comparing the two database types has been a rapidly moving target. If you are on Essbase 7x or an early version of System 9, you will see more differences than noted in the discussion below.

Let's start with the most important point – what does the user see? The beauty of ASO and BSO databases is that front-end tools like the Excel Add-In, Smart View, and Web Analysis really don't care if the database is BSO or ASO (even MaxL sees only minor differences between the two). They both seem like multidimensional databases that have Zoom In and Zoom Out and Keep Only and Remove Only and Pivot and all that nice stuff. There are some minor differences, but for the most part the database type is pretty much transparent to the end-user.

What else is the same? Both types of databases are defined by their outline. Most dimension and member properties like dimension type, data storage (store, never share, label only), consolidation tags and aliases are consistent for both ASO and BSO databases. How you build dimensions and load data is essentially the same. Certain rule files properties are database type specific but the overall interface and steps are the same.

Calculating the databases is where we really begin to see the differences between ASO and BSO. ASO databases, after data values are loaded into the level 0 cells of an outline, *the database requires no separate calculation step*. From any point in the database, users can retrieve and view values that are aggregated for only the current retrieval. ASO databases are smaller than block storage databases, enabling quick retrieval of data. For even faster retrieval, pre-calculate data values and store the pre-calculated results in aggregations. You can add in calculated members with member formulas in ASO. The syntax for the formulas is MDX.

On the other side of the house, BSO databases have member formulas also but they use a different syntax: Essbase calc script syntax. In most cases, you will need to aggregate the BSO database after performing a data load. You will use the default calc script or one that you manually create to roll up all of the values for the dimensions in the database. These BSO calc scripts can perform complex business logic and allocations.

Write back is another differentiator. For block storage databases, users can write back to any level in the database if they have permissions while aggregate storage databases only allow write back to level zero members.

Under the covers, the two types of databases are radically different. ASO outlines have two types of hierarchies: stored and dynamic. BSO outlines define dense and sparse dimensions. ASO databases are stored in a series of tablespaces while BSO databases are stored in a series of index and page files. How you tune each database is very different.

All of these concepts are covered in much greater detail in the remainder of this book but we wanted to have one place to summarize the great ASO vs. BSO debate.

Tip!

General guideline - Use ASO for applications as the default starting database; definitely use when requirements dictate large numbers of dimensions and members that simply "roll up" (i.e. minimal complex calculations are required).

General guideline - Use BSO for applications that require complex calculations and write back capabilities to any level.

The Essbase Database Administrator's Guide has a handy set of tables that compare the BSO vs. ASO features. Look for the "Comparison of Aggregate Storage and Block Storage" chapter:

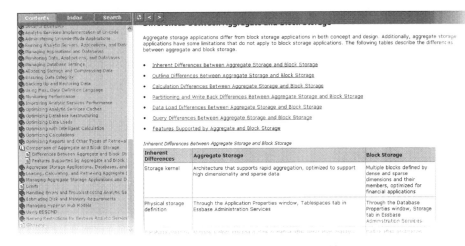

So let's now review our current Juggle applications. What we've built so far is pretty puny compared to what is possible for aggregate storage databases. But the Juggle CEO has big plans for JWC: global domination of the Juggling service industry with millions of customers across the globe and wolverine jugglers on every corner. She wants to own the birthday party, convention entertainment, and wedding reception circuit for entertainment. Everyone will know the JWC name.

To support this planet dominating enterprise, we'll need a set of Essbase applications to help us manage performance and make decisions. We'll want to review sales data across customers, regions, types of juggling (e.g. regular wolverines vs. flaming wolverines), by juggler, by wolverine sales managers, and more. We'll want to understand the pricing across regions and how we can effectively price our juggling services to gain market share and maintain high margins. We'll want to see how expenses relate to revenue and margin. Do our highly paid Level 5 wolverine juggling gurus really generate more revenue than the starting Level 1 wolverine juggling interns? You can see how our simple Juggling applications could increase in dimensions and members exponentially. With these types of requirements, ASO makes perfect sense as the Essbase database type.

Without further ado, let's explore the more advanced topics of aggregate storage databases.

Chapter 13:
ASO Aggregations

We've already learned that for ASO databases, after data values are loaded into the level 0 cells of an outline, the database requires no separate calculation step. From any point in the database, users can retrieve and view values that are aggregated for only the current retrieval. ASO databases are smaller than block storage databases, enabling quick retrieval of data values. For even faster retrieval performance, you can pre-calculate data values and store these pre-calculated results in aggregations.

INTRODUCTION TO AGGREGATIONS

Bear with us as we introduce some new terms and definitions. First terms: input cells and aggregate cells. Aggregate storage databases have two types of cells: input and aggregate cells. Input cells are the level zero intersection of members for all dimensions (see the dark cells depicted below).

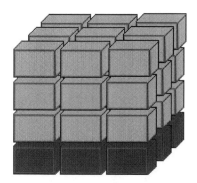

Aggregate cells are basically the rest of the cells other than the Accounts dimension and other dynamic hierarchies. Aggregate cells will never include dynamic hierarchies. Aggregate cells are calculated dynamically upon retrieval unless an aggregation process is run (more on the aggregation process in just a minute). Remember, we can load data to an ASO database and immediately retrieve data at any level.

Second term: aggregate views. Aggregate views are collections of aggregate cells. The aggregate views contain pre-calculated data values for an intersection of members from each dimension in the database and are based on the order of dimensions in the outline. The aggregate view table below stores precalculated results for level 0 Account members, level 0 Years members, level 1 Months members(Q1, Q2, Q3,Q4), level 1 Transaction Type members, level 1 Payment Type members, and so on.

Dimension	Level
Accounts	0
Years	0
Months	1
Transaction Type	1
Payment Type	1
Promotions	0
Age	0
Products	2
Markets	3

A collection of aggregate views are called an aggregation. To further confuse us, the process of creating aggregations is called "aggregation". In the aggregation process, an algorithm selects and stores "most taxing" queries. When dynamic queries are processed at runtime, Essbase achieves increased speed by leveraging nearest stored view.

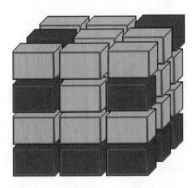

You will also hear the term materialization. Materialization is the phase during the aggregation process that actually Note!   calculates and stores the data values.

So why wouldn't you pre-calculate data values for faster retrievals? The main considerations are that aggregations can be a lengthy process and require extensive disk space. While not common, some default aggregations can result in an increase in database size of more than 40 percent more than just the input data alone. You want to balance query time and storage space, so the key is to run aggregations for the most queried data and not all data. Get the most bang for your buck.

PERFORM AN AGGREGATION

The process to aggregate an ASO database is as follows: First, select aggregation views to calculate. Fortunately for us, Essbase provides a number of mechanisms to help us identify and control the most beneficial aggregate views. Essbase analyzes how calculating and storing combinations of views will affect average query response time and storage size. Essbase then creates an internal list of those aggregate views. You can then pick and choose from the list of views, select all views and if desired at the end, save the list in the form of an aggregation script for later use.

Once the aggregate views are selected, you run the aggregation where Essbase will calculate and store the values for the aggregate views. This portion of the process is called materialization as we mentioned earlier.

Recap – Create Aggregate Views and Materialize

Helpful
Info

1. Select an aggregation task.
2. Specify aggregate view selection criteria.
3. Display the aggregated views.
4. Save and/or materialize the aggregation.

Let's run a basic aggregation for our ASOSamp.Sample database. Make sure data has been loaded to the database (you can use the dataload.txt and dataload.rul).

1. Right click on the ASOSamp.Sample database and select *Design aggregation:*

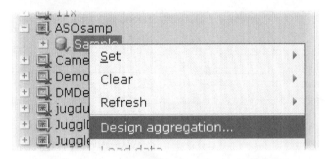

2. Select Aggregation Task:

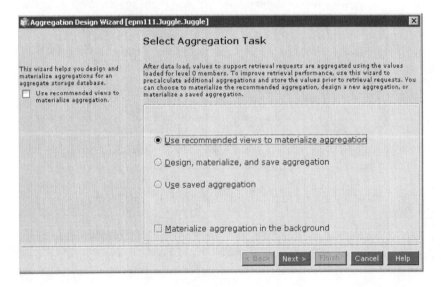

The *Use recommended views to materialize aggregation* option combines aggregate view selection and materialization into one step (you can't configure or change). If the database contains values from previous aggregations, Essbase will display a prompt for you to keep or drop existing values. Always drop values if the data in the database has changed. Essbase then selects what it thinks are the best set of aggregate views based on query time and storage resources.

Use saved aggregation will allow you to choose from a list of existing aggregations to apply (you would have saved these in an a previous process).

Design, materialize, and save aggregation separates the aggregate view selection and materialization process into two steps. This option gives you more control over the selected aggregate views. Available options for *Design, materialize, and save aggregation* include:

- Consider existing aggregate views
- Specify Stop criteria for Selection process
- Start aggregate view selection
- Save and materialize aggregation

3. For our exercise, choose *Design, materialize and save aggregation*:

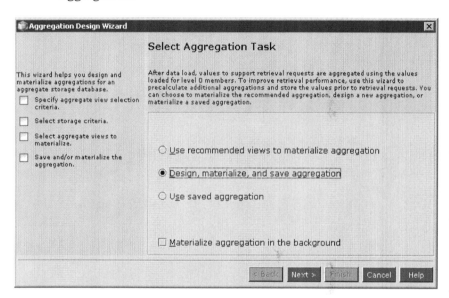

4. Click *Next.*
5. Choose *Replace existing aggregate view selection*:

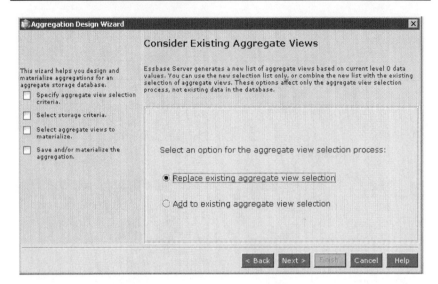

Replace existing aggregate view selection should be used when existing views are *not* optimal based on new data. *Add to existing aggregate view selection* should be used when previously selected views are optimal based on new data. Using an existing selection will reduce the time needed to materialize views.

6. Click *Next*.

The next section defines any stop criteria for the aggregation process:

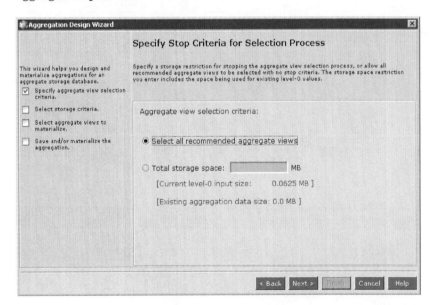

You then choose whether to select all recommended aggregate views or select all recommended aggregate views up to a specified storage limit. Limiting the storage space is helpful if disk space is an issue for you.

Tip!

To specify a multiplier of database size limit, use MAXL:

```
execute aggregate process on database
         ASOSamp.Sample stopping when total_size
         exceeds 1.3 ;
```

...would stop the aggregation after 30% growth

1. Choose *Select all recommended aggregate views.*
2. Click *Next.*
3. Click the *Start* button to start the aggregate view selection process:

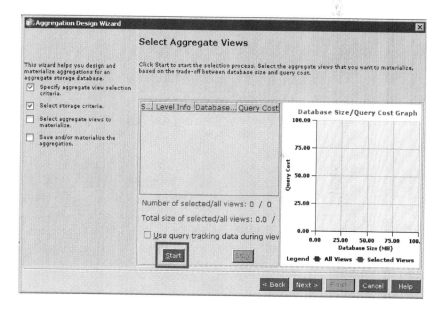

If you have turned on query tracking, you will want to check the option *Use query tracking data during view selection* (more on this in just a minute).

4. Click *OK* once the selection process is complete and we see the aggregate view listing and data query size/cost graph displayed:

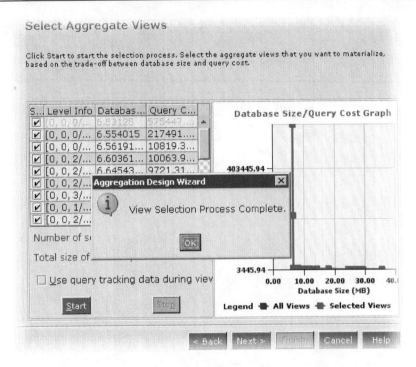

The aggregation wizard displays the following information:

- Level information (level numbers for each aggregate view)
- Database size (estimated size if that view and all other views it depends on is materialized)
- Query cost (average retrieval time for retrieving values from the aggregate view)
- Number of selected views
- Total size of selected / all views

The maximum number of views allowed are 1,023:

Select	Level Info	Database Size...	Query Cost
✔	[0, 0, 0/0, 0, 0...	6.53125	575447.4901...
✔	[0, 0, 0/0, 1, 1...	6.554015	217491.2514...
✔	[0, 0, 0/0, 1, 1...	6.5619173	10819.31911...
✔	[0, 0, 2/0, 0, 0...	6.6036186	10063.91116...
✔	[0, 0, 2/0, 0, 1...	6.6454396	9721.312100...
✔	[0, 0, 2/0, 1, 1...	6.661364	9557.734484...
✔	[0, 0, 3/0, 0, 1...	6.769894	8966.482355...
✔	[0, 0, 1/0, 0, 1...	8.1200485	8061.583022...
✔	[0, 0, 2/0, 0, 1...	8.156075	7931.618307...
✔	[0, 0, 1/0, 0, 0...	8.479492	7481.384739...
✔	[0, 0, 2/0, 0, 0...	9.090838	7147.731675...
✔	[0, 0, 3/0, 1, 1...	9.184105	6961.879754...
✔	[0, 0, 2/0, 0, 0...	9.951621	6651.162077...
✔	[0, 0, 2/0, 0, 1...	12.063818	6174.517114...

Number of selected/all views: 24 / 24

Total size of selected/all views: 35.41232 / 35.41232 MB

The Database Size / Query cost graph illustrates in graphical format the same information with database size down one axis and query cost down another axis:

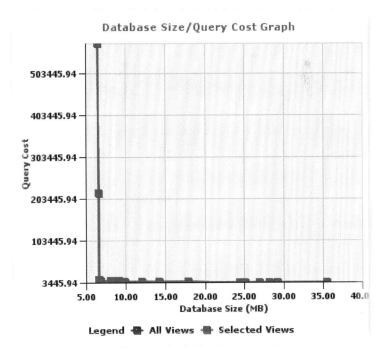

You can check or uncheck the aggregate views to materialize. As you check or uncheck the aggregate views, the size and graph will update to reflect the change. Notice in our ASOSamp.Sample listing, Essbase has listed the views in the order it thinks is most optimal. By selecting the first two aggregate views only, you see a big improvement in query performance with minimal impact to database size.

5. Select the first two aggregate views only:

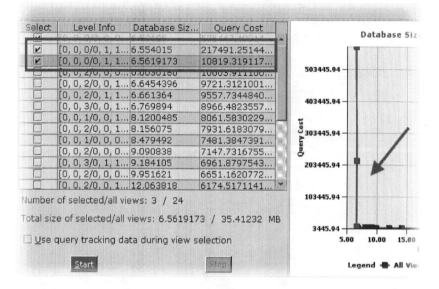

You goal is to achieve the best query performance with the smallest database size. The ASOSamp.Sample graph isn't really a good example because of the small data size. Let's look at something a bit more realistic. In this first example, the arrow is pointing to the selection for all of the aggregate views. Notice that many of the views will increase the size significantly without really helping on query performance. This probably isn't the best aggregate view selection:

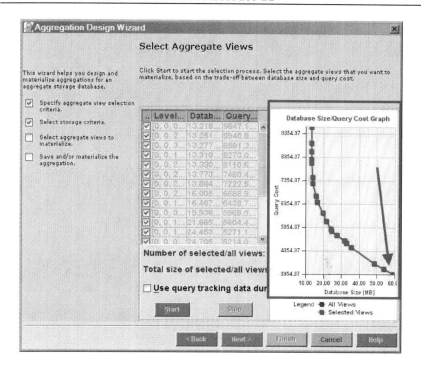

However if we only chose the first one or two aggregate views where the arrow is pointing on the database size / query cost graph, we'd be missing out on some big performance improvements with minimal storage impacts:

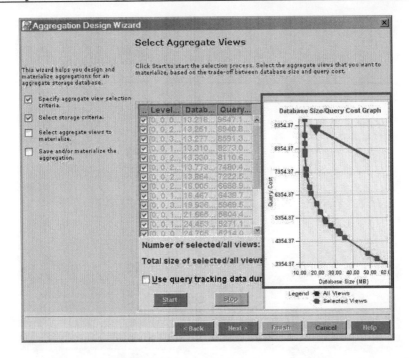

Usually you want to select the views that put you around this point in the graph:

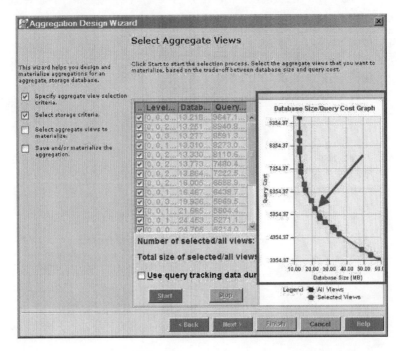

To recap, we want to select the aggregate views that have high query benefits without much impact on the database size.

6. Select the remaining aggregate views you feel will be most beneficial for ASOSamp.Sample.
7. Click *Next*.

In this last step, we will optionally save the aggregation script and run the materialization (AKA the precalcuation of data values for the selected aggregate views). Saving and re-executing aggregation scripts are useful for outlines that do not change. The scripts are saved in the database directory as .csc file.

Only one aggregation can be materialized at a time.

Tip!

8. Check the option to *Materialize aggregation*.
9. Check the option to *Replace existing aggregation:*

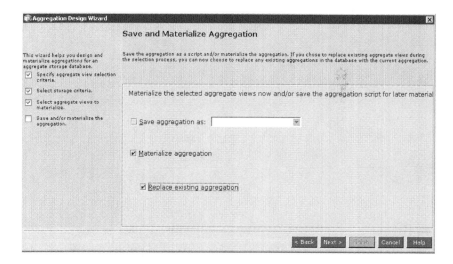

In many cases, you may want to add an aggregation to existing aggregations in the database. In those instances, do not check *Replace existing aggregation*.

10. Click *Next* and the aggregation will begin. You should see a message that looks like:

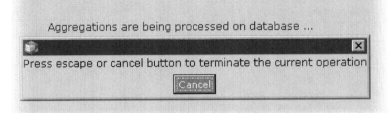

You'll be notified once the aggregation is complete:

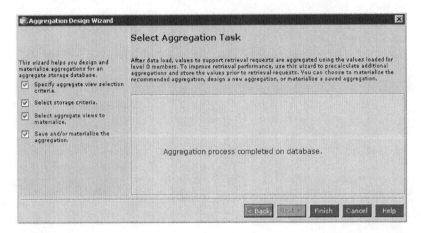

Notice the steps we've done so far have been manual through the Administration Services Console. You can also automate aggregations using MaxL, choosing to aggregate in a single phase and / or executing saved aggregation scripts.

Note!

Is there a way to tell how long an aggregation will take? Yes, by running the aggregation. Sadly, we're serious.

Often times you will want to clear aggregations like when new data is loaded into the database so precalculated values are no long valid. You can clear aggregations in both Administration Services console and in MaxL.

To clear an aggregation,
1. Right click on the database.
2. Select *Clear >> All aggregations:*

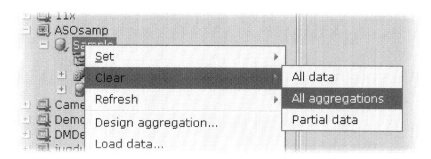

QUERY TRACKING

As an administrator you can turn on query tracking to help optimize the aggregate views chosen during the aggregation process. Query tracking tracks the members and data that are users retrieving in reports and analysis. Essbase then uses this information to create a more optimal aggregate view listing.

To turn on query tracking,
1. Right click on the database and select *Query Tracking >> Enable.*

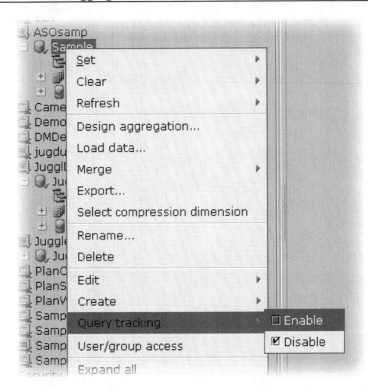

After query tracking has run for a reasonable period, rerun the aggregation process so that aggregate views will be created based off the gathered statistics. To use query tracking information, simply check *Use query tracking data during view selection:*

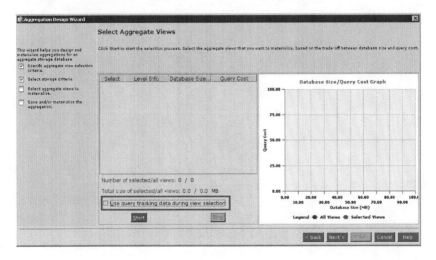

There is some overhead with query tracking, so we don't recommend you enabling this feature all the time. Turn this feature on periodically to gather current user usage information and apply to aggregate view selections.

Note! Query tracking usage information is held in memory. The following actions will clear query tracking usage statistics: loading or clearing data, materializing or clearing an aggregation, and turning off query tracking.

QUERY HINTS

Query hints are another way to improve the aggregate view generation as you, the Essbase administrator help Essbase understand what types of queries will likely occur for a database. They are essentially "soft restrictions" for aggregate view definitions. Essbase takes the query hints into consideration when creating aggregation view listings. User based view selection will override query hints.

To define a query hint,

1. Open the outline.
2. Select the *Query Hints* tab.

Note! You may be prompted to upgrade the sample application outlines. This is a one-time step sometimes required to upgrade an outline to the current version.

In the example below for ASOSamp.Sample, we know that most of our reports will pull level zero months for product categories.

3. Double click on *Time*.
4. Select *January* using the Member selection tool:

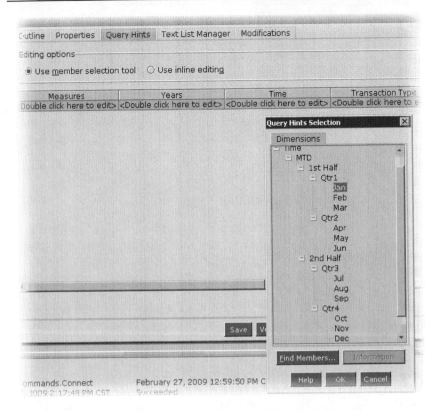

By selecting January, Essbase will know that any member at this level is likely to be queried (which means you don't have to define a query hint for every single month).

5. Double click on *Years* and try to define a hint. Notice that hints are not allowed for dynamic hierarchies.

6. Double click on *Products*.

7. Select *Personal Electronics* and click *OK:*

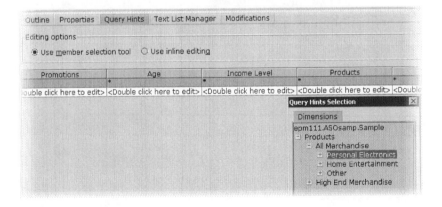

8. Click *Save* to save the query hints, retaining all data if prompted.

If a member is not specified in the hint, Essbase understands that any member can be used in the aggregate view.

Note!

Query hints cannot contain dynamic, label only or shared members.

Now to take advantage of these query hints, you need to rerun the aggregation design wizard and materialization process.

INTELLIGENT AGGREGATIONS

The later System 9 versions of Essbase introduced a new concept of intelligent aggregations. You can now define "hard" restrictions for a dimension, allowing you to exert more control over the aggregate views that Essbase identifies. This is helpful when you understand what the users will be querying and reporting. Intelligent aggregations are different than query hints which simply provide suggestions to Essbase ("soft" restrictions). Intelligent aggregations provide specific instructions for Essbase in aggregate view identification.

Available options include:

- Default (no restriction for primary hierarchy, no aggregation for alternate hierarchies)
- Consider all levels
- Do not aggregate
- Consider top level only (you only query top level)
- Never aggregate to intermediate levels (you only query level zero or top dimension)

To define a hard restriction (AKA intelligent aggregation) for a dimension,

1. Right click on a stored dimension and select *Edit member properties*.
2. On the Information tab, choose the *Level Usage for Aggregation*:

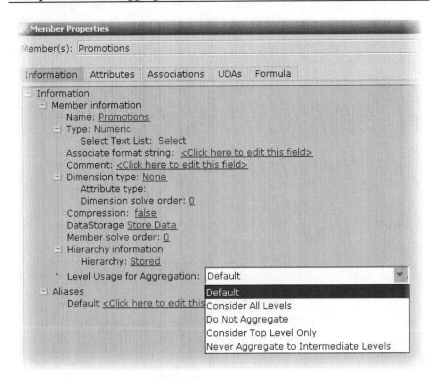

3. Click *OK* and save the outline.

To take advantage of the new settings, rerun the aggregation selection process and materialization.

IMPACT OF NEW DATA LOADS TO AGGREGATE VIEWS

What happens to the aggregate views after a new data load? The aggregates don't go away. When you load data into an ASO database with aggregations, "materialization on the fly" will take place during the load. The values in the aggregation are recalculated. However, the old aggregate view definition may not be optimal based on the new data set loaded so you may choose to clear the aggregations and rerun the aggregate view selection process.

You've learned the first tip in increasing retrieval performance in our aggregate storage databases. Before we learn some other tuning and optimization tips, we need to first understand the aggregate storage databases from a more technical perspective, "under the covers" if you will.

Chapter 14:
ASO Under the Covers

We now begin our less than exciting topic of "ASO Under the Covers" where we will introduce tablespaces, directory structures and restructuring. Snort some caffeine because while this isn't quite as exciting as building your Essbase outline and retrieving data, it is important to understand some of the underlying structures for aggregate storage databases.

If you ask some of the greatest minds in the business how ASO works, you'll hear the same resounding answer: "It's a black box" or "it is top secret and hard to understand". Under the covers, our handy Essbase developers designed a database to handle more dimensions and members, smaller batch windows for loads and aggregations of sparse data, and smaller database footprint. If you're familiar with blocks and dense / sparse, those concepts don't apply. Aggregate storage databases stores data in highly optimized aggregation nodes.

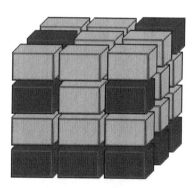

Let's jump into some more details about ASO "under the covers".

ESSBASE ASO DIRECTORY STRUCTURE

First, we'll tackle the Essbase directory structure. When you install Essbase, it creates various folders and files. In the 11x version, Essbase uses a system variable called ESSBASEPATH to denote where Essbase was installed. Older versions of Essbase used a system variable called ARBORPATH which you still see hanging around in 11x in various places. You refer to these environment variables as %ESSBASEPATH% and

%ARBORPATH% in Windows and $ESSBASEPATH and $ARBORPATH in UNIX. Because both variables are the same, we will refer to it generically as "arborpath" because that's what it's been for more than 15 years.

- arborpath\bin stores Essbase executables, the Essbase.cfg configuration file, the Essbase.sec security definition file, and the Essbase.bak backup security file.
- arborpath\app stores server-based applications (more on this shortly).
- arborpath\client stores any client based files and applications.
- arborpath\docs stores online documentation.
- arborpath\locale contains the character-set files necessary for multi-language use.

Need To Know – Essbase Executables

Helpful Info

Stored in *arborpath*\bin
- Essbase.exe – Essbase server agent process
- Esssvr.exe – application process
- Essmsh.exe – MaxL shell
- Esscmd.exe – Esscmd command line interface

Stored in *eas*\Server\bin
- Starteas.exe – start the Administration Server executable
- Admincon.exe – Administration Services Console application

The *arborpath*\app directory contains all of the application files. An application will contain a single database in the case of ASO, one to three databases in the case of BSO, and one to five databases if you have Planning Workforce and CapEx. A database will contain one outline file. Objects like report scripts, calc scripts, and rules files can be stored at the application or database level.

The official definitions for application and database are as follows: An application is the management structure containing one or more Essbase databases and related files. A database is the repository of data that contains a multi-dimensional storage array. Each database consists of a storage structure definition (outline), data, security, and optional objects for ASO databases like aggregation scripts and rules files.

Let's take a look at the directory structure for the arborpath\app folder:

Tip!

You can store rules files, aggregation scripts, calc scripts, and report scripts at the application OR database level.

ASO TABLESPACES

Aggregate storage databases utilize tablespaces for data file and work file storage and retrieval. Each ASO application has 4 tablespaces: Default, Temp, Log, and Metadata. These tablespaces will show up as folders under the application folder. The Default tablespace stores the data structure and database values. The Temp tablespace is a temporary work space for the application and is used during data loads, aggregations and retrievals. The Log tablespace houses a binary transaction log file of default tablespace updates and the Metadata tablespace stores information about the file locations, files, and objects contained in the database.

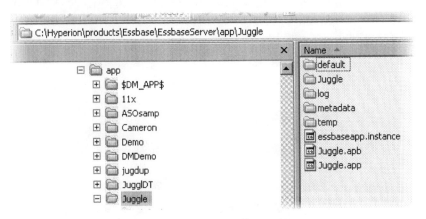

For the default and temp tablespaces, you can define multiple locations and sizes. A file location specifies a physical disk space for storing database files. Each tablespace may contain one or more file locations and can span multiple physical drives and/or logical volumes. You can also define tablespace "location" properties like the directory path locations, maximum disk space to be used for each location, and maximum file size allowed for each location. For example, you set the Max File Size to 16 MB, a .dat file will be created and loaded until it reaches the 16 MB limit. When the limit is met, another .dat file is created.

```
Ess00001.dat (16MB)
Ess00002.dat (8 MB)
```

You cannot change the location or size of the metadata and log table spaces.

To control and manage the tablespaces for your aggregate storage database, use the Tablespace Manager.

1. In the Administration Services Console, right click on the Juggle application.
2. Select *Edit Properties:*

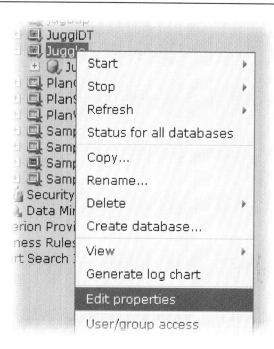

3. Choose the *Tablespaces* tab:

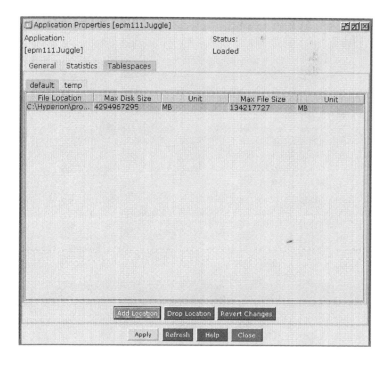

From this window you can edit the file locations for the default and temp tablespaces (by selecting either the default or temp tabs). Once you have chosen the desired tablespace, simply click in the existing file location and make the desired changes:

General	Statistics	Tablespaces		

default	temp			

File Location	Max Disk Size		Unit	
C:\Hyperion\pro...	4294967295	MB		13
	Unlimited			

Click the *Add Location* or *Drop Location* to add and remove locations.

4. Close the Juggle properties window.

SIZING TABLESPACES

During the data load and aggregation process, data is stored in both the Temp and Default directories. ASO will always build the full .dat file in the temp tablespace while the default tablespace still has the production .dat open. Hence, for your maximum database size you have to plan on **at *least* 3 times your maximum bloated .dat size**. We recommend you play it safe since there is no guarantee that the operating system is not "paging the buffer" (which sounds naughty, by the way). Basically, make sure you have plenty of disk space for your ASO databases.

ASO FILES

Let's also review some of the other files that you will see in your application and database directory folders:

Directory or File	Location	Description
appname.app	*ARBORPATH*\app\ *appname*\	Application file containing application settings
appname.LOG	*ARBORPATH*\app\	Application log file

	appname\	
dbname.db	*ARBORPATH*\app\ *appname**dbname*\	Database file containing database settings
dbname.dbb	*ARBORPATH*\app\ *appname**dbname*\	Backup of database file
dbname.ddb	*ARBORPATH*\app\ *appname**dbname*\	Partition definition file
dbname.otl	*ARBORPATH*\app\ *appname**dbname*\	Outline file
dbname.otl.kee p	*ARBORPATH*\app\ *appname**dbname*\	Temporary backup of *dbname*.otl (created by operations that modify the outline and write it to a new file.)
trigger.trg	*ARBORPATH*\app\ *appname**dbname*\	Trigger file
essn.dat	*ARBORPATH*\app\ *appname*\default\ *ARBORPATH*\app\ *appname*\log\ *ARBORPATH*\app\ *appname*\metadata\	Aggregate storage data file

Can you open and edit any of these files directly? No! And don't try it: doing so may cause database corruption.

RESTRUCTURING FOR ASO

Restructuring of your Essbase database takes place after the outline changes, like when you add new, edit, and delete members and dimensions. Any and every change forces Essbase to restructure the database, so think of it as "re-saving" the database. This can be a time consuming process depending on the type of restructure and database size.

If any of you guys have used earlier versions of aggregate storage databases, you know that when we used to make changes to an ASO outline, the entire data set would be cleared during the restructure process. Thankfully not so in our later 9x and 11x versions of Essbase. You've already seen (if you've been following along) that we can make many types of changes to the ASO outline and the data will be restructured to store the new outline changes. We are usually prompted with the following message:

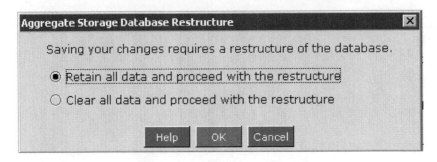

In most cases, we select *Retain all data and proceed with the restructure.*

A number of factors will play into the duration and storage size required for restructuring as well as whether or not you will have to clear data before a restructure.

A "light" restructure with low performance impact will take place when you make the following types of changes: renaming a member, changing a formula, and changing an alias. A slightly more intensive restructure takes place when you make those same changes to an alternate hierarchy or attribute dimension. If any aggregate views have been created using the updated attribute dimension or alternate hierarchy, they will be cleared, requiring the user to rerun any aggregations.

If you delete or move a member, a full outline restructure will take place which could take some time. Make sure to have up to three times the size of the database available so this restructure can complete without error.

A full restructure will take place and aggregation views will be cleared for a hierarchy that is moved, deleted or added. Changing the top member of a stored hierarchy from label only to stored (and vice versa) and changing dynamic hierarchies to stored hierarchies (and vice versa) will have the same end result.

Full restructures of ASO databases will require 3x the database size.

Tip!

If you add, delete or move a standard dimension, data will be cleared from the database and you'll have to reload data, recreate aggregation views and run the materialization.

The Essbase DBAG (Database Administrator's Guide) provides additional examples of outline changes and the types of restructures that will take place. Check it out for more detailed information.

Still awake? Now that you have a pretty good understanding of aggregate storage databases, let's jump into some tips and tricks for tuning and optimization as well as some design best practices.

Chapter 15:
Design and Optimize for ASO

Our juggling database is fast as lighting like most Essbase databases are but as we add in our millions of juggling customers and thousands of markets, we may begin to see some performance issues. Essbase is inherently fast but you need to design and tune your databases the "right" way. The "right" way isn't black and white unfortunately; tuning and optimization isn't an exact science and results are not always predictable. Design and tuning tips will help in some cases and not in others. We recommend you test, test, and test some more to arrive at the optimal result for each database. And test and tune periodically as your database grows and evolves over time.

We've already covered one way to improve retrieval performance in aggregations for ASO. In this chapter we'll provide a number of other tips and best practices so that you can achieve the best performance possible for your aggregate storage databases.

DIMENSION AND HIERARCHY SETTINGS

Stored versus Dynamic versus Multiple Hierarchies

Which dimensions should be stored versus dynamic versus enabled for multiple hierarchies? Does it matter? Yes! If you tagged every dimension dynamic, you would probably have a very slow database. Tag dimensions as stored whenever possible. Definitely use stored hierarchies for your really big dimensions (the ones with thousands and millions of members). Remember stored dimensions will perform a straight aggregation of members. Only the plus consolidation tag is allowed and no member formulas. Also note dimensions tagged "Accounts" cannot be stored.

Use the dynamic hierarchy setting for dimensions and hierarchies that need to be calculated and not aggregated. Dynamic hierarchies allow multiple consolidation symbols and member formulas written in MDX. All calculations are performed at retrieval time and are not part of any aggregate view selection.

Dimensions enabled for multi-hierarchy can contain hierarchies that are either stored or dynamic. Multi-hierarchy enabled dimensions allow you to build alternate rollups with shared members. Non shared members must occur in the outline before the shared members. The first hierarchy in a multi-hierarchy enabled dimension cannot contain shared members. By enabling multiple hierarchies, you can effectively use stored members and dynamic calculated members when needed.

Accounts

Why should a dimension be tagged "Accounts" in aggregate storage databases? The answer to this question differs depending on your Essbase version. (The answer is also slightly different for block storage databases). If you are using Essbase 11 ASO, the main reason to tag a dimension Accounts is to take advantage of time balance features (time balance first, last or average for an account). If you choose to make another dimension Accounts, you can still achieve "Time Balance" functionality via an analytic dimension (check out the appendix on building analytic dimensions).

By default, the Accounts dimension is the compression dimension. The Accounts dimension is a dynamic dimension that allows non additive unary operators.

 If you use an Essbase version prior to 9.3, the Accounts dimension is the dimension used for compression with no capabilities to change. Beginning in 9.3.1, you can choose other dimensions as the compression dimension.

Note!

Accounts dimensions in block storage databases allow a feature called expense reporting tags. This feature is not available for aggregate storage databases. If you want to build this logic into aggregate storage databases, simply use UDAs and member formulas (remember, we added this logic to our variance calculation in our Juggle database).

If your accounts dimension in your aggregate storage database contains a large number of members, you may want to consider *not* tagging the dimension as Accounts. By making the accounts dimension just a regular stored dimension that is aggregated, you might find some big performance improvements. But you don't want to add expenses to revenue! The way around this is to use UDAs to flip signs during data loads (under *Options >> Data Load Settings* within a rules file):

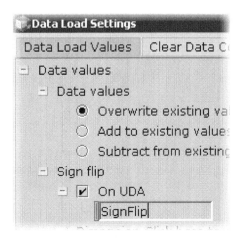

The caveat is the user will have to understand some signage differences. The resulting outline would look like the following:

```
- Account Stored # Default # <2>
  - Margin (+) <2>
    - Op_Income (+) <2>
        Net_Revenue (+)
        Op_Expense (+) (UDAS: Expense, Signflip)
      Other Exp (+) (UDAS: Expense, Signflip)
```

Another alternative for large account dimensions would be to use multiple hierarchies, allowing for more aggregates to be stored. The aggregate members in a stored hierarchy and an alternate rollup with shared member(s) to use non + consolidation tags:

```
- Account Multiple Hierarchies Enabled <3> (Label Only)
  - Op_Expense Stored # Default # (+) <3>
        Marketing_Exp (+)
        Admin_Exp (+)
        Travel_Exp (+)
  - Margin Dynamic (+) <2>
    - Op_Income (+) <2>
        Net_Revenue (+)
        Op_Expense (-) (Shared Member) (UDAS: Expense)
      Other Exp (-) (UDAS: Expense)
```

Time

Next we move on to the dimension tagged "Time". We've already learned that Time works with Accounts time balance tags. In block storage databases, Time allows "to-date" functionality but not for aggregate storage databases. So how do you accomplish to date functionality in ASO databases? If you are using an Essbase version prior to 9.3.1, create alternate rollups in the Time dimension. In 9.3.1 forward use analytic dimensions to achieve to date views. Analytic dimensions are dynamic dimensions that use member formulas to create different "views" of the data. In the example below, we created a PeriodView dimension to calculate to-date values. First, we created a "base" or "input" member to load data. Then we added to date members with member formulas, using Sum and PeriodToDate functions:

```
PeriodView Dynamic <3>
    Base (+)
    M-T-D (+) [0: Sum(PeriodsToDate([Period].Generations(3), Period.CurrentMember))]
    Q-T-D (+) [0: Sum(PeriodsToDate([Period].Generations(2), Period.CurrentMember))]
 Account Accounts Dynamic Compression <2>
```

If you are using time balance tags, make sure to use Aggregate function instead of Sum.

```
PeriodView Dynamic <3>
    Base (+)
    M-T-D (+) [0: Aggregate(PeriodsToDate([Period].Generations(3), Period.CurrentMember))]
    Q-T-D (+) [0: Aggregate(PeriodsToDate([Period].Generations(2), Period.CurrentMember))]
```

Other design ideas for the Time dimension: Time is a good candidate for compression. If you don't use this dimension as the compression dimension, make it stored or use multiple hierarchies if member formulas are required.

Attributes

Don't forget about attribute dimensions in aggregate storage databases. Even though we can build a database with 20+ dimensions doesn't mean that some of those dimensions wouldn't be better served as attribute dimensions. Retrieval time is similar to other hierarchy members and internally they are treated as a shared roll-up. Attribute dimensions can be used as part of Query Tracking. One big benefit (depending on your requirements) is that attribute dimensions are not displayed by default in adhoc queries using Smart View, Web Analysis or other tool. So from an end user perspective, their view isn't "cluttered" with a long list of dimensions. Here is the default query for ASOSamp.Sample database in Smart View (notice no attribute dimensions):

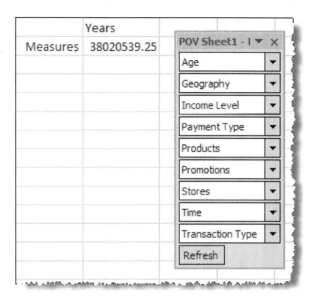

The easiest way for a user to query an attribute dimension is using the Smart View Query Designer:

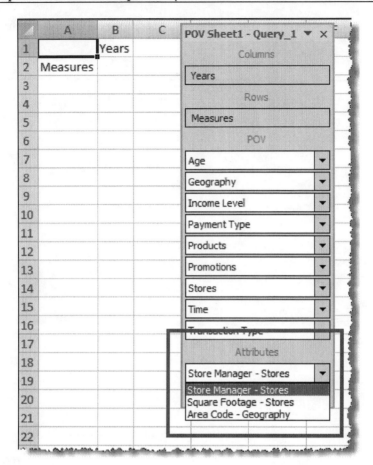

Tip!

Remember varying attribute dimensions are not available for aggregate storage databases so if an attribute needs to vary over Time or other dimension, make it a regular dimension.

Now that we've covered some design tips and tricks, let us turn our attention to optimization of aggregate storage databases. We've already discussed aggregations but there are a number of other alternatives to tune your ASO database.

COMPRESSION

You can decrease the size of the aggregate storage database which improves performance (smaller databases, faster queries) using a feature called compression.

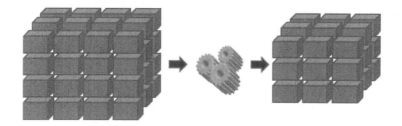

To compress an ASO database, you simply tag a dimension to be the "compression dimension". In previous releases, compression was tied to the Accounts dimension and is the default compression dimension in current versions. Beginning in version 9.3, any dynamic dimension can be used for compression. The compression dimension influences the size of the compressed database. It is not mandatory but helps overall performance. The goal is to optimize data compression but maintain end user retrievals.

Compression Dimension Rules

Helpful
Info

- Dynamic dimension
- Single dynamic hierarchy
- No attributes
- No associated base members for attribute dimension

Evaluate and Set the Compression Dimension

The cool thing about ASO compression is that Essbase helps you choose a compression dimension by estimating what the database size would be depending on which dimension is tagged for compression.

To evaluate and or select a compression dimension,

1. Right click on the database and select *Select compression dimension:*

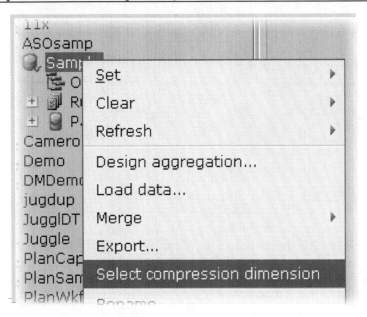

2. The available dimensions will display with the expected
    level zero database size.

Note Measures is selected as the compression dimension
and the expected level 0 size is significantly smaller than the other
dimension alternatives:

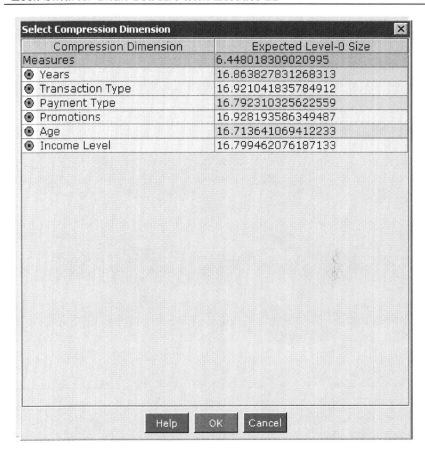

3. If you'd like to change the compression dimension, double click on the desired dimension.
4. Click *OK*.

Another way to view compression settings and get more detailed information is under the database properties.
1. Right click on the database and select *Edit Properties*.
2. Select the Compression tab:

Notice we see the same level 0 database size displayed in MB but we also see a number of other metrics that help us in our evaluation of the best dimension for compression. The *Stored Level 0 Members* displays the number of stored level zero members for the dimension (imagine that). You want this number to be low. Dimensions with many level zero members do not perform well when tagged as Compression.

Compression is more effective if values are grouped together consecutively versus spread throughout the outline with #missing in between. Essbase creates a bundle of 16 data values. The *Average Bundle Fill* is the average number of values stored in a group or bundle. The number will be between 1 and 16 where 16 is the best average bundle fill value.

Average Value Length is the average storage size in bytes required for the stored values in cells. The average storage size will be between 2-8 bytes, where 2 is the targeted value. Without compression, 8 bytes is required to store a value in a cell. With compression, it takes few bytes and the smaller the amount the better. Rounding data values can help compression as it reduces the average value length.

The compression dimension can also be specified in the outline editor.

1. Open the outline editor.
2. Right click on a dimension and select *Edit member properties*.
3. Select the Compression type to be *True:*

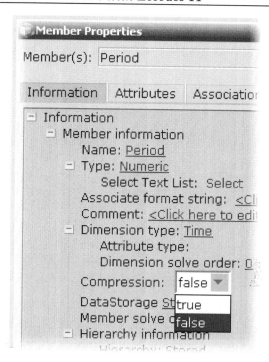

Changing compression requires a full restructure which could take some time. Perform this change during off hours when users are not in the system.

Compression Tips

If you are using compression, make sure to consider these tips. Ideally the compression dimension should be the column headers of your data source file. Time is an excellent candidate for compression dimension, especially if you have fiscal year as a separate dimension. The best compression is achieved when the leaf level member count is evenly divided by 16. And finally watch out for dimensions with many level zero members. This could negatively affect performance.

FASTER DATA LOADS

ASO and BSO databases share some commonalities in the data load process. We've already learned that data sources include both text files and relational databases. We can load one or more data sources at the same time and those sources can be loaded with or without rules files depending on the data layout. If multiple sources are used, choose *Overwrite existing values*, *Add to existing values*, or *Subtract from existing values*.

These concepts hold true for both BSO and ASO. However, the way the data is stored in ASO is very different than BSO (tablespaces versus page and index files). And more importantly, your aggregate storage databases are going to be much bigger than BSO databases with millions of members and 20+ dimensions. This means you are going to be loading some really big files. Because we have this requirement of loading large volumes of records, the ASO data load process provides buffering and parallel capabilities (not available for block storage databases).

Load Buffer for Multiple ASO Sources

Because the data files are potentially very large for aggregate storage databases, a temporary load buffer is used for loading multiple files (loading a single load file does not involve the buffer).

In Administration Services, when you load multiple sources in a single step, the load buffer is automatically used. Two additional options to define include *Aggregate Use Last* and *Resource Usage*:

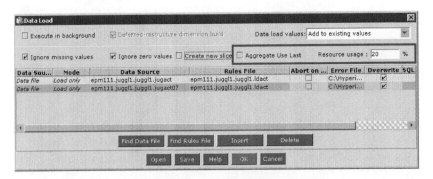

Aggregate Use Last option tells Essbase what to do with multiple values for the same cell. By default Essbase will sum up the values in the load buffer for each cell. However, if you requirements dictate, you can check *Aggregate Use Last* to load the value of the cell that was loaded last into the load buffer.

The *Resource Usage* option controls how much cache a data load buffer can use. This setting is defined in a percentage between .01 and 1. The total of all data load buffers created on a database cannot exceed 1 (so if you are performing multiple loads concurrently don't set all of them to use 100% of the cache).

You can also use the load buffer through MaxL statements. When you load multiple files, the first step in the process will be to initialize the load buffer to accumulate the data. Next, Essbase reads in the data sources into the load buffer. Finally the data will be loaded from the load buffer into the database.

```
/*Initialize the load buffer*/
alter database ASOSamp.Sample initialize load_buffer
     with buffer_id 1
     resource_usage .5;

/*Read the data sources into the load buffer*/
import database ASOSamp.Sample data from server
     data_file 'file_1' to load_buffer with
     buffer_id 1 on error abort;
import database ASOSamp.Sample data from server
     data_file 'file_2' to load_buffer with
     buffer_id 1 on error abort;
import database ASOSamp.Sample data from server
     data_file 'file_3' to load_buffer with
     buffer_id 1 on error abort;

/*Load data from the buffer into the database*/
import database ASOSamp.Sample data from load_buffer
     with buffer_id 1;
```

The import statements do not need to be continuous. As long as the buffer exists, the database is locked from queries, aggregations and data loads by other means.

Presorting multiple data source loads will improve performance even though the buffer always sorts: A sort-sort-merge-sort will be faster than a nonsort-nonsort-merge-sort. You won't see as dramatic a difference as when you apply sorting in BSO loads, but it is still important on very large loads and time critical incremental loads.

Concurrent Loads

Multiple data load buffers can exist. So this means you can load data into multiple buffers at the same time, giving us yet another way to speed up data load timing. This method is called concurrent loading. Using separate MaxL sessions, you load data into the Essbase database with different load buffers. Once the data loads are complete, you commit the multiple data load buffers in the same operation (which is faster than committing each buffer by itself).

Here's an example:

MaxL Session 1:

```
alter database ASOSamp.Sample
initialize load_buffer with buffer_id 1
     resource_usage 0.5;
import database ASOSamp.Sample data
from data_file "dataload1.txt"
to load_buffer with buffer_id 1
on error abort;
```

MaxL Session 2:

```
alter database ASOSamp.Sample
initialize load_buffer with buffer_id 2
     resource_usage 0.5;
import database ASOSamp.Sample data
from data_file "dataload2.txt"
to load_buffer with buffer_id 2
on error abort;
```

When data is fully loaded, use one commit statement to commit all of the load buffers:

```
import database ASOSamp.Sample data
from load_buffer with buffer_id 1, 2;
```

We've shared some tips for the full data loads for ASO databases, but what if only a small subset of my data changes? Do I have to reload everything? Let's next discuss incremental data loads for ASO databases.

Trickle Feeds & Slices

In the most recent versions of Essbase, you'll hear about the new feature "trickle feeds" or near real time data access. What exactly does this mean? Historically, users were not able to access an ASO database when it was being loaded. So in order to load the database, you would have to load in off hours or kick everyone out of the system.

Today is a different story. An aggregate database can store data in multiple "slices". The main database slice is created when you perform the main data load. This often occurs on a nightly or weekly basis.

With multiple slices, you can load additional slices without impacting the main slice, allowing users to remain in the database. The idea is that you can provide near real time data updates to an ASO database, hence the saying "trickle feeds". Imagine data is a stream that trickles into your Essbase ASO database. An incremental data load will perform much faster than reloading the entire record set. You can then merge all incremental slices into the main database slice or merge all incremental slices into a single data slice, leaving the main database slice unchanged.

In Administration Services you can load data to a new slice by checking the *Create New Slice* option:

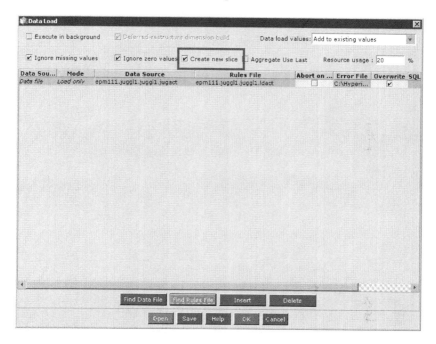

On a periodic basis, possibly nightly or weekly, you will want to merge the slices into one main slice or merge all incremental slices together into one slice. To merge slices,

1. In Administration Services, right click on the database and select *Merge>>All slices into one* or *Merge >> Incremental slices only:*

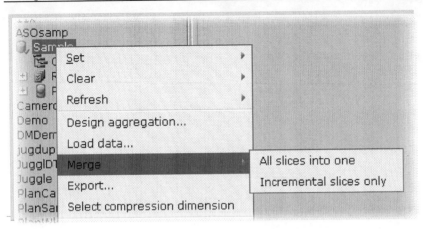

Dynamic aggregations are performed across the necessary slices to provide accurate query results. Different materialized views might exist within a slice as compared to the primary slice of the database.

Using the load buffer during incremental data loads improves performance.

Tip!

Now you know how to incrementally load data but what if you need to clear the slice before the incremental load? The annual budget is loaded and static while current month actuals are changing on an hourly basis. Your desired process is clear the current month actual data and keep the static budget data. Enter partial data clears.

PARTIAL DATA CLEARS

Essbase 11 now allows partial data clear for data sets in an ASO database. For example, our actual data is dynamic and needs to be refreshed often but the budget data is static (no need to reload). Two types of partial clears are available: physical and logical. Physical clears completely remove cells from a database while logical clears remove cells in the database by creating offsetting cells in a new slice.

See the illustrations below to help understand how this feature works:

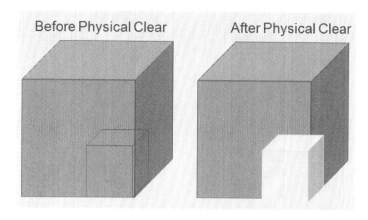

A physical clear removes the cells from the database.

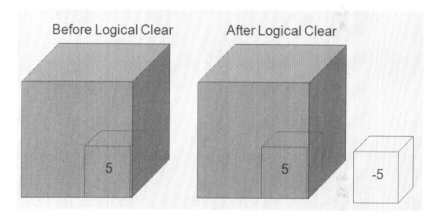

A logical clear creates offsetting cells in a new slice, a faster alternative to physical clears (in many cases, significantly faster).

What is the impact to upper levels? Essbase recognizes that values are changed and displays correct query results. Essbase doesn't rematerialize the aggregation: you have to reprocess aggregations.

You will use a combination of MaxL and MDX to clear a defined set of data. The region of data to be cleared will be identified using MDX:

```
CLEAR {Jan, Feb, Mar}
```

Tip!   Upper level or level zero data can be cleared.

A new MaxL command was introduced in version 11 to clear a region. The following statement logically clears a region identified by '*MDX-SET-EXPRESSION*':

```
ALTER DATABASE DBS-NAME CLEAR DATA IN REGION 'MDX-
    SET-EXPRESSION' ;
```

The following statement physically clears a region identified by '*MDX-SET-EXPRESSION*':

```
ALTER DATABASE DBS-NAME CLEAR DATA IN REGION 'MDX-
    SET-EXPRESSION' PHYSICAL;
```

There is a limit to the number of slices created for an ASO database (remember, logical clears create additional slices). The recommended process is to run the physical data clear at night to clean up the new slices and re-optimize the cube.

What is the impact to query performance when using partial clears? After the immediate clear, both options are a bit slower. Logical clears are slower because you have to combine two slices to view the correct data set. Physical clears result in slower performance too because you haven't processed any aggregations. After the materialization of aggregation, physical clears will always result in faster query performance.

In summary,

	Physical Clear	*Logical Clear*
Cube is locked for update and export operations during clear	Yes	Yes
Queries continue to process during clear	Yes	Yes
Time to clear	Slower	Faster
Time to clear	Proportional to input data size	Proportional to region being cleared

Other ASO Data Load Tips

Other data load optimization tips include: Don't include fields that are applicable to BSO (they will be ignored). Load level zero data only. If #Missing is specified, the cell will be removed from the database. Ignore zeros and #missing values whenever possible. Currency name and currency category are not supported. If time is compression, make sure those columns are across your headers in your source file.

OPTIMAL MDX MEMBER FORMULAS

As with any code writing, it is possible to write inefficient, overly complex MDX member formulas. Let's walk through some examples that our friend, Steve Liebermensch, shared at the Kaleidoscope user conference.

The following member formula calculates a 3 month average transactions contribution % to the total 3 month average transactions:

```
Round( ( (
([Time].CurrentMember,[Products].CurrentMember,[Tran
    sactions]) +
([Time].CurrentMember.Lag(1),[Products].CurrentMembe
    r,[Transactions])
+
([Time].CurrentMember.Lag(2),[Products].CurrentMembe
    r,[Transactions])
) /
(([Time].CurrentMember,Ancestor
    (Products.CurrentMember,
Products.Generations(2)),[Transactions]) +
([Time].CurrentMember.Lag(1),Ancestor
    (Products.CurrentMember,
Products.Generations(2)),[Transactions]) +
([Time].CurrentMember.Lag(2),Ancestor
    (Products.CurrentMember,
Products.Generations(2)),[Transactions]) ) )
,4)
```

How can we optimize this member formula?

1. Remove unnecessary functions like rounding. Leave rounding to the reporting tool:

```
Round( ( (
([Time].CurrentMember,[Products].CurrentMember,[Tran
      sactions]) +
([Time].CurrentMember.Lag(1),[Products].CurrentMembe
      r,[Transactions])
+
([Time].CurrentMember.Lag(2),[Products].CurrentMembe
      r,[Transactions])
) /
(([Time].CurrentMember,Ancestor
      (Products.CurrentMember,
Products.Generations(2)),[Transactions]) +
([Time].CurrentMember.Lag(1),Ancestor
      (Products.CurrentMember,
Products.Generations(2)),[Transactions]) +
([Time].CurrentMember.Lag(2),Ancestor
      (Products.CurrentMember,
Products.Generations(2)),[Transactions]) ) )
,4)
```

2. Avoid unnecessary references to CurrentMember. Essbase already assumes current member for dimensions in the Essbase database:

```
( (
([Time].CurrentMember,[Products].CurrentMember,[Tran
      sactions]) +
([Time].CurrentMember.Lag(1),[Products].CurrentMembe
      r,[Transactions])
+
([Time].CurrentMember.Lag(2),[Products].CurrentMembe
      r,[Transactions])
) /
(([Time].CurrentMember,Ancestor
      (Products.CurrentMember,
Products.Generations(2)),[Transactions]) +
([Time].CurrentMember.Lag(1),Ancestor
      (Products.CurrentMember,
Products.Generations(2)),[Transactions]) +
([Time].CurrentMember.Lag(2),Ancestor
      (Products.CurrentMember,
Products.Generations(2)),[Transactions]) ) )
,4)
```

3. Don't use 5 functions when 1 function will do the same thing. In our example, we replace 3 CurrentMember

functions and 2 lag functions with the Sum and LastPeriods functions.

```
( (
([Time].CurrentMember,[Transactions]) +
([Time].CurrentMember.Lag(1,[Transactions])
+
([Time].CurrentMember.Lag(2),[Transactions])
) /
(([Time].CurrentMember,Ancestor
        (Products.CurrentMember,
Products.Generations(2)),[Transactions]) +
([Time].CurrentMember.Lag(1),Ancestor
        (Products.CurrentMember,
Products.Generations(2)),[Transactions]) +
([Time].CurrentMember.Lag(2),Ancestor
        (Products.CurrentMember,
Products.Generations(2)),[Transactions]) ) )
,4)
```

4. Direct References are faster than Functions. If a member formula will always use a specific member, use the member name:

```
Sum(LastPeriods(3),Transactions)/
Sum(LastPeriods(3),
(Ancestor (Products.CurrentMember,
Products.Generations(2)),
Transactions))
```

We replaced Ancestor (Products.CurrentMember, Products.Generations(2) with the specific member name, All Merchandise. The ending result should look like the following:

```
Sum(LastPeriods(3),Transactions)/
Sum(LastPeriods(3),([All Merchandise],
Transactions))
```

5. Add a condition to evaluate the formula when data exists (why perform logic if support data is missing?):

```
Case When Not
IsEmpty(Sum(LastPeriods(3),Transactions)) Then
Sum(LastPeriods(3),Transactions)/
Sum(LastPeriods(3),
([All Merchandise],Transactions))
End
```

In Essbase 11x a new function was introduced to help perform calculations for data combinations that exist – nonEmptyMember.

6. Break up complicated formulas by using additional members. In our example, we create a member called *Last 3 Month Transactions* with the following member formula:

```
(LastPeriods(3),Transactions)
```

We then add the member formula to the *Three month average transactions contribution %* member:

```
NonEmptyMember [Last 3 Month Transactions]
Sum(LastPeriods(3),Transactions)/
Sum(LastPeriods(3),([All Merchandise],Transactions))
```

To recap, when it comes to MDX member formulas, simplify, simplify, simplify. And don't forget to use the handy Technical Reference Guide.

AGGREGATE STORAGE CACHES

The aggregate storage cache is memory used to speed up data loads, aggregations and retrievals for ASO databases. Data is held in memory which provides performance improvements because it is always faster to go to memory versus disk. 32 MB is the default cache size which supports 2 GB of level zero data. Use the size of input level data (level 0 data) to determine cache size so 2 GB of input data requires 32 MB aggregate storage cache or 4 GB of input data requires 64 MB aggregate storage cache. The cache incrementally increases until the maximum cache size is used or OS denies additional allocations.

To set the aggregate storage cache,
1. Select the application and right click.
2. Select *Edit Properties*.

3. Select the General tab.
4. Set the value next to *Pending cache size limit (MB)*:

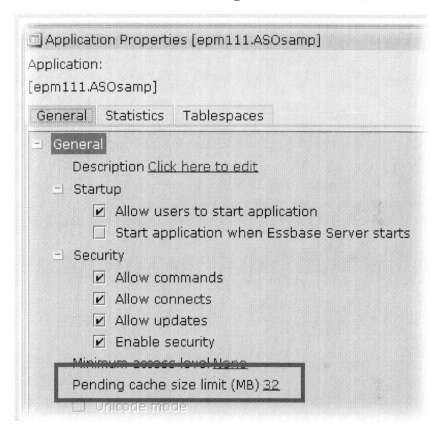

5. Click *Apply*.

The cache size is affected by the number of application threads. Essbase uses multiple threads to divide the aggregate storage cache during materialization. If you increase the number of threads specified in configuration settings, then you should increase the aggregate storage cache, increasing the cache by the same factor as the threads.

Multithreading

Helpful
Info

Essbase is a multithreaded application. Multi-threading ensures high performance in client server environments. The default number of threads is related to the number of licensed ports. You can change the number of threads used by the Essbase agent or Essbase server using AGENTTHREADS, AGTSVRCONNECTIONS, and SERVERTHREADS settings in the Essbase.cfg. More on the Essbase agent, Essbase server, and Essbase.cfg later in the book.

To see how effective the cache is being used, view cache statistics in Administration Services console under *Database Properties >> Statistics*. Look for the following cache statistics:

- Cache Hit Ratio
- Current Cache size
- Current Cache size limit

The Cache Hit Ratio tells you how often Essbase goes to the cache (or memory) to present data to the user. You want this number to be close to 1.

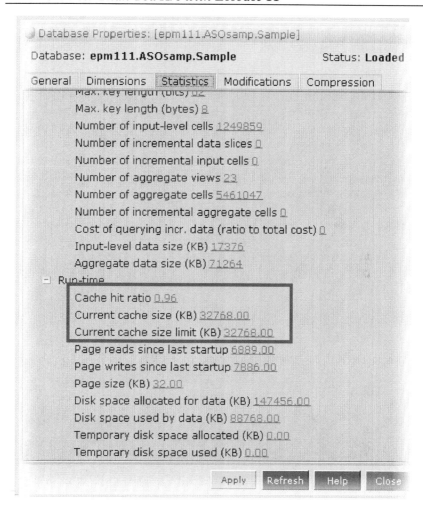

OUTLINE PAGING

Essbase preloads part of the outline into memory (instead of loading the entire outline into memory). This "paging" feature enables Essbase to handle very large outlines (e.g. 10 million or more members - that is a lot of juggling customers). The outline is organized into pages of 8192 bytes.

ASO outlines may be bigger than BSO outline files and these large outlines can increase data retrieval time. The factors in determining outline size include:

- Numbers of members
- Available memory for Essbase
- Amount of memory in Essbase allocated for other uses

- Amount of memory required for each member
- Operating System

So is there a way to optimize Outline paging when you encounter outline performance issues? The Outline Paging Cache is used to achieve balance between memory usage and retrieval times. An algorithm using the least recently used members takes place. Pages loaded into the cache will stay there until Essbase has to make room for new pages. Content is organized based on locality (siblings are probably on the same page). This means faster retrievals for related sets of data.

The default cache is set to 8 MB. The page size is 8192 bytes so 1024 pages can be loaded into the cache at once.

To determine the outline paging cache hit rate, run the following MaxL statement:

```
query application appname get opg_cache statistics;
```

If the hit rate is < 90%, then increase the OPGCACHESIZE. You will set the OPGCACHESIZE in the essbase.cfg (the maximum size is 500,000 KB):

```
OPGCACHESIZE 12280
```

Note!

The Essbase.cfg is the main configuration file for the Essbase server. We discuss this file and its settings in more detail in the Essbase Administration section later in the book.

Restart Essbase so the updated cache setting can take effect.

Two other Essbase.cfg settings can be used to help build *really* big outlines. PRELOADMEMBERNAMESPACE turns off the preloading of the member namespace. PRELAODALIASNAMESPACE – turn off preloading of the alias tablespace. By default, Essbase will try to load the member and alias namespaces into memory. If there's not enough memory, they are left on the disk and paged in and out on demand. Turn off these settings as a TEMPORARY measure when you need to build a really, really big outline. Turn the settings back on after the outline is built.

COMPACT THE OUTLINE

Just when you thought there wasn't any other possible way to improve ASO performance, we introduce our last ASO tip, compact the ASO outline. When you delete a member in an ASO outline, the member is marked as deleted but remains in the file. So the outline file grows as members are added and deleted. Compacting the outline will restructure the outline. It will not clear data. Users and processes must be out of the system during outline compacting.

1. To compact an outline, right click on the outline and select *Compact:*

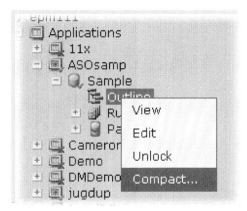

1. Choose foreground or background.
2. Click *OK*.

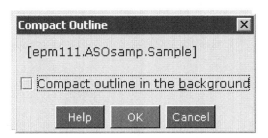

And with that, we'll conclude the "Become an Essbase Administrator" section. You made it! But we're not done yet. We're not satisfied with making you a knowledgeable Essbase administrator who can build ASO databases. We want to make you a *Master* Essbase administrator, fully fluent in both ASO and BSO speak. Hold on to your seats as we drive headlong into Essbase block storage option databases.

.

Block Storage Option (BSO) Databases

Chapter 16:
Create a BSO Application

You now know ASO backwards and forwards, but what is this BSO thing about which we continue to speak? Back in the ASO vs. BSO chapter, you learned the high level differences and heard some new concepts like dense and sparse. The biggest thing to recall from that chapter was that BSO databases provide complex calculation capabilities and write back to any level. So let's explore the other ~~white meat~~ Essbase database type and create a BSO application for our juggling wolverine company.

We want to create a budgeting application that allows users to input budgets by customer category and then we'll allocate those budget numbers down to the individual customer. That's not possible with ASO but it's very easy with BSO. Let's get it started in here (background music: *Let's Get It Started* by the Black Eyed Peas).

CREATE A BSO APPLICATION

To create a BSO application and database in Administration Services (this should sound familiar),

1. Select *File >> New*.
2. Choose Block Storage Application:

3. Select the Essbase Server and specify a new application name *Jugbud*:

4. Click *OK*. You now have an application with no databases within it. This is completely useless, so don't stop now.
5. Right click on the application you just created and select *Create Database*.
6. Your server and application should already be selected, so type in a new database name *Jugbud*.
7. Click *OK*.

That's it. The same steps as the creating the ASO application and database. From there you can open the outline and begin adding members manually if you would like, just like ASO outlines.

Create a block storage application called JugBud.JugBud.

Try It!

DEFINE DIMENSION TYPES AND MEMBER PROPERTIES

We've already covered dimension types and member properties earlier in the book. Most of the same dimension types and member properties that were applicable to aggregate storage option databases are also applicable to block storage option databases. Please refer to the earlier chapter, Create an ASO

Application, for more details on dimension types and member properties.

To recap,

Dimension Types

Dimensions can be assigned a dimension type which enables specific functionality. Valid dimension types for BSO databases:

- Accounts
- Date Time
- Time
- Country (BSO only)
- Currency (BSO only)
- Attribute

Currency and country dimension types are used for the currency module which you shouldn't really use. You can define logic for currency conversions a bit more effectively yourself (email us at info@interrel.com to learn more – we've hit our page limit on content for this book).

Note!

Attribute dimensions in block storage databases can vary over other dimensions (more on this in just a bit).

Try It!

Add the following dimensions to your outline:
- Period (Time dimension type)
- Accounts (Accounts dimension type)
- Customer
- Scenario
- Year

Consolidation Operators

Consolidation operators tell Essbase how to roll up the members in the outline. Valid consolidation operators for BSO databases:

- Addition (+)
- Subtraction (-)
- Multiplication (*)
- Division (/)
- Percent (%)
- No consolidate (~)

- Never consolidate (^)

Note! Never consolidate (^) will not aggregate a member up across any dimension in the Essbase database (e.g. prices, index) while no consolidate (~) will not aggregate a member up for the dimension in which it resides but will aggregate for all other dimensions (e.g. Actual, Budget).

Data Storage Properties

The Data Storage property tells Essbase how the member should be stored. Valid data storage options include:
- Store: Store the data value with the member.
- Never share: Do not allow members to be shared implicitly.
- Label Only: Create members for navigation and grouping. These members usually won't make sense from a logical consolidation standpoint.
- Shared Member: Share data between two or more members.
- Dynamic Calc and Store: Do not calculate the data value until a user requests it, but store the data value immediately after the retrieval. (Applicable to BSO only)
- Dynamic Calc: Do not calculate the data value until a user requests it, and then discard the data value. (Applicable to BSO only)

Let's spend a bit more time on the data storage properties for BSO databases as they differ slightly from ASO.

When should you set a member to *Store* in a BSO database? When you will need to load data or input data to that member. Set a member to store if that member has a large number of children. Most of the times, your large sparse dimensions will be set to Store. (What is a sparse dimension? We'll get there in just a few sections.)

When should you set a member to Dynamic Calc? In most cases, use the *Dynamic calc* property for your variances, ratios, and averages. You can also set upper level members of a hierarchy to dynamic calc when that member has just a few children. Often times you set upper levels of the Accounts and Time dimensions (and other dense dimensions) to Dynamic Calc to help reduce your database size.

When should you use Dynamic Calc and Store? Virtually never, actually. We recommend sticking to Dynamic Calc unless you have little used sparse members with very complicated formulas.

When should you use Never Share? When you have a parent that only has one child. Essbase has a built in feature called Implicit Sharing, a mischievous function that can cause confusion in your Essbase databases. Essbase tries to be smart for us. When a parent only has one child, the values for both the parent and the child will always be the same, right? So Essbase decides to only store one value, the child value, which reduces your database size. But this causes issues in loading or inputting data for the parent, who dynamically pulls the data value from the child.

When should you use Label Only? Use Label Only for members like "Scenario", "Ratios", or "Drivers", members whose sole purpose in life is to organize the dimension and hierarchy: members for which it never makes sense to add their children together. A member marked as Label Only will automatically pull the value of its first child when referenced. Because of this, when we make a member Label Only, we will often make its first child have a plus and the other children have a tilde to designate that only the first child is rolling to the member. This is entirely to help indicate what's going on in Essbase to a user who might not know that a Label Only member pulls the value from its first child.

In this example below, it makes no sense to add Actual and Budget together, so we flag Scenario as Label Only:

Expense Reporting

The Expense Reporting property is a new property, only available for block storage option databases. It is a simple flag that tells downstream calculations and reports whether a positive variance is good or bad. If you're over your target on revenue, everyone is happy. Of course, the opposite is true when you spend too much on Office Supplies. Well, not everyone will be upset but you don't want to be making enemies in the Finance Department when it comes time for them to cut you the bonus check for those positive-variance Revenues, right?

Let's walk you through an example. If you budget $1,000,000 in revenue and you make $1,100,000, that's a favorable variance of $100,000. Expenses are quite the opposite: if you budget $1,000,000 in marketing expenses and you spend $1,100,000, that's an unfavorable variance of $100,000. In general, you want expense data to have lower actuals than budget.

To allow for this, Essbase uses the property called Expense Reporting. Tag all of your expense accounts with Expense Reporting and Essbase will calculate the variance correctly when using the @VAR or @VARPER functions. Essbase will show a positive variance when Actual data is higher than Budget for revenue or metric accounts. Essbase will show a negative variance for those expense accounts tagged with the "Expense Reporting" property:

	Jan	FY2007		
	Actual	Budget	Variance	
Net_Rev	100	75	25	
Op_Expense	100	75	-25	
Op_Income	#Missing	#Missing	#Missing	

Set the Variance Reporting Expense property to True for all measures where budget should be higher than actual.

The Expense Reporting tag is found on the first tab of the Member Properties window, second from the bottom:

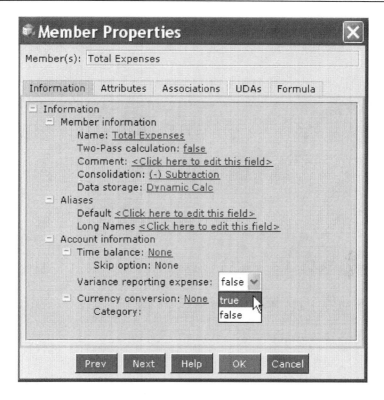

Member Formulas

Block storage option databases also allow member formulas but they use calc script syntax versus MDX. You may notice a few immediate differences between calc script syntax and MDX syntax – the use of double quotes around member names (vs. brackets) and the inclusion of semicolons.

Mathematical functions define and return values based on selected member expressions. These functions include most standard statistical functions. An example with a mathematical function would be the member formula for the "Variance":

```
@VAR (Actual, Budget);
```

Conditional operators allow tests based on criteria. The member formula to calculate "Commission" is:

```
IF (Sales > 1000)
     Sales * .02;
ELSE
     10;
ENDIF
```

In English-speak, if Sales is greater than 1000, then Commission is equal to Sales times 2 percent, otherwise Commission is equal to 10.

Functions can also be used in member formulas. The member formula for the member "Market Share" uses an index function:

```
Sales % @PARENTVAL (Markets, Sales);
```

In other words, Market Share is equal to the Sales for the current member as a percent of the current member's parent data value for the Markets dimension.

The member formula for the member "Mar YTD" uses a financial function:

```
@PTD(Jan:Mar);
```

The member formula for "Payroll" shows how to use conditional or Boolean criteria:

```
IF (@ISIDESC (East) OR @ISIDESC (West))
     Sales * .15;
ELSEIF (@ISIDESC(Central))
     Sales * .11;
ELSE
     Sales * .10;
ENDIF
```

To put it in English, for all of the members under and including East and West, Payroll is equal to Sales times 15 percent, for all members under and including Central, Payroll is equal to Sales times 11 percent, and for all other members, Payroll is equal to Sales times 10 percent.

Tip!

Don't forget, since Essbase 9, you can use substitution variables in member formulas.

Tip!

The syntax for member formulas is almost identical to the syntax used in calc scripts. The calc script chapter provides more detail on Essbase calc syntax.

Note!

Member formulas must end with a semicolon. If the member name has spaces, you must enclose the member name in double quotes.

Two Pass

The two pass member property is another BSO only member property. Two Pass tells Essbase to "come back and calculate this member at the end." Why is this important? Let's look at an example.

The Accounts dimension is calculated first (we'll learn this shortly) so Profit % is calculated based on input sales and profit. Once we roll up the Time dimension, the monthly Profit % is added together and placed in Q1's Profit %:

	A	B	C	D	E	F
1		Jan	Feb	Mar	Q1	
2	Profit	100	100	100	300	
3	Sales	1000	1000	1000	3000	
4	Profit %	10%	10%	10%	30%	
5						

Hmmm... something's not right there. We want Profit % to recalculate once the quarter and year totals for Profit and sales have been calculated. Tag the Profit % member with the two pass member property and Essbase circles back to calculate the correct percent after it's finished everything else:

	A	B	C	D	E	F
1		Jan	Feb	Mar	Q1	
2	Profit	100	100	100	300	
3	Sales	1000	1000	1000	3000	
4	Profit % (tagged as two pass calc)	10%	10%	10%	10%	
5						

We accomplished this same thing using solve order in ASO databases but solve order does not exist for BSO databases.

Time Balance Attributes

Just as you did in an ASO database, you can assign a Time Balance tag to Accounts members, telling Essbase how the specific account member should roll up the dimension tagged Time. For example, you probably would tag Headcount as Time Balance Last – Skip Missing (versus summing up the headcount values of months to quarters to years). "Skip" options tell Essbase what to do in the event of a missing or zero value. The one difference in Time Balance between ASO and BSO databases is that BSO databases allow you to skip None, Missing, Zeroes or Missing and Zeroes. ASO databases only allow you to skip Missing values.

UDAs

You can create user defined attributes for members like you did in aggregate storage databases. UDAs work the same way, providing a way to reference a group of members for analysis, calculations, or data loading.

Edit Member Properties

By now you are the expert in setting member properties, but just in case, to edit member properties,

1. Right click on the member.
2. Select *Edit Member Properties.*
3. The Member Properties window will display (like an old friend):

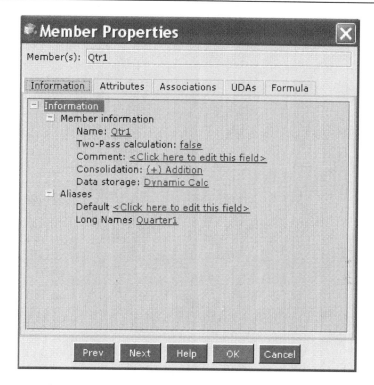

4. Assign the various member properties per your design on the Information tab or UDAs tab or Formula tab.

5. Click *OK* when you are finished.

Build the following members and hierarchies into the JugBud outline.

Try It!

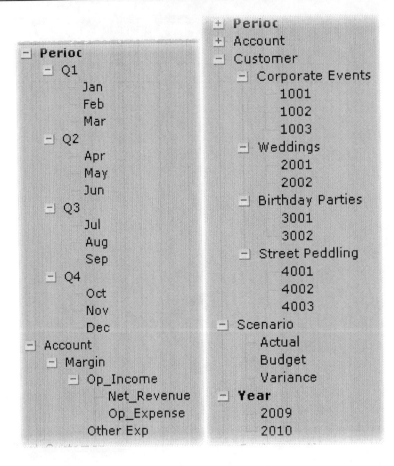

Let's define the member properties for the jugbud.otl. Set the following member properties:

Try It!

Member	Property
Account	Dynamic Calc, Accounts Dimension Type
Op_Expense	-
	Expense Reporting
Other Exp	-
	Expense Reporting
Op_Income	Dynamic Calc
Margin	Dynamic Calc
Q1, Q2, Q3, Q4	Dynamic Calc
Period	Dynamic Calc, Time

	Dimension Type
Scenario	Label Only ~
Actual, Budget	~
Variance	Dynamic Calc
	Two Pass
	@VAR(Actual, Budget);

```
Outline: jugbud (Active Alias Table: Default)
  - Period Time <4> (Active Dynamic Time Series Mer
    + Q1 (+) <3> (Dynamic Calc)
    + Q2 (+) <3> (Dynamic Calc)
    + Q3 (+) <3> (Dynamic Calc)
    + Q4 (+) <3> (Dynamic Calc)
  - Account Accounts <1> (Dynamic Calc)
    - Margin (+) <2> (Dynamic Calc)
      - Op_Income (+) <2> (Dynamic Calc)
          Net_Revenue (+)
          Op_Expense (-) (Expense Reporting)
          Other Exp (+) (Expense Reporting)
  + Customer <4> {Customer Manager}
  - Scenario <3> (Label Only)
      Actual (~)
      Budget (~)
      Variance (~) [Formula: @VAR(Actual,Budget);]
```

Dynamic Time Series

Dynamic time series (DTS) allows end users to retrieve 'to-date' totals from the Essbase BSO database. To enable DTS, you must tag a dimension Time. You then assign a description to the generation, identifying whether year-to-date, quarter-to-date, history-to-date, etc. should be used.

To set DTS,

1. Open the Outline Editor.
2. Right click and select *Dynamic Time Series*:

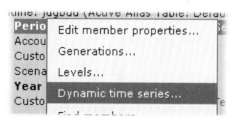

3. Check the box for the series you wish to enable.

4. Specify the generation number that correlates to the appropriate series.
   E.g., if quarters are at generation 2, then Q-T-D is 2.
5. Add a name if desired (this can be used in report queries):

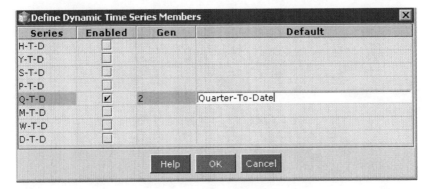

Series	Enabled	Gen	Default
H-T-D	☐		
Y-T-D	☐		
S-T-D	☐		
P-T-D	☐		
Q-T-D	☑	2	Quarter-To-Date
M-T-D	☐		
W-T-D	☐		
D-T-D	☐		

6. Click *OK*.

Try It!

For the JugBud outline, define DTS so that we can perform Q-T-D analysis.

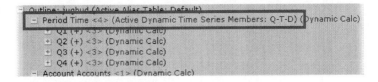

Note!

Dynamic Time Series is only available for BSO databases.

DEFINE A VARYING ATTRIBUTE DIMENSION

We've already learned that reducing the number of dimensions is important in Essbase, especially BSO databases. So one alternative that we can use to add dimensionality without increasing the database size is attribute dimensions. Attribute dimensions function like regular dimensions in that you can build hierarchies, add aliases, and perform cross tab reporting. They are different than a regular dimension in that they are dynamically calculated and tied to a base dimension. (For more information on attribute dimensions, check out the Attributes chapter earlier in the book.) A regular associated attribute member cannot vary across dimensions: it is tied to its base member. However, in 11x for block storage option databases, you can now build in varying attribute dimensions.

A varying attribute dimension is a dimension that can change across one or more other dimensions in a BSO database. This new Essbase 11 feature allows you to store data for situations where attributes can change: for example, an employee hierarchy (over time) or a product packaging hierarchy (over different markets). End users can analyze data based on a current view point or historical point in time (AKA differing perspectives). The dimensions for which an attribute varies are called the independent dimensions.

Yes, varying attributes are awesome. The main disadvantage is that varying attribute dimensions are available for block storage applications only.

To define varying attributes, you must first enable them for the database.

1. Open the JugBud outline.
2. Select the *Properties* tab.
3. To enable varying attributes, set *Varying attributes enabled* to true:

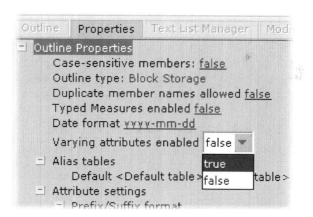

4. Save the outline.

Our juggling wolverine company has two customer managers, Larry and Bob, who can manage different customers at different times (in these trying economic times, constant reorganization is not only inevitable but fun). We need to set up a varying attribute called Customer Manager.

5. Right click on Customer and select *Add Sibling*.

6. Type in the new attribute dimension name *Customer Manager.*

7. Right click on *Customer Manager,* select Edit Member Properties.

8. Set the Dimension type to *Attribute* and attribute type to *Text.*

9. Click *OK.* (If you receive the following message, click *Yes* to continue.)

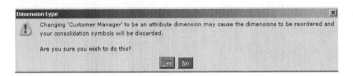

10. Add two children to the dimension: "Larry" and "Bob: The dimension should look as follows:

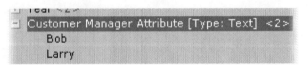

11. Right click on the Customer dimension member and select *Edit member properties.*

12. Select the Attributes tab.

13. Select Customer Manager and click the *Assign* button.

14. Once Customer Manager has been associated to the Customer dimension, select *Customer Manager.*

15. Check *Period and Year* as the independent dimensions (the dimension for which the attribute will vary):

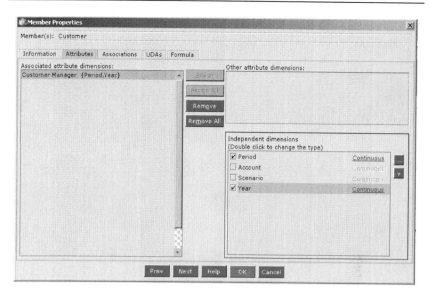

Note we've defined the Customer Manager attribute to vary over Periods and Year. This allows us to define a range that spans two dimensions. (e.g. the start range as 2008 Jan and the end range as 2009 Jul.) You will also notice the independent dimensions are highlighted in bold font in the outline editor:

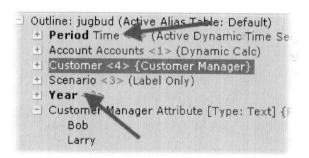

16. Click *OK* from the Customer Member Properties window.

17. Select customer member 1001.
18. Right click and select *Edit Member Properties*.
19. Select the Associations tab.
20. Under Available Attributes, expand Customer Manager and select *Bob*.
21. Click the *Add Range* button:

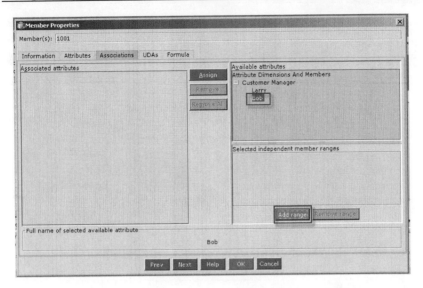

Next you define the start range and an end range (in this case month). In our example, Bob manages 1001 from January 2009 through September 2009 and Larry takes over that customer beginning in October 2009. (Bob was tired of sitting the sidelines as a wolverine sales manager so he grabbed some flaming juggling wolverines at the OpenWorld event and attempted to join the ranks of wolverine jugglers. Let's just say it didn't quite work out for Bob. Juggling wolverines is much more difficult than it looks, especially when they are on fire.)

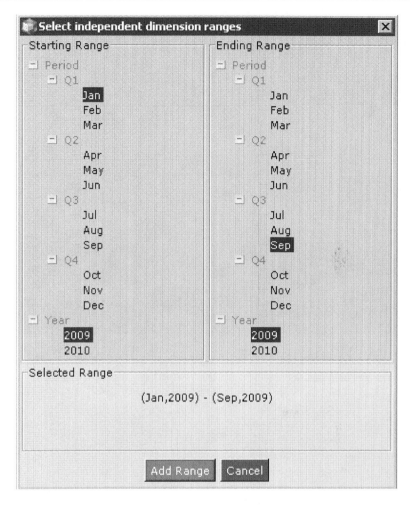

22. Click *Add Range*. The Add Independent Dimension Ranges window will close and you are returned to the Member Properties window.
23. Click the *Assign* button in the Member Properties window to assign the newly added range for Bob.
24. Select Larry.
25. Click the *Add range* button.
26. Define the start range as Oct 2009 and the end range as Dec 2010.
27. Click *Add Range*.
28. Click the *Assign* button.
    The end result should look like the following:

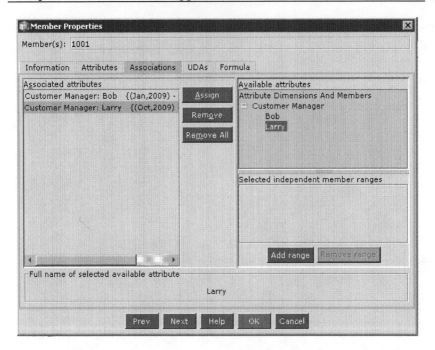

29. Assign Bob as the Customer Manager for 1002 Jan 2009 – Oct 2009 and Larry as the Customer Manger Nov 2009 – Dec 2010.
30. Validate and save the jugbud outline.

Varying Attribute Dimension Rules

Helpful Info

- Attributes can only vary along the same level.
- Continuous dimensions must act as a single dimension – e.g. Year and Period
- Independent members must be stored, level 0 members

You're ready to analyze the Customer Manager in Smart View. Or are you? We probably need to load some data first. How do you load data for block storage databases? Does BSO require a separate calculation step? Now that you've successfully created an outline with dimensions, hierarchies, and members, built a varying attribute dimension and Bob has recovered from the flaming wolverine incident, we can move on to other important block storage concepts like building dimensions, loading and calculating data.

BUILD DIMENSIONS AND LOAD DATA

We're happy to say the process to build dimensions and load data for block storage option databases is the same as the process for aggregate storage option databases.

Dimensions are built from text, spreadsheet, or relational sources with rules files using generation, level or parent/child formats.

Data is loaded from text or relational sources using free form if the source is in the appropriate layout or using rules files. However, some ASO concepts like slices, trickle feeds and load buffers are not possible in block storage databases.

Try It!

Create a text file (or email us at info@interrel.com for a copy of ours) and load some data for the JugBud database.

For more information on building dimensions, please refer to the chapter "Add Thousands of Members" and for more information on loading data, please refer to the chapter "Load Data."

DENSE AND SPARSE

Now that we've created our base BSO outline, we need to review some key concepts related to the Essbase BSO structure (not applicable to ASO databases). Get ready to impress your coworkers with complicated concepts like "dense" and "sparse" and "optimized block structure".

First, let's define member combination. A member combination is the intersection of members from each dimension. See the following examples of member combinations for the Sample.Basic outline:

Year Time (Active Dynamic Time Series Members: H-T-D, Q-T-D) (Dynamic Calc)
- Qtr1 (+) (Dynamic Calc)
- Qtr2 (+) (Dynamic Calc)
- Qtr3 (+) (Dynamic Calc)
- Qtr4 (+) (Dynamic Calc)

Measures Accounts (Label Only)
- Profit (+) (Dynamic Calc)
- Inventory (~) (Label Only)
- Ratios (~) (Label Only)

Product {Caffeinated, Intro Date, Ounces, Pkg Type}
- 100 (+) (Alias: Colas)
- 200 (+) (Alias: Root Beer)
- 300 (+) (Alias: Cream Soda)
- 400 (+) (Alias: Fruit Soda)
- Diet (~) (Alias: Diet Drinks)

Market {Population}
- East (+) (UDAS: Major Market)
- West (+)

Example member combinations:

- Qtr1->Profit->100->East->Actual
- Year->Profit->100->East->Actual
- Jan->Sales->100-10->New York->Budget
- Jan->Sales->100->New York->Budget

Tip! The symbol "->" is known as a cross dimensional operator in Essbase (more on this later). For now, when you see the "->", think of the word "at". We are referencing the data value at Qtr1 at Profit at 100 at East at Actual.

Dense data is data that occurs often or repeatedly across the intersection of all member combinations. For example, you will most likely have data for all periods for most member combinations. You will most likely have data for most of your accounts for member combinations. Time and accounts are naturally dense.

Sparse data is data that occurs only periodically or sparsely across member combinations. Product, Market, and Employee dimensions are usually sparse:

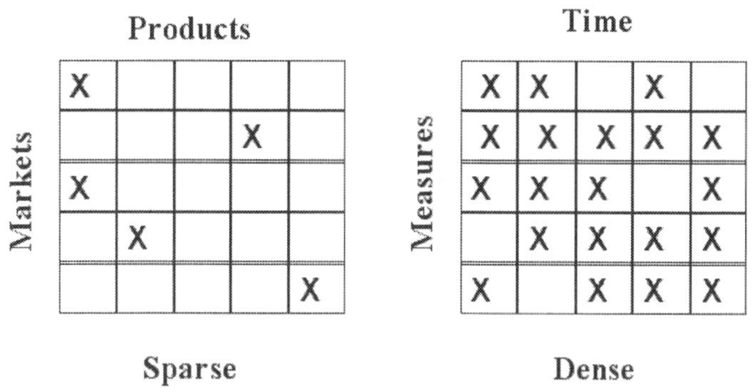

Products   Time

Markets	X					
				X		
	X					
		X				
					X	

Sparse

Measures	X	X		X	
	X	X	X	X	X
	X	X	X		X
		X	X	X	X
	X		X	X	X

Dense

You as the administrator will assign a dense / sparse setting to each dimension. This will dictate how the Essbase database is structured.

To define dense or sparse for a dimension,
1. In Administration Services, open the outline.
2. Select the Properties tab.
3. Scroll down to the Data Storage section:

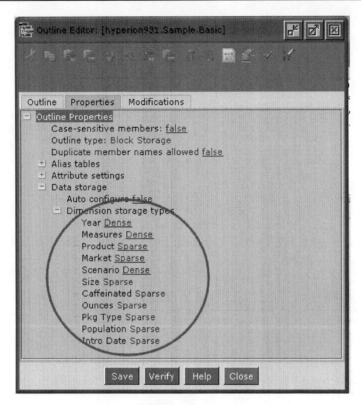

4. Choose the Dense and Sparse settings from the drop down box for each dimension:

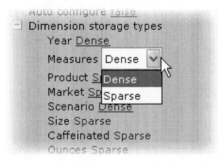

Tip!

Disable Autoconfiguration. Autoconfiguration of dense and sparse dimension provides only an approximation and cannot take in account the nature of the data loaded into the database or the requirements of calc scripts.

Set the following dense / sparse settings for the dimensions in jugbud.otl):

- Account: Dense
- Period: Dense
- Scenario: Sparse
- Customer: Sparse
- Year: Sparse

Try It!

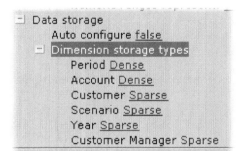

Why can't you change the dense / sparse setting for the Customer Manager dimension? If you answered "customer manager is an attribute dimension and attribute dimensions are always sparse", pat yourself on the back. You're coming along, my fledgling administrator.

BLOCK STRUCTURE

The Essbase database is composed of a number of blocks. A block is created for each intersection of the sparse dimensions. In the example below, Market and Product are sparse. See a block for each sparse member combination in the example below:

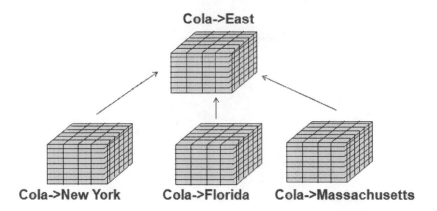

Cola->East

Cola->New York   Cola->Florida   Cola->Massachusetts

There are four types of blocks:

- Input blocks are blocks where data is loaded or input.
- Calculated blocks are blocks that are created through consolidation or calculation.
- Level zero blocks are blocks that are created from the level zero members of all dimensions.
- Upper-level blocks are all blocks that contain at least one upper level member (non-level zero).

Each block is made up of cells. These cells are created for each intersection of the dense dimensions. In the example below, Time, Measures, and Scenario are dense dimensions. See the cells for each dense member combination in the example below (we've highlighted one specific cell Profit at Jan at Actual):

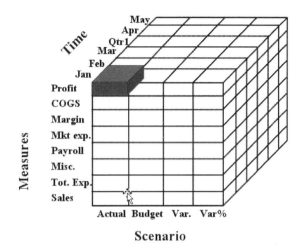

OUTLINE CONSOLIDATION

Essbase is built to perform outline consolidations. You assigned a consolidation attribute to each member that tells Essbase how to perform the consolidation, whether it should add to the total, subtract from the total, and so forth. Unary operators include +, -, *, /, %, and ~. The consolidation will use these operators and follow the path of the hierarchies for each dimension.

So what does outline consolidation and dense/sparse have to do with each other? Essbase will perform dense calculations first and then sparse calculations. The default calculation order for Essbase is the following:

- First, Accounts
- Second, Time
- Third, remaining dense dimensions
- Fourth, remaining sparse dimensions
- Two Pass Calculation (covered in a later chapter)

Let's follow the path of an Essbase consolidation to help you better understand. In the example below, the highlighted cells indicate cells loaded with data.

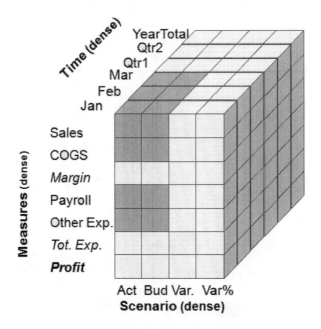

Next you see those cells populated with the Accounts dimension calculation (see Profit, Margin, Tot. Exp).

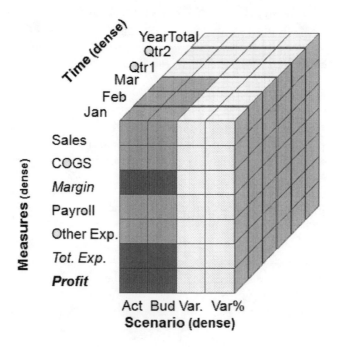

Finally the cells in the upper portion of the block represent those cells populated with the Time dimension calculation (Qtr1, Qtr2, YearTotal).

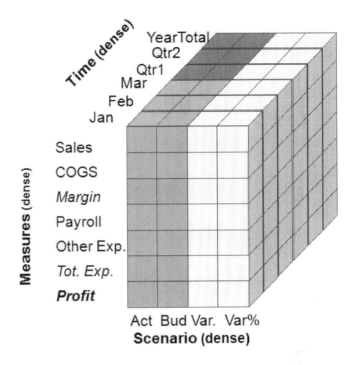

Why doesn't the variance and variance % members show calculated data values? 99% of the time you will tag these two members with the dynamic calc property so data will never be stored and in most cases, you won't need to calculate the Scenario dimension (and in most cases, this is probably a sparse dimension instead of a dense dimension but we're getting a bit ahead of ourselves).

Here is another view of this dense calculation. Data is loaded to Sales and COGS members for each month. We are looking at the block for Vermont, Cola, and Actual (there's that cross dimensional symbol that means "at").

Vermont -> Cola -> Actual

Accounts	Jan	Feb	Mar	Qtr1
Sales	124.71	119.43	161.93	
COGS	42.37	38.77	47.28	
Margin				

First we consolidate the Accounts dimension, calculating the Margin member.

Vermont -> Cola -> Actual

Accounts	Jan	Feb	Mar	Qtr1
Sales	124.71	119.43	161.93	
COGS	42.37	38.77	47.28	
Margin	82.34	80.66	114.65	

Next we consolidate the Time dimension, calculating the Qtr1 member.

Vermont -> Cola -> Actual

Accounts	Jan	Feb	Mar	Qtr1
Sales	124.71	119.43	161.93	406.07
COGS	42.37	38.77	47.28	128.42
Margin	82.34	80.66	114.65	277.65

Once the Dense calculation is complete, the sparse calculation is next. The Vermont -> Cola -> Actual block and the New York -> Cola -> Actual block are added together to create the East -> Cola -> Actual block.

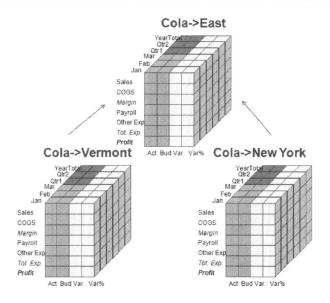

DEFAULT CALC

Unlike aggregate storage databases, block storage databases require a separate calculation step. The default calc is the simplest method for calculating Essbase databases, performing outline consolidations and calculating formulas as they appear in the outline. The default calc runs a "Calc All" calc script against the Essbase database.

Outline consolidations (sometimes called "unary operators") are those little plus, minus, divide, multiply, percent, and "no consolidate" signs that you place on individual members in the outline:

```
⊟Measures
  ⊟Profit (+)
    ⊞Margin (+)
    ⊞Total Expenses (-)
  ⊞Inventory (~)
```

In this snippet of Sample.Basic, you see that "Margin" has a plus sign next to it and "Total Expenses" has a minus sign. These are unary operators. When a default calculation occurs on Sample.Basic, the data in these two members will consolidate together and be saved in the Profit member. "Inventory" has a tilde next to it (AKA "No Consolidate") so it won't be added to the data from "Profit" and stored in Measures.

The other type of calculation that occurs during a default calculation is the members in the outline with formulas will have their formulas evaluated:

>   ⊟ **Ratios (~)**
>   ├ **Margin % (+) [Formula: Margin % Sales;]**
>   └ **Profit % (~) [Formula: Profit % Sales;]**

When the default calculation occurs, the formula on "Margin %" will evaluate and take margin as a percentage of sales.

Note!

In Sample.Basic, Margin %, Profit, and Measures are not actually stored members, so no data is really stored into these members.

To launch the default calc,

1. Select the database.
2. Right click and select *Execute Calculation*:

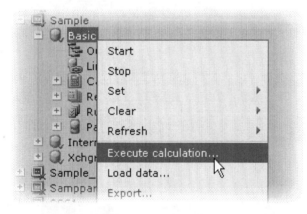

3. Select Default calc.
4. Check "Execute in Background" (this frees up the Administration Services console for other tasks):

Execute Database Calculation ☒

[hyperion931.Sample.Basic]

State: Data values have been modified since the last calculation

Calculation script

(default)
BudSet
MyCalc

☑ Execute in the background

| Help | OK | Cancel |

5.   Click *OK.*

Data will be consolidated for all dimensions and members.

Run the default calc for the wolverine juggling budget application.

Try It!

Our next chapter will introduce us to the powerful calculations that are possible with Essbase block storage option databases.

Chapter 17:
Calculate with Calc Scripts

In the previous chapter, we discussed using outline consolidations and member formulas. Quite often, these tools provide all the calculation power an application will need. However, as member formulas start to reference other levels or other dimensions, they can get very complex, very quickly. In Sample.Basic, the Budget member has no formula. Let's say you're in charge of setting goals for the remainder of the year. We don't want our goals to be reasonable or obtainable (else everyone would reach them), so we want to set every "Budget" member to be exactly fifty percent greater than the "Actual" number from last year. The problem is that this calculation would be very complex, and probably not a good thing to store directly in the outline as it may change frequently, so we'll need to override the default calculation. Calc scripts to the rescue...

WHAT IS A CALC SCRIPT?

At this point, you're probably asking yourself "What the heck is a calc script?" If you're not, then you're skipping the headings that introduce each section. A calc script is short for "calculation script" and it allows you to override the standard outline calculations and take complete control of how your database derives its numbers. While most of the time calc scripts are run at regular intervals to do simple things like aggregate subsets of your database, they can also be run sporadically such as at the start of budgeting season when you want to run your allocation processes with each what-if iteration.

A calc script is really just a sequential series of commands, equations, and formulas. It is stored in a standard text file with a .CSC extension, so you can even open them in Notepad if you want to. Here's the calc script that will set all of your budget values to 50% above your actuals:

```
/* Creates Initial Budget */
SET UPDATECALC OFF;

CLEARDATA Budget;
Budget = Actual * 1.5;
CALC ALL;
```

You might have noticed that this calc script actually does a few things beyond just creating the budget, but we'll get to those in due time.

There are a lot of reasons to use a calc script. If you're not happy with the order that Essbase uses to calculate the members and dimensions, a calc script can easily override the default order. If you don't want to calculate the entire database, a calc script can be written to only calculate the current month. If you want to clear data or copy data from one place to another, calc scripts can do the job. Want to create formulas that aren't in the outline? Calc scripts are there for you. Calc scripts will even let you perform allocations and multi-pass calculations. When one of the end-users passes you a multi-stage allocation calculation that would make most Excel gurus run home crying to their mommies, you can just tie on your cape and write an Essbase Calc Script to save the day.

CREATE A CALC SCRIPT

Normally, people edit their calc scripts in Administration Services. It is possible to create and modify calc scripts in your favorite text editor, but only nerds do this. Since I'm a nerd, I'm completely okay with that. [Other Author's Note: Edward wrote that last line. I, Tracy McMullen, am definitely not a nerd (not that there's anything wrong with that).]

There are some definite advantages to using your own text editor. Text editors tend to let you see more lines at once, allow better find and replace functionality, have better line numbering, and provide greater printing options than Administration Services' built-in Calc Script Editor. If you do create your calc script in an external editor, it is very easy to copy and paste the body into Administration Services, or you can also save your calc script as a text file in the appropriate database directory (when you do this, remember to save the file with a .CSC extension).

My First Calc Script

For now, let's pretend that you're not a nerd for a second and use Administration Services to create your first calc script.

1. In Administration Services, select the database.
2. Right click on the database and select *Create* >> *Calculation Script*:

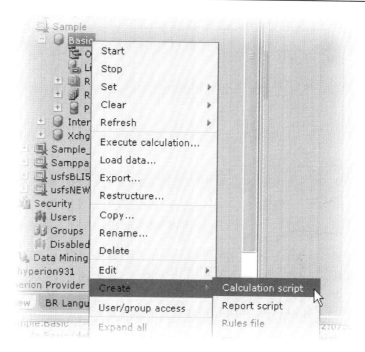

You can also create a calc script by going to the menu and choosing *File >> New >> Scripts >> Calc Script Editor*.

Tip!

3. The Calculation Script Editor window will display:

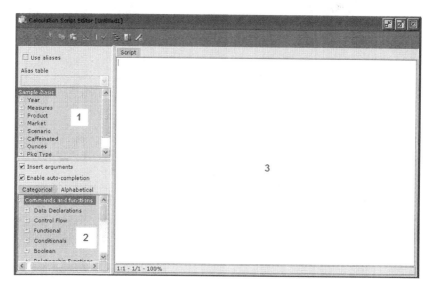

This editor has three main panes:

1. Outline. This pane helps you to select members from the outline and add them automatically to the calc script being edited.

2. Functions. This pane lets you select functions and commands and add them to the calc script being edited. The check boxes above this pane determine if arguments to the functions and commands will be inserted as well.

3. Data entry. This is where you actually type your calc script. While you could live without panes one and two (though it would be a royal pain), all of the power of calc scripts is entered into pane three.

The calc editor (as we'll call it from now on) has a toolbar at the top of the screen just below the menu:

While most of the buttons are the same ones you'd see in fancy Windows applications like Notepad, the rightmost three icons are calc editor specific. The check mark icon validates the syntax of your calc script. The outline icon associates an outline with your calc script. You'll need to do this if you don't see an outline in the outline pane (pane one, remember?). The final icon (the green down arrow next to a cash register receipt) runs the calc script that's open in pane 3. We're not going to be using the toolbar for right now, but go right ahead if you'd like to. It's a free country.

Note!

If you are in Cuba, then you're not actually in a free country but rather are under the ironclad grip of a communist dictatorship. Hopefully this won't stop you from using the toolbar, though.

Simplest Calc Script

While it's small in stature, it's powerful in nature. This single line will aggregate all of the dimensional hierarchies in your outline, calculate all of the formulas attached to members, perform time balancing on time balanced members, and does it all quickly using "intelligent calculation". We'll be covering more sophisticated calc scripts throughout this chapter, but you should always remember that no matter what we create, we'll always have the power of default.

```
CALC ALL;
```

Try It!

Create a new calc script for JugBud. Type "CALC ALL;" into the data entry pane. Go up to the menu and choose *Syntax >> Check Syntax* (or press *Ctrl-Y*). After you see the validation message, go up to the menu to *Options >> Execute Script* (or just press *F5*) to calculate JugBud.JugBud.

Calc Script Syntax

There are a few simple rules to follow when writing a calc script:

1. End every statement with a semicolon.
2. You do not talk about fight club.
3. You can break a statement onto multiple lines, but the end of the statement must have a semicolon.
4. If a member name contains spaces or starts with a number, surround it with "double quotes."
5. Start comments with /*
6. End comments with */
7. Statements must have a semicolon at the end.
8. Calc scripts are not case-sensitive.
9. Spaces between member names, commands, and functions do not matter.

There are many more rules, but these are the important ones that people tend to forget and then wonder for hours why their calc scripts aren't working. Here's a calc script that demonstrates several of those syntax rules:

```
/* Increase Opening Inventory */

"Opening Inventory" =
 "Opening InVeNtOrY" * 1.1;
```

Notice that the first line is a comment and it has the appropriate start and end characters. "Opening Inventory" has a space in the member name, so it's surrounded by double quotes. At the end of the entire statement (although not at the end of the comment), there's a semicolon. (You can tell the calc script language was written by a programmer, because only programmers end sentences with semicolons ;) Finally, observe that the second instance of Opening Inventory uses wacky cases just to show you that calc scripts are indeed *not* case-sensitive (unless you have explicitly told Essbase to behave otherwise).

SIMPLE CALCULATIONS

One of the simplest calculations you can perform is to tell Essbase to do the calculation for a single member. In a production system, this is the leanest, meanest calc script you can write, and is used when you want the script to finish in the quickest possible time.

Calculate Single Members

Imagine for a moment that the "Variance" member in Sample.Basic was stored and not dynamically calculated. We've just loaded data and we want to tell Essbase to calculate the formula on "Variance" and leave the rest of the outline alone. All we have to do is spell the member name and add a semicolon:

```
Variance;
```

How do you think you'd modify the calc script to calculate both Variance and Variance %? Hopefully it's something like this:

```
Variance;
"Variance %";
```

Notice that we have to use double quotes around "Variance %" due to the space in the name.

Tip!

If you want to be safe about it, put double quotes around all member names (even "Variance"). It doesn't hurt anything, and it does help you identify your member names quickly during troubleshooting exercises.

The technique of specifying a member name on a line by itself can be applied to members that do not have formulas but do have members aggregating into them. Imagine that we have just loaded data in Sample.Basic to the great state of Texas. Now we want to roll-up the Texas numbers to the top of the Market dimension:

```
South;
Market;
```

The nice thing about this script is that it doesn't bother rolling up totals that haven't changed. There's no Texas in the North (thankfully) so we know we don't need to modify the totals for North.

It's also possible to temporarily override the formula in the outline for a member. Let's return to our earlier example where we were an evil budget manager trying to set our budgets slightly higher than our actuals so no one could ever meet their numbers. To do this in a calc script, we just set up an equation with Budget on the left-side of the equal sign:

```
Budget = Actual * 1.5;
```

This script will set the budget to be 50% greater (notice that we're multiplying times 1.5) than actuals. If you're really in need of a raise, you could set the profit of your company to double what it should be:

```
Profit = Profit * 2;
```

Forgetting that the above calc script is probably illegal (thanks, Senator Sarbanes, wherever you are), it is interesting in that it puts the member "Profit" on both sides of the equation. It's also useful to understand that every time you run it Profit will double, so make sure you only run scripts like this once.

Tip!

There are better ways to increase your company's profitability than writing an illegal calc script.

Intelligent Calculation

Before we go any further, you have to learn the command to turn off intelligent calculation. Intelligent calculation allows Essbase to remember which blocks in the database need to be calculated based on new data coming in, and which haven't been impacted (and don't need calculation). Intelligent calculation is wonderful when you're running a default calc.

But (there is always a "but") intelligent calculation is the devil's work when you're running a calc script. Think about the budget calc script from earlier:

```
Budget = Actual * 1.5;
```

Do we want this calc script only to operate on so called "dirty blocks" or do we want all budgets throughout the entire system to be set 50% above actuals? If we leave intelligent calculation turned on during the running of our calc, Essbase will only calculate our new budgets for blocks that have recently been loaded with data. That's definitely not what we want, as some business units will escape with a sensible quota. We definitely can't have that!

The good news is that you don't have to turn off intelligent calculation for the entire database: you can just tell Essbase to ignore it during the calc script with this command:

```
SET UPDATECALC Off;
```

If you want to turn Intelligent Calc on again later in the script (maybe you want a "CALC ALL" command at the end of your script to calculate just the dirty blocks), include the command SET UPDATECALC ON; and everything past that point will work "intelligently. We recommend that you include the command to turn intelligent calculation off at the top of every calc script. If there's a case where you actually want to use it, go ahead and remove the line on a case-by-case basis. Leaving it out is courting disaster (and take it from a guy who dated disaster back in high school: you don't want to be courting her).

Calculate Entire Dimensions

As we've already mentioned, there's a simple command that you can include in a calc script that tells Essbase to evaluate all your member formulas and do all of your outline aggregation. While "CALC ALL" is great and powerful, there are times when you only want to calculate specific dimensions. For instance, what would we do if we just wanted to calculate Sample.Basic's Product dimension? We have a new command for this called "CALC DIM" (short for calculate dimension):

```
CALC DIM (Product);
```

This line calculates the Product dimension doing both outline aggregation (such as rolling all the Colas up into the parent value) and member formulas, if they exist for members in that dimension. If we want to calculate multiple dimensions using this command (say, Market and Product), just separate them with commas:

```
CALC DIM (Market, Product);
```

Remember how we said that "CALC DIM" not only does aggregation but also member formulas? Well, how many member formulas are there in the Market and Product dimensions? That's right - none, so "CALC DIM" is wasting time looking for formulas that you know aren't there. For dimensions that don't have formulas, there's a faster command that only does aggregation:

```
AGG (Market, Product);
```

Note!

"AGG" can only be used on sparse dimensions. If you have a dense dimension with no formulas that you only want to aggregate, you cannot use "AGG." You must use the "CALC DIM" command.

Calculate a Subset of Data

While calculating entire dimensions makes you feel very powerful, sometimes you just want to calculate a portion of the database. For instance, let's say you just updated your budgets but you didn't touch actuals. How could you ignore the Actual member? Well it turns out that there's an optional argument to the "CALC ALL" command called "EXCEPT". You use it to calculate everything except specific dimensions (DIM) or members (MBR). If we didn't want to calculate actuals, we'd say:

```
CALC ALL EXCEPT MBR (Actual);
```

It's also possible to list multiple members. Say that we didn't want to calculate Texas and New York (no offense to either state). We'd list the members separated by commas:

```
CALC ALL EXCEPT MBR (Texas, "New York");
```

If there's an entire dimension you don't want to calculate, replace "MBR" with "DIM":

```
CALC ALL EXCEPT DIM (Measures) ;
```

While this method may be fun at first, it's not nearly the most powerful method for limiting a calculation to a small portion of the database. Remembering Wolverine Jugglers, Incorporated, let's say we just loaded our budgets for next year for the street peddling we do on "System 9th Ave". Now we just want to calculate our accounts dimension for that one member, ignoring the rest of the database. The "CALC ALL EXCEPT..." method from above is really used to do the majority of a database and not just a smidgen, so we need a new command: "FIX" and its sister command "ENDFIX".

If we just want to calculate "System 9th Ave", we put this in double quotes after the "FIX" as such:

```
FIX ("System 9th Ave")
        CALC DIM (Account) ;
ENDFIX
```

Tip!

While the indentation is not necessary, it helps make it easier to see which commands the FIX affects.

"FIX" and "ENDFIX" are called sandwich commands because one command is like the top layer of bread and the other as the bottom with lots of things thrown in between. For instance, we could choose to calculate a few specific accounts:

```
FIX ("System 9th Ave")
        Op_Income;
        Margin;
ENDFIX
```

It's also possible to give list multiple members in a FIX as long as you separate them with commas:

```
FIX ("Essbase 7th Street", "System 9th Ave")
        Op_Income;
        Margin;
ENDFIX
```

Let's say you only loaded budgets to next year (which for our purposes, we will call "NY") for both the customers above. Here's one way to accomplish that by nesting one "FIX" within another:

```
FIX ("Essbase 7th Street", "System 9th Ave")
    FIX (NY)
            Op_Income;
            Margin;
    ENDFIX
ENDFIX
```

Note!

Each "FIX" must conclude with an "ENDFIX". It is not necessary to end a "FIX" or "ENDFIX" statement with a semicolon, but it doesn't hurt anything to use one either.

While this is a valid method, two "FIX"es are not necessary. You can list members from multiple dimensions within one "FIX" command, and this is the traditional way to do it:

```
FIX ("Essbase 7th Street", "System 9th Ave", NY)
    Op_Income;
    Margin;
ENDFIX
```

Tip!

Using "FIX" commands on sparse dimensions will speed up the performance of your calculations, because it limits the number of blocks pulled into memory to just what's listed in the "FIX" statement.

Two new commands were introduced in Essbase 9.3: EXCLUDE / ENDEXCLUDE (you may see these new commands referred to as "Unchanged Cells"). The new commands will calculate everything except what is defined in the EXCLUDE statement. Think opposite of a FIX / ENDFIX. The following calculation will calculate everything except Essbase 7th Street:

```
EXCLUDE ("Essbase 7th Street")
Calc Dim (Accounts, Product):
ENDEXCLUDE
```

Point to Another Member

While you're inside a "FIX" command, blocks outside are ignored. What if you want to refer to values from blocks that aren't being retrieved into memory? Surely there must be a way, you cry out of quiet desperation. Stop your incessant bawling, because there is indeed a way. It's called the cross-dimensional operator. Its job is to point to another member in the database and it looks like this:

```
->
```

Note! There is no "cross-dimensional operator" symbol on your keyboard. You type this in by pressing dash followed by a greater than symbol.

If we wanted to set net revenue for the Hyperion User Conference equal to net revenue for the Oracle User Conference, we could write a calc script that looks like this:

```
FIX ("Hyperion User Conference")
     Net_Rev = Net_Rev->"Oracle User Conference";
ENDFIX
```

What exactly is this doing? On the right-side of the equation, we told Essbase to get the value from net revenue for the Oracle User Conference. The left-side of the equation told it to put the result in net revenue, but which net revenue? Well as you see from the "FIX", we told Essbase to only calculate the Hyperion User Conference, so it will put the value into net revenue for the Hyperion User Conference.

Whenever possible, try to avoid cross-dimensional operators. They're unseemly and slow. For instance, if we had to add another account, we would have to include it within the "FIX":

```
FIX ("Hyperion User Conference")
 Net_Rev = Net_Rev->"Oracle User Conference";
 Op_Expense = Op_Expense->"Oracle User Conference";
ENDFIX
```

We could remove the need for the cross-dimensional operator (called "cross-dim" for short) by pivoting the customer and account dimensions. That is, we'll put the account dimension in the "FIX" and the customer dimension inside the "FIX":

```
FIX (Net_Rev, Op_Expense)
  "Hyperion User Conference" =
      "Oracle User Conference";
ENDFIX
```

This is much easier to read, and more flexible as well. It's obvious now that we're focusing on two specific accounts and setting one conference to be equal to another.

Tip!

If you find yourself repeating a cross-dim to the same member, it might be possible to pivot a dimension as above to remove the need for the cross-dim.

It is also possible to string cross-dims together to point to more and more specific intersections in the database:

```
FIX ("Hyperion User Conference", CY)
  Net_Rev = Net_Rev->NY->"Oracle User Conference";
ENDFIX
```

Net_Rev->NY->"Oracle User Conference" is called a "member combination. This is how the on-line documentation refers to the intersections of members via cross-dimensional operators.

Clear Data

Have you ever had one of those days when everything was going wrong and you just wanted to wipe out the entire day and start over? Fortunately, it's much easier to do this in Essbase than it is in reality. If we wanted to clear all of the data in our cube, we'd need the following little calc script:

```
SET UpdateCalc Off;
CLEARBLOCK All;
```

The first line (as no doubt you'll recall from a few pages ago) tells Essbase to operate on all blocks in the database and not just the dirty blocks. The second line tells Essbase to clear all the blocks in the database.

Try It!

Go ahead and create the calc script above and run it against JugBud (reload the data afterwards).

This script will run extremely quickly, and when it's finished, it will certainly appear that your database is empty, but if you look closely, it's not. Look out on your server's hard drive and you'll see that the .PAG file still exists. The reason that "CLEARBLOCK" runs like a paparazzi after Angelina Jolie is that all it does is blank out the index entries: the pointers to the corresponding blocks in the page file. Since it can no longer find the blocks, they might as well be blank.

Tip!

"CLEARBLOCK" will leave your database fragmented. Remember to defragment your database periodically to improve performance (see the Tune and Optimize chapter for more information on fragmentation).

A powerful way to use "CLEARBLOCK" is within a "FIX" statement. We want to blank out our Sample.Basic budget so that we can try again (our last attempt at the budget was horrendous, let's be honest), so we write this script:

```
FIX (Budget)
     CLEARBLOCK All;
ENDFIX
```

Remember that "CLEARBLOCK" will clear out entire blocks by removing the pointers, but in Sample.Basic, Budget is in the Scenario dimension and Scenario is a dense dimension. Since Budget is in every block in the database? Does it remove all the blocks? No, "CLEARBLOCK" is smart enough to only clear out index entries when the entire block is not being "FIX"ed on. In cases where just a portion of a block needs to be cleared, "CLEARBLOCK" will read the blocks into memory, clear out the necessary slices, and write the blocks back out to the page file. As such, "CLEARBLOCK" when used inside a "FIX" on a dense dimension is noticeably slower.

If you want to blank out a specific dense member, there's a simpler way than including a "CLEARBLOCK" inside a "FIX" on that dense member:

```
CLEARDATA Budget;
```

The "CLEARDATA" command allows you to specify a single member (in our case, budget). Do not use this on a sparse member, because the "CLEARBLOCK" command will always be faster. It is also possible to use a cross-dim operator on the right-side of a "CLEARDATA" command. If we wanted to clear out only our sales budget, we could write:

```
CLEARDATA Budget->Sales;
```

If you need to clear out multiple dense members, do not write your script like this:

```
CLEARDATA Actual;
CLEARDATA Budget;
```

This will result in multiple passes through your database since Essbase will not know to clear your data from actual and budget during a single pass. In this case, go back to using the "CLEARBLOCK" command within a "FIX":

```
FIX (Actual, Budget)
     CLEARBLOCK All;
ENDFIX
```

At various times, you'll want to make sure that all of the aggregated blocks in your database are cleared. For instance, if you're about to recalculate all of the totals in your database, it's faster if Essbase doesn't have to read the old totals into memory before writing out the new ones. There is an argument you can use in place of "All" called "Upper":

```
CLEARBLOCK Upper;
```

This command will clear all of the upper-level blocks in your database. As before with the "All" argument, "CLEARBLOCK Upper" can be used within a "FIX" statement. A related argument is "NonInput":

```
CLEARBLOCK NonInput;
```

This will clear out all the blocks that haven't had data directly input to them. Assuming we're following best practices and only entering data into level-0 blocks, this command will only clear out the upper-level blocks like "CLEARBLOCK Upper".

A new argument was added for the CLEARBLOCK command in Essbase 9.3: "CLEARBLOCK Empty" which removes #Missing blocks from the database. The "CLEARBLOCK Empty" command sets values to #MISSING and if the entire block is empty, Essbase will remove the block. This is helpful if you've run the CREATEBLOCKONEQ to create blocks and may have unnecessarily created blocks with no data.

```
CLEARBLOCK Empty;
```

There's one other way to clear data. You can set a member equal to #Missing:

```
Budget = #Missing;
```

While this is valid syntax (and we've even seen a few sub-par consultants use it), it's just weird. Stick to "CLEARBLOCK" or "CLEARDATA".

Copying Data

There are two common ways to copy data. The first is with a simple equation:

```
"Budget"="Actual";
```

This equation copies the Actual data over to the Budget data. Depending on the settings in your database, this method may or may not create blocks. The way to be sure you create all necessary blocks is by using the "DATACOPY" command. It takes two arguments: a member to copy the data from and a member to copy the data to. This command accomplishes the same thing as the line of code above, but with added comfort that there will be no block creation shenanigans:

```
DATACOPY "Actual" TO
        "Budget";
```

Both of these methods can be used within a FIX command. Do not use multiple "DATACOPY" commands on dense members:

```
DATACOPY Jan TO Feb;
DATACOPY Feb TO Mar;
```

In the case of Sample.Basic, this calc script will actually cause two passes through the database since Time is a dense dimension. In this case, the first method of setting one member equal to another would be better.

Tip!

To oversimplify, use the equation method on dense members and the "DATACOPY" method on sparse members.

IF and Its Other Brother, ENDIF

You learned earlier how easy it is to use the "IF...ENDIF" sandwich commands (technically, they're functions, but since they don't start with @, we like to think of them as commands) inside of a member formula. As a refresher, let's say we wanted to check and see if our number of dropped wolverines exceeded our number of juggled wolverines. If so, let's fire everybody (i.e., set headcount equal to zero). Here's what this would look like if you made it the member formula for "Headcount" in the outline:

```
IF (Avg_Wolverines_Juggled < Avg_Dropped_Wolverines)
    Headcount = 0;
ENDIF
```

Now since this is attached to the Headcount member, it's technically not necessary to specify "Headcount =" on the third line. As a matter of policy, we don't tend to include it, because if the "Headcount" member gets renamed, the member formula reference to it will *not* rename. As such, we'd write the formula like this:

```
IF (Avg_Wolverines_Juggled < Avg_Dropped_Wolverines)
    0;
ENDIF
```

Now, if you just type this into a calc script and verify it, you'll get the following message:

"Error: 1012061 The CALC command [IF] can only be used within a CALC Member Block"

First of all, note that the error message calls "IF" a command, so we were right all along about it not being a real function, on-line documentation be damned. To translate the error message into semi-English, "IF" can only be used in a member formula.

"Uh, oh," you say, "but I want to do IFs in a calc script. Is now the time for ritual suicide?"

While it may indeed be, don't do it over this, because there's a simple work-around: create a temporary member formula within your calc script that contains the needed "IF". You do this by specifying the member that you want to assign the temporary formula and then include the formula in parentheses. For example:

```
Headcount
    (
    IF (Avg_Wolverines_Juggled <
                Avg_Dropped_Wolverines)
            0;
    ENDIF
    )
```

Notice "Headcount" at the top and the parentheses surrounding the "IF...ENDIF". Voila! The calc script will now validate and run successfully.

FUNCTIONS

Everything we've done up to this point has been focused around using the calculation commands. There are also at least 135 functions that let you do most of the interesting things that Microsoft Excel functions can do (like absolute values, statistical deviations, and internal rate of return calculations) and many things that Excel functions cannot (like return the parent value of the current member in a hierarchy and allocate values down across a hierarchy).

 These are the very same functions that you used when creating member formulas. With very few exceptions, all of Note! the functions can be used both in member formulas and calc scripts.

To make it easier to find the functions in the on-line help, Hyperion segmented the functions into several nebulous categories. Some of the categories are easily understood (like "Boolean"). Some, like the mysterious "Miscellaneous" category, are not.

Boolean

Boolean functions return True or False (actually, they return a 1 for True and a 0 for False). Boolean functions are generally used inside an "IF" or an "ELSEIF". One of the common boolean functions is "@ISMBR" and it's used to tell if a specific member is being calculated. Let's say that we want to set budgeted sales equal to 123.45:

```
IF (@ISMBR (Budget))
     Sales = 123.45;
ENDIF
```

It's possible to put a cross-dim operator inside the "@ISMBR". All parts of the cross-dim must be true for the entire statement to be true. In this example, the current intersection being calculated must be "New York" and "Budget":

```
IF (@ISMBR (Budget->"New York"))
     Sales = 123.45;
ENDIF
```

It's even possible to list several members in an "@ISMBR" separated by commas. For instance, if we only want to set New York and California sales, our script would look like this:

```
IF (@ISMBR ("New York", California))
     Sales = 123.45;
ENDIF
```

At times, you might want to check to see if the current member is in a range of members. For instance, say you want "COGS" to be set to 500 if the month being calculated is between January and June. To do this, separate the two members (in this case "Jan" and "Jun") with a colon:

```
IF (@ISMBR (Jan:Jun))
     COGS = 500;
ENDIF
```

You might sometimes see "Jan::Jun" with a double-colon between the two members. The single-colon method returns all members from "Jan" to "Jun" that are at the same level. The double-colon method returns all the members from "Jan" to "Jun" that are at the same *generation*. Unless your outline contains ragged hierarchies, the single- and double-colon methods will return the same list. For simplicities sake, we tend to use a single colon.

There are at least fifteen other Boolean functions, some of which are actually helpful (@ISCHILD, @ISGEN, and @ISLEV, among others).

Relationship functions

Relationship functions are used to lookup values at intersections elsewhere in Essbase. Generally, the value being looked up is in the same database, but it doesn't have to be (the extremely helpful but slightly slow "@XREF" functions looks to other databases).

One of the common needs is to look at the value at a parent member. For instance, say Sample.Basic had a stored member named "Product Share" that needed to show each level-0 product's sales as a percentage of its parent's sales:

```
"Product Share" =
    Sales / @PARENTVAL (Product, Sales);
```

The first argument to the "@PARENTVAL" function is the dimension for which you want to take the value at the parent. If we had a "Market Share" member, we could calculate it like this:

```
"Market Share" =
    Sales / @PARENTVAL (Market, Sales);
```

Mathematical, Statistical, and Forecasting

Mathematical functions perform standard arithmetic type calculations such as absolute value, integer, and factorial. The "@VAR" function used in Sample.Basic to calculate variances is, for no apparent reason, a mathematical function.

While simple statistical functions like maximum and minimum are found in the Mathematical category, advanced statistical functions get their own category: Statistical.

There are also some statistical type functions that have to do with moving sums, averages, minimums, and so on. These functions are found in the Forecasting category along with "@SPLINE" which finds a curve most closely fitting a range of data and "@TREND" which predicts the future (well, kinda). If you're ever curious how "@TREND" comes up with its trend calculations, the programmers at Oracle were kind enough to put the formulas in technical reference documentation. Here's a snippet of the "Algorithm for Triple Exponential Smoothing (TES)." Sing along if you know the melody:

@TREND

Back to main @TREND topic.

Algorithm for Triple Exponential Smoothing (TES)

$Ylist$ $y_1, y_2, ..., y_K$

$Xlist$ $x_1, x_2, ..., x_K$

TES with period T (if T is not given, it is assumed to be $T = 1$)

$x_1, x_2, ..., x_K$, $y_1, y_2 ..., y_K$ are input to TES, x is forecast value

$$a_i = (1-c)^{x_{i+1} - x_i} \quad d_i = (1-d)^{x_{i+1} - x_i} \quad e_i = (1-e)^{x_{i+1} - x_i}$$

Note: When $Xlist$ is missing, the exponents disappear.

Default $c = .2$
             $d = .05$
             $e = .1$

Step 1,

$$S_1 = y_1$$

$$b_1 = \frac{y_2 - y_1}{x_2 - x_1}$$

$$I_1 = 1$$

We'll bet you are wishing you hadn't slept through your statistics class in college right about now.

Member Set

Member Set functions simply return lists of members. These are commonly used in "FIX" commands. Say that we wanted to focus on just aggregating products in the East region. Rather than hard-code all the members in "East," we could use a member set function called "@CHILDREN":

```
FIX (@CHILDREN (East))
     AGG (Product);
ENDFIX
```

Essentially, the "@CHILDREN(East)" portion of the "FIX" is replaced by a series of members before the calc script runs. In essence, the calculation actually performed is this (once the "@CHILDREN" is evaluated):

```
FIX ("New York":"New Hampshire")
      AGG (Product);
ENDFIX
```

Or to put it another way (not using the single-colon range indicator):

```
FIX ("New York", "Massachusetts", "Florida",
    "Connecticut", "New Hampshire")
      AGG (Product);
ENDFIX
```

A common request is to calculate all of the members from a certain member on upwards to the top of the dimension. For instance, let's say you just loaded a value to the great state of Utah (thought we were going to say "the great state of Texas," didn't you?). You want to aggregate this value up through the Market dimension, but you don't want to aggregate the entire dimension (since nothing else has changed). Use the "@ANCESTORS" function on a line by itself:

```
@ANCESTORS (Utah);
```

Remembering that member set functions essentially return lists of members, the script is exactly the same as this request:

```
Utah;
West;
Market;
```

Note!

If a member set function returns any dynamic calc or dynamic calc and store members, they will not be evaluated

What if you wanted to calculate just the regions in the Market dimension? You could use the "@CHILDREN" function on a line by itself:

```
@CHILDREN (Market);
```

Range and Financial

Range functions (sometimes called "Financial" functions just to be contrary) operate on a range of members. The most commonly used range function is "@PRIOR" which looks to earlier members in the outline and "@NEXT" which looks to later members in the outline. Both of these functions assume that you want to look forward and backward through the dimension marked as the "Time" dimension if you do not otherwise specify a range. As such, many people think of them as time-specific, but they do not have to be.

The member "Opening Inventory" in Sample.Basic uses the "@PRIOR" function to refer to the prior month's "Ending Inventory":

```
IF (NOT @ISMBR(Jan))
      "Opening Inventory" =
                    @PRIOR ("Ending Inventory");
ENDIF;
```

The "IF (NOT ..." is used to make sure that we don't try to look back to the prior period if we are in the month of January (because Sample.Basic only contains one year of data, this wouldn't make any sense).

Allocation

Allocation functions allocate summarized higher level values down to detailed members. This is often used for top-down budgeting or targeted forecasting (when values are often loaded to parent members and then spread downward). There are only two functions. "@ALLOCATE" allocates values down a single dimension and its more impressive counterpart "@MDALLOCATE" which allocates values down multiple dimensions simultaneously.

Try It!   Look up the syntax for "@ALLOCATE" in the on-line help and create a calc script using it. Don't use any of the optional arguments for right now: there are too many to deal with right now what with everything else going on in your life and all.

While the allocation functions are powerful, they're not very efficient at complex allocations. If you find that using these functions is slow, you can generally improve performance by "rolling your own" allocations in the form of a more complicated calc script.

Date & Time

Date & Time functions change dates in the form of strings to numeric dates. This category only has one function in it at the moment, "@TODATE", which makes me wonder why they didn't just put this function in the Miscellaneous category. Somehow, we think the marketing department is involved.

Miscellaneous

Miscellaneous is the category for functions that don't have a place elsewhere. The "@TODATE" function should be here, but it's not. Instead, you get the bizarre "@CALCMODE" function which changes the way Essbase calculates a member and three string manipulation functions (@CONCATENATE, @NAME, and @SUBSTRING).

Custom-Defined

Custom-defined functions are whatever you want them to be. It is possible to write your own functions in Java, register them with Essbase using the MaxL "create function" command, and call them from a calc script as if they were part of the native language.

One of the best uses of CDFs (custom-defined functions) is for iterative type calculations (such as the common retail metric "Weeks of Supply") that would take up pages in a calc script but are just a few lines of custom Java code. Other CDFs we've seen include a better implementation of internal rate of return than the "@IRR" function that comes with Essbase and a function that checks a weather database to pull back high and low temperatures.

Create a calc script to aggregate the jugbud.otl.

Try It!

```
SET UpdateCalc Off;

AGG (Customer) ;
```

Wow – we only have to calculate one dimension because Year, Accounts, Scenario, and Fiscal Period are dynamically calculated or don't require a calculation.

Create a calc script to perform an allocation of Other_Expenses down to each customer for Budget based on last year's actual.

Try It!

```
SET UpdateCalc Off;

FIX (Budget, @LEVMBRS(Customer,0))
"Other_Expenses" = "Other_Expenses"->Customer *
    ("Other_Expenses" -> Actual ->"2009"/
    "Other_Expenses" -> Actual ->"2009" ->
    Customer);
ENDFIX
```

EXPORTING SLICES OF DATA IN A CALC SCRIPT

Data Export Commands

Starting in Essbase 9.3, a new calc script command can be used to export slices of data from Essbase cubes. It is extremely fast and if you use the binary form of the export, it is faster than a traditional Essbase database export.

The new command, "DATAEXPORT", leverages the calc engine as a native function and is faster than report scripts and JEXPORT. You simply use the new command in a calc script and embed within a Fix statement to define the data slice for export. Output formats include delimited text files or a relational database table. There are a number of set commands that define information for the export like:

- SET DATAEXPORT DECIMAL <n>
- SET DATAEXPORTCOLFORMAT "ON" OR "OFF"
- SET DATAEXPORTCOLHEADER <DIMENSION NAME>
- SET DATAEXPORTLEVEL "ALL" OR "LEVEL"- OR "INPUT"

Here is an example export script that exports Actual revenue data for the West Region for all Versions to a text file:

```
Script

//ESS_LOCALE English_UnitedStates.Latin1@Binary

SET DATAEXPORTOPTIONS
   {
   DataExportPrecision 2;
   DataExportLevel "LevelInput";
   DATAEXPORTCOLFORMAT ON;
   DataExportColHeader "Year Total";
   DataExportDynamicCalc OFF;
   };


FIX( Actual,
     (@DESCENDANTS("Version")),
     (@DESCENDANTS("West Region")),
     (@DESCENDANTS ("All Revenue Accounts"))

   )

DATAEXPORT "File" "," "C:\usfs\inputEXP.txt" ;


ENDFIX
```

You can also export directly to a table in your data warehouse. The syntax for that option would be:

```
SET DATAEXPORTRELATION "DSN"
DATAEXPORT "DSN" "[dsn_name]" "[table_name]"
     "[user_name]" "[password]";
```

You need to create the relational table beforehand with the appropriate columns and then use load rules to load the exported data set into the target cube.

Binary Calc Export / Import Commands

One other new option for exporting data is the Binary Export/Import calc command. This option moves or copies out data blocks in a compressed encrypted format to a text file. This is a fast backup method and also allows you to embed the commands in fix statements so that you can easily export out slices of data. Binary export/import ignores fixes on dense members (it copies entire blocks – intersection of sparse dimensions). You can also use the import command to import in the export text files. The exported file can only be imported into a database with the same dimensionality. The syntax for binary export / import is as follows:

```
DATAEXPORT "BINFILE" "[file_name]";
DATAIMPORTBIN "[file_name]";
```

 Create a calc script to export budget data the jugbud.otl.

Try It!

```
Set UpdateCalc off;


SET DATAEXPORTOPTIONS
    {
    DataExportPrecision 2;
    DataExportLevel "LEVEL0";
    DataExportColFormat On;
    DataExportColHeader "Period";
    DataExportDynamicCalc Off;
    };


FIX( (Actual),("2008"),
      (@DESCENDANTS("Customer")),
      (@DESCENDANTS ("Account")),
      (@DESCENDANTS( "Period"))
    )

DATAEXPORT "File" "," "C:\LEV0EXP.txt" ;

ENDFIX
```

WHERE DO WE GO FROM HERE?

Learning everything there is to know about calc scripts would take several years, we're fairly certain. We are considering writing a sequel to this book that focuses entirely on calc scripts. We are sure we could fill at least 400 pages with non-stop, wall-to-wall, hot, steamy, calc action. We are also sure that it would sell no more than 100 copies world-wide including the fifty copies we bought just to prove to our families that we had more than just one book in us.

Rather than drag this chapter on any further, we'll point you in the right place for further information: the Essbase Technical Reference. From within Administration Services, click on Help>>Information Map. When this comes up, click on Technical Reference to be taken to a bounty of detailed, look-up information:

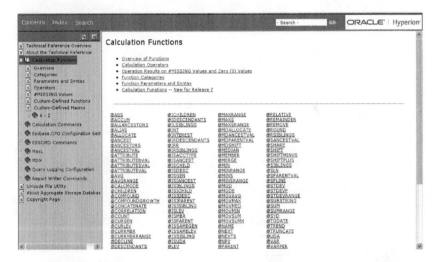

The "Calculation Functions" section contains details on all of the @Functions. The "Calculation Commands" section is where you go to find information on all of the commands that can be used in a calc script that don't start with an @ symbol. Several of the calculation functions contain examples showing you how to use them. While they're not in depth, they're plentiful, so maybe that makes up for it.

If you'd like to pre-reserve an advance copy of "Look Smarter than You Are with Calc Scripts: Essbase Goes Hardcore," please e-mail info@interrel.com. If we get 100 advance orders, we'll start writing. Don't hold your breath.

Chapter 18:
True Essbase BSO Ghost Story

Just when you thought you couldn't keep your eyes open a second longer (don't worry, calc script syntax does that to all of us), we bring you a story that will keep you awake at night, peeking out from under the covers and looking for the ghosts of Essbase. This story is 100% true. Disbelieve if you dare.

As told by a client who shall remain nameless (with a bit of dramatization added for the reader's entertainment)...

It was a dark and stormy night. I was working late, all alone in the dimly lit office. We'd closed out the GL just that morning and I was responsible for updating our Essbase financial reporting application. I'd run our monthly process of building the dimensions and loading and calculating the database. But something wasn't right. The hairs on the back of my neck tingled with the sensation of doom. I opened my check worksheet and held my breath as I hit Retrieve. Time froze. The numbers weren't tying.

I don't understand, I told myself, trying to ignore the tremble in my voice. Please, please, I begged as if that would help the situation. It didn't and I knew I had to do something.

Trying to find some inkling of courage, I zoomed in on the numbers, again and again until I couldn't believe what I was seeing. I screamed in terror. Some of the data was double counted in my Organization dimension. How could that happen?

Closing my eyes, not standing to look anymore, I reached for the phone. I fumbled the numbers twice before getting it right.

"Tracy, what's happening? What's happening to my numbers?" I whispered, hoping the consultant could make things right again. "Help, please help."

"Calm down," Tracy reassured. "You have to calm down and explain to me exactly what happened."

Knowing that I wasn't alone anymore helped a bit. My eyes darted around before resting on my Monthly load checklist. I ran the dimension build process to update the Organization dimension, run the data load process from GL, and then run the Actuals calculation script.

"I think I know what's happening," Tracy said. "Did you have any reorganizations this period?"

"How did you know?" I asked, shocked because I hadn't mentioned that fact. The IT department had broken up the Infrastructure department into two departments: Networking and

Hardware. That was where my data issue was occurring. I still had a value for the Infrastructure member when the cost centers rolling up to Infrastructure should have been remapped to the two new departments. In fact, the cost centers had been remapped. I'd checked. So how was there still data in the Infrastructure member?

Here is my Check Worksheet. The red cells should be blank but they still have a data value, which is doubling the expense amounts:

A	B	C	D	E	F	G	H
	Product	Actual					
	Jan	Feb	Mar	Apr	May	Jun	Jul
	Expense	Expense	Expense	Expense	Expense	Expense	Expense
Infrastructure	100	100	100	100	100	100	
Networking	50	50	50	50	50	50	50
Hardware	50	50	50	50	50	50	50
Applications	250	250	250	250	250	250	250
Custom Development	100	100	100	100	100	100	100
IT	550	550	550	550	550	550	450
Support & Admin Services	1000	1000	1000	1000	1000	1000	1000
Total Company	4000	4000	4000	4000	4000	4000	4000

"Ghost data," Tracy said.

I shuddered. "A ghost?"

"Yes, here's what happened. You first ran your dimension build process that moved all cost centers from the Infrastructure department to the two new departments. This left the Infrastructure member as a level zero member with data still stored in that member. Then you ran your load and calc process, which aggregated the Org dimension, including the amount still stored in the Infrastructure member. This is what we call ghost data."

"How do I get rid of ghost data?" I asked, picturing a large contraption similar to what the Ghostbusters used in the movie.

"Simple. You need to update your process to clear upper level members before you run the dimension build process. Picture how this would work. You clear upper level members, which would clear the Infrastructure department. You can clear upper level data manually in Administration Services or via a calc script using the CLEARBLOCK command. Then you run the dimension build which would remove the cost centers from the Infrastructure department and move them to the new departments. But that's OK because any data in the Infrastructure member has been cleared. You load and calc as always. The end result – no ghost data."

So the moral of the story is your overall Essbase BSO load and calc processes (in most cases) should follow this order:

1. Clear data for upper level members.
2. Update dimensions.
3. Load data.
4. Calculate.

The one case where this process will not apply: if you load data at upper levels. If you load budget or targets to upper level members in your database, you will not want to ever clear data for upper level members. For these databases, be especially mindful of the ghosts of Essbase as you update and move members in your dimensions.

Chapter 19:
BSO Under the Covers

To become an all knowing, all seeing Essbase administrator, you have to understand some of the more complex aspects of Essbase. So let's pull back the covers and take a look.

ESSBASE BSO DIRECTORY STRUCTURE

Next we will tackle the Essbase directory structure. We've already covered some of these items in the sister chapter "ASO Under the Covers" but in case you missed that section, we'll recap here. Prepare for a bit of déjà vu. The Essbase directory structure contains folders and files created when you install the program. In the 11x version, Essbase uses a system variable called ESSBASEPATH for this directory structure. Older versions of Essbase used a system variable called ARBORPATH which you still see hanging around in 11x. You refer to these environment variables as %ESSBASEPATH% and %ARBORPATH% in Windows and $ESSBASEPATH and $ARBORPATH in UNIX. Because both variables are the same, we will refer to it generically as "arborpath" (continuing to kick it old school).

- arborpath\bin stores Essbase executables, the Essbase.cfg configuration file, the Essbase.sec security definition file, and the Essbase.bak backup security file.
- arborpath\app stores server-based applications (more on this shortly).
- arborpath\client stores any client based files and applications.
- arborpath\docs stores online documentation.
- arborpath\locale contains the character-set files necessary for multi-language use.

Need To Know – Essbase Executables

Stored in *arborpath*\bin
- Essbase.exe – Essbase server agent process
- Esssvr.exe – application process
- Essmsh.exe – MaxL shell
- Esscmd.exe – Esscmd command line interface

Helpful
Info

Stored in *eas*\Server\bin
- Starteas.exe – start the Administration Server executable
- Admincon.exe – Administration Services Console application

The *arborpath*\app directory contains all of the application files. An application will contain databases. For ASO databases, we will only have a single database but for block storage databases, we may have up to three databases (more if you are using Planning and the Workforce Planning or Capital Expenditure modules). Each database will contain one outline file. Other objects like calc scripts in BSO databases and rules files can be stored at the application or database level.

The official definitions for application and database are as follows: An application is the management structure containing one or more Essbase databases and related files. A database is the repository of data that contains a multi-dimensional storage array. Each database consists of a storage structure definition (outline), data, security, and optional calculation scripts, report scripts, and rules files.

Let's take a look at the directory structure for Sample.Basic:

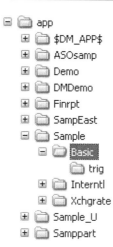

You can store rules files, calc scripts, and report scripts at the application OR database level. If you have a calc script that will be run against one or more databases, store this script at the application level once instead of being replicated at the database level.

Tip!

CALCULATE THE BLOCK SIZE

We've already learned the basics about the Essbase block structure. Blocks are composed of dense members. In the case below, Measures, Time and Scenario are dense dimensions. The dense members, like Jan at Profit at Actual, make up the cells within the block.

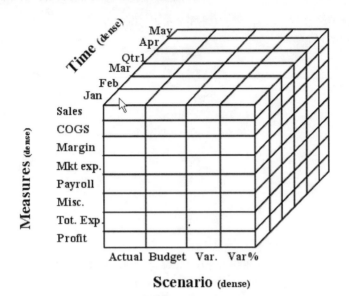

A unique block is created for each intersection of the sparse members. Product and Market are sparse dimensions in the example below. A block is created for Cola at New York, for Cola at Florida, for Cola at East, and so forth.

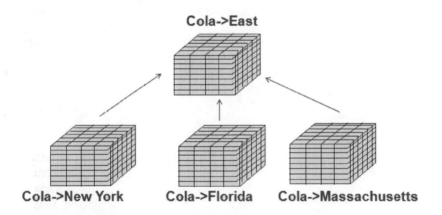

So what else is there to know? And why do you care? Oh, if only we could go back to the innocence of a new Essbase administrator. Everything seemed so simple – dimensions, hierarchies, and spreadsheets.

For some reporting and analysis databases, you may not need to worry about this. But we can imagine you will be building larger database with thousands and thousands of members with complex calculation and reporting requirements. So why do we need to dig deeper into the Essbase structure? Understanding these components helps us more effectively tune and optimize our Essbase databases. Let's start digging.

First, we will learn how to calculate block size. Data block size is determined by the amount of data in a particular combination of dense dimensions. Data block size is $8n$ bytes, where n is the number of cells that exist for that combination of dense dimensions. Here is an example:

Measures (Dense): 40 stored members
Time (Dense): 17 stored members
Scenario (Dense): 2 stored members

Block size = 40 * 17 * 2 * 8 = 10880 bytes or 11 KB

Note! Use the number of stored members when calculating block size not the total number of members.

Despite what the Essbase Database Administrator's Guide says, we recommend a block size of about 8 KB. Larger block sizes will hurt parallel calculations (which is what most of your calculations will be these days). Too small block sizes may result in an increased index file size. This forces Essbase to write and retrieve the index from disk, slowing calculations When in doubt, error on the side of smaller. That is, 1 KB is better than 40 KB. Unless you're using 64-bit Essbase (in which case 1+ MB block sizes are not abnormal), avoid blocks larger than 40 KB and strongly avoid blocks larger than 100 KB.

Tip! As with anything Essbase, these guidelines are not definitive and are just a starting point. Hence, the term "guideline". We have implemented applications that violated the block size guideline and still realized fast performance.

Let's calculate the block size for our wolverine juggling application. We have three dense dimensions right now: Account, Period, and Scenario. The period dimension has 12 stored members (the upper level members are dynamically calculated so we will exclude those from the block size calculation):

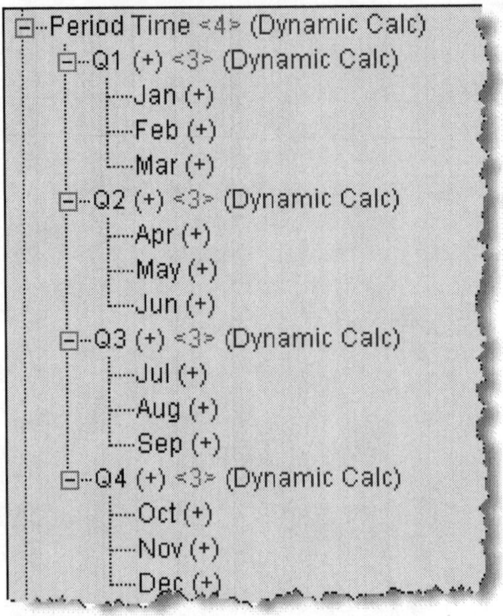

The account dimension has eight stored members:

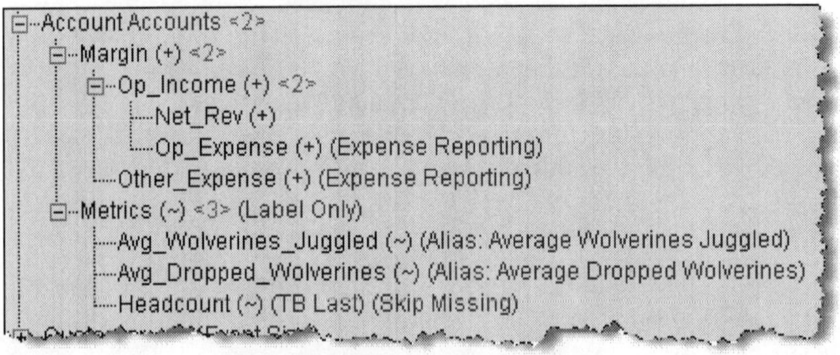

The scenario dimension has three stored dimensions (Variance is dynamically calculated):

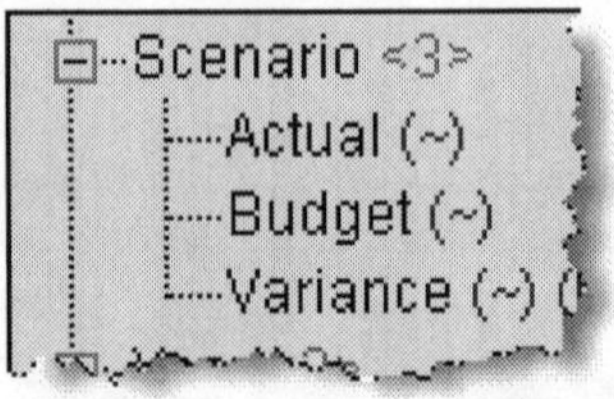

So the block size for the wolverine juggling application is 12*8*3*8 = 2304 bytes or 2 KB.

Calculate the block size for the juggling wolverine application if we changed the Scenario dimension from dense to sparse.

Try It!

Oh, we forgot to mention that Essbase also calculates the block size for you. Select the database and right click. Select *Edit >> Properties*. Select the Statistics tab:

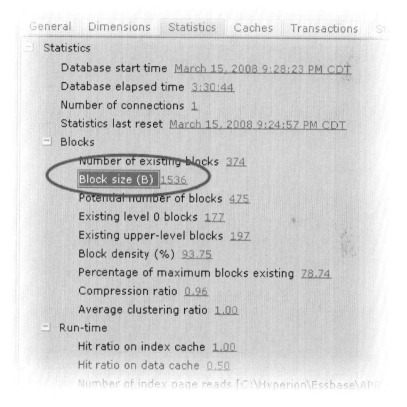

So why did we teach you how to calculate block size? One, it is important to understand the concept of what members make up a block. Getting the block size to a reasonable size is important in tuning. You can reduce block size by making more members dynamic and changing a dense dimension to sparse. Two, you may want to use this calculation when you are performing an initial design to figure out your starting point dense and sparse dimensions.

CALCULATE THE NUMBER OF BLOCKS

So now we know the size of the data blocks. But how many blocks could we possibly have? A block is created for each unique intersection of stored sparse members. So to calculate the total possible blocks, multiply the number for stored members for each sparse dimension. Here is an example:

Product (Sparse): 19 stored members
Market (Sparse): 26 stored members

· Number of Possible Blocks = 19*26 = 494

This time we will mention up front that Essbase also calculates the total possible blocks for you. Select the database and right click. Select *Edit >> Properties*. Select the Statistics tab again:

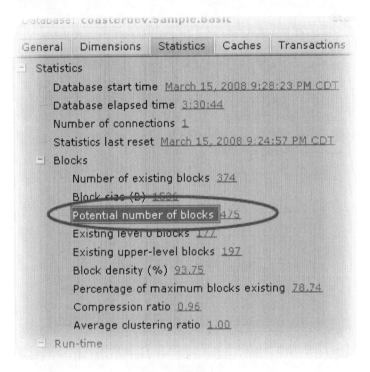

When you see this number for a production database, you may get really scared. This number will probably be really big, sometimes into the quadrillions. But remember, we've tagged these dimensions sparse for a reason. The likelihood that data exists for every single combination is very, very rare. So we recommend you understand this concept but don't worry about it any further (don't you just love it when the teacher teaches you something that you won't ever really use?). In certain cases, really large potential block counts (in excess of 100 trillion) can cause inefficient calcs, so watch out if you see this occurring.

The more helpful statistic is the number of existing blocks. Make sure you have loaded and calculated the database before you check this statistic. Go back to the Statistics tab under Database Properties:

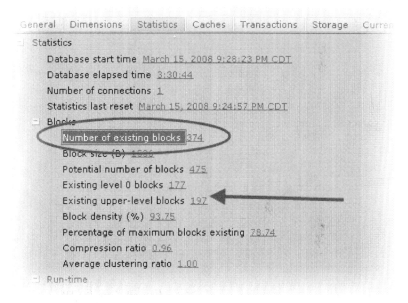

While you are there, note that Essbase also tracks the number of existing level-zero blocks and upper level blocks.

INDEX AND PAGE FILES

The index file is a file that contains pointers to all of the different blocks in the database. The index file is named ess*n*.ind and is stored in your database directory (n starts with 00001 and increments by 1 every time the file size reaches 2 GB). Essbase uses this file to locate the blocks that are requested during Essbase operations.

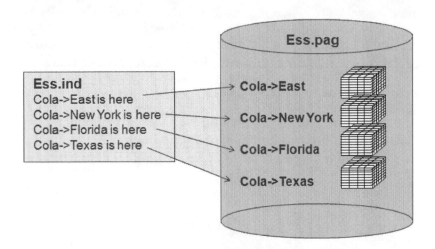

Data is stored in page files, named ess*n*.pag and stored in the database directory (also starting with 00001 and incrementing every 2 GB). These files are stored in the database directory. Essbase uses both the index and page files when performing operations on data blocks.

Try It!

Find the index and page files for the juggling wolverine application. Let's open the page files and take a look at the data. WAIT! We caught you again. This was another trick "Try It!" Do not open the page or index files. Ever. Leave these files alone always (unless you are backing them up). You cannot view data via the page files or a list of sparse blocks in the index file. If you open these files, not only will you see quite a bit of mumbo jumbo, you will probably corrupt your application and database. Don't say we didn't warn you.

Memory (index and data caches) can be set aside to help performance during operations. The index cache stores a portion or all of the index in memory for quicker access. The data cache stores a portion of the data blocks in memory for quicker access. We'll show you how to define these memory caches in the tuning and optimization chapter.

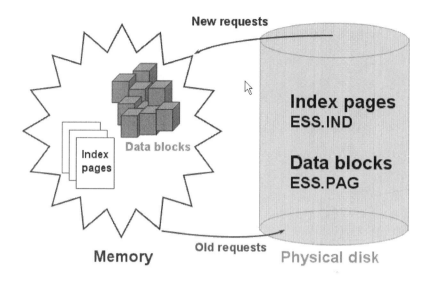

Did you know that interRel Consulting provides free concierge service for every paying client? Just kidding. We wanted to make sure you were still awake and paying attention through this valuable but dry and slightly boring section (OK, really boring section).

RESTRUCTURING FOR BSO

Restructuring of your Essbase database takes place after the outline changes, like when you add new, edit, and delete members and dimensions. Any and every change forces Essbase to restructure the database, so think of it as "re-saving" the database. This can be a time consuming process depending on the type of restructure and database size.

A full restructure, the most time consuming type of restructure, will take place when an outline is updated with the moving, deletion, or addition of a member from a dense dimension. This will reorganize every data block in the page file and regenerate the index. A re-calculation will also be required.

A sparse restructure is a much faster type of restructure, and takes place when you move, delete, or add a member from a sparse dimension. This type of restructure regenerates the index file but does not restructure the data blocks.

An outline restructure is the last type of restructure and will take place when you make a change that impacts the outline only, like changing an alias or member formula. This restructure will not regenerate the index file or restructure the data blocks, so is very quick indeed.

Note! Each action you perform on an Essbase outline will cause some type of restructure. For a full list of the actions and what type of restructure will occur, see the Essbase Database Administrator's Guide and search for a table called "How Actions Affect Databases and Restructuring".

If your restructuring times are taking too long and impacting your users, consider the following tuning tips:
- If you change a dimension frequently, make it sparse.
- Use incremental restructuring to control when Essbase performs a required database restructuring.

INCREMENTAL RESTRUCTURING

One way to optimize your Essbase application is to enable incremental restructuring. This option will help with performance if you make frequent changes to your outline. Essbase will defer restructuring if possible, not restructuring either the index or affected blocks until the time that the block is accessed.

There are a few actions that will cause restructuring even if you have turned on incremental restructuring:
- Add or delete a non-attribute dimension.
- Delete a stored member of a sparse dimension.
- Change a dimension from sparse to dense or dense to sparse.

Note! You cannot use incremental restructuring if you use LROs in your database.

To turn on incremental restructuring for a database, all databases in an application, or all databases in all applications, update the Essbase.cfg file with the INCRESTRUC setting.

```
INCRESTRUC Sample Basic TRUE
```

RESTRUCTURE DATA OPTIONS WHEN SAVING AN OUTLINE

Once your application is up and running, sooner or later you will need to update an outline for a database that contains data. When you save an outline with data attached, you will be prompted with the following restructuring options: "All data", "Level zero data", "Input data" or "Discard all data". In most cases (if you've added, moved, or deleted members or changed storage properties), you will need to recalculate the database, so we recommend choosing input or level 0 data to restructure. This allows you to restructure a smaller data set which is much faster than the entire data set. If you've just made outline changes like aliases or change that doesn't require a recalculation, you could select a restructure of "All Data".

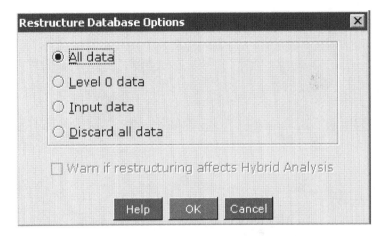

Try It!

We've just checked the block size for our juggling budget wolverine application and it is too big (larger than the 8 KB guideline). If we change the Scenario dimension from dense to sparse. What type of restructuring will occur? Ding, ding, ding – a full restructure. How would the block size change?

Chapter 20:
Design and Optimize for BSO

There is so much to be said about designing and tuning Essbase for BSO we could write another full book (Look Smarter Than You Are with Essbase: Tuning Faster than the Speed of Light). For an introduction, this chapter will succinctly list different tuning and optimization steps that you can take for your Essbase applications.

Disclaimer: **There isn't simply one right answer when it comes to tuning.** Some of the tuning guidelines can contradict other tuning guidelines. Optimizing can have different perspectives: are you tuning for calculations or retrievals or both? In some databases, these tuning tips will have significant impact and in other databases, the tuning tips won't. Make sure you test, test, test. Did we say that tuning wasn't an exact science?

One further warning, most of the information in this chapter is for 32-bit Essbase not 64-bit Essbase. 64-bit Essbase addresses far more memory (up to 2 exobytes), more threads, and more hard drive data at once, so the majority of these optimization tips simply do not apply.

TUNE THE INDEX CACHE

The index cache is a reserved set of memory that is used to store all or a portion of the index file for quick access. You want to try and place as much of the index file into memory as possible to help with performance.

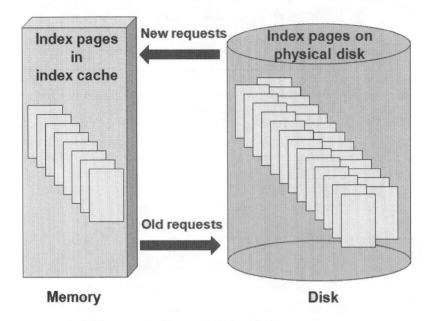

Here is a guideline for setting the index cache:

Set the index cache equal to the combined size of all ess*n*.ind files, if possible. If you can't do that, then size the index cache as large as possible. Do not set this cache size higher than the total index size, as no performance improvement will be realized and you'll be consuming memory that other processes might need to use. It is possible that the index can be too large: Essbase will spend more time looking in the index cache than it would use by giving up and reading from the hard drive. In other words, if your index is 1,750 GB, don't set your index cache to 1,750 GB.

Here's an example: the index size for Sample.Basic is 8024 KB. We have enough memory on the server, so we will increase the index cache to 8024 Kb.

Note!

The default amount of RAM Essbase allocates to caching the index is a paltry single megabyte (1024 Kb). This is the value that it's been since the initial release of Essbase when RAM cost more than a good, sturdy mule, and as much as we love Essbase, it's moronic that they haven't increased this default to a much higher level. Oracle, please increase the default values for index and data cache so we can stop complaining. In the meantime, we recommend using 100 Mb as your default for new databases.

To set the index cache:
1. Select the database.
2. Right click and select *Edit >> Properties*.
3. Select the Caches tab:

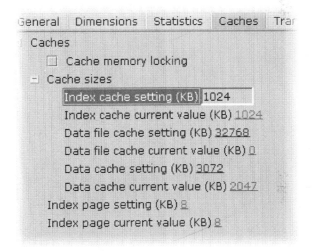

4. Enter the new index cache value.
5. Click *Apply*.

Note!

Be aware. In some places, like in Caches, Essbase will reference KB (Kilobytes) for size. In other places, Essbase will reference B (bytes).

TUNE THE DATA CACHE

The data cache is the memory set aside to hold data blocks. You'll want to place as many blocks in memory as possible, but with the caveat that too much places a management burden on the system and can hurt overall performance.

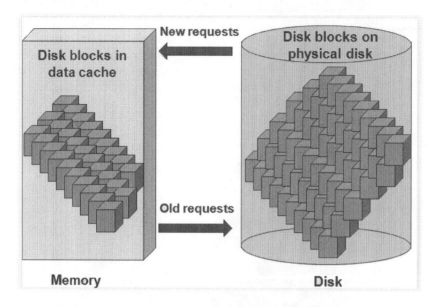

A guideline for setting the data cache is to set the data cache to 0.125 times the combined size of all ess*n*.pag files with a minimum value of about 307,200 KB (the default is only a miserly 3 Mb, and we're forcing back another diatribe on stupid defaults that never get increased). Consider increasing this value even further if you have a high number of concurrent users and they're complaining about retrieval times during peak times. Another time to further increase the Data Cache is when you have calculation scripts that contain functions that operate across sparse ranges and the functions require all members of a range to be in memory, for example, when using @RANK and @RANGE.

Here's an example of the recommended initial setting: the page size for your database is 3 GB. We have more than enough memory on the server, so we will increase the data cache to .125 * 3072000KB or 384,000 KB which equals about 300 Mb.

To set the data cache:

1. Select the database.
2. Right click and select *Edit >> Properties*.
3. Select the Caches tab:

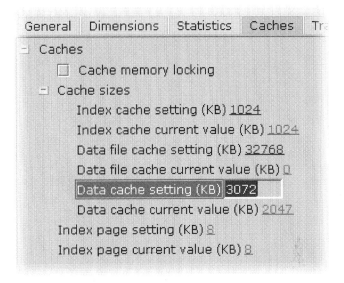

4. Enter the new data cache value.
5. Click *Apply*.

The priority for cache tuning is as follows:
1. Index Cache
2. Data File Cache (if using Direct I/O, which you shouldn't be 99% of the time)
3. Data Cache

Tune the index and data caches for the wolverine juggling application.

Try It!

The new cache settings will not take effect until the database is restarted.

Note!

   Cache hit ratios will tell you how well your caches are being utilized. The ratio will tell you the percentage of time that a requested piece of information is available in the cache. As a general rule, the higher the ratio, the better. The goal for the index cache ratio should be close to 1. The goal for the data cache ratio should be 1, but values as low as 0.3 are acceptable. Why so low for data cache ratio? Your page files are a lot bigger than the index file.

The chances that you can fit all of the page files or data into memory is pretty slim to impossible.

To view the cache ratios, right click on the database and select *Edit >> Properties*. Select the Statistics tab to view hit ratios:

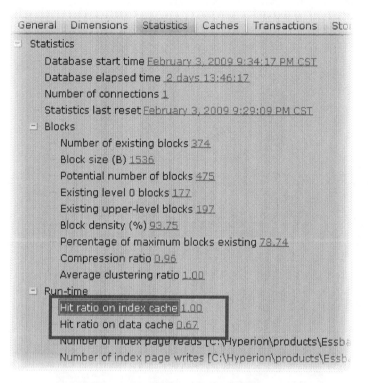

TUNE THE CALCULATOR CACHE

Warning – this topic is confusing. We'll give you the background information related to calculator cache but when all is said and done, use this cache when the database has at least two sparse dimensions, and either you calculate at least one, full sparse dimension OR you specify the SET CACHE ALL command in a calculation script. Be prepared to read this section at least two or three times for full comprehension.

The best size for the calculator cache depends on the number and density of the sparse dimensions in your outline. First let's review a few terms:

The bitmap is a highly efficient mechanism that is used to very quickly tell the Essbase Calculation Engine whether a block exists or not at a given location. As the engine will not have to perform this lookup by reading the index file (which is relatively slow), and large Essbase databases can have a massive number of potential blocks, this little time saving for each potential block location can save a very large amount of time overall.

The bitmap dimensions will be the sparse dimensions from the database outline that Essbase fits into the bitmap until the bitmap is full. Each member combination of the sparse dimensions placed in the bitmap occupies (wait for it) 1 bit of memory. There must be enough space in the bitmap for every member combination of a sparse dimension for it to be placed in the bitmap, so we will need to make sure we size the cache to be large enough for what we want to load into the bitmap.

The anchoring dimensions are the remaining one or more sparse dimensions in the database outline that do not fit into the bitmap.

The calculator cache controls the size of the bitmap, therefore controlling the number of dimensions that can fit into the bitmap.

In case you found that section too simple, here are some equations:

- Calculator cache = Bitmap size in bytes * Number of bitmaps
- Bitmap size in bytes = Max ((member combinations on the bitmap dimensions/8), 4)
- Number of bitmaps = Maximum number of dependent parents in the anchoring dimension + 2 constant bitmaps
- Minimum bitmap size is 4 bytes

There are a few different ways to define the calculator cache. The default calculator cache size is set in the essbase.cfg. You can also set the size of the calculator cache within a calculation script, at which time the setting is used only for the duration of that script.

This is definitely one of those settings that you will want to test to get the maximum performance from your calc scripts, but be prepared to spend a lot of time tweaking the settings to get it just right.

DEFINE COMPRESSION METHOD

Attention readers: this section is for the IT geeks in the audience (OK, maybe this entire chapter is for the IT geeks). When Essbase stores blocks to disk, it can compress the blocks using one of several different algorithms to save space. When a compressed block is requested, Essbase will uncompress the block before sending the data into the main engine for further processing. Luckily this is all happening behind the scenes, so you can just make your choice and Essbase will handle all these details for you.

No compression is an option, but you should only use it in production if your average block density is more than 50%.

zLib compression is good for very sparse data.

Index value pair (IVP) is good for large blocks with sparse data though you don't directly assign this compression type. Use index value pair when your blocks are very large, say more than 1Mb and your have just a few values loaded per block.

Bitmap is the default and is good for non-repeating data. If bitmap compression is chosen, then Essbase can choose between bitmap and index value pair compression types for the best fit.

RLE or run length encoding compression type is good for blocks with many zeroes or repeating values. If RLE compression is chosen, then Essbase can choose between RLE, bitmap, and index value pair compression types for the best fit.

To set compression,

1. Select the database.
2. Right click and select *Edit Properties*.
3. Select the Storage tab.
4. Select the desired compression type:

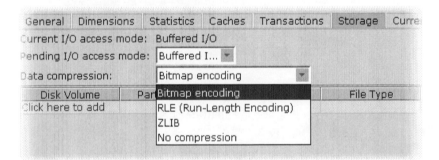

5. Click *Apply*.

Note!

The storage tab will tell you the size of your database (both index and page files):

Data/Index File Type	Size	Status	Name
Index	8216576	Open	C:\Hyperion\products\Essbase\EssbaseServer\APP\Sample\Basic\...
Data	573368	Open	C:\Hyperion\products\Essbase\EssbaseServer\APP\Sample\Basic\...

Dimension order within your outline will make a difference with respect to optimizing compression. If you think of a block on disk like a spreadsheet, the first dense dimension determines the columns in the page file. Compression then works from left to right, top to bottom. Historically, people said that Accounts should be the first then Time the second dense dimension:

	A	B	C	D	E	F
1		Budget				
2		Sales	COGS	Margin	Exp	Profit
3	Jan	100	50	50	30	20
4	Feb	100	50	50	30	20
5	Mar	100	50	50	30	20
6	Apr	120	50	70	30	40
7	May	120	50	70	30	40
8	Jun	120	50	70	30	40
9						

That said, we almost *always* recommend using RLE compression under Essbase 7.x and later. When using RLE compression, you should switch the order of dimensions, listing Time as your first dense dimension, then Accounts, so that Essbase can take advantage of the high probability of values repeating in successive periods (especially in budget scenarios):

	A	B	C	D	E	F	G
1		Budget					
2		Jan	Feb	Mar	Apr	May	Jun
3	Sales	100	100	100	120	120	120
4	COGS	50	50	50	50	50	50
5	Margin	50	50	50	70	70	70
6	Exp	30	30	30	30	30	30
7	Profit	20	20	20	40	40	40
8							

QUICK APPLICATION DESIGN TIPS

Minimize the number of dimensions

The general rule for the number of dimensions in a block storage database is 5-9 dimensions. Make every one of them count! You will want to avoid dimensions that do not offer descriptive data points. This will help reduce complexity and size of database.

Remember that adding a dimension increases the size and complexity of a database *exponentially*, not arithmetically.

Avoid Repetition in dimensions

Repeating members indicates a need to split dimensions, thereby reducing redundancy. In the example below, we repeat FTE, Average Hourly Rate (AHR), and Expense dollars for every payroll account. A better design would be to split the metrics from the Accounts dimension.

Before: 1 Dimension (Payroll):

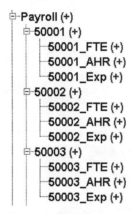

After: 2 Dimensions (Payroll and Metric):

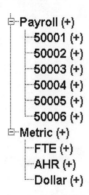

Although this rule might seem to contradict the first tip in this section about minimizing the number of dimensions, this one is really about making sure you have the *right* number of dimensions given a specified analytical requirement. Repeating members can become awkward for end-users and causes a potential maintenance nightmare for administrators.

Avoid interdimensional irrelevance

This occurs when many members of a dimension are irrelevant across other dimensions. For example, Product and Customer dimensions will probably not be needed in a Human Resources headcount analysis database. Another example would be an Asset Category dimension placed in a sales analysis application.

The important point here is not to try to meet everyone's requirements into a single database. Split databases into meaningful analytical domains with common dimensions wherever possible.

DIMENSION ORDER WITHIN THE OUTLINE

Here is another tuning tip related to the order of dimensions within an outline. Dimension ordering within outlines is critical to your overall Essbase performance. You will want to test different iterations of dimension orders to determine the optimal structure. Historically, outlines were ordered from largest dense to smallest dense and then smallest sparse to largest sparse (sometimes called the "hourglass" format). This works well when parallel calculation is not utilized. Since Essbase 6.5, though, everyone is using parallel calculation, so an improved method for ordering the dimensions was created.

First a few definitions:

Dense dimensions are the dimensions that define the internal structure of the data block. They should reside at the top of the outline.

Aggregating Sparse dimensions are dimensions that will be calculated to create new parent values. These dimensions should reside directly below the last Dense dimension in the outline. Placing these dimensions as the first Sparse dimensions positions them to be the first dimensions included in the calculator cache. This gives them an ideal location within the database for optimized calculation performance.

Non-Aggregating Sparse dimensions are dimensions that organize the data into logical slices. Examples include Scenario, Year or Version. It is not crucial for these dimensions to be included in the calculator cache because their members are typically isolated in FIX statements.

With this in mind, try the following guidelines to create an optimal outline order (sometimes called a "dress form" or an "hourglass on a stick"):

1. Time (assuming it's a dense dimension)
2. Largest Dense Dimensions

3. Smallest Dense Dimensions
4. Smallest Aggregating Sparse Dimensions
5. Largest Aggregating Sparse Dimensions
6. Non-aggregating Sparse Dimensions

Example – An Employee Analysis Database:

Dimension	Type-Stored Member Count	Density After Calc	Density After Load	Data Points Created
Time Periods	D – 21	85%	85%	-
Accounts	D – 94	3 %	2%	-
Scenarios	AS – 9	22%	11%	199
Job Code	AS – 1,524	.56%	.23%	853
Organization	AS – 2,304	.34%	.09%	783
Versions	NAS – 7	19%	19%	-
Years	NAS – 7	14%	14%	-

D=Dense, AS=Aggregating Sparse, NAS=Non-Aggregating Sparse

Outlines can be ordered based on dimension stored member count or on dimension density. Ordering by stored member count is the easy option but may not be as accurate as ordering by dimension density. In the example above, the optimized outline should follow this order (assuming we order the outline based on dimension density and our other rule, Time first and then Accounts):

Original Dimension Order (Typical Hourglass)	Optimized Dimension Order (Modified Hourglass)
Accounts (D)	Time Periods (D)
Time Periods (D)	Accounts (D)
Years	Job Code (AS)

Versions	Organization (AS)
Scenarios	Years (NAS)
Job Code	Versions (NAS)
Organization	Scenarios (NAS)
Employee Status (Attr Dim)	Employee Status (Attr Dim)
Fund Group (Attr Dim)	Fund Group (Attr Dim)

To figure out the density of a dimension, set that dimension to dense and set all other dimensions to sparse. Load and calculate the database with that single dimension set to dense. Check the block density value in Administration Services. Right click on the database and select *Edit Properties*. Select the Statistics tab and scroll down to find the block density:

Tip!

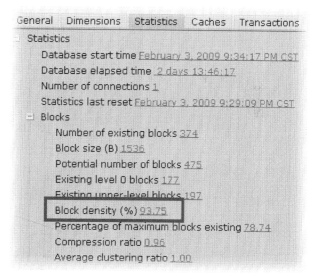

Try It!

Order the dimensions in the juggling wolverine application per the guidelines above.

OTHER OUTLINE TIPS

Here are a few other quick tips related to outlines. Avoid large flat sparse dimensions like an Employee dimension with 10,000 employees rolling up to a total. Adding additional levels into the hierarchy will speed up retrievals and aggregations. If you want to optimize the outline for fast retrievals, place the most queried sparse dimensions as the first sparse dimension in the outline.

OPTIMIZE DATA LOAD RULES

Make sure your source data file follows a reverse order of the outline: Non-aggregating sparse dimensions, aggregating sparse dimensions, and finally the dense dimensions (assuming your outline follows the dress form model).

Outline Order	Data File Order and Sort
Time Periods (D)	Scenarios (NAS)
Accounts (D)	Versions (NAS)
Job Code (AS)	Years (NAS)
Organization (AS)	Organization (AS)
Years (NAS)	Job Code (AS)
Versions (NAS)	Accounts (D)
Scenarios (NAS)	Time Periods (D)
Employee Status (Attr Dim)	
Fund Group (Attr Dim)	

Tip!

If you ever forget the order for an optimal data load file, do a columnar export. Look at the order of the dimensions in the file (and the dense dimension across the columns). Match your input file to the order of the dimensions in the export file.

Other tuning tips for faster data loads include using dense dimension members for data column headers and avoid using the single "data field". For example, an optimized data file with columns for each period will load much quicker than a file with only one data value per line and the periods going down the rows.

Avoid unnecessary columns in the source data file. For example, your data file has columns for period, account, product, sales manager, product description, and product introduction date. Unless your rules file updates the product dimension and loads data, take out the extraneous columns like sales manager, product description, and product introduction date. For large data loads, every little bit counts.

Copy data load files directly to the Essbase server. It is faster to load from the server than the client where the network can sometimes become a bottleneck.

And lastly, pre-aggregate records before loading. Here is a data file where the Jan records will have to be added together during the load process:

```
01/01/2007, Jan, California,Caffeine Free Cola, Sales, 145
01/02/2007, Jan, California,Caffeine Free Cola, Sales, 123
01/03/2007, Jan, California,Caffeine Free Cola, Sales, 132
01/04/2007, Jan, California,Caffeine Free Cola, Sales, 145
01/05/2007, Jan, California,Caffeine Free Cola, Sales, 102
01/06/2007, Jan, California,Caffeine Free Cola, Sales, 116|
```

Here is an optimized data file with records pre-aggregated by month. This is a very simple task for any relational database.

```
Jan, California, Caffeine Free Cola, Sales, 762
Feb, California, Caffeine Free Cola, Sales, 775
Mar, California, Caffeine Free Cola, Sales, 862
Apr, California, Caffeine Free Cola, Sales, 700|
```

Review the load file that we created for the wolverine juggling application. Is this rules file optimized per the guidelines above? If not, then optimize.

Try It!

OPTIMIZE CALCULATIONS

We get a lot of calls that ask "Why does my calc script take 5 hours?" or "How can I get my calc time down?" Changing a number of the database and outline settings can significantly impact your calculation time. These settings are discussed in other sections of the book, but here are a few more tips.

Calculate only those dimensions requiring calculation. For example, do you need to rollup Scenario (Actual + Budget)? If all of the upper level members in your Accounts dimension are dynamic, do you need to calculate Accounts? Nope. By utilizing a lean and mean "CALC DIM" or "AGG" with only the dimensions that need it, you'll shave valuable time from your calc scripts.

"AGG" and "CALC DIM" are not the same. "AGG" is faster for straight aggregation of sparse dimensions with no member formulas so use this when you can. There are some cases where a sparse dimension with 7+ levels may CALC DIM faster than it AGGs, but this is rare.

 You cannot "AGG" dense dimensions. Your dense dimensions should be dynamic, so you should not be using Note! CALC DIM.

In general, use "Fix" on Sparse dimensions and use "If" on Dense dimensions if you're going to be doing different logic on different members from the same dimension. If you need to do a bunch of logic against a set of members of a dimension (dense or sparse) and you don't need to do *different* logic against different members of that dimension, always use a FIX.

Try to calculate in parallel vs. serial mode when possible. How do you this? First, let's make sure we understand serial and parallel calculations. Serial calculation is the default calculation mode where each calc is executed using a single thread. Parallel calculation can be set at the system, application, database or calc script level. Essbase generates a series of tasks and schedules them to run on up to 4-8 threads (8 threads for 64bit Essbase) using the CALCPARALLEL setting. Each thread can run on a separate CPU, allowing you to distribute calculation tasks for faster performance. Parallel calculations are used for straight forward calcs; the more complex or dependent calculations will always run in serial mode.

Essbase uses the CALCTASKDIM setting to define the parallel task list. CALCTASKDIM tells Essbase how many sparse dimensions to consider when determining a task schedule for parallel processing of cube aggregations. The default value is one, which means that Essbase will only consider the last sparse dimension for defining a task list.

You can define CALCPARALLEL in the following ways:
- In essbase.cfg – `CALCPARALLEL appname dbname n`
- In calc script – `SET CALCPARALLEL n;`
  - N = 1 to 4/8; default is 1

You can define CALCTASKDIMS in the following ways:
- In essbase.cfg – `CALCTASKDIMS appname dbname n`
- In calc script – `SET CALCTASKDIMS n;`
  - N = 1 to number of sparse dimensions
  - Use when fixing on the last sparse dimension

If the last sparse dimension in the outline does not contain multiple members to FIX on and CALCTASKDIMS is still the default, then Essbase will not parallelize the calculation no matter how many threads you devote to the calculation. In general, setting the number of CALCTASKDIMS to high values has negative return. Essbase calc performance can be greatly reduced by asking for it to analyze too many dimensions when determining a task list. Testing is the only way to determine the optimal CALCTASKDIM settings for your cube/calc environments.

Essbase will modify CALCPARALLEL and CALCTASKDIMS settings when using the CALC CACHE. Essbase will write in the log that it has adjusted the number of CALCTASKDIMS because of the use of the CALC CACHE. In these situations, testing has shown better performance when using parallel calculations over optimal CALC CACHE settings.

Other last general calculation optimization tips: Simplify the calculation if possible by using unary calcs instead of member formulas, and member formulas instead of logic within a calc script. Take advantage of built-in Essbase functionality like Dynamic Time Series whenever possible.

OPTIMIZE RETRIEVALS

You *can* speed up data retrievals by increasing the value of two retrieval-specific buffer settings. These buffers hold extracted row data cells before they are evaluated or sorted. If the buffer is too small, retrieval times can increase with the constant emptying and re-filling of the buffer. If the buffer is too large, retrieval times can increase when too much memory is used when concurrent users perform queries. The default buffer is set to 10KB for 32-bit platforms and 20 KB for 64-bit. As a rule, don't exceed 100KB for either buffer.

To set the retrieval buffers,

1. Right click on the Database and select *Edit Properties*.
2. Go to the General tab and set the retrieval buffers:

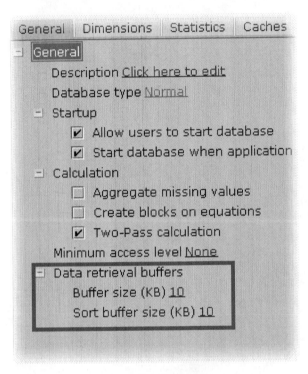

FRAGMENTATION

Fragmentation can be a potentially crippling side-effect of frequently updated databases that use one of the compression techniques mentioned earlier in this chapter. Let's assume that we have a very simple block with only eight cells:

100	#Missing	#Missing	#Missing
#Missing	#Missing	#Missing	#Missing

Any one of the compression methods would work well on this, but for the sake of example let's assume Run-Length Encoding is used and is able to compress the data storage component to 32 bytes (8 Bytes for the 100 and 24 Bytes to compress all the

#Missing values together). Then, a user writes some budget data to this block:

100	150	200	#Missing
#Missing	#Missing	#Missing	#Missing

This block will now require 48 Bytes to store (8 Bytes for each number, and 24 Bytes for the #Missing values). Fragmentation happens because Essbase can't fit 48 Bytes back into the original 32 Byte location and it is written to the end of the file. The original block still remains in the file, but there is no corresponding pointer in the index file so it is lost forever but still taking up space. Actually, it's not quite forever. Essbase tracks empty space in the database directory in a .esm file.

Now that you understand fragmentation, an alarm should be going off for all budgeting application administrators – Ding, Ding! Budgeting not only involves frequent updates, but also calc scripts that expand block size. Fragmentation also runs rampant when data load rules aren't sorted properly and blocks are written to the .pag file, then updated later in the load and re-written to a new block location.

Tip!

Go to the Statistics tab in your database properties and look at the Clustering Ratio. While this number is just a sample and will not be exact, you want it to be as close to 1.00 as possible. If it drops below .7, you should consider defragmenting your database and if it goes below .5, defragment as soon as you have available downtime.

To eliminate fragmentation, you can export the data from the database to a file, clear all data from the database and reload from the export file (see the Backup and Recovery section in "A Day in the Life of an Administrator" chapter). This workaround (and various other unseemly workarounds like adding "dummy members" to dense dimensions) was the only method to defragment an Essbase cube until recently. Newer versions of Essbase MaxL support a command called **alter database [database name] force restructure** which removes all fragmentation from the database.

Try It!

Defrag the wolverine juggling application by exporting the data to a file, clear all data, and reload the exported data file. What happened to the size of the database on disk?

COMMIT ACCESS

Commit access in Essbase tells the engine how and when to save the data to the physical disk. This concept will be familiar if you have worked in-depth with relational databases. When you run an update statement against a SQL database, you must run a commit after the fact to ensure changes are saved to the database. Commit access in Essbase works similarly.

When you use uncommitted access, Essbase writes the data blocks to disk when the commit level is reached. The default commit level is set to 3000 blocks. So let's say you are performing a data load, once 3000 blocks have been loaded (triggered by the arrival of the 3001st block), they will commit to disk. Essbase will then continue with the load, committing again once 3000 more blocks are loaded. So Essbase is going back and forth writing to disk (also called I/O or input/output) which could impact performance. By increasing the Commit level, you will be sending more data fewer times, and by decreasing this value you will be sending less data more times.

Committing by rows is for environments where there is a risk that the data load process will be interrupted mid-stream and the administrator will want to continue the load from a logical starting point. For example, if the Commit setting is equal to 1000 rows, Essbase will save the blocks to disk at this interval. If the load fails on the $3,462^{nd}$ record, there will be a record of 3,000 rows successfully saved into the Essbase database and the administrator can restart the load from record 3,001. Yes, this will reload the records from 3,001 to 3,461 redundantly, but better that than losing data.

You can also set the commit blocks to zero. With this setting, Essbase will only write to disk at the completion of the entire transaction (in our example, this is at the end of the data load). This can dramatically improve performance, BUT (and that was a big ass "but") this can significantly fragment the page file (see section on Fragmentation). Only do this if you're running calculations infrequently as part of a periodic batch updating process, but if you are, setting commit blocks to zero can reduce your calculation time by more than half on bulk aggregations.

To change the Commit setting,
1. Select the database.
2. Right click and select *Edit Properties*.
3. Select the Transactions tab.
4. Select either Committed or Uncommitted access.
5. If you chose Uncommitted access, next define the synchronization point:
    a. Commit blocks OR
    b. Commit rows

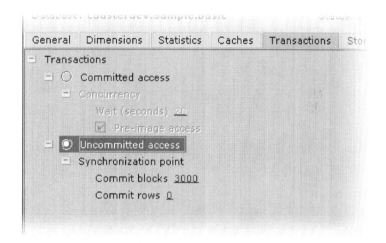

6. Click *Apply*.

Congratulations! If you've made it this far, you are in the home stretch. We are in the last two miles of the Essbase marathon. You've created and tuned the databases, but how do you manage them? You are in some degree of pain, your feet are killing you, you are dehydrated, and you just want to fall down and collapse. Grab an energy bar, some Gatorade, and keep going. You are almost there. You can do it!

Essbase Administration

Chapter 21:
Introduction to Essbase Security

SECURITY OVERVIEW

You've built your database, loaded data, and in the case of BSO databases, calculated. The anticipation is killing you. Finally you are ready for analysis. But all you see is #NoAccess. Oh, that's right. We haven't covered one of the most important parts of Essbase, security. Let's discuss that now.

Essbase provides flexible security that can be implemented from a high level down to the individual cell level. Cell level? You mean I can control which cells in my body I want to grant access to and even to whom to grant them access? Well, then let me begin by granting Angelina Jolie access to every single...

No, not those cells, dreamer. By cell level, we mean down to a single intersection in the database. For example, you can define write access for product 100 for January for gross revenue for actual for FY07 for the west region. Do we recommend this level of security? No, that would be a nightmare to maintain, but if your requirements dictate that kind of madness, you go for it. The next three chapters will teach you how.

In Essbase System 9 and 11, security is managed in the Shared Services Console (remember, Shared Services is part of the Foundation Services layer of System 9 / Oracle EPM System). Shared Services is where you will manage the security for all of your Hyperion products.

Could you implement security within Administration Services (just like you did in Essbase 7x)? Technically, yes. You can use Essbase security instead of Shared Services if (and this is a big if) you are only using Essbase and the Excel Spreadsheet Add-in. If you use any other product like Financial Reporting, Planning or Financial Management, it probably makes sense to implement and manage security in Shared Services.

Chapter 22 is dedicated to managing security in Shared Services and Chapter 23 is dedicated to managing security in Administration Services. But before we jump into the details of each tool, we will review Essbase security concepts that are the same whether you manage security in Essbase or in Shared Services.

First, let us discuss the different types of users within Essbase. Essbase has four different kinds of users: Administrators (a.k.a. supervisors), Provisioning Managers (a.k.a. user managers), Application Managers (a.k.a. application designers), Database Managers (AKA database designers) and End Users.

Note! The types of users changed names slightly between Essbase 7x and System 9 (but in this instance you can easily map the new names... not so with some of the other System 9 roles and user types).

Administrators (AKA god-like supreme beings) have full access to all Essbase components and applications. User managers can manage security access but cannot update or access applications.

Provisioning Managers manage security access in Shared Services for the server and specific applications and databases. They grant End Users Read, Write, Calculate or Filter access. Read access and Write access provide either read or write access to the entire database. Calculate access allows an End User to run calculations, either all calculations or specific calculations. Filter access defines an End User's access at a more detailed level (filters are discussed below). A Provisioning Manager cannot access or update the application unless they have been granted another Essbase role.

If your administrator is Satan, application managers are demons who run some of the circles of hell. Application Managers can manage applications but they cannot update security (although one user could be assigned both of these roles). An application creator can be defined at the application level and the database level. The Application Manager can perform the following:

- Modify or delete the application.
- Create, modify or delete the database within application.
- Assign user access privileges at the application or database level.
- Define and assign filter objects anywhere in the application.

Note! When we said above "if your administrator is Satan," that was what we in the literary biz call "an analogy." Despite what you may think, demons are probably not administering your servers.

Database Managers are the low-people-on-the-totem pole in the world of Essbase administrators (maybe they get to watch over some of hell's outer rings). Don't feel too bad, database managers. You still have full control of your own database world and you don't have the headaches that come with being a (god-like) supervisor. The Database Manager can perform the following:

- Modify or delete the database.
- Assign user access privileges at the database level.
- Define and assign filter objects anywhere in the database.
- Remove data locks within the database.

End Users can have read, write, calculate or filter access. Read and write are pretty straightforward roles, providing either read or write access to the entire database. Calculate access allows the users to run calculations (either all calculations or specific calculations which the provisioning manager assigns). Let us now review database filters and filter access, because they're just cool.

DATABASE FILTERS

Database filters apply detailed End User Essbase security to a slice of the database (even down to the cell level). Filters can grant four types of access to specific dimensions and members: None, Read, Write, or MetaRead. None, Read, and Write access rights are pretty straightforward and specify an End User's access to the data. Though it's mostly obvious, we'll provide an example anyway (can you guess who gets paid by the word?): Read access set within a filter allows Read-only access to data in specific cells of the database.

MetaRead is more complicated, because it doesn't grant access to the data itself. MetaRead security applies a level of security for metadata so that an End User can view only part of the Essbase outline hierarchy. Setting filter access to MetaRead restricts the End User's view to specific members or sections of an Essbase outline hierarchy.

In the example below, the user has access only to the West Region. Because their filter is set to MetaRead access to West region in the Market dimension, they can view only the West portion of the hierarchy:

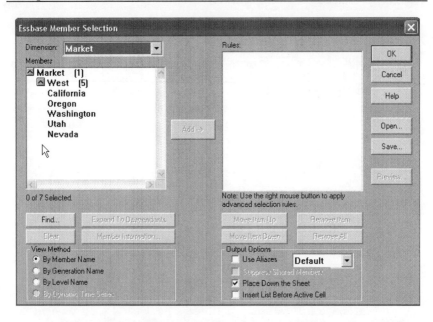

If the user had Read access to the West region instead of MetaRead access, they would be able to view the entire Market hierarchy yet would still only have access to West region data. They would receive the message "#NoAccess" for data points other than the West region descendants.

Here we switched the user's access from MetaRead to read and now the user can see the full hierarchy:

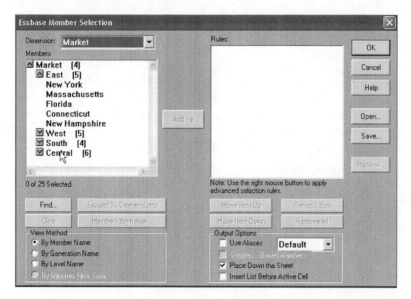

But the user can only see data values for the descendants of West:

	A	B	C	D	E
1			Sales	Product	Actual
2	East	Year	#NoAccess		
3	California	Year	47442		
4	Oregon	Year	19992		
5	Washingto	Year	19036		
6	Utah	Year	17305		
7	Nevada	Year	29156		
8	West	Year	#NoAccess		
9	South	Year	#NoAccess		
10	Central	Year	#NoAccess		
11	Mar	Year	#NoAccess		
12					
13					

MetaRead security offers the following benefits:
- Improves the ease of use when users can only see a small number of the members
- Provides privacy so extranet users can't see the existence of other extranet users (such as vendors)
- Provides privacy so that users of sensitive applications (i.e., Payroll) can't see the existence or *non-existence* of specific members (like a company reorganization where a department may be eliminated)

CREATE A DATABASE FILTER

Let's create the database filter for the West group of users. This filter should only allow access to the West region of the Market dimension. We do not want the West users to be able to see the other members of the Market dimension. What type of filter access should be assigned? That's right – MetaRead.

1. Within Administration Services, navigate to the application and database where you will be creating the filter.

Note! Be aware! Filters are created in the Application / database section of Administration Services, not the Security section. This is because filters are always associated with an application and database.

2. Right click on the Sample.Basic database and section select *Create >> Filters*:

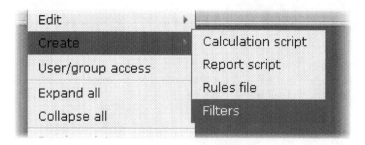

3. The Filter Editor window will open.
4. Type in the name of a filter in this case 'F_West'.
5. Under Access, select *"MetaRead"*:

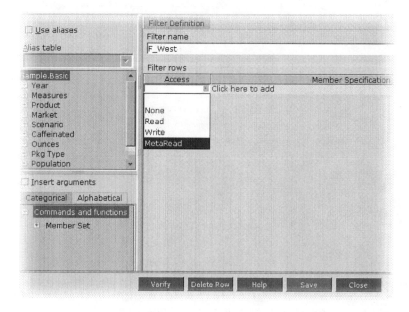

Dimension References in the Filter Editor

- The dimension reference area allows you to navigate the outline within the Filter editor window.
- You can search for a member.
- You can insert a member name into the filter definition area.

Helpful
Info

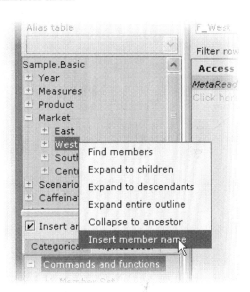

Available Functions in the Filter Editor

- Lists available functions and operators available for filters.
- Enables the administrator to insert arguments for functions.
- Assists the administrator with the formula syntax.
- Enables auto-completion and speeds up filter creation.

Helpful
Info

6. Next, place your cursor in the Member Specification box.
7. Under the Commands and functions section of the Filter Editor, expand the Member Set grouping and look for '@DESCENDANTS'.
8. Double-click on '@DESCENDANTS' when you find it. This should insert the function into the Member Specification box:

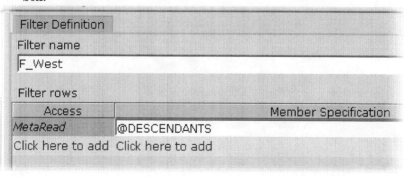

9. Place your cursor after the first parenthesis. We need to insert the desired member in between the parentheses – in this case, West.
10. In the dimension reference portion of the Filter editor, expand the Market dimension to find the West member.
11. Right click on West and select *Insert Member Name*:

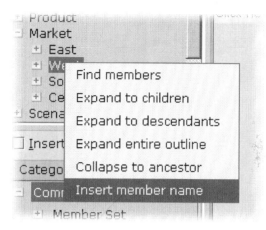

12. This should insert the function into the Member Specification box.

You can further define the filter by specifying a specific generation number or generation name. These settings are optional (as denoted by the square brackets - [ ]).

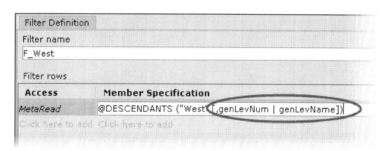

We are choosing descendants in this case because we want this filter to allow MetaRead access to West's descendants.

Tip!

If we wanted to give access to both West *and* West's descendants, we would put the letter "I" right after the @ sign: @IDESCENDANTS. "I" before the function name means to include the member itself. Depending on your security requirements, you may choose to use the "I" or not.

Note! You don't have to use the dimension reference or available functions sections in the Filter editor. If you know the syntax and exact member name, you can type directly into the Member Specification box. This will impress people.

Filter Definition	
Filter name	
F_West	

Filter rows

Access	Member Specification
MetaRead	@DESCENDANTS("West")
Click here to add	Click here to add

13. Click on the *Verify* button.

14. Check the message panel for any errors.

15. Select *File >> Save* or the *Save* button to save the filter.

In our example, we only defined access on one dimension, but you could define access on multiple dimensions. We could have also locked down Accounts, giving read access to Net Income accounts but not balance sheet accounts. We could have granted write access to the budget scenario and read access to Actual.

If a filter has overlapping member specifications, access is set by the following rules:

- A filter that defines a more detailed dimension combination list takes precedence over a filter with less detail.
- If the preceding rule does not resolve the overlap conflict, the highest access level among overlapping filter rows is applied.

The access level for unspecified members is the inherited access level of the database.

INHERITANCE RULES

Rule one: try to be the heir to billions so that when everyone else in the family dies (of *natural causes*), you can inherit everything! [Tracy's note to Edward: not *those* kinds of inheritance rules. Good idea, though.]

As we discussed earlier, users can be grouped together and assigned to a group. Security settings and filters are applied to those groups. Users inherit all privileges defined for their group. Though, sometimes group security assignments may conflict with each other. How does Essbase handle conflicting security group and user assignments?

Let's use the following scenario to explain. The minimum access for the database is set to Read. The Budget group has write access to the Budget scenario and all regions via the filter F_Budget. Shaq is a member of the Budget office group. Shaq as an End User is assigned Write access to the West Region. Chuck is an Essbase End User and is not a member of any group. So here are the rules of inheritance:

Default minimum access will apply for all users. So Chuck has read access to the entire database.

If a user has more detailed access privileges than the default (via a filter), those assignments will take precedence. Shaq is a user so by default has Read access to the entire database. However, he is a member of the Budget group which has a higher level of security – filter access to Write to the Budget scenario. The Budget group's Write access will take precedence over the default Read access.

The Budget group has Write access to all Regions but Shaq only has Write access to West. User access overrides group access, so Shaq's individual security takes precedence and he will be able to write only to the West region.

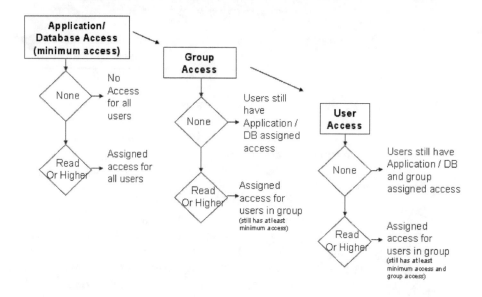

Now that you have the security basics, go to the next chapter if you will use Shared Services for security management or to Chapter 23 if you are going to manage security in Administration Services.

Chapter 22:
Manage Security in Shared Services

INTRODUCTION TO SHARED SERVICES

Shared Services is part of the Foundation Services layer of System 9 and Oracle EPM System 11. Components of Shared Services include:

- User Provisioning
- Enterprise Performance Management Architect (versions 9.3 and later)
- Life Cycle Management (11x)
- Core Services

Core Services is better known as the underlying "plumbing" for Oracle EPM System: session management, authentication and authorization, repository services, and logging and usage.

User provisioning allows you to maintain Oracle EPM System security for all products. The one exception: if you use Financial Reporting, Web Analysis, Interactive Reporting, or Production Reporting, you will assign document permissions in the Workspace.

You create a user once, assign the user to groups, assign the user to roles, and assign application access. A common set of roles is available across products. The interface for User Provisioning is called the Shared Services Console in version 11 and the User Management Console in System 9 (it is the same console, they just renamed it in version 11).

User provisioning provides single sign on across the Oracle EPM System / Hyperion products (you can even implement single sign on between external systems). Users can externally authenticate to LDAP, MSAD, NTLM or other third party tools. User provisioning is bundled with OpenLDAP for native Shared Services users and groups.

Two security layers exist in Shared Services. The first is the user authentication layer that validates the user id and password. The authentication can be native or external. The second layer is the product specific authorization that grants the user access to the Hyperion products and applications. Shared Services manages the product specific authorization.

Next we will delve into the capabilities of the Native Directory of Shared Services. The Native Directory manages and maintains the default Shared Services user accounts required for Hyperion products. It is the central repository for all Hyperion provisioning information and stores the relationships between users, groups, and roles. The backend database is OpenLDAP and is easily corrupted, so back up this repository often.

The basic steps to get Shared Services up and running are as follows (see the installation and production documentation for the details):

1. Install and configure Shared Services.
2. Set up external authentication.
3. Install and configure the Oracle EPM System / Hyperion products.
4. Register the products with Shared Services.

Finally, let us recap the applicable Essbase roles that are available in Shared Services (these should look familiar):

Power Roles include:
- Administrator (a.k.a. god-like Supervisor)
- Provisioning Manager
- Application Manager (AKA Application Designer)
- Create / Delete Application
- Database Manager (a.k.a Database Designer)
- Load / Unload Application

Interactive Roles include:
- Calc
- Write
- Filter

View Roles include Read access.

The Provisioning Manager role, another god-like role, allows you to assign and grant security. If a user only has the provisioning manager role and not the other Essbase roles, this person can only maintain security.

PRE-REQS TO USING SHARED SERVICES & ESSBASE

Prerequisite steps must be taken before you can manage Essbase security in Shared Services. Assuming Shared Services,

Essbase, and Administration Services have been installed, you will need to convert native Essbase users to externally authenticated users through a process called "Externalize Users":

You'll externalize the Essbase users only once and the important thing is you can't go back. Never. Ever. To underscore the importance of this, Essbase uses the word "really" in the warning message. This is serious business for serious consideration.

Note!

Don't click Yes to this message until you've read all of the installation and product documentation related to setting up Shared Services and Essbase (or your handy consultants have reviewed the considerations with you). The documentation is a few hundred pages not one of which is even as interesting as this sentence.

Clicking on *Yes* will take you from native Essbase security mode to Shared Services security mode. (Dorothy, you're departing Kansas on a one-way trip to Oz.) For the complete set of installation and configuration instructions and details on the process to migrate Essbase users to Shared Services users, please read the installation documentation. (Sorry!)

LOG INTO THE USER MANAGEMENT CONSOLE

To log into the Shared Services Console, the main interface for Shared Services,

1. Log into the Workspace: http://server:19000/workspace.
2. Select *Navigate (steering wheel icon) >> Administer >> Shared Services Console*:

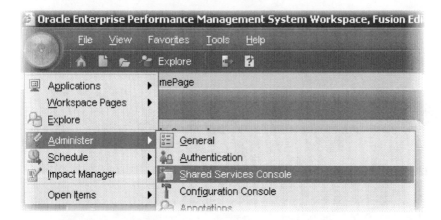

3. The Shared Services Console window will display:

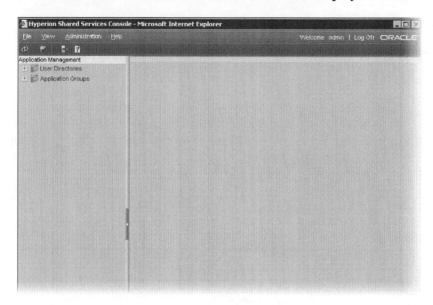

Note! To manage Essbase security in Shared Services, your Shared Services administrator must grant you the Provisioning Manager role for the Essbase server or specific Essbase application and databases.

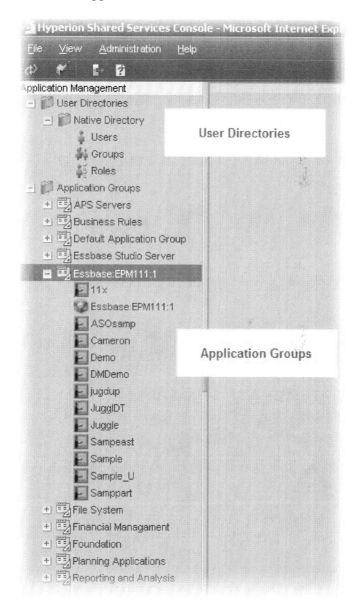

The navigation panel on the left portion of the window controls the main content area. For example, if you select "User Directories", the main content area will allow you to search and display the users. The User Directories section groups native and external directories. The Application Groups section lists all of the products registered with Shared Services (this used to be called Projects in System 9). By default, a separate application group will be created for each Oracle EPM System / Hyperion product that you install and configure through the configuration utility. Your Essbase server(s) will display as follows: *Essbase: servername:1:*

CREATE A NATIVE GROUP

In general, you will want to use Group security assignments as much as possible. Groups reduce the overall maintenance for your security application. You define security once and as users come and go, they can be added to and removed from groups. If security requirements change, you update the group security once vs. many times for individual users. Specific to Shared Services, you can use external or native groups which can contain both native users and external users. Native groups that can contain other groups are called nested groups.

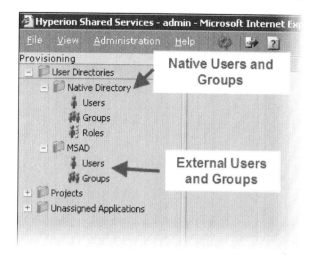

 Note!

Externally authenticated groups cannot be managed with Shared Services. That means you can't modify the users in the group, though you can assign security to the group.

 Tip!

The same group can be used across multiple applications and databases. This is actually a pretty good practice.

Let's walk through an example. End users of the Sample.Basic application will only have access to their market. We will create a native group for the West market:

1. Within Shared Services, select Groups.
2. Select *File >> New*
     or
   Right Click on *Groups* and select *New*:

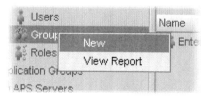

3. The Create Group window displays.
4. Type in the group name and description:

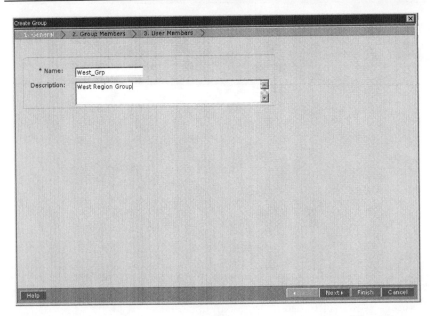

5. Click the *Next* button to advance to the Group Members tab.
6. Select desired available groups (either native or external). Search for specific groups if you'd like.
7. Select the arrow icons to assign the selected groups:

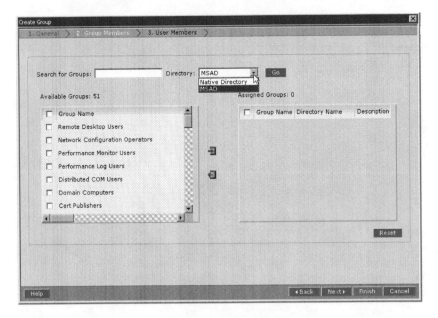

8. Click the *Next* button to advance to the User Members tab.
9. Select desired available users (either native or external). Search for specific users if you'd like.
10. Select the arrow icons to assign the selected users:

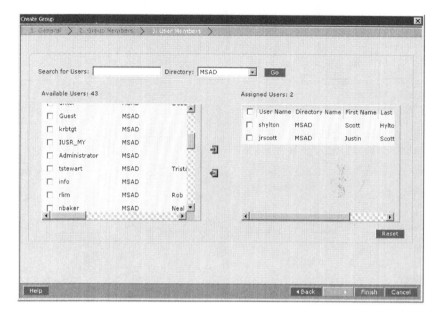

11. Click *Finish*.

CREATE A NATIVE USER

Shaquille O'Neal has finally decided to retire from the NBA and pursue a career in business performance management (go with us on this one: it could happen). This is good news for us, because our wildly successful wolverine juggling business has recruited Shaq to be the manager for the West Region (pretend that we've added a Market dimension to our juggling wolverine application). Let's create a new Shared Services native user, 'Shaq' and assign him to the West Region group.

1. Within Shared Services, select *File >> New* (you should have Groups selected).

   or

   Right click on Users and select *New*:

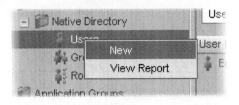

2. The Create User window displays.
3. Type in the user id "Shaq", name, password and other information.

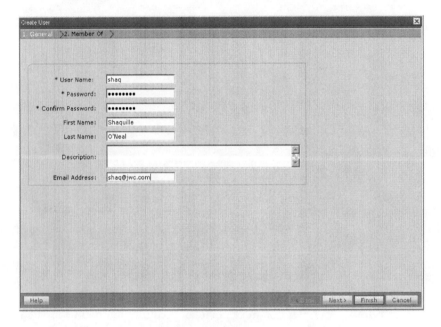

4. Select *Next* to advance to the Group Membership tab.
5. Click the *Go* button to list all groups or search for a specific group:

6. Select desired available groups, using the arrow icons to assign the user to specific groups. We'll assign *Shaq* to the West group:

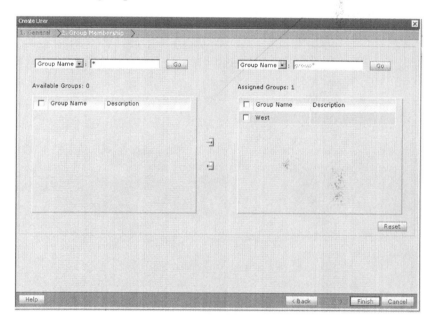

7. Click *Finish*.

Try It!

Shaq will need to input budgets for the West region in the Sample.Basic application. Create a new "Budget" group and assign Shaq to this group.

Try It!

Shaq has recruited our favorite NBA star, Charles Barkley to join the juggling wolverine business. Since his role will be defined later, create a new user chuck, but don't assign him to any groups at this point.

VIEW USERS AND GROUPS

Sometimes it's fun to see a list of users. To view users:

1. Select the Users in the left pane.
2. Search for a specific user or click *Search:*

A number of search options are available for filtering the user list:

- User Property: First Name, Last Name, User Name, Description, email
- Group
- View: active, inactive or all users

Follow the same steps to view groups. This is not nearly as fun, because groups usually don't have cool names like "Shaq".

PROVISION USERS AND GROUPS

So far we we've created users and groups but we haven't assigned any roles or application access. Next, we'll go through the steps to provision a user. So what exactly are we doing when we provision a user? You are assigning a role for the user; for example, you are giving a user read or write access to an Essbase database or Content Publisher role for Reporting and Analysis modules (which means they can create adhoc queries and save them in their personal directories).

Note! The steps to provision a user and group are the same. If you need to provision a group, right click on the group and select Provision. Follow the steps provided below.

To provision a user,

1. Right click on the user and select *Provision*:

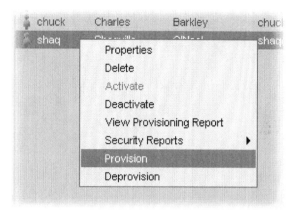

2. The Available Roles section will display on the left. You should see your Essbase server listed as Essbase:*servername*.
3. Expand the Essbase server. The server will display first, and the list of Applications will follow. As you continue to expand the hierarchy, the Essbase roles will display:

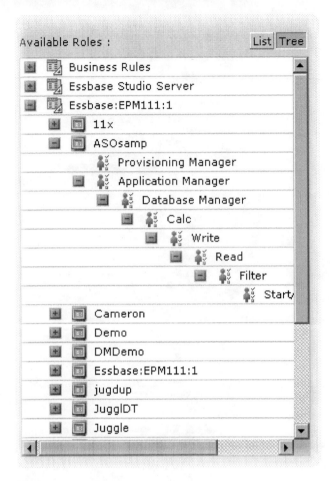

Note you can view the roles by list view. Click on the *List* button:

4. First assign server access for the user:

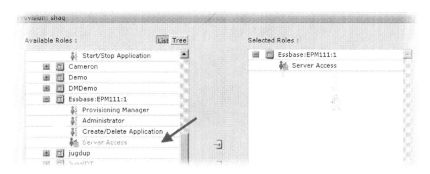

5. Next, choose the desired role and use the arrow icon to move the role over to the Selected Roles section:

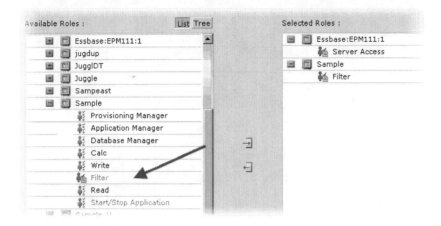

6. Click the *Save* button to save the role assignments. A Provision Summary report will display:

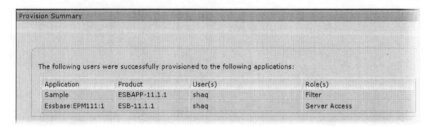

If you want to assign filter or calculation access, you're not finished yet. You still need to assign the actual filter or calculations.

7. Navigate to the Application Groups section in the Shared Services Console.
8. Expand the Application Groups section.
9. Double click on the application or right click on the application and select *Assign Access Control:*

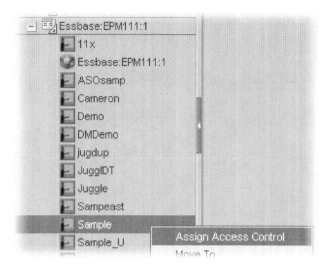

10. Refresh the available user or group list by selecting Available Users, Available Groups or Available Users & Groups from the drop down. Click the *Refresh* button:

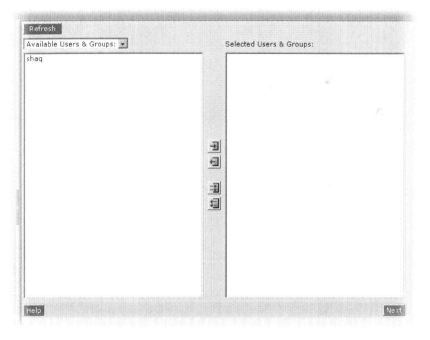

11. Select the desired users or groups and use the arrow icons to move them over to the Selected section.

Select the users or groups by placing a check mark next to their name. Select the desired filter and/or calc scripts to be assigned:

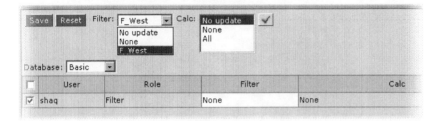

12. Click the check icon:
13. Click the *Save* button to save the assignments. A successful status message should display:

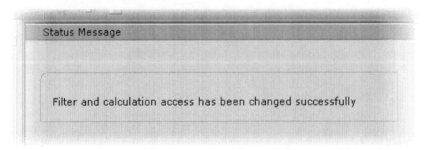

To assign whether a user (or group) is an Essbase user or Hyperion Planning user:

1. Navigate to the Application Groups section in the Shared Services Console.
2. Expand the Application Groups section.
3. Double click on the Essbase server or right click on the application and select *Assign Access Control:*

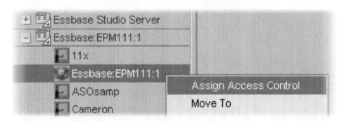

4. Select the users or groups by placing a check mark next to their name. Select None, Essbase, or Planning for the user.

5. Click the check icon:

	User Name	Supervisor	Create/Delete Application		User type
☑	shaq	No	No	Essbase	

Save Reset User type: None / Essbase / Planning ☑

6. Click the *Save* button to save the assignments. A successful status message should display.

MAINTAINING ESSBASE SECURITY

In the User Management Console, you can easily maintain your Essbase security. To edit a user or group, simply right click and select *Properties*. The User / Group window will display and you can update descriptions and memberships. You can delete groups (or users) as necessary.

In Administration Services, you can right click on the Security section and select *Manage users and groups*. This option will launch the User Management Console:

From time to time users can become deactivated (or disabled). It is also possible to do this manually if a user is being a royal pain in the rump. To re-activate (or to manually deactivate) a user:

1. In the Shared Services Console, find the user.
2. Right click on the user and select *Activate* or *Deactivate* (depending on your objective):

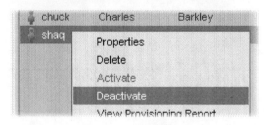

Next, you will need to synchronize security between Shared Services and Essbase, essentially pushing security to Essbase and updating the Essbase.sec file.

Note!

To oversimplify its importance, Essbase.SEC is the Essbase security file that stores information about users, groups, passwords for native security, privileges on applications and databases, and some application/database properties. DO NOT OPEN THIS FILE DIRECTLY EVER. It may be the single most important file in your Essbase installation, and we will cover this file in a later chapter.

In Administration Services, you can right click on the Security section in the Enterprise View and select *Refresh security from Shared Services:*

For automatic updates, use the following configuration settings within Essbase.cfg file. (What's the Essbase.cfg file? The two-second answer for this question is: it is the main configuration file for the Essbase server.)

- CssSyncLevel = Automatic User Synchronization (synchronizes security information for a specific user and any related groups when the user logs in to Analytic Services)

- CssRefreshLevel = Automatic Refresh refreshes the status of all users, groups, and applications for an Analytic Server at Analytic Server start up
- SharedServicesRefreshInterval = Schedule automatic refreshes

The CSSRefreshLevel setting does not affect the SharedServicesRefreshInterval setting.

Even though you will manage security in Shared Services for Essbase, you can view some security for Essbase in Administration Services. In Administration Services, double click on Users or Groups under the Security section to view a list of users and groups:

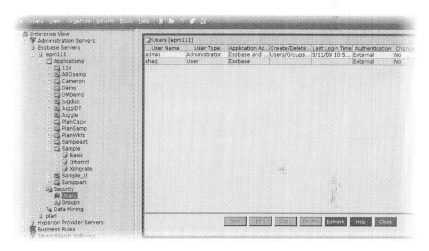

A list of users or groups will display with their attributes. Notice that the buttons to manage security (*New, Edit, Copy, Delete*) are disabled.

RUNNING SECURITY REPORTS IN SHARED SERVICES

You can run predefined reports to understand role assignments for users and groups in Shared Services (although as of version 9.3 you could not view a report displaying the user-group assignment). To run a security report,

1. From the Administration menu option in the Shared Services Console, select *Administration >> View Provisioning Report*:

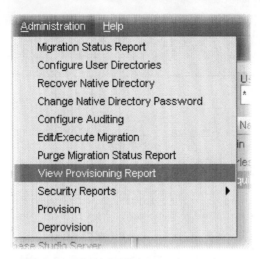

2. Select the desired options for the report.
    -   Filter by users, groups, roles
    -   For user or role
    -   Show effective roles
    -   Group by (defines how the report will be structured):

Select *Show Effective Roles* as *Yes* if you want to see all of the security that is applied to a user either by the explicitly assigned security or by the security inherited from group security assignments. In most cases, choose yes for *Show Effective Roles*.

3. Click *Create Report* button:

4. Click *Print Preview* to preview and print the report.
5. Click *Export to CSV* to export the report content to a comma delimited file.

COPY PROVISIONING

Shared Services provides capabilities to copy provisioning where you can copy all user, group, and role information from one application to another. To use this feature, the applications must be in the same product and product version, and you must be a Shared Services Administrator or Provisioning Manager of the source and target applications.

1. From Shared Services Console, expand Application Groups.
2. Select the application whose provisioning information you want to copy.
3. Right-click and select *Copy Provisioning*.
4. On the Copy Provisioning frame, select the application to which you want to copy provisioning information.
5. Click *Save*.

Note!   We have seen some instances where the Shared Services backend database gets corrupted when you try to copy provisioning information (in the early versions of System 9). Make sure you consistently back up the Shared Services OpenLDAP repository and relational database.

Before we conclude, we want to give you these last tips for implementing Essbase security in Shared Services.

Tip!

1. Set up external authentication to corporate user directory.
2. Leverage external user groups where possible.
3. Create native groups where necessary.
4. Assign users to groups.
5. Assign roles to groups.
6. Assign application specific access to groups.

Once security is set up for your Essbase application, your users are ready to retrieve and report. Happy analyzing!

Chapter 23:
Manage Security in Administration Services

WARNING – read this chapter only if your company chooses to manage security in *native Essbase security mode,* using Administration Services to create users and groups and assign application access. You can do this *if and only if* you are using just Essbase and the Excel Spreadsheet Add-in. (Technically, you could use native Essbase security in scenarios with other products but please contact your friendly consultants to discuss considerations and limitations.)

Note!

If you are still using Essbase 7x, the steps to manage security in Essbase 7x may be slightly different than those documented here for Essbase 11x.

SET DEFAULT ACCESS

In native Essbase security mode, you can define default security access for a database. To set application or database default access,

1. Right click on the application or database.
2. Select *Edit Properties*.
3. On the General tab, set the Minimum access level to either None, Read, Write, Calculate or Database Manager:

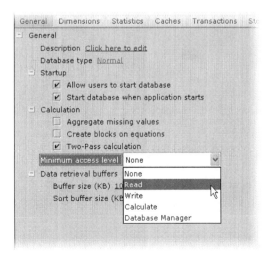

4. Click *Apply* to save the change.

CREATE A GROUP AND ASSIGN SECURITY

In Essbase you will want to use Group security assignments as much as possible. Groups reduce the overall maintenance for your security application. You define security once and as users come and go, they can be added and removed to groups. If security requirements change, you update the group security once vs. many times for many users.

Note!

The same group can be used across multiple applications and databases. We stated that in an earlier chapter, but you probably skipped that part (it was boring, we'll admit).

Let's walk through an example. End users of the Sample.Basic application will only have access to their market. We will create a group and assign security for the West market.

1. Within Administration Services, select *File >> New >> Group*

    or

Right Click on *Groups* under the Security section and select *Create Group*:

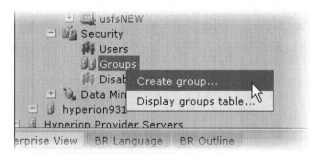

2. The Create Group window displays.
3. Type in the group name.
4. Specify Group Type:
    - Administrator
    - User
    - Application access type

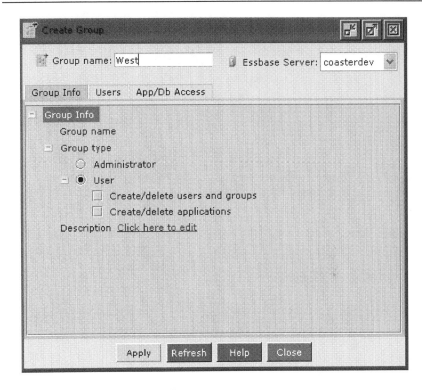

5. Select the Users tab.
6. Select desired available users.
7. Select the < (or the << to assign all users):

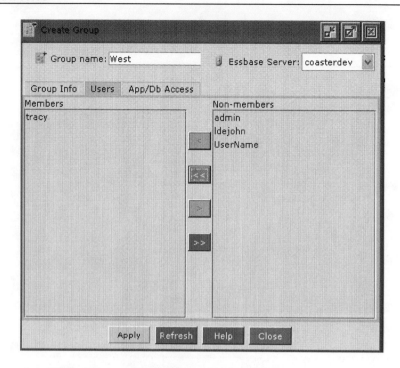

8. Click the App/Db Access tab. By default, users do not have access to any application or database:

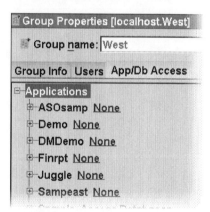

To assign access,

9. Select the desired application and select *"Access Databases"* from the drop down box to the right of the selected application:

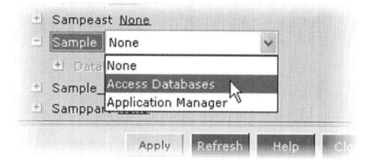

10. Select the database and then the desired access from the drop down box (for example, Filter access):

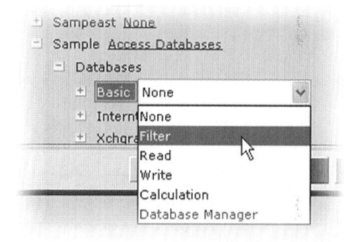

Available options include:
- None – The user or group will have NO access to the database.
- Filter – The user or group will have filter access that allows specific access to certain members or dimensions. After assigning Filter access you must assign a specific security filter that you have already created.
- Read – The user or group will have Read access to the entire database.
- Write – The user or group will have Read and Write access to the entire database.
- Calculation – The user or group will have Read and Write access to the entire database, plus access to

run all database calculations or specific calculations.

- Database Manager – This allows the user or group to update the Essbase database through Administration Services console, for example, they can change dimensions, write calc scripts, create load rules.

In this example, we are creating a group that has read access to the West market. What access should we assign? If you answered 'Filter', you are correct. If you answered "42," then you are a geek who spends way too much time reading Douglas Adams. [Edward: But I answered 42!] [Tracy: Exactly.]

11. Select the filter to assign to the group (more on filters in just a few pages).

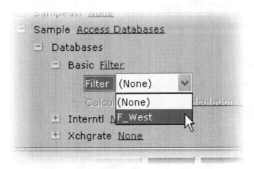

12. Click *Apply* and the group should be created with the assigned security privileges.

CREATE A USER AND ASSIGN SECURITY

Like in the last chapter that you probably didn't read (or else, why would you be reading this chapter?) Shaq has decided to retire from the NBA and pursue a career in business performance management. While the basketball world is devastated, this is good news for us. Our hugely successful wolverine juggling business has recruited Shaq to be the manager for the West Region (pretend that we've added a Market dimension to our juggling wolverine application). Let's create a new user, 'Shaq' and assign him to the West Region group.

2. Within Administration Services, select *File >> New >> User*

or

Right click on *Users* under the Security section and select *Create User*:

6. The Create User window displays.
7. Type in the user name "Shaq".
8. Specify authentication method and enter password if necessary.

With Essbase 7x, System 9, and version 11, you can authenticate against the Essbase server or an external provider like Microsoft Active Directory or LDAP. There are additional configuration steps required for external authentication (see the installation guides for more information). For this example, we will choose Essbase authentication.

9. Specify User Type.
    *   Administrator
    *   User
    *   Application access type

In this example, we choose 'User'.

10. Select the Groups tab.
11. Select desired available groups.
12. Select the < (or the << to assign all groups). We'll assign the user, Shaq, to the West group.
13. Click *Apply*.

Now if we wanted to assign user-specific security to an application, we could do so by selecting the App/Db Access tab and follow the same steps for assigning database access security. But we are leveraging groups for all security assignments (remember that best practice tip). So we are done with the process of creating the user, Shaq.

Try It!

Shaq will need to input budgets for the West region in the Sample.Basic application. Create a new "Budget" group and assign Roger to this group.

Try It!

Shaq has recruited Charles Barkley to join the juggling wolverine biz. Create a new user "chuck" but don't assign him to any groups at this point.

MAINTAINING ESSBASE SECURITY

In the Administration Services console, you can easily maintain your Essbase security. Use "Copy" functionality when you need to create a group (or user) that is exactly the same as another group (or user) with one or two slight changes. Use the "Edit" functionality when you need to edit group (or user) access. You can delete groups (or users) as necessary.

Double-click on Groups or right click on Groups in the Enterprise View panel. Select *Display Groups table* to maintain Essbase groups. Double-click on Users or right click on Users and select *Display Users table* to maintain Essbase users:

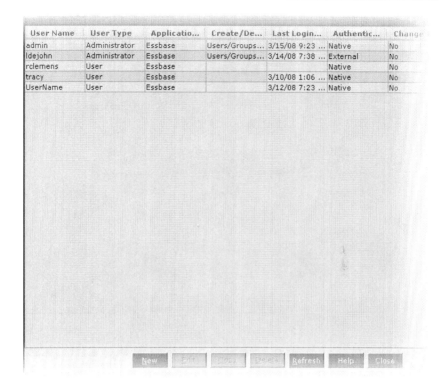

Right click on any user (or group from the group view) and a number of available actions are displayed, such as edit properties, enable or disable a user, copy a user, and so forth:

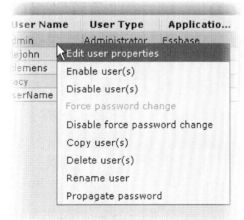

From time to time users can become disabled (for example, they've entered in the wrong password three times or you disabled them because they're stealing your food from the office refrigerator). To re-enable (or to manually disable if the refrigerator thing happens again), double-click on *Disabled Usernames* under Security in the Enterprise View panel. The Disabled Usernames window will display. Move the users from Disabled to Enabled (or vice versa depending on your objective) and click *Apply*.

Once security is set up for your Essbase application, your users are ready to retrieve and report. Happy analyzing!

[Edward: I just had an episode of déjà vu.]

[Tracy: *I* just had an episode of déjà vu.]

Chapter 24:
Essbase Administration

We've taken you through the process of creating an application and assigning security but what about the day to day tasks of an Essbase administrator? Sipping pina coladas, taking walks at midnight... if only that were true. Now let's jump into what your job will really be like. Here are some of the daily tasks you will perform.

ESSBASE AGENT

First, let's review the Essbase Agent, otherwise known as essbase.exe (on Windows) or ESSBASE (on UNIX). The Essbase Agent starts and stops all applications, manages security, and in controls the flow of communications. It is THE CRITICAL piece of Essbase. It can be started in the foreground as active operating window but you must stay logged in to keep the server up. The recommended method is to start the Essbase Agent in the background. In the "A Day in the Life of an Essbase Administrator" section, we reviewed commands to communicate with the Essbase Agent.

ESSBASE SERVER

The Essbase Server is the component that actually does all the heavy data work. An esssvr.exe (Windows) or ESSSVR (UNIX) process is started for each Essbase Application that is created. This process handles all database activity, and this design wisely isolates other Applications from any evil-doing that goes on in a rogue Application (you know, the ones that hang out by the bike racks after the books are closed).

ESSBASE.CFG

The Essbase.cfg file is the main configuration file for Essbase, and it is simply a text file stored in the arborpath\bin directory. Administrators may add or change parameters and values in this file to customize Essbase functionality. Most of these settings apply to the entire Essbase Server. Essbase reads the configuration file at startup of the Essbase Agent and every time an Application is loaded. Be aware of the potential requirement to restart the system or an application when you are making changes to this file.

In this file you can define settings that control TCP/IP ports and connections, define how detailed you would like your log files, specify cache settings for performance improvements, define query governors for the server or specific application, and much more highly technical gobbledygook. Here is a sample Essbase.cfg file:

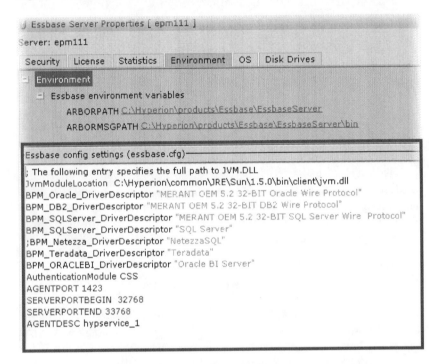

For a full listing of the Essbase.cfg settings, see the Technical Reference provided by Hyperion.

To update the Essbase.cfg,

1. In the Administration Services console, right click on the Essbase server and select *Edit >> Properties*.
2. Choose the Environment tab.
3. Update the parameters by typing directly in the Essbase.cfg.
4. Restart the Essbase server for settings to take effect.

The "old school" way to update the Essbase.cfg settings is as follows:

1. Edit the file in text format with any text editor, such as Windows Notepad.

2. Enter each setting on a separate line in the file. You do not need to end each line with a semicolon.
3. Make sure the file is named essbase.cfg,
4. Save the file in the arborpath \ bin directory.
5. Restart the Essbase Server or the Essbase Application after changing the configuration file.

```
essbase.cfg - Notepad
File  Edit  Format  View  Help
;  The following entry specifies the full path to JVM.DLL
;  JvmModuleLocation  C:\Hyperion\common\JRE\Sun\1.4.2\bin\client\jvm.dll
;This statement loads the essldap.dll as a valid authentication module
;AuthenticationModule LDAP essldap.dll x;
EssbaseLicenseServer C:\Install
AnalyticServerId 1
UPDATECALC FALSE
CALCCACHEHIGH  150000000
CALCCACHEDEFAULT 50000000
CALCCACHELOW  20000000
CALCNOTICEHIGH 20
CALCNOTICEDEFAULT 10
CALCNOTICELOW 5|
```

View the settings defined in your Essbase.cfg file.

Try It!

ESSBASE.SEC

The Essbase.sec stores information about users, groups, passwords for native security, and privileges on applications and databases. It also stores many application and database properties. This isn't a file you can open and read but it is critical to your Essbase server. It lives next door to essbase.exe in the arborpath\bin neighborhood.

Each time that you successfully start the Essbase Server, a backup copy of the security file is created (named essbase.bak). You can restore from the last successful backup by copying essbase.bak to essbase.sec. If you have a corrupt application, you often times will need to recover from the security file backup as well as recreate the application from scratch.

Find the Essbase.sec file on your server and take a look at the security settings assigned. WAIT! This was a trick "Try It!" *Do not* open the Essbase.sec. You don't ever open up this file and read it. To view security, go to the Security section in Administration Services.

Try It!

Since Essbase 9.3, you can export the Essbase.sec into a readable file. In Administration Services, right click on *Security* and select *Export security file:*

You can also use MaxL statement export security. The MaxL syntax is as follows:

```
EXPORT SECURITY_FILE to DATA_FILE file_name;
```

The resulting file will be available:

```
exp_sec.txt - Notepad
File  Edit  Format  View  Help
Essbase security file dump:          Fri Feb 29 11:32:27 2008
Company:                             interRel
Registered Username:                 admin
Essbase installation date:           Wednesday, November 28, 2007 1:45:21 PM
Essbase Location:                    CoasterDev.interrel.com:1423
EAS Location:                        CoasterDev.interrel.com:10080
MyOlapEnabled:                       DISABLED
All HSS identity migrated:           Yes
Encoding:                            UTF8
Product Version:                     9.3.1
Security File Version:               22.0
Number of Ports:                     65535
Named User license. 65535 user server
Maximum Possible Planning Users:  65535
Maximum Connection allowed per user/port:65535
Security:                            ENABLED
Default Access Level:                None
Logins:                              ENABLED
Auto-Logout time (seconds):          3600
Auto-Logout check interval:          300
Currency:                            ENABLED
SQL:                                 ENABLED
Aggregate Storage (ASO):                 ENABLED
Spreadsheet Macros:                  ENABLED
Read Only Spreadsheet:               DISABLED
Read Only Spreadsheet Macros:        DISABLED
64-bit port:                         ENABLED
Spreadsheet Addin:                   ENABLED
Reports:                             DISABLED
Busines Rules:                       ENABLED
EDS (High Concurrency):              ENABLED
Crystal:                             ENABLED
Limited SKU Appman:                  DISABLED
Limited SKU Spreadsheet:             DISABLED
Single-User Essbase:                 DISABLED
Development Server Option:           DISABLED
Block Storage (BSO):                 ENABLED
MultiCube:                           ENABLED
Hyperion Integration Server Option:  ENABLED
EssbaseObjects:                      ENABLED
Visual Explorer:                     ENABLED
Triggers:                            ENABLED
DataMining:                          ENABLED
SAPBW:                               ENABLED
```

If you scroll down through the file, you will notice stored user information as well as database information.

```
exp_sec.txt - Notepad
File  Edit  Format  View  Help
                    APP: usfsNEW  ; Manage
                    DB:  usfsNEW  ; APP: usfsNEW  ; Manage
                    DB:  usfsNEW2 ; APP: usfsNEW  ; Manage


   ldejohn                       User
           Default Access:           Administrator
           HSS Identity:             msad://OBJECTGUID=\24\3a\94\ec\6f\d4\17\41\8c\ea\de\5a\20\2d\81\d7?USER
           HSS Identity Migrated:    Yes
           Last Login:               Monday, February 25, 2008 3:51:29 PM
           Password Expires on:      NOT SET
           User Locked out:          FALSE
           Change Password on next Login:FALSE
                    APP: Coaster1 ; Manage
                    DB:  Demo    ; APP: Coaster1 ; Manage
                    DB:  Ver1    ; APP: Coaster1 ; Manage
                    DB:  Ver2    ; APP: Coaster1 ; Manage
                    DB:  Ver0    ; APP: Coaster1 ; Manage
                    DB:  CoasStor ; APP: Coaster1 ; Manage
                    DB:  Backup  ; APP: Coaster1 ; Manage
                    DB:  Coaster ; APP: Coaster1 ; Manage
                    DB:  BackStor ; APP: Coaster1 ; Manage
                    APP: Bery    ; Manage
                    DB:  AFE     ; APP: Bery    ; Manage
                    DB:  FinAD   ; APP: Bery    ; Manage
                    DB:  FinPE   ; APP: Bery    ; Manage
                    DB:  Prod    ; APP: Bery    ; Manage

**** Applications:
      Demo              Created by:          ???
           Default Access:           None
           Connects:                 TRUE
           Commands:                 TRUE
           Updates:                  TRUE
           Security:                 TRUE
           Loadable:                 TRUE
           Autoload:                 FALSE
           Lock Timeout:             3600
           Data Storage Type:        Multidimsional Data Storage
           LRO File size Limit:      NOT SET
           Application Type:         NONUNICODE
           Application Locale Description:English_UnitedStates.Latin1@Binary
              ion Type:      ESSBASE
```

MANAGE THE ESSBASE SERVER

You will definitely need to know how to start and stop the Essbase server. Essbase will stop responding at some point no matter how good of an administrator you are.

Note!

There will be many, many times when something happens in Essbase and you just don't know what caused it. Prepare yourself for the unknown at times. Let the force guide you (not really, let the knowledge you gain from this book guide you).

To start Essbase, type "**essbase password**" at any command line or double-click on Essbase.exe in Windows environment. You can also start the Essbase Server from the Hyperion Solutions program group in the start menu. Any of these steps will start the Essbase server in the foreground. You can create a script to start Essbase in the background which is recommended for production instances. You don't want anyone to see an open command line window on the server and hit the X button. No more Essbase.

Other commands that you might use for managing the Essbase Server:

START *appname*	Starts the specified application.
STOP *appname*	Stops the specified application.
USERS	Displays a list of all users connected to the Analytic Server.
PORTS	Displays the number of ports installed on the Analytic Server and the number of ports in use.
LOGOUTUSER user	Disconnects a user from the Analytic Server and frees a port. This command requires the Analytic Services system password.
PASSWORD	Changes the system password that is required to start the Analytic Server. This command requires the Analytic Services system password.
COMPACT	Enables compaction of the security file when the Agent is running. Essbase compacts the security file automatically each time the Agent is stopped.
DUMP filename	Dumps information from the Analytic Services security system to a specified file in ASCII format. If you do not supply a path with the file name, the file is saved to the bin directory. Requires the Essbase system password.
VERSION	Displays the Analytic Server software version number.
HELP	Lists all valid Agent commands and their respective functions.
QUIT and EXIT	Shuts down all open applications and stops Analytic Server.

START AND STOP AN APPLICATION

Before users can connect to an application, it must be started. There are a few different ways to start an application.

- Using the Essbase Server Agent window, type **Start application_name**
- Using Administration Services, right click on the application and select *Start >> Application*.

- Using MaxL, type `alter system load application`
  `application_name`
- Applications can be configured to startup automatically with the Essbase Server. Update this property under Application Properties in Administration Services.

Once the application has been started, data and user security is enabled and each database can be started. Users can connect to the application and administrators can change settings of the application.

At times you will want to stop an application. Careful! Stopping applications while actions are in progress could cause database corruption. The steps to stop an application are similar to the Start steps:

- In the Essbase Server Agent window, type `Stop`
  `application_name`
- Using Administration Services, right click on the application and select *Stop >> Application.*
- Using MaxL, type `alter system unload application`
  `application_name`

START AND STOP A DATABASE

You must also start a database to allow users to connect. When the database is started, the entire index cache is committed to memory. What is an index cache? Don't worry about this for now. We'll cover index caches in an upcoming *master* chapter.

To start a database, use one of the following methods:

- Using the Essbase Server Agent window, type `Start`
  `application_name database_name`
- Using Administration Services, right click on the database and select *Start >> Database.*
- Using MaxL, type `alter system load database`
  `database_name`
- Databases can be configured to startup automatically with the Essbase Server. Update this property under Database Properties in Administration Services.

The same caution we noted above related to stopping an application applies to databases as well. Stopping databases while actions are in progress could cause database corruption. Once the database is stopped, all data is unloaded from memory and committed to disk. The steps to stop an application are similar to the Start steps:

- In the Essbase Server Agent window, type `Stop database_name`
- Using Administration Services, right click on the application and select *Stop >> Database*.
- Using MaxL, type `alter system unload database database_name`

Try It!

Shaq kicked off a huge query against our juggling wolverine application and the application has stopped responding. Stop and restart the application to resolve the issue (note – this may not always work but it is one of the first things you try).

VIEW THE SERVER LOG FILE

You are going to have to troubleshoot at some point. Really? Errors? Issues with Essbase? Yes, yes, and yes. The Essbase Server log file is one of your first starting points when investigating an issue. The server log file is stored in the main Essbase folder as ESSBASE.log. This log file captures all server activity, including user logins, application level activities, and database activities. We can see that Shaq, the end user, logged in at 7am on Tuesday. We can see that Charles Barkley renamed an application at 10am (glad we're paying the big bucks for those hardworking users).

You can view this log file through Administration Services. Select the Essbase server from the Enterprise View panel in Administration Services. Right click and select *View >> Log*:

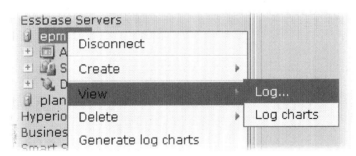

Choose Starting Date and enter the desired start date in most cases. Your log files will get really big and if you open the entire log file, be prepared to wait.

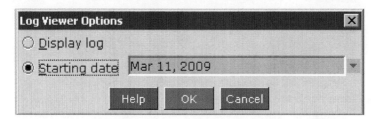

Have you ever tried to read text in a foreign language? Just a little confusing, right? Well, prepare yourself for a similar experience with the Essbase server log files:

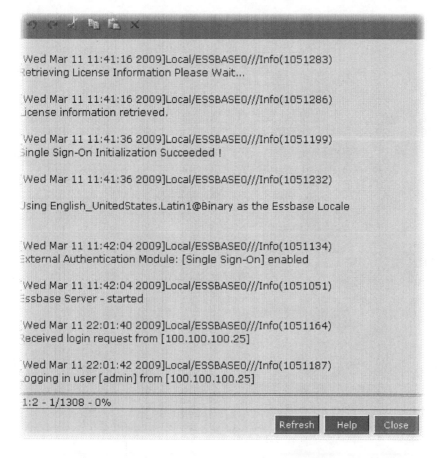

Actually, interpreting the log files isn't that bad. We'll give you a brief translation course on some of the common messages. Here are some example Startup Messages that you will see in the Essbase.log. We see the Sample application is loaded and started, and then the database Basic is loaded.

```
[Tue Nov 06 07:54:16
     2006]Local/ESSBASE0///Info(1051061)
     Application Sample loaded - connection
     established
[Tue Nov 06 07:54:16
     2006]Local/ESSBASE0///Info(1054027)
     Application [Sample] started with process id
     [1300]
[Tue Nov 06 07:54:18
     2006]Local/ESSBASE0///Info(1054014) Database
     Basic loaded
```

Here is an error message captured in the log file when user admin tried to rename an application. He received an error message stating that an application already existed with the name 'Testing'.

```
[Tue Nov 06 08:00:04
     2006]Local/ESSBASE0///Info(1051001) Received
     client request: Rename Application (from user
     admin)
[Tue Nov 06 08:00:04
     2006]Local/ESSBASE0///Error(1051031)
     Application Testing already exists
[Tue Nov 06 08:00:04
     2006]Local/ESSBASE0///Warning(1051003) Error
     1051031 processing request [Rename
     Application] - disconnecting
```

Here is an example of the messages you will see when you stop the Sample application and shutdown the Essbase server.

```
[Tue Nov 06 08:00:46
     2006]Local/ESSBASE0///Info(1054005) Shutting
     down application Sample
[Tue Nov 06 08:00:52
     2006]Local/ESSBASE0///Info(1051052) Hyperion
     Essbase Analytic Server - finished
```

Congratulations! You now speak Essbase-log-ish (like Elvish except that you might actually put this on your resume).

Tip! Periodically archive off the Essbase.log file. Smaller log files can help with performance. In 11.1.1.1, Oracle moved the Essbase.log location to hyperion\logs\essbase and app logs to hyperion\logs\essbase\app\.

Try It! Take a look at your Essbase.log file. Look for instances where applications are started and users have logged into the server. Find them?

VIEW ESSBASE SERVER PROPERTIES

Within Administration Services you can view Essbase server level properties like username and password management settings, version information, server statistics, and OS/CPU and Memory information.

Within Administration Services, right click on the Essbase server. Select *Edit >> Properties*. Select the Security tab:

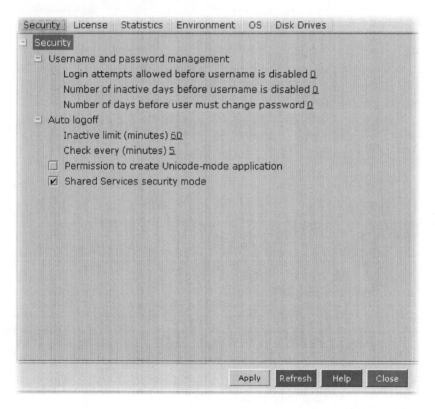

Let's say we decide to set "Login attempts allowed before username disabled" to 3 and set "Number of inactive days before username disabled" to 365. If a user enters an invalid password, after three tries, the username is disabled. If a user hasn't logged into the server in a year, their username is disabled (don't waste those precious, costly Essbase licenses).

Select the License tab. This used to provide pretty important information back when Hyperion was still an independent company. Want to see what version you've installed, what additional components are installed, and when does the license expire? Beginning in Essbase 9.3.1, all of the additional components are installed with Essbase (no additional licensing required):

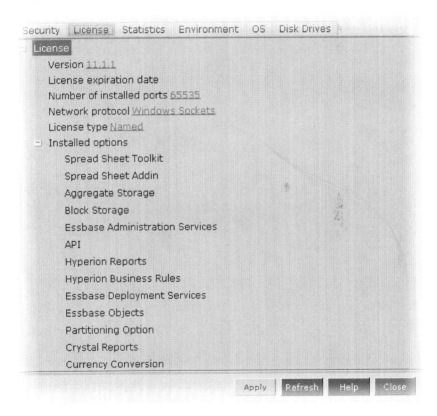

On the remaining tabs, you can view server statistics, environment information, and other hardware related information.

What is the inactive limit on your server? What version of Essbase are you running? Check out these settings and more for the Essbase server.

Try It!

VIEW SERVER SESSIONS

You can view current activity for the server: Who's connected? For how long? And more importantly, what are they doing? It is fun to be big brother. For example, you receive a call from a user complaining that performance has slowed significantly on the Essbase server. You check out the current sessions and see that Roger Clemens kicked off an application copy that has brought the system to its knees.

To view Sessions, right click on the Essbase server select *Edit >> Sessions* in the Enterprise View panel:

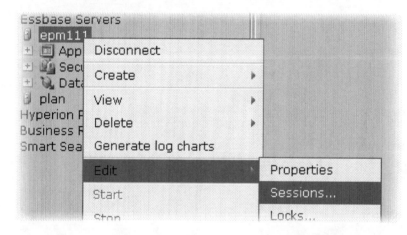

From the Sessions module, you can log off and kill users from their sessions. Why would you want to kill someone? No matter how much of a pacifist you may be, you will want to kill someone in your Essbase world.

You will definitely receive this call at some point. "I just accidentally drilled down to Dimbottom on the Product dimension which has 10,000 products. Now my computer is frozen." What is the resolution to this problem? View sessions and log off or kill this particular user. Killing may be a bit drastic but sometimes it's required. Don't worry – killing a user in Essbase is quite legal.

To log off or kill, select the desired option from the dropdown at the top of the Sessions window:

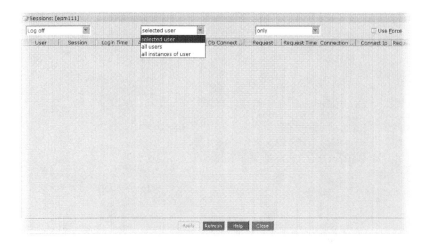

Select User, All Users or All Instances of User. Select On Server, On selected Application, or On selected Database (the available options here depend on your two previous selections). Select Use Force (if necessary).

So we have some flexibility with logging off or killing. In our request above, we may only have to kill the user for a specific database. You may need to log all users off of a particular application just before the monthly load and calc takes place. You may need to log all users off of a server before nightly backups run.

As an almighty Essbase administrator, see what the minions in your domain are doing right now. View the current sessions for your Essbase server.

Try It!

SERVER DATA LOCKS

Essbase will lock cells when they are being updated whether it is through Essbase Add-In lock and send, data load, or calculation. Once the update is complete, the lock is released. Occasionally locks are not released. You select *Essbase >> Lock* in the Essbase Add-In and then Excel crashes. You may want to periodically check for data locks or you may get a call from a user saying that Essbase won't accept their data changes.

To view data locks, right click on the Essbase server and select *Edit >> Locks*:

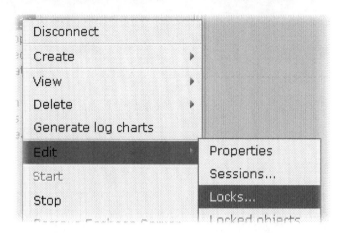

From the Locks window, you can view locks by application, database, and user. You can unlock locks by selecting *Unlock* (very tricky, we know).

LOCKED OBJECTS

Similar to data locks, you can also have locks on Essbase objects. Remember how you are prompted with the following message each time you edit an object:

Most of the time we say "Yes" because we don't want anyone else to change the object while we are viewing or editing it. Once we save our changes and close the object, the object lock is released. But what happens if your computer freezes and causes you to reboot while you had the act.rul data load rule open? You weren't able to successfully close the rules file within Administration Services so the lock remains on the rules file.

You can unlock the rules file in the Locked Objects window. To view locked objects, right click on the Essbase server and select *Edit >> Locked Objects:*

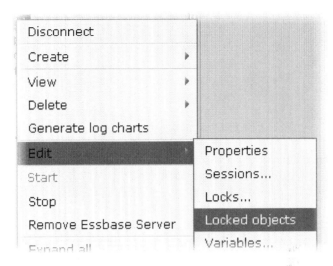

From the Locked Objects window, you can view locked objects by application, database, and user. You can unlock locked objects by selecting *Unlock*:

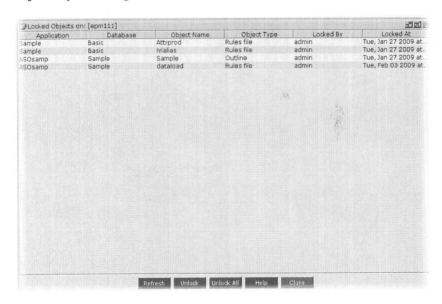

Try It!

See if you have any data locks or locked objects on your Essbase server.

VIEW AND EDIT APPLICATION PROPERTIES

The application properties and statistics tabs provide some helpful options to administrators. Remember, this is where we set the default minimum security for an application. You may want to enable "Allow Users to Start Application" for rarely used applications. This way the application and database won't take up precious memory if it is not being used. When the application is needed, it will start when the user tries to connect via the Essbase Add-In or other reporting tool. This will, however, add a bit more initial response time for the user. Alternatively, if you have a highly used application, you can check "Start application when Analytic Server starts" because you know this application will need to be started and you can save some time for the first user to connect. This is also where you can define an application as a Unicode application (more on this later).

To view and edit application properties,

1.   Select the application.
2.   Right click and select *Edit Properties*.
3.   The Application properties window will display:

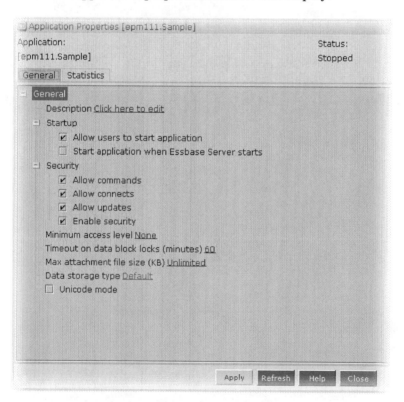

Try It!

Change the minimum access to our wolverine juggling application to Read. Allow the application to start when Essbase starts.

VIEW APPLICATION LOG FILE

The Application log file displays all activity for an application and its databases. There is a different application log file for each application. The log file name is the *application_name.log* and is stored in the application App file. This file tracks activity for the specific application, including the "who" and "when" of an operation and any errors of operations. For example, we can see Shaq ran a calc script on Monday at 12 p.m. We can see that Charles performed a series of retrievals on Tuesday at 1 p.m. (more big brother capabilities).

You can view this log file through Administration Services. Right click on the application and select *View >> Log*:

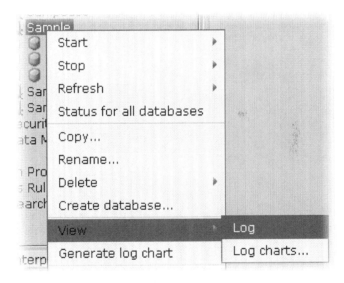

Choose Starting Date and enter the desired date in most cases. Your log files will get really big and if you open the entire log file, be prepared to wait.

The application log file will display:

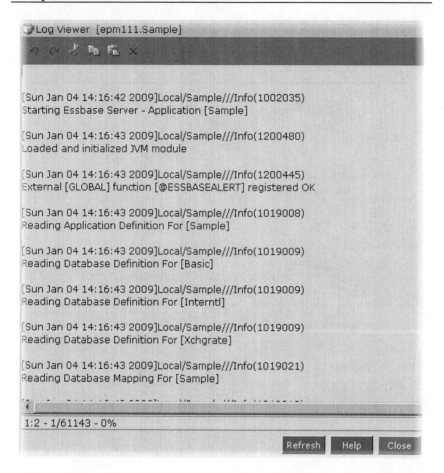

Let's learn more Essbase-log-ish. Here are some example Startup Messages that you will see in the application log file. Essbase writes information about the dimensions and members in the outline, such as the dimension sizes and dynamic calculation information, to the application log.

```
[Tue Nov 06 08:47:14
     2006]Local/Sample///Info(1002035) Starting
     Essbase Server - Application [Sample]
[Tue Nov 06 08:47:15
     2006]Local/Sample///Info(1200480) Loaded and
     initialized JVM module
[Tue Nov 06 08:47:15
     2006]Local/Sample///Info(1019008) Reading
     Application Definition For [Sample]
[Tue Nov 06 08:47:15
     2006]Local/Sample///Info(1019009) Reading
     Database Definition For [Basic]
[Tue Nov 06 08:47:15
     2006]Local/Sample///Info(1019021) Reading
     Database Mapping For [Sample]
[Tue Nov 06 08:47:15
     2006]Local/Sample///Info(1019010) Writing
     Application Definition For [Sample]
[Tue Nov 06 08:47:15
     2006]Local/Sample///Info(1019011) Writing
     Database Definition For [Basic]
[Tue Nov 06 08:47:15
     2006]Local/Sample///Info(1019022) Writing
     Database Mapping For [Sample]
[Tue Nov 06 08:47:15
     2006]Local/Sample///Info(1013202) Waiting for
     Login Requests
[Tue Nov 06 08:47:15
     2006]Local/Sample///Info(1013205) Received
     Command [Load Database]
[Tue Nov 06 08:47:15
     2006]Local/Sample///Info(1019018) Writing
     Parameters For Database [Basic]
[Tue Nov 06 08:47:15
     2006]Local/Sample///Info(1019017) Reading
     Parameters For Database [Basic
```

Essbase also writes information about the outlines for each database to the application log.

```
[Tue Nov 06 08:47:15
     2006]Local/Sample///Info(1019012) Reading
     Outline For Database [Basic]
[Tue Nov 06 08:47:15
     2006]Local/Sample///Info(1007043) Declared
```

```
      Dimension Sizes = [20 17 23 25 5 3 5 3 15 8 6
      ]
[Tue Nov 06 08:47:15
      2006]Local/Sample///Info(1007042) Actual
      Dimension Sizes = [20 14 20 25 4 3 5 3 15 8 5
      ]
[Tue Nov 06 08:47:15
      2006]Local/Sample///Info(1007125) The number
      of Dynamic Calc Non-Store Members = [8 6 0 0 2
      ]
[Tue Nov 06 08:47:15
      2006]Local/Sample///Info(1007126) The number
      of Dynamic Calc Store Members = [0 0 0 0 0 ]
```

Here is an example of an error message in an application log file. The user Admin tried to load data to the Sample.Basic but the data file contained the member '500-10' which does not exist in the outline. We are told that zero records were loaded (the rules file was most likely set to abort on error).

```
[Tue Nov 06 08:49:52
      2001]Local/Sample///Info(1013210) User [admin]
      set active on database [Basic]
[Tue Nov 06 08:49:52 2001]
      Local/Sample/Basic/admin/Info(1013091)
      Received Command [DataLoad] from user [admin]
[Tue Nov 06 08:49:52 2001]
      Local/Sample/Basic/admin/Info(1003040)
      Parallel dataload enabled: [1] block prepare
      threads, [1] block write threads.
[Tue Nov 06 08:49:52 2001]
      Local/Sample/Basic/admin/Error(1003000)
      Unknown Item [500-10] in Data Load, [0]
      Records Completed
[Tue Nov 06 08:49:52 2001]
      Local/Sample/Basic/admin/Warning(1003035) No
      data values modified by load of this data file
[Tue Nov 06 08:49:52 2001]
      Local/Sample/Basic/admin/Info(1003024) Data
      Load Elapsed Time : [0.11] seconds
[Tue Nov 06 08:49:52 2001]
      Local/Sample/Basic/admin/Info(1019018) Writing
      Parameters For Database [Basic]
```

Take a look at the wolverine juggling application log file. What date and time did we load data most recently? How long did the default calculation take place?

Try It!

Managing Log Files

We recommend you archive log files on a periodic basis (depends on the level of activity on an application). These files can become quite large and could slow performance. Application log files should be stored in Logs in your Oracle EPM / Hyperion install folder (e.g. hyperion\logs\essbase\app\). Within Administration Services, after you've made a backup of the file, you can clear the file.

View Log Charts

Starting in version 7, Essbase added log charts, which help you review and understand Essbase activity much better than those easy-to-read log files (by "easy-to-read," we mean "easier to read than Edward's handwriting"). With log charts, Essbase-log-ish is no longer required.

To view the log file in chart format, select the application in Administration Services. Right click and select *View >> Log Chart:*

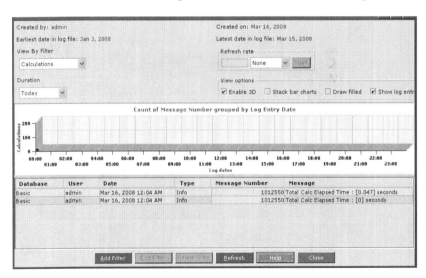

You can filter Log charts by predefined filters: errors, warnings, calculations, data loads, and spreadsheet queries:

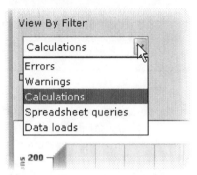

OTHER APPLICATION TASKS

Via Administration Services, several other actions for applications are available. Select an application in the Enterprise View panel and right click. These are the other actions you can perform on applications. You can copy, rename, and delete applications from Administration Services:

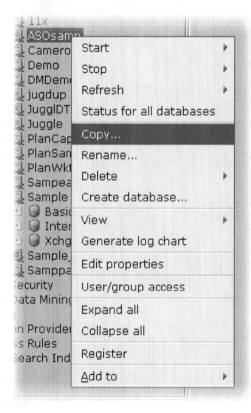

When you copy an application, all objects will be copied within Essbase including the outline, rules files, report scripts, calc scripts, and data. During the copy process, users are prohibited from accessing both the 'from' and the 'to' applications. You can copy across servers if desired.

Try It!

We need to create a development version of the wolverine juggling application. Copy the wolverine juggling application, creating DevJug (we love to be creative with our 8-character limit for application and database naming since we're not using Unicode).

VIEW AND EDIT DATABASE PROPERTIES

Get to know your database properties! You can define startup options and default access privileges for databases just as you can applications. Database properties will vary depending on the database type, ASO versus BSO.

To view and edit database properties,
1. Select the database.
2. Right Click and select *Edit >> Properties*.

ASO Database Properties

Important information is displayed for ASO databases including dimension settings, member counts, and other helpful ratios and statistics. You can manage compression settings and much more via database properties.

General tab:

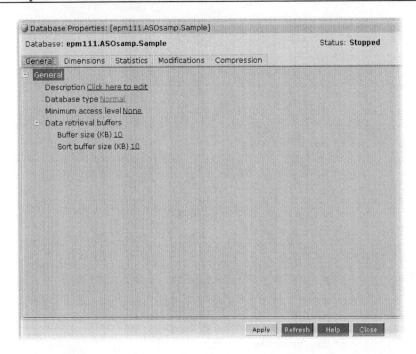

The Dimensions tab lists the dimensions and their member counts:

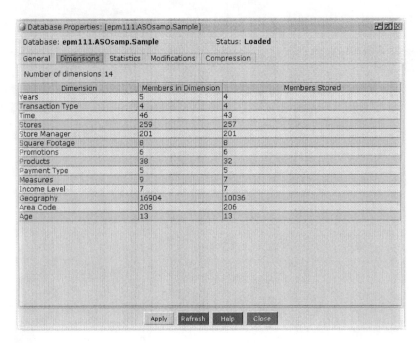

The Statistics tab lists aggregate storage statistics:

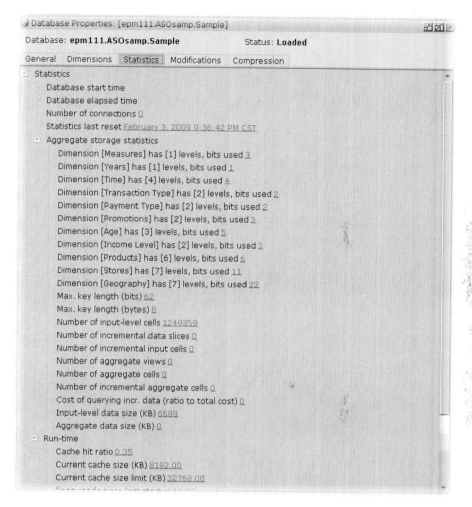

The Compression Tab was discussed earlier in the book under Tune and Optimize for ASO:

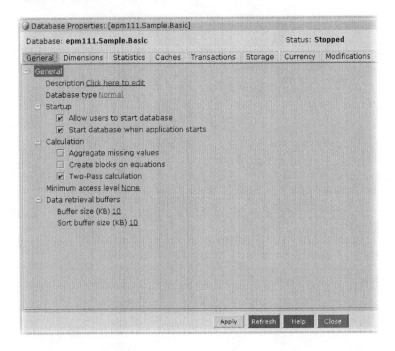

BSO Database Properties

Important information is displayed for BSO databases including dimension dense / sparse settings, member counts, and other helpful ratios and statistics. You can manage commit settings, cache settings, data storage volumes, and much more via database properties.

Database level settings like startup options and data retrieval buffers are defined on the General tab:

The Dimensions tab presents the dimensions in a helpful table, labeling dense and sparse settings and giving you a count of all members and stored members:

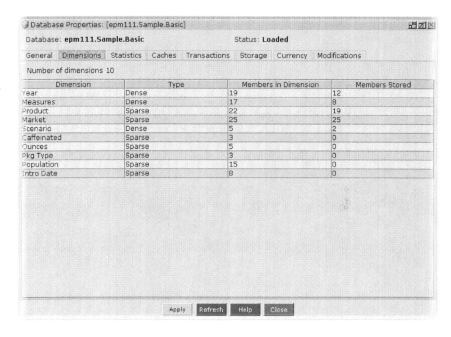

BSO statistics like cache hit ratios and block size are available on the Statistics tab:

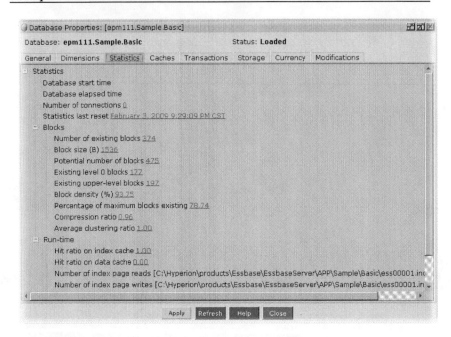

Cache settings are defined on the Caches Tab:

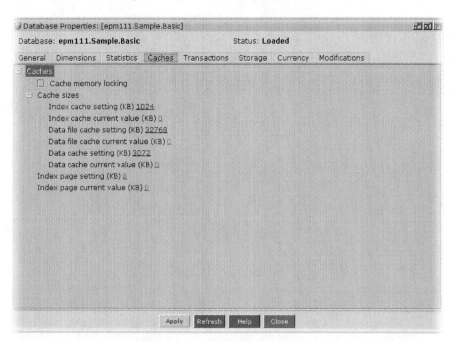

Commit settings are defined on the Transactions Tab:

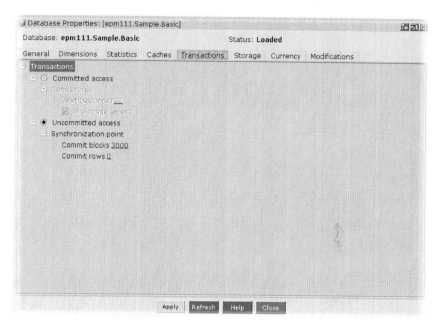

BSO compression and index and data file volumes are specified on the Storage Tab:

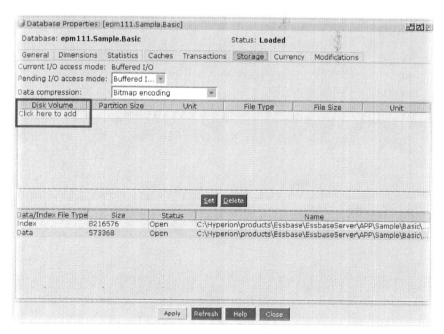

The Modifications tab lists any recent updates to the database:

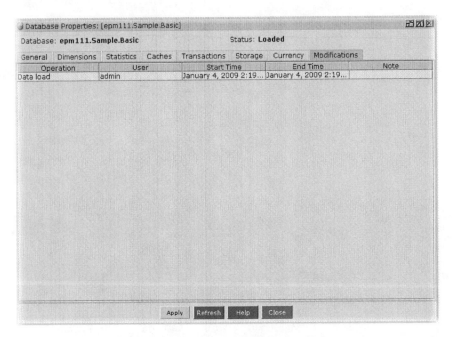

OTHER DATABASE TASKS

Via Administration Services, you can perform several other actions for databases. Select the database and right click. These are the other actions you can perform on databases. You can copy, rename, and delete databases from Administration Services. You can clear data from a database, clearing either upper levels blocks, non-input blocks, or all blocks. You can load data, calculate, export, or restructure data:

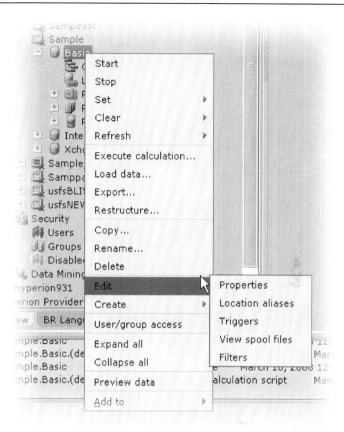

Those same notes we mentioned about copying applications also apply to copying databases. All objects will be copied within Essbase including the outline, rules files, report scripts, calc scripts, and data. During the copy process, users are prohibited from accessing both the "from" and the "to" databases. You can copy across servers if desired.

Some database actions are ASO specific like Merging slices and Query Tracking:

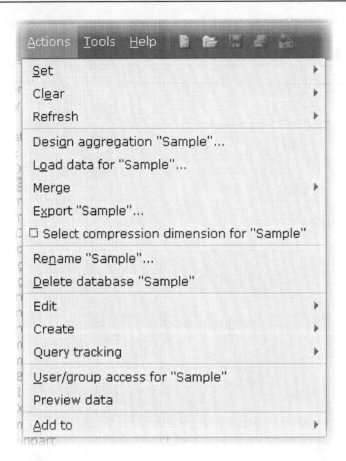

Other actions are specific to block storage databases like launching calculations or using transaction replay:

See – we told you that Essbase Administration isn't always fun in the sun. Thankfully you now have the tools to manage the day to day administration tasks. But we can't forget one of the most important action items for you as an administrator – backups!

Chapter 25:
Backups and Recovery

This will probably never happen to you. Well, maybe. Actually, this will probably happen more than once in you Essbase career. An Essbase database will crash just before close and you need to get the data back. Fast. Because the CFO is standing over your shoulder saying "Where are my reports?" At first you think, "Can I book my Southwest flight without him seeing"? (wanna getaway?) but then you remember that you have a proven, tested backup and recovery plan and process. You are not like the guy who spills beer over all of the fans at the basketball game. We can't stress how important it is to backup your applications. Listen to us – this is *really* important.

BACKUP / RESTORE FOR BSO

Version 11x introduces new backup and restore functionality for block storage option databases. This new Backup and Restore feature backs up and restores all the necessary files for a BSO database (previously you had to manually perform this process). During the backup process, the database is placed in read-only mode and files are archived to the specified location. When a restore is launched, the database is locked while the files are restored from the archive folder. The backup and restore feature is available in the Administration Services Console and MaxL.

Note! Backup and restore is not available in Essbase Studio.

Note! Because Planning creates block storage option databases, you can use the backup and restore feature on Planning databases.

In the example below, we will archive a database called "11x".

To backup a BSO database,

1. In the Administration Services Console, right click on the database and select *Archive Database*:

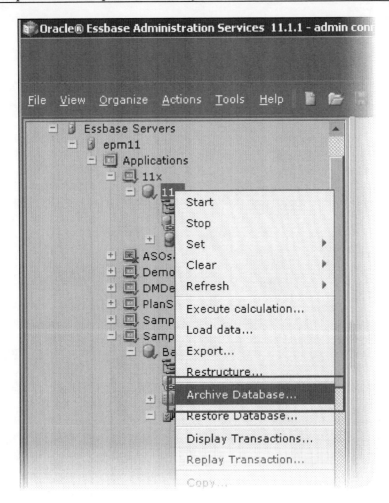

2. Provide a name for the archive:

3. Optionally, select *Force archive* and/or *Archive in the background*. Force archive will replace any existing archives that exist with the same name.
4. Click *OK*.

5. A file will be created in the essbasepath\app directory:

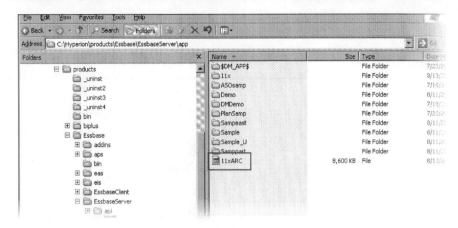

Then use your third party backup tools to backup the archive files created by Essbase.

So now when the Essbase server goes down or a database crashes and the CFO is breathing down your neck, rest assured you have a good backup file. So how do you get it back up? Fast.

To restore a database,

1. If necessary, place the archive files are placed in the Essbase\app folder.
2. Right click on the database and select *Stop* to stop the database.
3. Right click on the database and select *Restore Database*.

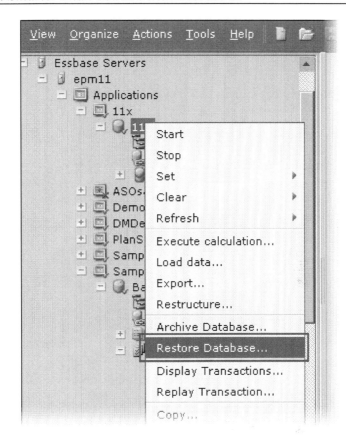

4. Choose the restore file from the drop down box:

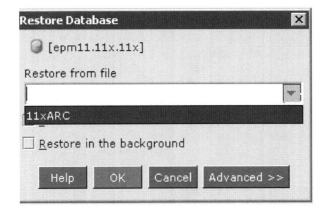

5. Optionally choose to *Force Restore* and/or to *Restore in the background*.

6. Click *OK*.

Ta-da! Like magic, the database is restored (along with some of the CFO's face color).

Archive the JugBud application.

Try It!

TRANSACTION LOGGING / REPLAY

Another new feature that goes along with backup and restore is the transaction logging and replay capability. Essbase can now track operations in the database like data loads, calculations, and data submissions from Smart View or the Excel Add-in.

Because the events are tracked, the administrator can then display and replay those transactions. The administrator can choose to replay all transactions from a certain point or she can pick and choose the transactions to replay.

The real power comes with using backup and restore along with transaction logging / play back to restore a database to a previous state. This will probably never happen... wait, actually this could definitely happen. Your budgeting and planning database crashes just after lunch and plans are due at the end of the day. You backup on a nightly basis so you could restore from last night's backup. However, your chances of getting the plan data changes from the morning were pretty slim. Now in Essbase 11, you can use transaction replay to get those data changes back, restoring the BSO database fully with minimal data loss (picture Essbase as a superhero with a big "S" emblazoned across its chest).

The replay for data loads uses a reference or pointer to the data source file (not the actual file). If the underlying data file changes, the new data will be loaded to the database.

Tip!

First you have to enable transaction logging for the desired database (by default, transaction logging is not enabled). To turn on transaction logging, update the essbase.cfg with the following setting.

```
TransactionLogLocation AppName DbName LogLocation
         Native Enable
```

For example:

```
TransactionLogLocation Sample Basic
         c:\hyperion\trlog native enable
```

In this example, we'll enable transaction logging for our 11x database.

1. In the Administration Services console, right click on the Essbase server and select *Edit >> Properties*.
2. Choose the Environment tab.
3. Update the TransactionLogLocation parameter in the Essbase.cfg by typing:

```
TransactionLogLocation 11x 11x c:\hyperion\TRLog
         NATIVE ENABLE
```

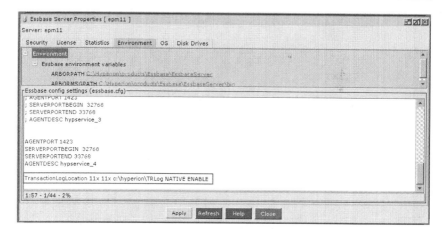

4. Click *Apply*.
5. Restart the Essbase server.
6. Create the directory and folder if necessary (we created a TRLog folder in the Hyperion directory to store the transaction log files). The name must match exactly or the application won't start.

7. Right click on the application and select *Start* to start the application.

8. Right click on the database and select *Start* to start the database.

9. Right click on the database and select *Display Transactions*:

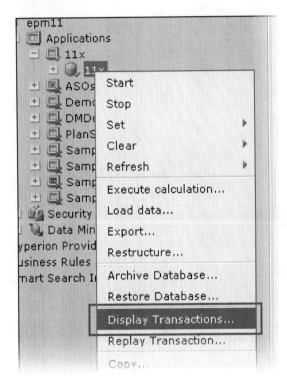

10. Display transactions based on one of the following options:
    - Based on last replay time
    - Since a specific date and time

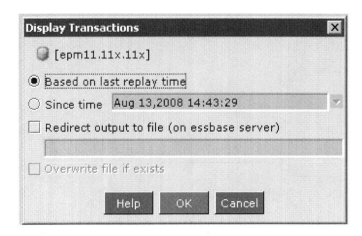

11. Check the Redirect output to a file if desired (and optionally overwrite the file if it exists).
12. The Transaction List displays:

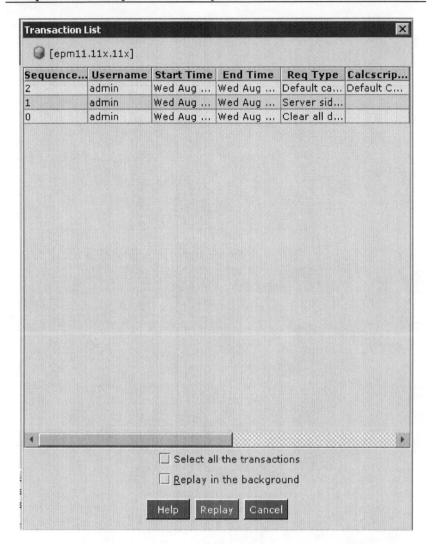

The following columns are shown: Sequence, username, start time, end time, action (or req type), Calcscript name, dataload file, dataload file type, rules file, rules file location, sql or ftp file user name. (For you existing admins, admit it – you are saying – "Wow, this is really cool. What took so long?")

So what transactions have taken place for the 11x database? If we adjusted the columns you would see that first (Sequence 0) all data was cleared by the user *admin* Wednesday, August 1, 2008, beginning at 8:01 am and ending at 8:02 am. Next (Sequence 1) we see that user *admin* loaded data using the calcdat.txt Wednesday, August 1, 2008, beginning at 8:05 am and ending at 8:06 am. And finally (Sequence 2), we see the default calc script was run by admin on Wednesday, August 1, 2008, beginning at 8:07 am and ending at 8:08 am.

To replay a single transaction, select the desired transaction and click *Replay*.

13. Select 0 and select the *Replay* button (to clear all of the data).

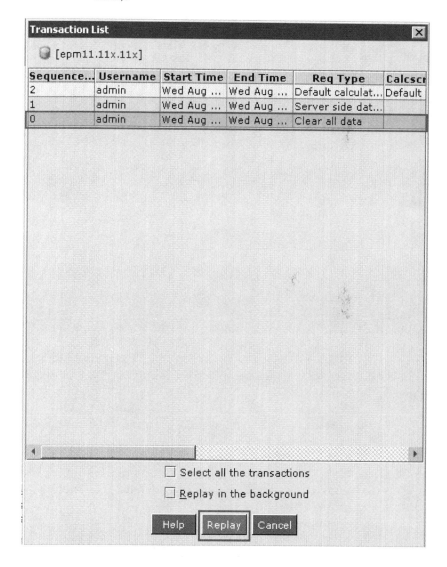

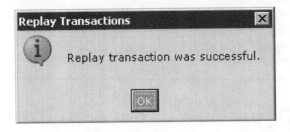

Optionally, we could have chosen to select all transactions and replay in the background.

So back to our midday budget crisis... because you turned on transaction logging for the budget database, you can easily recover last night's archive file, restoring the database. Next you can then replay all transactions that have taken place since the backup, returning the plan data to its original state just before the crash. Because of the quick recovery, we think we see a budget increase for a certain Essbase DBA salary.

Enable transaction logging for the JugBud database. Load data and run a calc script for JugBud. Test viewing and replaying transactions.

Try It!

EXPORTING THE DATA

The second method for backups is data exports. Exporting will copy data to a text file that you specify. You can export all data, level zero data, or input-level data for BSO databases and level zero data for ASO databases. The thing with exports is that it only exports data. Essbase objects like outline files, rules files, etc. are not included so you will need to use file system backups for those items.

So if we have to do a file system backup anyway, why export? Use exports when you want to transfer data across platforms, when you want to back up only a certain portion of the data (level 0 blocks), or when you want to create an exported file in text format, rather than binary format. If you have a copy of the outline and data export, this can be a quick way to recover a corrupted database.

To perform a data export,
1. Select the database.
2. Right click and select *Export* or Select *Actions >> Export "dbname"*:

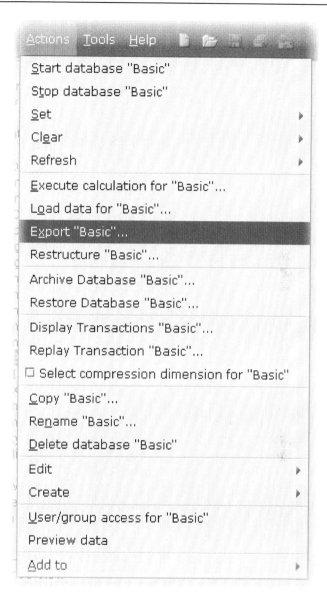

3. Specify the name for the exported data file.
4. Choose the export option:
   - BSO - All data, Level 0 blocks, or Input blocks
   - ASO – Level 0 blocks
5. Choose either column or non-column format.
   Column format often facilitates loads to relational databases or other systems. Non-column format is faster for loading

or reloading to the Essbase database. Column format exports are not available for ASO.

6. Select "Execute in the background" in most cases:

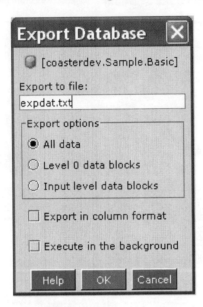

The export file is by default placed in the \arborpath\essbase\app directory.

To reload an exported file, you will follow the same steps to load any data file though you won't need a rules file.

1. Right click on the database and select *Load Data*.
2. Select *Find Data File* and navigate to the exported data file.
3. Specify the error file location and name.
4. Click *OK* to load the data.

If you are reloading a level zero export or input level export file for a BSO database, the database must be recalculated.

Tip!

Don't forget about the binary data export commands; these are other good options for exporting data sets for backup purposes.

BACKUPS FOR ASO

File system backups are the best method for aggregate storage databases.

To backup an ASO database,

1. Stop the application.
2. Using the File system to back up the *arborpath\app\appname* folder.

The following ASO files must be copied:

Appname.app	*\ARBORPATH*app*\appname*
Appname.log	*\ARBORPATH*app*\appname*
Dbname.db	*\ARBORPATH*app*\appname*
Dbname.db	*\ARBORPATH*app*\appname\dbname*
Dbname.dbb	*\ARBORPATH*app*\appname\dbname*
Dbname.ddb	*\ARBORPATH*app*\appname\dbname*
Dbname.otl	*\ARBORPATH*app*\appname\dbname*
Dbname.otl.keep	*\ARBORPATH*app*\appname\dbname*
Trigger.trg	*\ARBORPATH*app*\appname\dbname*
Default	*\ARBORPATH*app*\appname\default*
Temp	*\ARBORPATH*app*\appname\temp*
Log	*\ARBORPATH*app*\appname\log*
Metadata	*\ARBORPATH*app*\appname\metadata*
Essn.dat	*\ARBORPATH*app*\appname\default*

To restore files from a backup,

1. Stop the application and databases.
2. Replace the files on disk with the corresponding files from the backup.

Now let's review a few rules for file system backups. You can use the file system backup to restore application files (same server, same application name, same database name). You cannot use the platform file system to copy, move, rename, or delete applications and databases. When an application or database is altered through the file system, the Essbase security file is unable to recognize the changes. The only files that can be managed through the file system are:

- Rules files for dimension builds and data loads (.rul)
- Data load or dimension build text files

- Calculation scripts (.csc)
- Report scripts (.rep)
- MaxL scripts (.mxl or any extension)

BSO BACKUPS THE OLD FASHIONED WAY

In the olden days of backups, before we had the 11x backup and restore feature, we had to walk to school every day in the snow with no shoes and prepare the Essbase server and applications ourselves for file system backup. To do this,

1. Place database in read-only ("archive") mode. Using MaxL, type **alter database begin archive**
2. Perform backup using third-party backup utility, backing up the entire Essbase directory or specific files.
3. Return database to read-write mode. Using MaxL, type **alter database end archive**

BEGINARCHIVE commits any modified data to disk, switches the database to read-only mode, reopens the database files in shared, read-only mode and creates a file containing a list of files that need to be backed up. By default, the file is called archive.lst and is stored in the *ARBORPATH*\app\appname\dbname directory. ENDARCHIVE switches the database back to read-write mode.

It is important to back up all .ind and .pag files related to a database because a single database can have multiple .ind and .pag files. These files could be placed on different volumes so make sure you are backing up everything.

These are the key BSO files to backup (these are captured for us in the 11x Backup feature):

ess*n*.ind	*ARBORPATH*\app*appname**dbname*
ess*n*.pag	*ARBORPATH*\app*appname**dbname*
dbname.esm	*ARBORPATH*\app*appname**dbname*
dbname.tct	*ARBORPATH*\app*appname**dbname*
dbname.ind	*ARBORPATH*\app*appname**dbname*
dbname.app	*ARBORPATH*\app
dbname.db	*ARBORPATH*\app*appname**dbname*
x.lro	*ARBORPATH*\app*appname**dbname*
dbname.otl	*ARBORPATH*\app*appname**dbname*

Database object files (.otl, .csc, .rul)	*ARBORPATH*\app*appname**dbname*

Just as we did for an ASO database, to restore files from a backup,
1. Stop the application and databases.
2. Replace the files on disk with the corresponding files from the backup.

Do not move, copy, modify, or delete any of the following files: essn.ind, essn.pag, dbname.ind, dbname.esm, dbname.tct. Doing so may result in data corruption.

CRITICAL FILES TO BACKUP

Don't forget to backup the following files along with your application and database files:

essbase.sec	*ARBORPATH*\bin
essbase.bak	*ARBORPATH*\bin
essbase.cfg	*ARBORPATH*\bin

Finally a last piece of advice: Regularly test your backup and recovery process. We know some of the smartest Essbase administrators who thought their backup process was working correctly but found out otherwise at the most critical time. Trust us. When you get that 2 a.m. I-need-my-data-where-is-it-and-how-could-you-be-asleep-when-the-sky-is-falling call from your panicked boss, you can calmly say "I'll have the database up shortly sir." No need for any throwing of quad ten pump venti vanilla lattes.

Chapter 26:
Sharing Data

As your Essbase environment grows, you will most likely have a number of different Essbase databases (if not, you are not leveraging Essbase to its full potential – go build some cubes!) The next inevitable question – how can you share data across your Essbase databases? A number of ways exist to share data across databases and in this chapter we'll provide an introduction to most of them.

CALC EXPORT COMMANDS/LOAD RULES

We've already discussed one easy and fast way to extract slices of Essbase block storage data using a calc script command DATAEXPORT. This command allows you to extract data to text file or relational table from a calc script. Placing this command within Fix statements and If statements allows you to isolate the desired data to be pulled. You then can load the extracted data to a source cube using a load rule. The full process can be automated and scheduled to run as needed. For more information on using the DATAEXPORT command, please revisit the calc script chapter.

INTRODUCTION TO PARTITIONING

Partitioning has been around for a long, long time, back since the days of good ole Essbase Application Manager (if you don't know what this is, congratulations: you haven't been using Essbase since before dirt was invented). A partition is a definition that connects data between Essbase databases. Depending on the type of partition, data can be shared directly between databases (transparent partition), copied from one database to another (replicated partition), or used as a predefined launching point from one database to another (linked partition):

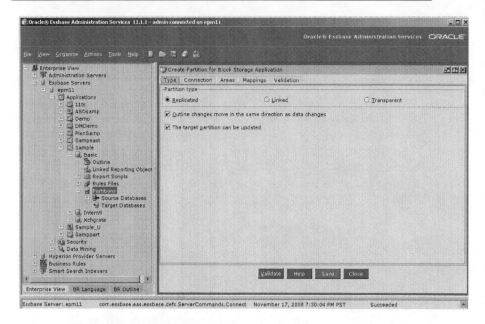

Transparent Partitions

Transparent partitions place a direct link from a target database to a source database. A subsection of the target database is defined and directly linked to the source database. When a user accesses the defined shared section of the target database, data is retrieved directly from the source database. This type of partition allows for real time data to be shared between two databases.

Replicated Partitions

Replicated partitions are similar to transparent partitions. However, instead of the target database containing direct links to the source database, data from the source database is copied into the target database.

Transparent vs. Replicated Partitions

Although transparent partitions allow for real time data, it can be taxing on sensitive networks. Retrievals times can be slower when you are accessing a transparent partition. These days, networks usually have the bandwidth to handle transparent partitions. However, if you have a slow network, you may encounter performance issues with transparent partitions. A replicated partition may not have real time data, but it can be a lot faster for retrievals and easier on your network as data is retrieved directly from the target database. You can schedule your database copies during off peak times and still have the same data between the source and target databases. Replicated partitions tend to be the optimal solution if you have data that doesn't change often and/or you have a slow network.

For both of these types of partitions, the dimensions between the databases do not have to be the same. You can define mappings to handle differences in outlines between the source and target database.

Linked Partitions

Linked partitions do not actually share data across databases. They are predefined links between databases that allow a user to jump from one database to another when drilling into a database. The advantage of using a linked partition is that you are not restricted to the dimensionality of the target database. Data is not physically transferred from one database to another.

Comparing Partitions

Let's now summarize some of the key aspects of partitioning.

Requirement / Restriction	*Replicated*	*Transparent*	*Linked*
Real time data		X	X
Limited Network Traffic	X		X
Limited Disk Space		X	X
Faster calcs	X		
Small database size		X	X
Faster retrievals	X		X
Seamless to the user	X	X	
Connecting databases with different dimensionality			X
Easy Recoverability	X		
Less synchronization			X
Attribute based queries		X	X
Frequent updates and calculations		X	
Update data at the data target		X	X
Contextual Differences			X
Batch updates and simple	X		

Requirement / Restriction	Replicated	Transparent	Linked
aggregations			

ASO vs. BSO Partition Considerations

Target	Source	Replicated	Transparent	Linked
BSO	BSO	Y	Y	Y
BSO	ASO	N	Y	Y
ASO	ASO	N	Y	Y
ASO	BSO	Y	Y	Y

Partitions can be created in the Administration Services Console using the Partitioning Wizard or in MaxL. Below is a quick glimpse of the Partitioning Manager where we are defining the sections of the source and target databases to connect:

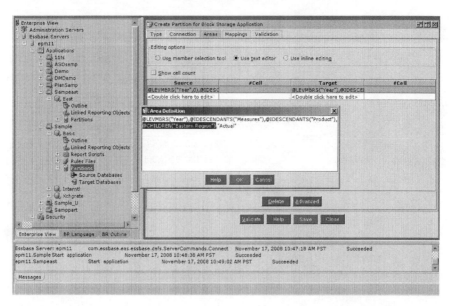

Notice we can use functions to define the sections of the database (e.g. level-0 members of the Year dimension, descendants of Measures, descendants of Product, and children of Eastern Region in the Market dimension are selected in the example above). A number of tools in the Partitioning Wizard help us create valid partitions like member selection and "Show cell count".

Now that we've discussed sharing larger data sets in calc export commands and partitions, let us turn our attention to another data sharing alternative called XREF.

@XREF FUNCTION

Intuitively, you can think of the @XREF function as a partition that only applies to one member. This function retrieves data from a database at a cell level. You can use this function in a member formula and Essbase will retrieve data at the specified data intersection into the database. If you make the member a dynamically calculated member, it will retrieve the data when the member called, like a transparent partition. If it's a stored member, it will retrieve that data when the outline is calculated. In this respect, the formula is like a replicated partition.

The syntax for the @XREF function is

```
@XREF(LocationAlias [,MbrList])
```

The LocationAlias is a predefined description that references an Essbase server, application, database, username, and password. This saves you from having to save login information inside a calc script or formula that calls @XREF.

MbrList is a list of members to point to when Essbase queries the database mentioned in the Location Alias. This list is similar to the mapping section of a database. The calc engine will first reference all common members in the cell that is currently being accessed. However, if the source has dimensions that do not coincide with the target, the member list will specify which members to use.

For example, consider the following formula:

```
Sales = @XREF(sourceDB, Revenue);
```

Assume that Sales is a measure in the data target database and that Revenue is a member in the data source database. This formula will map the Sales member in the target to the Revenue member in the source database. When Sales is retrieved, Essbase will actually retrieve the value of Revenue in the source database. Note that the source database is the database with the location alias, sourceDB.

@XREF vs. Partitions

When you design the database, considerations must be made to determine whether or not to use @XREFs or partitions. If you only want to share a few members, @XREFs are the best choice. @XREFs work well between databases in the same application since they are sharing the same memory. Partition management is designed to handle data sharing for large groups of members well. However, it is usually more work than it's worth to manage a partition for just a few measures. In this case, it is better to make the few measures calculated @XREF formula. Retrieval and calculation performance is another factor. Dynamic @XREFs can be costly especially if those members are used in calculations in the target database. A stored XREF member or replicated partition could address calculation and retrieval issues.

OTHER DATA SHARING ALTERNATIVES

Data Synchronization in EPMA

If you are using Oracle Hyperion Enterprise Management Architect, EPMA, to manage your Planning and Financial Management applications, you can also use the Data Synchronization Module. This module allows you to share data between Planning, Financial Management, Essbase (ASO and BSO), Profitability and Cost Management applications from the following sources: Financial Management, Planning, Essbase (BSO), Profitability and Cost Management, flat files, and Interface Tables. Interface tables are tables that are defined in EPMA that access relational databases directly. This allows for changes to flow directly from the relational database into the source application.

There are some caveats to using Data Synchronization. All applications that are used as data sources must be managed by EPMA. If you use a flat file, the format is very specific. The file must be delimited with the final column being the data field. It will not accept fixed length fields. This method is recommended if you are already using EPMA to manage the majority of your applications.

MDX Scripts and Report Scripts

You can run MDX scripts for both ASO and BSO databases to extract data sets from Essbase. Report scripts are also available for block storage databases. Result sets can be written to a text file that is then loaded into a target Essbase database using data load rules files.

JEXPORT Command

The JEXPORT command allows you utilize the flexibility of Java programming language to extract data from databases. You can use JEXPORT to create a Java script that specifically states what section of the database to extract. While this is technically possible, the new calc export commands do essentially the same thing much faster.

ETL TOOLS

As most folks on the planet know, Oracle is one of the (if not THE) leading data warehousing solution available. With data warehousing comes ETL tools (data Extraction, Transformation and Load), solutions that help us move data from system A to system B. Up until this point we've focused on data integration between Essbase databases. You may have bigger requirements to integrate data from Essbase to other systems along with other enterprise data integration needs. Oracle provides a number of ETL tools to share data between Essbase and Oracle EPM System tools along with almost any other system. We'll focus on the solutions that work with Essbase here.

ODI – Oracle Data Integrator

Oracle Data Integrator (ODI) is Oracle's current strategic direction for a comprehensive ETL tool (although if you want to be technical about it, ODI is an ELT tool: extraction, load, and transform). Built in adapters exist for Essbase, Planning, Financial Management and most other source transactions systems, allowing you to easily integrate data across your enterprise.

FDM – Financial Data Quality Management

Where ODI is a true ETL tool, mostly used by the IT types, Financial Data Quality Management (FDM) is an out-of-the-box data transformation and validation tool for the more business oriented individuals. Source-level financial data is fed to consolidation, reporting, planning, and analytical applications, with detailed audit trail and reconciliation capabilities.

HAL – Hyperion Application Link

In the old days of Hyperion, we used Hyperion Application Link (HAL) to build dimensions and share data across Hyperion products. HAL served as an ETL tool but was not as robust as a tool like ODI. HAL is set to be sunset in the future and existing customers should begin to plan for a migration to ODI.

We'll conclude with one last tip: One strong non-Oracle solution for extracting Essbase data (and Oracle EPM System data) is a product called Star Integration Server by StarAnalytics (http://www.staranalytics.com/).

So which data sharing option is the best? You've learned by now there isn't just one right answer. Depends on a number of factors like what needs to be shared, how often it needs to be refreshed, what are the sources, what are the targets, retrieval and calculation requirements, and more. Make sure you have a clear understanding of the requirements and the best alternatives should begin to stand out.

Chapter 27:
Automate with MaxL

You've learned most all of the tasks to build and maintain Essbase databases through the Administration Services Console. However, you certainly don't want to perform all of these tasks manually every day. Essbase of course has a scripting alternative to automate almost any Essbase task. MaxL is the scripting language for Essbase and is installed with every instance of the Essbase server, on all operating systems. These are some of the more common actions that MaxL is used for:

- Loading a database
- Building a dimension
- Altering a substitution variable
- View database statistics

Having a good knowledge of MaxL is absolutely essential to the smooth running of your Essbase environment. In addition to daily database updates and administration, developers can also automate repetitive tasks in order to speed up testing cycles, a trick that can save much stress when under tight deadlines.

Here is a sample MaxL script that will connect to the local Essbase server, unload the Sample application, then delete it.

```
LOGIN admin password ON localhost;
ALTER SYSTEM UNLOAD APPLICATION Sample;
DROP APPLICATION Sample;
EXIT;
```

EXECUTE MAXL

MaxL can be run in two ways: interactive and batch. Both methods use the essmsh executable (*ESS*base *MaxL SH*ell) at the command prompt. There is a visual editor for MaxL scripts in the Administration Services Console, but this is used for development only and is not normally used in production.

To run MaxL interactively, simply type **essmsh** at the command line and the MaxL interface will then be ready to accept your commands:

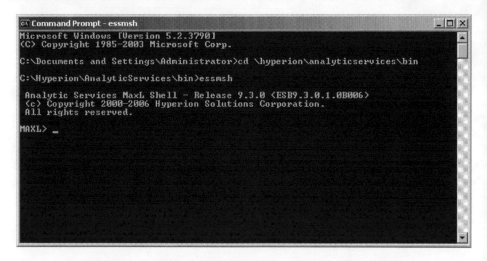

To run MaxL in batch mode, add the name of a script file as an argument to the command. MaxL will then read and interpret each line in succession until it reaches an EXIT command or the end of the file:

There are also MaxL interfaces for Perl and Java, but their usage is not covered in this book. More details of this can be found in the DBA Guide and Technical Reference publications.

SECURE MAXL

In Essbase 9.3, the ability to secure a MaxL script using public/private key pair encryption was introduced. In prior versions, the password would either be stored as clear text in the script or passed in as a variable from the command shell, which poses a security risk.

To create a key pair, run the MaxL shell with this argument: **essmsh -gk**

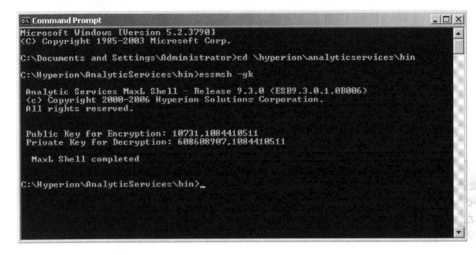

Then, to encrypt a script using this key pair, run: **essmsh -E [scriptname] [public key]** Note that this process creates a new secured script with the same name and a ".mxls" extension. To run this script you will need the corresponding private key: **essmsh -D [scriptname] [private key]**

If you try to run this script without the key you will see an error message, so don't lose the private key!

BASIC MAXL SYNTAX RULES

MaxL is neither case-sensitive nor space-sensitive, meaning you are free to format your scripts any way you see fit. The only general restrictions are that the file can only contain ASCII text, and every command must be terminated with a semicolon. Other than that, you can insert tabs, spaces, and new lines as you see fit to make the code easier to read.

Tip! Capitalizing the MaxL keywords only will make it much easier to identify which words are your variables and which are MaxL commands.

Application and Database names are case-sensitive on UNIX hosts, even in MaxL scripts.

Note!

However, there is an important difference between single and double quotes in MaxL. Single quotes tell the engine to translate the text they enclose literally, while double quotes allow for variable translation. Consider the case where we want to output the system environment variable ARBORPATH. Here are two different MaxL statements that attempt to do this:

```
ECHO 'ARBORPATH is $ARBORPATH'

ECHO "ARBORPATH is $ARBORPATH"
```

The first statement with single quotes will output literally **ARBORPATH is $ARBORPATH**, while the second will evaluate the variable first and output the desired result of **ARBORPATH is c:\hyperion\essbase**.

If you want to output a single quote, you need to enclose the entire statement in double quotes:

```
echo "Isn't Keira Knightley the cutest girl ever?";
```

Backslashes are considered special characters in MaxL, and need to be doubled up when specifying a Windows file location:

```
'c:\\hyperion\\essbase\\app'
```

LOGIN

The login command is used to connect to an Essbase server. The IDENTIFIED BY syntax is completely optional and was probably only included for script readability.

```
LOGIN [username] IDENTIFIED BY [password] ON
      [hostname]

LOGIN [username] [password] ON [hostname]
```

Tip! To run MaxL interactively and to easily login to the machine local to your session, type **essmsh -l [username] [password]** at the command line.

REDIRECT OUTPUT

Most of the time, you will schedule MaxL jobs to run in the middle of the night as part of an automated process. Of course, you will want to see everything that happened when you arrive at the office in the morning.

Redirecting the output of the script is usually the first command that you will issue in a script. The syntax for this is as follows:

```
SPOOL ON TO [File Name];
```

Tip!

There is no easy way to create a unique log file identifier in MaxL, but you can easily do this in most operating system command shells and pass a unique value in as a runtime variable (see the next session).

USE VARIABLES

There are three types of variables that you can use inside your MaxL scripts.

1. Environment variables from the operating system. If you want to reference a variable set in the operating system shell, you can reference it directly by name and prefixed with a dollar sign (e.g. $ARBORPATH)

2. Positional variables passed in on the command line. You can also add parameters to essmsh that will be translated to variables inside the script. For example, consider the script myscript.mxl that contains these commands:

```
ECHO "The third variable is $3.";
ECHO "The second variable is $2.";
ECHO "The first variable is $1.";
```

When you execute this script using this syntax:

```
essmsh myscript.mxl ten twenty thirty
```

The output will be:

```
The third variable is thirty.
The second variable is twenty.
The first variable is ten.
```

3. Temporary variables that you set inside the MaxL script. You may also want to set variables inside your MaxL scripts. To do this, use the following syntax:

```
SET myvariable = 'ten';
ECHO $myvariable;
```

MAXL ACTIONS

It can be overwhelming for first-time users to look at the large list of MaxL commands. However, everything becomes much simpler when you understand that there are only ten core actions.

The following table summarizes what each of these core actions does.

Alter	Change the state of an object.
Create	Create a new instance of an object.
Display	Show information about an object.
Drop	Delete an instance of an object.
Execute	Run a calculation or aggregation process.
Export	Output data or LRO's.
Grant	Assign security to users or groups.
Import	Load data, dimensions, or LRO's.
Query	Get information about an application or database.
Refresh	Reload partitioning information or custom Java function definitions.

SAMPLE MAXL STATEMENTS

The following sections will illustrate some of the most frequently used MaxL actions, and provide commentary on the nuances of the syntax.

Update an outline from a text file

The following statement will import dimensions from a text file (named products) using the rules file (named prod_bld) existing in the database directory. Note that the error file is being written to a common directory but the file name contains both the database name and the dimension being built for easy reference.

```
IMPORT DATABASE Sample.Basic DIMENSIONS
 FROM SERVER TEXT DATA_FILE 'products'
 USING SERVER RULES_FILE 'prod_bld'
 ON ERROR WRITE TO
       'c:\\hyperion\\MaxL_logs\\build.sample_basic.p
       roducts.err';
```

Load a database from a SQL source

This statement will load data from a SQL database. You don't have to specify the ODBC data source name as that is contained within the load rule itself (named sql_load).

```
IMPORT DATABASE Sample.Basic DATA
 CONNECT AS dbadmin IDENTIFIED BY dbpasswd
 USING SERVER RULES_FILE 'sql_load'
 ON ERROR WRITE TO
       'c:\\hyperion\\MaxL_logs\\load.sample_basic.er
       r';
```

Run a Calc Script

Of course, MaxL can run a calc script that you've already saved (in this example, the calc script named "Allocate" is executed). There are two ways to do this (both of these commands have the exact same result, it's your choice which you prefer to use):

```
EXECUTE CALCULATION 'Sample.Basic.Allocate';

EXECUTE CALCULATION 'Allocate' ON Sample.Basic;
```

A nice capability that is often overlooked is the ability to send custom calc commands directly from MaxL, which is incredibly useful when you want to test different settings or commands using variable substitution.

```
EXECUTE CALCULATION
  "SET UPDATECALCOFF;
   CALC ALL;"
ON Sample.Basic;
```

Create a user

When creating users, you most often use the OR REPLACE syntax to overwrite any existing users. This is important because no changes will be accepted by Essbase if there is a "User already exists" error thrown by the MaxL command. This example shows how to add a user authenticated externally against an LDAP server.

```
CREATE OR REPLACE USER 'Shaq'
 TYPE EXTERNAL WITH PROTOCOL 'LDAP'
 IDENTIFIED BY 'ou=Finance, dc=MyCorp,
     dc=com@ldapserver2:389';
```

Run an MDX Query

MDX queries are interesting in that they do not have an action of their own. Rather, you execute the entire MDX statement as an action itself.

```
SPOOL ON TO 'mdx_output.txt';
SELECT
 {Products.Generation(2).Members} ON ROWS,
 {Time.Level(0).Members} ON COLUMNS
FROM Sample.Basic;
SPOOL OFF;
```

RUN AS

A new "run as" feature allows supervisors to login in as another user. This is helpful when debugging someone's security access. It was introduced for batch bursting in Financial Reporting. Type in ESSMSH –la and provide the admin id, admin password, and the user to log in as (ESSMSH –la Username, password, usernameas).

ERROR HANDLING

Error handling in MaxL is a two-stage process. The first involves redirecting the script after the error occurs so no more statements are executed. In this example, we are testing for a login failure and if not successful then there is no point in executing the load and calculate commands so we divert the MaxL script immediately to the "no_login" error handling section.

```
LOGIN admin password ON server01;
IFERROR 'no_login';

ALTER SYSTEM LOAD APPLICATION 'Sample';
EXECUTE CALCULATION DEFAULT ON 'Sample.Basic';
EXIT;

DEFINE LABEL 'no_login';
EXIT;
```

The second stage takes place in the operating system command-line environment that is called **essmsh**. The **essmsh** process will return a 0 (zero) if everything was successful, but will return a non-zero number if an error was encountered. The operating system script will then be responsible for further actions.

Try It!

We want to perform hourly updates to our juggle application. Write a MaxL script to clear daily data logically and perform an incremental load during the day for the juggle application.

Try It!

Because of the large data source, record set for the juggle application, we want to break up the file and perform concurrent loads to the juggle application nightly. Write two MaxL scripts to perform a concurrent load process using multiple load buffers for the juggle application.

Try It!

Write a MaxL script for the nightly JugBud process: Clear upper levels, clear current month actual data (running a clear calc script), load current month actual data, and finally consolidate the database.

Chapter 28:
Introduction to Essbase Studio

As an Essbase administrator, we face a number of different challenges. We have many applications using the same or different dimensions, sourced from the same or different data sources, and often times share data. We have many dimension maintenance rules files and procedures and many data load rules files and dimension maintenance procedures. In versions prior to 11x, we had to use Essbase Integration Services (EIS) to allow drill through to relational detail and even those drill through capabilities were limited.

ESSBASE STUDIO DEFINED

Essbase Studio is the next generation tool for Essbase application building and administration. In version 11, you can use a combination of Administration Services Console and Essbase Studio to manage your Essbase databases.

Essbase Studio provides a single graphical modeling environment and single set of steps to create and deploy Essbase cubes. Studio integrates cube creation capabilities of EIS and Administration Services console. Other benefits of Essbase Studio include: reuse and consistency, standard methodology for deploying Essbase apps, and capabilities to manage change through impact analysis and artifact lineage.

At a quick glance, Essbase Studio:
- Creates, deploys and maintains cubes in a graphical modeling interface
- Unifies many sources for modeling including relational database files, Oracle Business Intelligence Server, Flat Files, and Enterprise Performance Management Architect (EPMA) Dimension Library
- Supports new 11 features like varying attributes and text and date lists
- Provides Catalog browsing and exploring
- Enables flexible drill through on members and/or the data to almost any source
- Utilizes role based security

The Essbase Studio Console is displayed below:

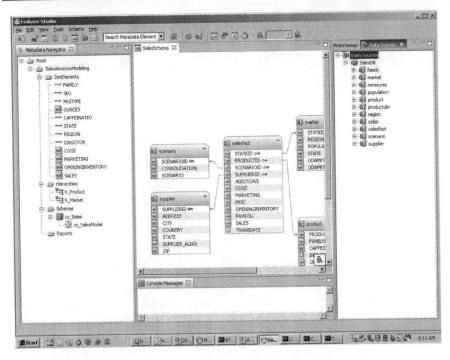

The Right Panel defines and manages data source definitions and mini schemas. The Left Panel lists the components to ultimately create an Essbase cube (Hierarchies, Logical elements, Measures, Cube schemas, Essbase Models AKA Essbase applications, Cube Deployments, Drill Through Reports). The Center Panel is the work area for editing objects.

The Essbase Studio process is as follows:
1. Create data source
2. Create mini-schema (similar to metamodel in EIS)
3. Create hierarchies
4. Create cube schema, creating hierarchies to ultimately be created in the Essbase database
5. Create Essbase model, defining the Essbase specific properties
6. Cube deployment wizard

A Mini-schema defines the star schema of joins between tables. It is similar to an EIS OLAP Model or metamodel. A Studio Connection wizard helps you create mini-schemas.

Hierarchies are created using columns and text fields from sources that are used in cube schemas. Hierarchies can have three different types: Standard, Measure, Calendar.

Cube Schemas are a series of related dimensions and hierarchies that will eventually be deployed as an Essbase cube. You define the accounts dimensions in the cube schema. The cube schema is similar to metaoutline

You define the Essbase specific properties like dense sparse, member formulas, and consolidation tags in the Essbase Model.

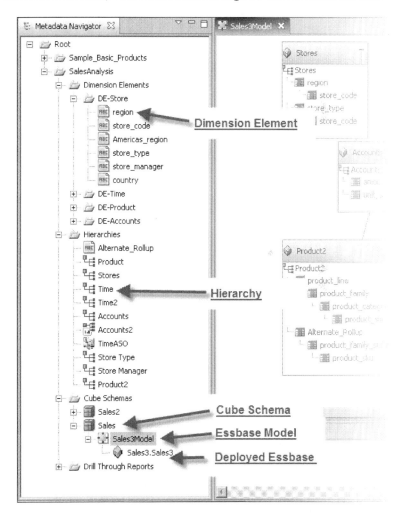

Here is an example of the Essbase Model display:

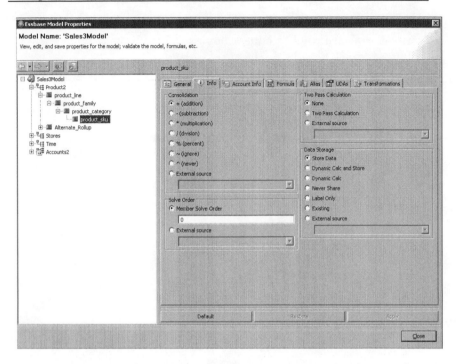

Options when deploying Essbase models include build outline only, load data only, build outline and load data, load members incrementally, delete members from an existing cube before loading, delete and restore data to an existing cube, and create and save a rules file only during deployment. Incremental loads are possible for dimensions and members (but not data).

DRILL THROUGH REPORTS

Essbase Studio provides drill through capabilities for end users. When the end user is performing analysis in Essbase, he can launch a drill through report that in most cases queries a relational table, pulling up additional details that are not stored in Essbase (think more detailed transactions or text based information). Drill through queries can be tied to members or data.

In the example below, we are creating a drill through report that is tied to the store code level, displaying store attribute information like Address, Phone number, Manager, and more. Users can launch a drill through report for a selected store code:

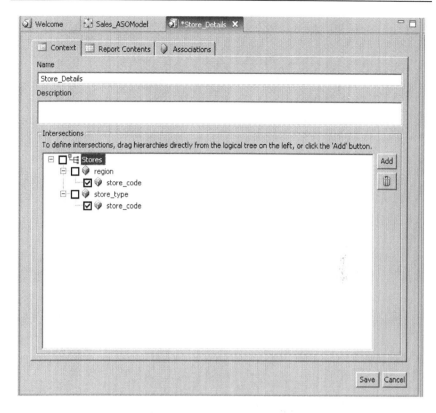

The columns that will be displayed in the drill through report are defined on the Report Contents tab. Report Content can be defined through a wizard or via manual SQL:

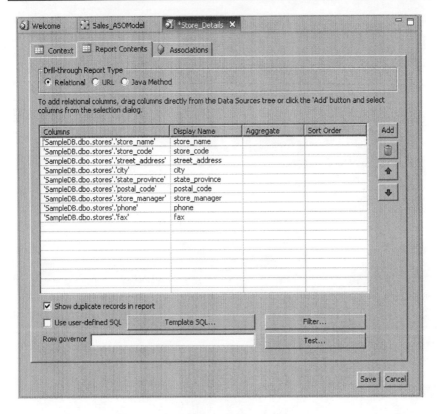

XOLAP

XOLAP cubes are cubes defined in the Essbase Studio that are entirely stored in a relational database. XOLAP stands for eXtending OLAP on Relational Database. It looks just like an ASO cube and can be used through any of the reporting analysis tools like Smart View or Web Analysis.

In summary, Essbase Studio is the future of Essbase Administration. In the current version, you cannot solely use the Essbase Studio. There are still a number of administrative tasks that require the Administration Services Console. Eventually all functionality will be moved to the Essbase Studio (at least that is what we've heard).

Chapter 28:
Other Essbase Features

As we drew up the outline for this book, we began with a list of fairly simple items. From an administrator perspective, we wanted to show you how to create, optimize, and manage the application. While we didn't want to overwhelm you, we still wanted to make you knowledgeable and able to dig in immediately.

But Essbase has *so many* features and functions that it is almost impossible to include in one book without overwhelming you. In addition, the book would probably weigh about 100 pounds (wait a minute, now that we've added in the ASO content, the book does weigh 100 pounds). There are still many topics that we can't cover in detail so in this section, we'll give you a brief overview of those additional topics.

INTRODUCTION TO UNICODE APPLICATIONS

Do you need to increase the length of your aliases? Do you need to roll out an application in a foreign language? Do you feel like you're stuck in a never-ending infomercial? Essbase fully supports Unicode applications for these reasons. Unicode applications use UTF-8 encoding form to interpret and store character text, providing support for multiple character sets. Let's take a look at the Sample_U.Basic application.

We can see that Sample_U has a different alias table for each foreign language plus an additional alias table for long names:

Notice, if we change the active Alias table in the Outline editor to German names, we can see the German aliases:

Note!   To set the active alias table, open the outline editor. Select the Properties tab. Under the "Alias tables" section, right click on the desired alias table and select "Set as active".

```
⊟ Outline: Basic (Active Alias Table: GermanNames)
  ⊕ Year (Alias: Jahr)
  ⊕ Measures [Alias: Umsätze)
  ⊕ Product (Alias: Produkt)
  ⊟ Market (Alias: Markt)
       ⊕ East (+) (Alias: Ost)
       ⊕ West (+)
       ⊕ South (+) (Alias: Süd)
       ⊕ Central (+) (Alias: Mitte)
  ⊕ Scenario (Alias: Szenario)
  ⊕ Caffeinated (Alias: Koffeinhaltig)
  ⊕ Ounces (Alias: Unzen)
  ⊕ Pkg Type (Alias: Art der Verpackung)
  ⊕ Population (Alias: Einwohner)
  ⊕ Intro Date (Alias: Datum der Einführung)
```

To set up a unicode application,
1. Setup a computer for unicode support by doing one of:
   - Install a font that supports UTF-8 encoding, or
   - Install a unicode editor
2. Set the Essbase Server to Unicode Mode via Administration Services or MaxL (use Server Properties).
3. Check the Unicode box when creating a new unicode-mode application.
4. You can also migrate non-unicode applications to unicode applications (but NOT the other way around).

It's important to understand that unicode is supported for Block Storage option databases only. Partitions cannot connect non-unicode mode databases to unicode mode databases and if you do partition unicode databases, all databases in the partition must use the same encoding.

REPORT SCRIPTS

Essbase comes with a report script engine that you can use to create reports. Do we recommend this? No. Oracle delivers much, much better reporting solutions using the Add-Ins and tools like Web Analysis, Financial Reporting and Interactive Reporting. Still report scripts can be helpful when extracting subsets of data from Essbase for online backups or feeding into other systems (at least they were before System 9.3 and the new calc export commands).

The report script editor is the text editor where you will create a report script. There are two types of commands in report scripts: extraction and formatting. The basic layout of a report script will contain a page, row, and column definition (sound familiar?).

```
<Page
<Row
<Column
```

Here is what a report script will look like in the report script editor:

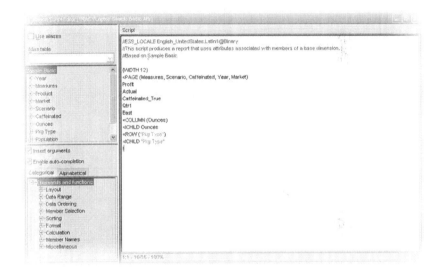

Here is an example of a report script that extracts a subset of data in a loadable format:

```
<COLUMN("Fiscal Year")
Sep Oct Nov Dec Jan Feb Mar Apr May Jun Jul Aug
<ROW("Market", "Scenario", "Accounts")
{TabDelimit}
{Decimal 2}
{NoIndentGen}
{SUPMISSINGROWS}
{SUPZEROROWS}
{RowRepeat}
{SupBrackets}
<Link (<DESCENDANTS("East") AND <LEV(Market,0) )
"Actual" "Budget"
<Link (<DESCENDANTS("Margin") AND <LEV("Accounts",0)
      )
!
```

Note!

// denotes a comment in report scripts.

Tip!

System 9.3 introduced a new calc script command that will allow you to extract subsets of data from an Essbase database. We recommend you take a look at this new command as a superior replacement for your data export report scripts.

WIZARDS, WIZARDS, WIZARDS

No, this section isn't part of the last Harry Potter installment (although we wish we had their special effects budget). Essbase comes with several wizards to assist you in various tasks, and Oracle is always adding more. Try it - select *File >> Wizards* from the Administration Services menu. The wizards are so easy to use we will let you get to know these magical creatures on your own:

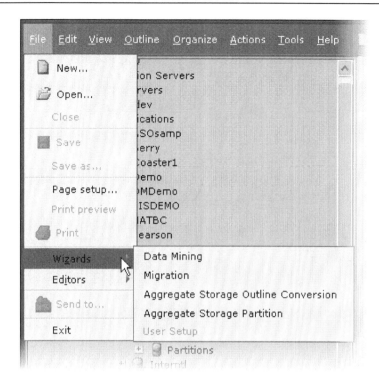

The User Setup wizard will walk you through the process of creating Administration Services users. The wizard will help map Administrative Services users to Essbase users.

The Migration wizard will walk you through the process of migrating (copying) applications and databases across Essbase Servers with no server downtime. You can copy from any platform to any platform (Window to Unix and back again). Migrations can be run in the background, freeing up Administration Services for other activities.

The remaining wizards are discussed in their own relative sections.

DATA MINING

Data mining is the process of searching through large amounts of data to find hidden relationships and patterns. Data mining results can be descriptive (provide information about existing data). For example, people who bought root beer in July also bought ice cream in July. The results can be predictive (forecast future trends.) For example, forecast next year's root beer sales based on this year's.

Note!   Data mining is not supported for ASO databases.

There are six data mining algorithms provided for creating new data mining models: simple regression, multilinear regression, clustering, association rules, decision tree, and neural net. Luckily, Essbase provides a wizard to assist in the creation of data mining models.

TRIGGERS

Triggers allow users to monitor data changes in Essbase. If data meets a trigger's rules, Essbase can send an e-mail or log the information in a file. An example of this would be to send an e-mail to the department manager if the wolverine juggling revenue in the Western region fell below the revenue for the same month in the previous year. Triggers are evaluated during the following system events: data load, calculation and lock and send from the Spreadsheet Add-In.

ESSCMD

We haven't mentioned ESSCMD in this book on purpose. Don't use ESSCMD (this is the old way of scripting in Essbase). Use MaxL for all Essbase scripting needs.

NO LONGER OPTIONAL ESSBASE COMPONENTS

A number of Essbase components now come standard with Essbase (previously they required additional licensing):
- SQL Interface provides the ability to load data directly from a relational table to Essbase using ODBC connectivity.
- Spreadsheet Toolkit provides the ability to create custom functions and applications in the Spreadsheet Add-In.
- Partitioning provides the ability to share dimensions and data between Essbase databases along with linking ("drill-to") capabilities.
- Application Programming Interface (API) provides the ability to develop custom applications on top of the Essbase platform.

- Visual Explorer provides a highly visual query and analysis interface for large data sets. (This one still has an extra cost.)

While it may have been a bit painful (and not the least bit boring), you've now developed a highly sought after skill that will aid you in creating well designed, finely tuned Essbase applications. You've reached the end of the road on this journey through Essbase. There are still a few helpful sections in the appendix so we encourage you read through that information. But we officially grant you *master* Essbase administrator (sniff, sniff...we are a bit teary-eyed. Our junior administrator is all grown up now.). So get out there, start diving into Essbase and apply everything that you've just learned. While we hope this book will be invaluable to all Essbase users and administrators, there is nothing like hands-on practice with the tool itself. Go out and look smarter than you are with Essbase.

Appendix A:
Note from the Authors

A NOTE ON VERSIONS

This book is based on System 11.1.1.1 Essbase. If you are on Essbase 6x, upgrade. Period.

If you're on Essbase 7x, 60% of the content in this book will apply to you. The main difference in System 9 and Essbase 7x is the security maintenance process, ASO improvements, and big new features mentioned throughout the book. In System 9, you will utilize the Shared Services User Provisioning to create users and groups and in Essbase 7x, you utilize the Administration Services console for managing security. Some of the menus, icons, and right click menus changed slightly from a navigation perspective.

If you are on Essbase System 9, 95% of the content in the book will apply to you. We've tried to highlight in most cases where new features were introduced in version 11.

Almost nine months after Hyperion 11x was first released only in English and only on Windows, localized versions of Hyperion are finally available. On April 2, 2009 EPM 11.1.1.2 was posted to edelivery.oracle.com with the level of fanfare normally reserved for the openings of small suburban strip malls. In other words, no announcement was made at all. In addition to localaized versions, 11.1.1.2 addresses a number of bugs (3 pages just for Essbase documented in the readme files).

A NOTE ON THIS BOOK

Our objective is to teach you Essbase. We've tried to be as detailed as possible but if we described every single click or button, you'd be 100 years old before you were ready to use Essbase. So we don't mention the fairly obvious tasks and buttons. For example, if there is a Close button, we probably skipped defining what this button does. Cancel means Cancel (doesn't save anything that you just did). Nothing tricky there. Once we've walked you through a specific step, we may not go into as much detail the next time.

APPENDIX B:
Intro to LCM

Life Cycle Management (LCM) is a new set of tools introduced with version 11 of Oracle EPM System that provides a consistent way for EPM products including Essbase to migrate applications, a repositories or individual artifacts across environments and operating systems. LCM is part of the Foundation services component of an Oracle EPM implementation.

The LCM tools are designed to facilitate the movement of objects in connected and disconnected environments for development, test & production.

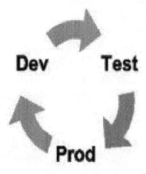

A connected environment is where dev, test, and prod environments are managed by a single Shared Services instance. A disconnected environmet is one where each logical environment (dev, test, prod) has its own Shared Services instance. Most user configurations will have disconnected environments.

Let's now review some of the features of the Oracle EPM Life Cycle Management.

Application Groups & File System Group

An application group in Shared Services essentially maps to a product like Essbase or Planning. Previously known as "projects" , application groups allow for more simplified management of the applications registered with Shared Services. A new application group called 'File System' is introduced in 11x to support disconnected migrations in LCM.

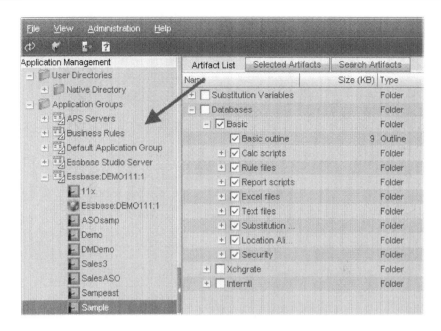

The File System Group references the artifacts that have been selected for migration to the file system as opposed to a target application in the same Shared Services environment. This is what allows for the support of disconnected Shared Services environments and will be used in most situations.

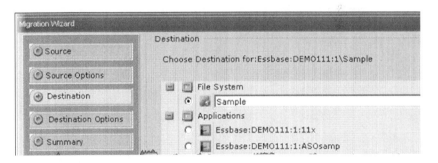

Each migration that is defined to have a file system destination will get a folder created on the Shared Services server that will contain the objects in scope for the migration. Additionally each user gets a named folder to help organize the migrations. The default location on the file system is <HYPERION_HOME>/common/import_export/<USER_NAME>.

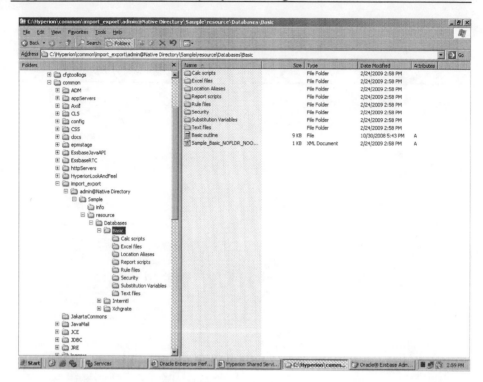

Application Artifacts

The Life Cycle Management tools can be used to manage a variety of artifacts from the different Oracle EPM applications. The supported applications & artifacts are currently:

- Essbase
  - Substitution Variables
  - Rule Files
  - Calculation Scripts
  - Report Scripts
  - Excel Files
  - Location Aliases
  - Security Filters

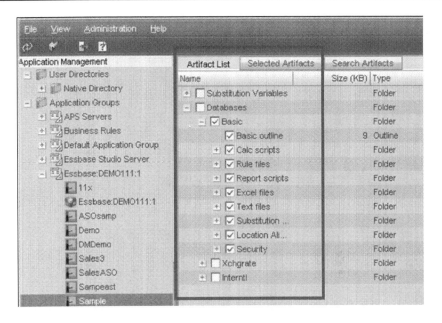

- Financial Management
  - Security
  - Dimension
  - Phased Submission
  - Rules
  - Documents
  - Forms
  - InterCompany
  - Journals
  - Member Lists
- Planning
  - Configuration
  - Relational Data
  - Global Artifacts
  - Plan Types
  - Security
- Reporting & Analysis
  - Financial Reporting
  - Interactive Reporting
  - Production Reporting
  - Web Analysis
- EPMA / Calc Manager
  - Application Metadata
  - Shared Dimensions
  - Dimension Access
  - Data Synchronization

- Profitability Management
  - o Driver definitions
  - o Stage definitions
  - o POV definitions

  - o Driver selections
  - o Assignments
  - o Application preferences
  - o Assignment Rules
  - o Assignment Rule selections
- Performance Scorecard
  - o Administrative Options
  - o Objects
- Shared Services (users & task flows)
  - o Native Directory (Security)
  - o Task flows

Migration Wizard

A migration is defined in the Shared Services Console utilizing the Migration Wizard. This wizard guides the user through the steps required to define an artifact migration. To migrate,

1. Select Source Artifacts
2. Define any Source Options
3. Select Destination – Either a specified folder for the file system or an application in the same environment.
4. Define any Destination options such as selecting dependent artifacts.
5. Review Summary & Execute the migration or save the migration definition to an XML file.

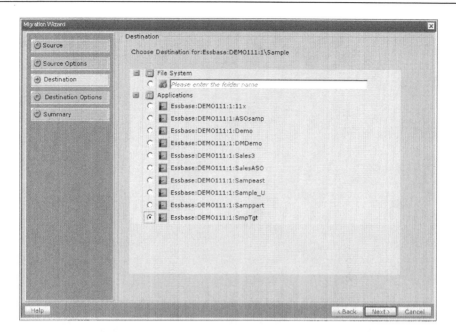

The saved migration definition file contains all the information about a migration (source, destination, artifacts for migrations, export and import options) and can then be used to automate migrations or is updated to execute the migration into a disconnected Shared Services environment. The migration definition file is in XML format.

Life Cycle Management Reports

The Life Cycle Management tools have reporting capabilities to assist in the management of LCM activities. The Migration Status Report provides migration status, migration date and time, and total number of artifacts migrated. The Compare Report provides comparison information of artifacts based on file dates. The Audit Report displays user LCM activities and must be configured prior to use.

Life Cycle Management Utility - Command Line Utility

The Life Cycle Management Utility is a command-line utility that provides an alternate way to migrate artifacts from source to destination. Lifecycle Management Utility can be used with a third-party scheduling service such as Windows Task Scheduler or Oracle Enterprise Manager.

```
C:\WINDOWS\system32\cmd.exe                                              _ □ ×

C:\Hyperion\common\utilities\LCM\9.5.0.0\bin>dir
 Volume in drive C has no label.
 Volume Serial Number is 7CED-1D75

 Directory of C:\Hyperion\common\utilities\LCM\9.5.0.0\bin

12/15/2008  08:40 PM    <DIR>          .
12/15/2008  08:40 PM    <DIR>          ..
12/15/2008  08:40 PM             2,490 hsslcmutility.bat
12/15/2008  08:40 PM             3,151 hsslcmutility.sh
12/15/2008  08:40 PM             1,437 invokeCLU.bat
12/15/2008  08:40 PM             8,190 Utility.bat
12/15/2008  08:40 PM             6,703 Utility.sh
               5 File(s)         21,971 bytes
               2 Dir(s)  10,441,723,904 bytes free

C:\Hyperion\common\utilities\LCM\9.5.0.0\bin>_
```

Conclusion

Life Cycle Management provides a powerful set of tools that can be used to facilitate many administrative tasks within an Oracle EPM Environment:

- Application migrations with cross-product artifact dependencies
- Security migrations
- Edit Shared Services Registry data
- Configuration of Oracle EPM System products in a mixed-release environment
- Enable or disable Secure Socket Layer (SSL) connections
- Perform other manual configuration changes
- Backup & Recovery (not intended for data)
- Bulk security updates
- Import and export artifacts for editing purposes
- Edit a single artifact
- Version control

In summary, Life Cycle Management is a big step forward for configuration and change management processes for the Oracle EPM System products.

Appendix C:
Advanced Essbase BSO Tuning

By Rick Sawa, Senior Technical Response Specialist, Oracle

It's not every day that someone "volunteers" to write part of our book for us. Rick Sawa has been optimizing Essbase cubes at Hyperion and then Oracle for eons (well, it seems like it at least). He read our book and felt that it could use another approach to Essbase optimization. We are pleased to be able to include his contribution as this appendix on "Advanced Essbase BSO Tuning." The style is definitely Rick's and we're sure you'll find lots of valuable information in this section. We did a mite of editing, but the hard work in authoring "Advanced Essbase Tuning" was brought to you by Rick Sawa at his finest. We're making him an honorary wolverine. Wolverines!!!

- Tracy McMullen and Edward Roske

There are three primary areas to the tuning of BSO Essbase. These are tuning the outline, tuning database settings (caches, etc.) and finally the tuning of database calculations or Business Rules.

We will break the contents down into the following areas of optimization:
1. Understanding the Caches
2. Tuning the Outline
3. Tuning Calculations
4. Tuning Settings in the Essbase.cfg File
5. Performance Metrics

UNDERSTANDING THE CACHES

The caches are the memory objects that Essbase uses to manage index and data pages. Every important aspect of BSO Essbase is impacted directly by data block design decisions, and the caches are no exception.

The block and index structures are the units of storage that Essbase works with and moves in and out of memory. Essbase provides five memory buffers for this purpose: the index cache, data cache, data file cache[1], dynamic calculator cache and the dynamic calculator cache compressed buffer[2].

Data Files (ESS*.PAG)

The default setting is for Essbase to use data compression, and bitmap is the default compression algorithm. Data blocks are stored on disk in compressed format. Blocks are compressed as they are written *into* the buffer *from* which they will be written to disk. There is, however, a little cart-before-the-horse going on here.

The stored or physical block resides within the data cache. Blocks are compressed into an additional buffer before being written to disk. When buffered I/O is used, *the operating system file cache* receives compressed blocks from Essbase *before the OS writes the data to disk*. When direct I/O is used, Essbase puts compressed blocks in its *data file cache* before *Essbase writes data to disk*.

Index Cache

Index pages reside on disk in ESS*.IND files, and on-demand within the Essbase index cache. When buffered I/O is being used, index entries are passed through the operating system data cache before being written to disk. When direct I/O is used, Essbase writes index entries directly to the ESS*.IND files.

Data Cache

Data blocks are retrieved into and/or written from the data cache. Blocks in the data cache are expanded to be equal in size to the number of stored cells multiplied by 8 bytes per cell.

Data File/OS File Caches

The Essbase data file cache is functional only when using direct I/O. Buffered I/O is the default setting. Using direct I/O means that Essbase manages the writing of data to disk. Data blocks are compressed before being passed into the data file cache. When buffered I/O is used, blocks are compressed and then passed through the operating system file cache.

---

[1] Only used when using Direct I/O else the Operating System data cache is used. The much misunderstood calc cache has nothing to do with data block and index movement. It is rather a sort of scratch pad to assist the Essbase calculator in block creation during sparse calculations.

[2] An additional cache can be configured to support hybrid analysis using the HAMEMORYCACHESIZE Essbase.cfg parameter. Its use will not be discussed in this Appendix.

Direct I/O Considerations

When using direct I/O it is important to adjust the operating system **not** to allocate memory for its file system cache. Changing this server configuration is performed by the role of the Server Admin. It is not the role of an Essbase Admin. The necessity of adjusting the operating system memory to support direct I/O infers that the server is dedicated to Essbase because the reduction of OS resources potentially starves other non-Essbase services of resources. It also reinforces Oracle's recommendation that for any given Essbase server either direct or buffered I/O be used, but not both.

Oracle recommends that the buffered or direct I/O setting be applied at the Server level. This means that for a single Essbase server, either all cubes will use direct I/O, or all cubes will use buffered I/O.

The Essbase DBA Guide recommends to set all ESS*.PAG files to be in memory when using Direct I/O. In order to do this, the Server at the OS level really should be configured to consume a known quantity of RAM.

The OS dynamically manages the File System Cache (FSC). How much RAM is devoted to the FSC is determined by the operating system and can fluctuate over time. Using both I/O options in Essbase, at the same time, forces the Essbase Admin to manage conflicting resource allocations. What are the conflicting requirements? Buffered I/O wants as much RAM as possible for the FSC, and Direct I/O wants as much RAM as possible for the data file cache (DFC). The DFC and the FSC both compete directly for RAM pertaining to disk I/O, which is common to both.

Dynamic Calculator Cache

Essbase also provides another user configurable cache to perform all dynamic calculations called the Dynamic Calculator Cache (DCC). The default setting for the DCC is 20 MB and data blocks are fully expanded there. This buffer is designed to support dynamic calculations for end-user queries.

Dynamic Calculator Cache Compressed Buffer

The administrator also has the option to configure and utilize another buffer called the *dynamic calculator cache compressed buffer* to help manage the dynamic calculator cache. As Essbase processes dense dynamic calc members, blocks become fully expanded within the DCC. In environments with heavy query activity, the admin has the option to adjust the amount of RAM devoted to the DCC as well as to configure Essbase to temporarily compress and set aside DCC blocks to improve query throughput. The DCC compressed buffer will be discussed below in the section dealing with the Essbase.cfg file settings.

Two forms of the Block – Which are really Four!

There are, then, essentially two forms of the data block. The stored block contains data that is persisted to disk (along with additional data block overhead). This version of the block is compressed into the OS or Essbase data file cache before it is written out to disk. We can refer to this as the compressed physical block.

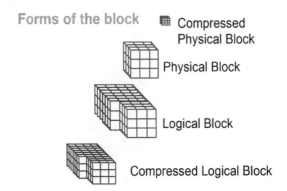

Forms of the block

▦ Compressed Physical Block

Physical Block

Logical Block

Compressed Logical Block

The fully expanded version of the block reserves memory to compute dynamically calculated members. This version of the block is held in the dynamic calculator cache and is compressed within the DCC compressed buffer when Essbase is configured to do so, and we can refer to the later as the compressed logical block.

Compression, Data Blocks and Memory

Index files are not compressed objects. Data (ESS*.PAG) files, however, are. Adding to the complexity of compression/decompression is the fact that the relative size of the data block differs depending on which buffer is being considered. Differences in block size derive from the particular cube specific use of member tags.

Figure 5 and Figure 6 depict the relative sizes of the data block in various locations. Note that the size of the data block is the same when it is resident on disk as it is in the data file or operating system data cache. In these locations, the block is in its smallest form.

Figure 5. Buffered I/O

OS File Cache (FSC)
Buffered I/O

Data *and* Index Pages are brought into RAM. In Buffered I/O we use the FSC.

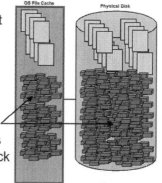

Note that blocks are compressed in this cache. And the block in this cache is the same size as the block that is stored on disk.

Figure 6. Direct I/O

Data File Cache (DFC)
Direct I/O

Data Pages are brought into Data File Cache. Index pages are brought into the Index Cache.

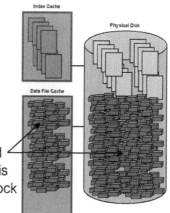

Note that blocks are compressed in this cache. And the block in this cache is the same size as the block that is stored on disk.

When blocks are moved into the data cache, they are uncompressed. They are the equivalent to the number of stored cells defined in the block – approximately eight bytes for every cell whose members are not tagged dynamic calc or label only. The block in the data cache is referred to as the physical or stored block.

When blocks are moved into the dynamic calculator cache, **they are fully expanded** to include eight bytes for every cell whose members are not tagged label only. The block in this location is referred to as the fully expanded, logical, or big block.

Finally, blocks that are managed within the dynamic calculator cache compressed buffer are fully expanded blocks that have been temporarily compressed and put aside to make more room in the dynamic calculator cache.

Proportioning RAM Allocations to the Caches

Allocate Essbase caches at values to enhance the likelihood that blocks reside in memory. Consider the following statistics from a customer model that contained 510,205 blocks with a data file of 483,495,437 bytes. The physical block size is 157352 bytes large, the fully expanded block is 257600 bytes in size.

Dividing the total data file size by the total number of blocks reveals an average compressed block size on disk of 965-bytes.

Consider the following chart:

		Data Cache Block Count	Dyn Calc Cache Block Count	Data File or OS Cache Block Count
Stored Block Size (bytes)	157,532	133	-	-
Expanded Block Size (bytes)	257,600	-	81	-
Compressed Block Size (bytes)	965	-	-	21,740
Number of Blocks	501,205	-na-	-na-	-na-
Data File Size (bytes)	483,495,437	-na-	-na-	-na-

To make the point, and for purposes of comparison, consider a cube that uses 20 MB for each of the data, dynamic calculator, and data file caches. The chart shows that 21,740 compressed blocks can be stored in the data file cache, with the data cache and the dynamic calculator cache only holding 133 and 81 blocks respectively.

When requests for data are made, there is a better chance that the block will be found in the data file or OS file cache because data block is compressed there, and it can hold more blocks. The chart supports configuring in favor of the data file/OS cache. However, the point is *not* to set the data, dynamic calc and index caches to their minimal settings. It is self-evident that the above settings would result in abysmal performance in a high concurrency query and business rule environment.

The objective of optimizing the Essbase caches is to favor the OS/data file cache by systematically determining the minimum "working set" of memory to support each processing activity in order to hold as many blocks in memory as possible.

Tuning for Batch Calculations

Batch tuning Essbase can be time consuming, but is relatively easy to accomplish.

During batch processing, new logins are prohibited. Then users are disconnected from cubes, and all user initiated processing is halted. Data is then loaded to cubes, calculated and/or moved between cubes as appropriate. Once complete, the cubes are released back to users.

The batch process assumes complete control of the environment. This permits the Admin to allocate 100% of Server resources to the process if desired or required, effecting maximum use of server resources and parallelism. To determine the optimal configuration, keep everything constant, and systematically test the impact of altering only one setting at a time.

For example, establishing the best setting for the index cache during a batch calc would involve consecutively running the same calc script. Every other cube setting remains fixed. Each run of the calc script occurs after the value of the index cache has been incrementally altered by some quantity. The optimal setting is revealed by the fastest calc time[3].

Tuning Runtime Queries and Business Rules

Using explicit and appropriate response time expectations[4], determine what the overall minimum memory requirement is to process user queries to meet that expectation. In initial testing[5], this is done as if for a single user, but it should be based on a worst-case scenario.

Then, using explicit appropriate response time expectations, determine the average minimum memory required to execute the worst-case business rule. Factor into those requirements the worst-case scenario for the expected rate of concurrency. Adding these together will help you better quantify the initial memory requirements of the Essbase component to your Planning application.

---

[3] A parallel methodology is applied to establish optimal parameters for every setting affecting Essbase server performance.

[4] Response times will be, of course, also dependent upon parallel processing abilities. We will discuss below in Essbase.cfg Settings the impact and use of CALCPARALLEL.

TUNING THE OUTLINE

We briefly discuss outline design issues here to the extent that they impact how much data is stored, and what data is dynamically computed. Organizational hierarchies are embedded in the Essbase outline and most of data is persisted. How a cube performs will partly depend upon the inter-relation between how many dimensions there are, how large the dimensions are (i.e. total members) and how deep the hierarchies in the dimensions are.

Complex business algorithms too can be embedded in the outline. Additional complexity accrues to cubes that need to embed business logic in formulae as well as calculation scripts. The performance characteristics of any given cube will be the combined impact of the use of member tags, outline consolidation (unary) logic, the use of formulae (and or calc scripts/business rules).

Each of these components is impacted directly by dense/sparse settings.

Query performance improves, as more of the data is precomputed. The dynamic calc member tag was one of the tools that Oracle programmer's provided Essbase designers to trade-off the cost of calculating data values on-the-fly for a reduced batch calculation.

How can we optimize blocks via the outline? Let us take a look at the advantages and disadvantages of using the Label-Only and Dynamic Calc member storage properties.

Label Only

It is an Essbase best practice to keep the size of the cube to a minimum by storing data only when necessary. In Figure 8, the block contains 60 cells (all members are stored):

Figure 8. No Label Only, No Dynamic Members

Block size: 60 cells

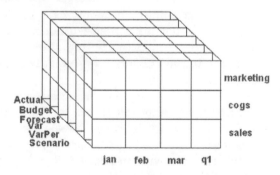

To minimize the amount of data that is persisted by Essbase make use of the Label Only tag on navigational members wherever possible. Tagging Scenario Label Only reduces the block size to only 48 cells.

Figure 9. Label Only, No Dynamic Members

Block size: now 48 cells

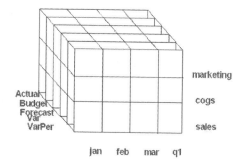

Dynamic-Calc Non-Store

Use Dynamic Calc non-store tags within the data block results in a block that has only 27 cells. We tagged the upper members of the dimension as dynamic calc; we left the place-holder members as Label Only:

Figure 10. Label Only, Dynamic Calc Members

Block size now 27 cells

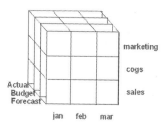

Whereas the Label only tag has some storage overhead effecting performance, dynamic calc tags have processing overhead effecting performance. Specifically the dynamic calc tag was introduced to **remove** the calculation of certain intersections completely from batch and procedural (i.e. scripted) calculations.

Figure 9 depicts the 48-cell block that will be materialized within the dynamic calculator cache. Figure 10 depicts the 27-cell block that will be materialized in the data cache. In this example, a block materialized in memory will consume 27*8=216 bytes in the data cache. When a dynamic calculation is involved, then a 384-byte block will be materialized in the dynamic calculator cache. Note that the "same" block occupies 600 bytes of RAM.

In summary, consider using label only and dynamic calc storage properties to reduce your block size which will in turn improve calculation times and overall performance.

Dynamically Calculated Members & Query Performance

Above we mentioned that as more data is persisted in the cube, query performance increases. Optimal query performance might be achieved by precalculating all database values. This would preclude the use of dynamic calc tags, and severely limit the overall size of the Essbase cube. And it might be that the use of dynamic calcs in upper-level dense members speeds up retrieval times because you are reducing how much data needs to be read from the hard drive. Reading from auxiliary storage is still about the slowest thing you can do in Essbase.

How to handle Consolidation and Formulae

The following are a general rules-of-thumb methodology when implementing dynamic calc tags and member formula:

1. Place member formulae in the outline (as opposed to calc scripts)
2. Ensure that inter-dimensional calculations are resolved *within* the data block. This objective will impact sparse-dense settings.

Both of these rules of thumb are unfortunately difficult to follow rigorously in Essbase for Hyperion Planning applications (more on this in the book, *Look Smarter Than You are with Hyperion Planning*).

TUNING CALCULATIONS

Natural Consolidations

A natural consolidation of an Essbase cube is invoked by issuing a CALC ALL[6] consolidation. These can be of two types. A consolidation can simply perform only aggregations. Here, the outline contains no member formulae, and all business logic is expressed by using unary operators. The cube is calculated in outline order according to the default calculation algorithm. Block creation is regular and predictable, and no CPU cycles are devoted to dense calculations.

---

[6] The equivalent results can be achieved using appropriate AGG or CALC DIM commands.

A slightly more resource intensive consolidation occurs when an outline has dense member formulae that reflect some of the business logic. In this natural consolidation, cross-dimensional references are resolved within the data block and performed as they appear in outline. The cube is calculated in outline order according to the default calculation algorithm and block creation and consolidation is regular and predictable.

These so-called natural consolidations represent ideal configurations. Reporting cubes are often very good candidates for natural consolidations. It would be considered a best practice from an overall Essbase perspective to convert cubes that do not involve write-back or procedural calculation to the aggregate storage option using MDX to replicate any formula requirements. ASO cubes are very efficient at storing data.

Focusing Calculations – FIXing and IFing

The objective of effective programming in Essbase is to isolate specific sections of the cube to increase calculation efficiency. Make as few passes over the database as necessary in order to achieve the desired results. The FIX statement pre-determines the correct data set and by working on a smaller set of data minimizes the operations performed by the calculator.

Figure 11. Focusing Calculations – FIX/ENDFIX

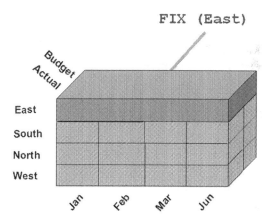

By this time you already know the Essbase adage to "FIX on sparse and IF on dense" dimensions. It is a good rule that can be used even more effectively after a little refining of understanding has been done.

First, it is important to understand when FIXing on dense dimensions is a problem, because it is not always problematic. It is only a problem in a badly written calc script where the FIX is exclusively on dense members. This will force Essbase to touch every block in the cube.

Let us review an example. Assume Time is dense and Region is sparse, consider the following calc script:

```
FIX (January)
      IF (Boston)
            Commands;
      ENDIF
ENDFIX
```

THIS CALC SCRIPT IS BAD! Every block will be touched with this Fix on January, a dense member.

Let's consider the classic case. Suppose that dense/sparse optimization exercises reveal the optimal configuration is to tag the Scenario dimension as dense along with Time and Accounts: this configuration creates the fewest, densest blocks. It is a classic configuration for financial applications to measure Accounts across time and for almost every scenario.

Add to this cube configuration the additional requirement to focus calculations for particular scenarios. In other words, different business logic applies for different scenarios. Consider the FIX statement that focuses on the Working Scenario when the Scenario dimension has been tagged dense:

```
FIX (Working)
      calculation logic;
ENDFIX
```

If there are 10,000,000 blocks in the database, everyone would contain the Working member, and the calculation would need to perform a cube scan of 10,000,000 blocks in order to complete.

What happens if Scenario is tagged sparse? First, it should be expected that the number of blocks in the cube would increase. When you reflect the density of the data in the index rather than the block, the result is block explosion[7]. Our hypothetical cube might now contain 45,000,000 blocks but only 3,000,000 of these reflect the Working scenario. So the calculation that focuses on the Working scenario touches 3 million rather than 10 million blocks, and our script can be expected to be about that much more efficient.

That is really all there is to understanding FIX...ENDFIX. Whereas FIX statements can certainly be expected to be more complex in

---

[7] The inverse happens when you tag a dimension dense that represents sparseness – you create a very large and very empty data block.

real world applications, the objective of focusing on subsets of data remains the same. In Essbase for Planning applications, users initiate what should be tightly focused business rule calculations that ideally process in a matter of seconds.

When do you consider using the IF statement? Use the IF statement when the logic dictates that FIXing is not possible. This happens when the logic of the calculation forces you to use two separate FIX statements to accomplish the task.

```
FIX (@DESC(East))
        Actual (
                IF (Boston)
                        Logic;
                ELSEIF (Stamford)
                        Logic;
                ENDIF
                )
ENDFIX
```

Figure 13 illustrates that only a portion of the blocks are included in the application of the if logic.

Figure 13. Using IF in a Calculation

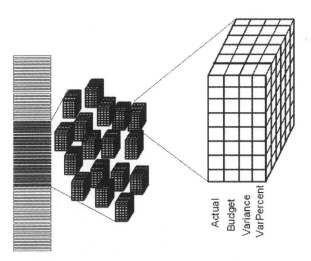

The objective is to minimize I/O described as either cube or index scan operations. Use FIX whenever possible and use IF to resolve logic to replace having to use multiple FIX statements across the same slice of data.

This logic:

```
FIX (Budget, Albany, Buffalo, "Jan 1999")
      IF (Albany)
            Sales=Sales*1.15;
      ELSEIF (Buffalo)
            Sales-Sales*1.2;
      ENDIF
ENDFIX
```

Is preferable to this logic:

```
FIX (Budget, Albany, "Jan 1999")
      Sales=Sales*1.15;
ENDFIX
FIX (Budget, Buffalo, "Jan 1999")
      Sales=Sales*1.2;
ENDFIX
```

Because the former will make the fewest scan across the data to complete.

In the final analysis, you *can* use FIX in the block, and you *can* use IF on a subset of blocks. The point is to use combinations of FIX and IF as required in order to process the calculation using as few I/O requests as possible.

Dense Dynamic Calc Dependencies

What happens when a script or outline contains a dynamic calc dependency? Essbase:

1. Pauses the calculation.
2. Computes the dynamic calc member as if it were performing a query retrieve (the caches involved depends on the specific configuration, but it could conceivably involve every cache).
3. Returns the value to the calculator engine.
4. Continues the calculation.

In order to process dense dynamic calc dependencies, Essbase may even materialize the logical block *within the dynamic calculator cache* to continue processing. The expanded block potentially is materialized in both the dynamic CALC CACHE and the data cache during a calculation depending on whether further processing involves updates to the stored block. The presence of BIG blocks within the data cache can seriously skew data cache sizing requirements.

Whether Essbase computes every cell in the big block is computationally dependent. The use of certain functions, currmbr() for example, can force Essbase to compute *every* dense dynamic cell during materialization and thus exacerbate processing requirements.

Whenever dense dynamic calc members are involved in a calc script, the dynamic calculator cache is used to initialize the fully expanded block. If the BIG block needs to participate in further calculations, (i.e. roll up to its parent) the batch calc will search the DATA CACHE first and then DYNAMIC CALCULATOR CACHE.

In summary, as long as a block needs to be read from and written to the kernel, it will have to be materialized in the data cache. A dense dynamic calc dependency will then determine whether a BIG block needs to be materialized. Based on whether that BIG block is dirtied during the batch calc, it might be materialized also within the data cache. Thus the same BIG block may exist in both dynamic calculator cache and the data cache. The BIG block is always initialized in dynamic calculator cache first, and whether it is moved into the data cache depends on whether any changes to the block need to be written back to the kernel.

TUNING SETTINGS IN THE ESSBASE.CFG FILE

In this section, we will discuss the use of and performance implications of several key configuration parameters. Where appropriate, cross-reference will be made to equivalent calc script command settings. We do not reproduce but rather complement the contents of Oracle Hyperion Technical Reference materials.

Parallel Calculation - CALCPARALLEL

This setting tells Essbase to use multiple (up to 8, depending on the operating system) processors for the calculation. How effective Essbase is at parallelizing a calculation is cube dependant. This means that Essbase will evaluate the specific outline to determine a task list that can be worked through in parallel. This setting needs to be used in conjunction with CALKTASKDIMS.

Parallel Calculation - CALCTASKDIMS

This setting tells Essbase how many sparse dimensions to consider when determining a task schedule for parallel processing of cube aggregations. The default value is one, which means that Essbase will only consider the last sparse dimension for defining a task list. If the last sparse dimension in the outline does not contain any aggregation points, and the system is configured at the default level, then Essbase will not parallelize the calculation no matter how many threads you devote to the calculation, or how many CPUs are available to be used.

It is a common strategy to move non-aggregating sparse dimensions to the bottom of the outline[8] in an attempt to optimize calculation times. Testing needs to determine what the best CALCPARALLEL and CALCTASKDIM settings are for a given calc script. These settings can be used procedurally in a calc script to the same effect as globally setting default values in the Essbase.cfg file. For very complex calculation script logic, it is possible to fine tune each aggregation section.

The objective is to enable Essbase to devise a task list that it can use to parallelize the calculation. Performance degradations can occur when configuring the calc to evaluate too many CALCTASKDIMS. Suitable testing is necessary to determine the optimal setting. Configuring the calculation use from one to three sparse dimensions has been found to be optimal, but an adjustment needs to be made when using CALCPARALLEL in combination with moving non-aggregating sparse dimensions to the bottom of the outline. For example, if the last three dimensions in the outline are non-aggregating dimensions, and parallelism is required, then start testing setting the CALCTASKDIMS at four, five and/or six to ensure that Essbase will consider appropriate dimensions to create its task list.

In general, setting the number of CALCTASKDIMS to high values has negative return. Essbase calc performance can be greatly reduced by asking for it to analyze too many dimensions when determining a task list. Once again, thorough testing is the only way to determine the optimal settings for your cube/calc environments.

Dynamic Calculator Cache

This cache is used to perform dynamic calculations. The dynamic calc tag was developed to enable designers to delay certain member calculations to query time. This assumes that the amount of time to compute the values dynamically will be transparent to the user at runtime, and does not affect batch or script driven calculation times. When a database calculation is coded to invoke dynamic calc members in a script, the purpose of the dynamic calc tag is completely defeated, and Essbase is forced to expand blocks fully in this cache during script/batch processes.

All dynamic calculator cache settings are configurable at the database level. Oracle strongly recommends that they be tuned per database to ensure optimal use of server resources. The amount of memory available to an application is determined by the OS and it is important not to over-allocate memory beyond that limit.

---

[8] Bottom of stored, not attribute, dimensions that is.

Tuning the dynamic calculator cache to handle dynamic calculations is a non-trivial task and strictly speaking depends on your database configuration. You should attempt to limit the use of dynamic calc tags to dense dimensions to defray the impact of unexpected resource requirements. It is just as important to ensure that no dynamic calc references occur during business rule processing. If dynamic calc tags on sparse members are necessary, it is equally necessary to study end user query behavior in-depth and configure the dynamic calculator cache appropriately.

DYNCALCCACHEMAXSIZE

This setting determines how much memory (20 MB default) a database will reserve for dynamic calculations. By default, if more memory is required, Essbase asks the OS for more RAM. Underestimating and overestimating this cache setting can cause overall poor system performance: Too many requests from the OS are expensive, and allocating too much memory to the buffer can starve the application of memory.

Essbase records the usage of the dynamic calculator cache in the application log.

It is important to note that dynamic calc processing of sparse members are not recorded in log entries, so the cost of their computation is not easily determined beforehand. A cube with an outline that uses dynamic calc tags on sparse members, and has business rules that reference dynamic calc members (dense or sparse), can seriously degrade overall system performance. In extreme cases, this can lead to application or even server-wide instability. This is the result of the unexpected resource demand for Essbase to process the dynamic calculations concurrently for the business rules and query requests.

DYNCALCCACHEONLY

The setting is used to restrict Essbase from making OS level requests for resources. If the Server Admin decides in favor of this restriction, then it is important to specify what Essbase needs to do when there is not sufficient memory in the dynamic calculator cache.

DYNCALCCACHEWAITFORBLK

This setting instructs Essbase to wait for memory to be freed within the dynamic calculator cache. If the setting is set to true, and the DYNAMICCAHCEBLKTIMEOUT setting has been exceeded, Essbase generates an error message. You can instruct Essbase to create a DYNCALCCACHECOMPRBLKBUFSIZE buffer to store blocks temporarily when the timeout has been reached. Overall application memory limits need to be respected.

DYNCALCCACHEBLKTIMEOUT

This setting specifies how long Essbase waits for memory to be freed within the dynamic calculator cache before generating an error message.

DYNCALCCACHECOMPRBLKBUFSIZE

Use this setting to specify an area of memory for Essbase to temporarily compress and store blocks to make room in the dynamic calculator cache. Essbase temporarily stores compressed blocks from the dynamic calculator cache into this buffer.

DYNCALCCACHEBLKRELEASE

Enables Essbase to create a temporary buffer for dynamic calculations in cases where the wait for space in the dynamic calculator cache has exceeded the specified wait time.

Miscellaneous Configuration and Calculation Settings

MEMSCALINGFACTOR

This setting applies only to 64-bit environments. It affects performance only to the extent that using it enables you to take advantage of the increased memory space available to 64-bit applications

CALCNOTICE/SET NOTICE

This setting causes Essbase to estimate the progress of a calculation. It is useful in development environments but is *not recommended for Production environments*. Consultants coordinate calc progress with the estimation of percent complete to gauge the effectiveness of different configurations. For example, a calculation is initiated and the output in the log is monitored for when the first percent completion notice appears. Once it appears, the duration is noted and the calculation is cancelled. A change is made to the cube, for example, a new sparse/dense configuration. The calculation is then re-initiated and monitored for the first completion notice. The calculation is cancelled, and the quickest completion notice message is assumed to point to the most efficient design.

CALCCACHE/SET CACHE

The calculator cache is an area of memory that can be set aside by Essbase to enhance sparse calculations *that create data blocks*. Specifically it is *not* a cache in the sense of a stash of index or data pages. It is better understood as a roadmap that tracks children and parents in support of block creation. By default, the CALCCACHE is on, and Essbase will use either 200000 bytes or whatever value is established using the CALCCACHEDEFAULT configuration setting.

Three values (HIGH, DEFAULT and LOW) for CALCCACHE are set in the Essbase.cfg file. Which specific value is used during a given calculation is controlled through the SET CACHE command. Essbase determines whether or not to use a calc cache based on the contents of the specific calculation script that is being executed. The developer can force the use of the calc cache in a calc script by issuing the SET CACHE ALL command.

The range of useful calc cache values depends on specific cube configurations and available memory resources. Performance results are thus cube dependant.

Essbase will modify CALCPARALLEL and CALCTASKDIMS settings when using the CALC CACHE. Essbase will write in the log that it has adjusted the number of CALCTASKDIMS because of the use of the CALC CACHE. In these situations, testing has shown that performance is better when favoring parallelism than it is when favoring the optimal CALC CACHE.

PERFORMANCE METRICS

What performance metrics should you use when tuning Essbase?

The only significant performance indicator is time. How long do things take to do? While not wanting to treat lightly the GUI aspects of an application that make life better for users, the very best GUI environment will ultimately be abandoned when response times are unacceptable.

Users concentrate on the following times: How long does it take to calculate a cube? How long does it take for the user to run business rules? How long does it take queries to complete? If you are using Hyperion Planning, you may also concentrate on aspects specific to the Planning interface like "How long does it take for forms to refresh?"

Administrators focus on batch times. How long does the nightly or monthly load process take? How long do backups and recovery take?

When you tune your Essbase databases, you will have to balance ALL of these factors. Hey, it isn't Rocket Science, it's Essbase!

Richard (Rick) Sawa has worked for Oracle-Hyperion for almost 9 years, starting back in 1998. He is currently working out of Columbus, Ohio as a Senior Technical Response Specialist within Oracle's Advanced Customer Support group. Formerly a Technology Development Manager to IBM, he was a key contributor to the IBM Redbook DB2 OLAP Server Theory and Practice (April 2001) as well as a contributor to the Michael L. Gonzales' IBM Data Warehousing, Wiley Publishing Incorporated, 2003. With approximately 19 years experience, Rick recently ('05-'06) worked for Informatica Corporation, and has pre-Hyperion experience as an independent BI consultant.

Appendix D:
Build Analytic Dimensions

Our last guest author put together a great white paper on building analytic dimensions in multi-dimensional databases. We wanted to share this whitepaper with you, showing new ways to expand your Essbase database design. Thank you Gary Crisci, Oracle ACE, for contributing this content. We now have two honorary wolverines.

- Tracy McMullen and Edward Roske

The use of an Analytic dimension in a multi-dimensional database is a design technique developers can use to enhance the analytic capabilities of their data model. In this appendix we will discuss what an analytic dimension is and how it can be leveraged with the MDX query language to provide end users powerful, built-in, analytic calculations, without adding additional overhead to the database. We will show some examples of analytic dimensions and some of the MDX code used to drive the calculations, including examples of scaling, time functionality (period to date and time balancing), commonly used statistics (Avg, Max, Min, etc.), and a new way to look at calculating some key performance indicators.

WHAT IS AN ANALYTIC DIMENSION?

An analytic dimension is a dimension added to a data model with one default stored member. All other members in the outline are calculated members, or label only members that are only used to help group related calculated members. Generally, the analytic dimension is not related to the subject data in the model. To this end, you will find there are some general categories for analytic dimensions and you will be able to reuse the same code in multiple models.

One particular benefit of an analytic dimension is the fact it adds almost no additional overhead to your existing database. This is due to the fact it only has one stored member. This particular point was critically important in block storage models. In aggregate storage models, this is less of a concern since ASO models support databases with many more dimensions than a BSO database could. Another benefit is the way an analytic dimension allows you to leverage one formula across a broad range of members within the database, limiting the number of calculated members in your database. You can literally replace hundreds or thousands of individual calculated members with one single calculated member in an analytic dimension.

While you can create an analytic dimension for many different reasons, there tends to be some general categories. As mentioned previously, you can have an analytic dimension that scales values, performs time functionality calculations like period to date and time balancing, or to drive a number of KPI's or statistical calculations. Scaling is a simple use of an analytic dimension and a good place to start understanding how they work.

Business case

Many end users of Essbase leverage Microsoft Excel to retrieve data from the database. One common issue with Excel is how to scale values when formatting reports. Reporting tools like Financial Reports and Web Analysis have scaling features built in. With Excel, it's a little tricky since there is no default-scaling feature. Power Excel users know how to use custom formatting functions in Excel to scale values, but this requires the user to go through the report an apply formatting on a per cell basis. If a user then decides to pivot or drill to more detail, some of the formatting could be lost. This also requires the end user to identify values that should not be scaled and format them differently, for instance, you might scale revenue values to thousands or millions, but you would not want to scale headcount.

One approach to solving this issue is to scale the values dynamically within Essbase, allowing users to retrieve scaled values into their spreadsheet(s). A common approach developers have used is to scale within an existing dimension, often the scenario dimension. In these models you would have a member [Actual] and then a calculated member [Actual 000's]. If you wanted millions then you would also have [Actual M's]. You would then repeat this for Budget, Forecast, and any of the other scenarios you have. This approach is undesirable for a developer because it requires that many members be created, each with a similar formula. From an end user perspective, this is also less desirable because the end user is now required to search through many members to find the one they need.

An alternative approach is to use an analytic dimension. Instead of adding multiple members to an existing dimension, the designer would add a new dimension to the model [Scale] and have one stored default member [whole_units]. All data values are loaded to [whole_units]. The developer can then add members like [in_Thousands] and [in_Millions] with member formulas to calculate the scaled values. End users simply select the scale member in their page heading and any values returned from any dimension combination will be scaled properly. Refer to figure 1.3.

CREATING AN ANALYTIC DIMENSION

Creating the analytic dimension is a simple process. Figure 1.1 shows an example of aggregate storage outline without any analytic dimensions. Figure 1.2 shows the same outline with a [Scale] dimension added to it

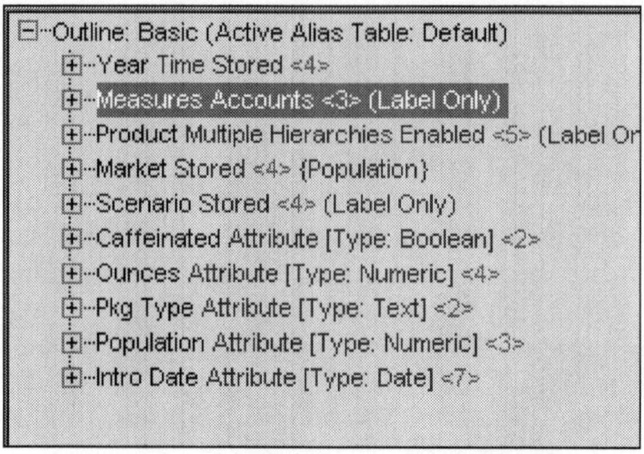

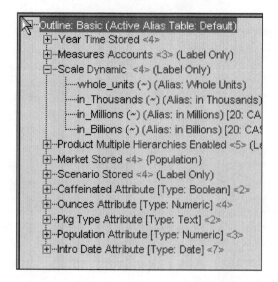

Figure 1.1

Figure 1.2

Take note the analytic dimension, in this case, the [Scale] dimension, is a Dynamic hierarchy, which allows the developer to add member formulas and set the members to non-consolidating (~).

For these members, the MDX formulas are simple.

```
[in_Thousands] = [Scale].[whole_units] / 1000
[in_Millions] = [Scale].[whole_units] / 1000000
```

In cases where you want to limit the scaling to certain members, you can tag the members in your outline with a UDA and modify the formula to this:

```
CASE WHEN IsUDA([Measures].CurrentMember, "NO_SCALE")
      THEN
      [Scale].[whole_units]
ELSE
      [Scale].[whole_units] / 1000
END
```

Figure 1.3 demonstrates the results of a retrieve.

	A	B	C	D	E
1		Year	Actual	East	Product
2		Whole Units	in Thousands		
3	Sales	27,740	28		
4	COGS	9,322	9		
5	Margin	18,418	18		
6	Total Expenses	5,762	6		
7	Profit	12,656	13		

Figure 1.3

TIME FUNCTIONALITY

Another use for analytic dimensions revolves around the need to perform time-based calculations within the data model. Period to date calculations are required in most models with a time dimension. In block storage databases, this was achieved with dynamic time series. At this time, ASO models do not provide native period to date functionality.

Another time-based issue faced in OLAP models is how to handle members that do not aggregate over time. Figure 1.4 shows how [Opening Inventory] for Qtr 1 is an erroneous number. The correct value should be 28,929, the last known inventory balance for the quarter.

	A	B	C	D	E
1		Actual	Whole Units	Market	Colas
2		Opening Inventory			
3	Jan	29,448			
4	Feb	29,124			
5	Mar	28,929			
6	Qtr1	87,501			

Figure 1.4

In BSO models, this was handled using the Time balancing feature. In ASO models, time balancing is first supported in v9.3.1. However, due to performance tuning and optimization techniques that are beyond the scope of this paper and certain other database design features like alternate roll-ups in the time dimension, which can interfere with ASO time-balancing functionality, there may be times when it is still necessary to calculate time balancing via MDX formulas.

Period to date

One approach to creating period to date functionality is to use alternate rollups. Figure 1.5 demonstrates an example of this method.

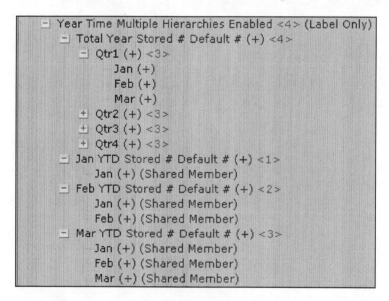

```
─ Year Time Multiple Hierarchies Enabled <4> (Label Only)
    ─ Total Year Stored # Default # (+) <4>
        ─ Qtr1 (+) <3>
              Jan (+)
              Feb (+)
              Mar (+)
        ± Qtr2 (+) <3>
        ± Qtr3 (+) <3>
        ± Qtr4 (+) <3>
    ─ Jan YTD Stored # Default # (+) <1>
          Jan (+) (Shared Member)
    ─ Feb YTD Stored # Default # (+) <2>
          Jan (+) (Shared Member)
          Feb (+) (Shared Member)
    ─ Mar YTD Stored # Default # (+) <3>
          Jan (+) (Shared Member)
          Feb (+) (Shared Member)
          Mar (+) (Shared Member)
```

Figure 1.5

A similar approach might involve using an MDX formula for a member.

```
[Mar YTD] = [Jan] + [Feb] + [Mar]
```

While either of these methods works, it again involves the need to create many extra members with either formulas or shared member associations. In this case, we were only looking at a time dimension with twelve months resulting in twelve Year to Date members. If the users also wanted Quarter to Date members the developer would have to create another twelve members. Now let's assume our model goes down to the daily level and the end users wanted Year to Date, Quarter to Date, and Month to Date functionality. You would literally need hundreds of members to drive each calculation and finding those members would be a burdensome experience for the end users. Clearly, in this example, an Analytic dimension is a more feasible solution.

Similar to the Scale dimension, the developer would add a new [View] dimension to the model as depicted in figure 1.6.

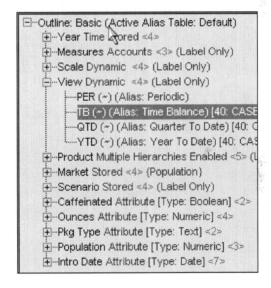

Figure 1.6

The new [View] dimension has four members. The first member is the default-stored member [Per] (alias: Periodic). The calculated members are [TB] (alias: Time Balance), [QTD] (alias: Quarter to Date), and [YTD] (alias: Year to Date).

The MDX formulas for QTD and YTD are fairly simple.

```
[QTD]  = SUM( PeriodsToDate( [Year].Generations(2),
        [Year].CurrentMember ), [View].[Per] )
[YTD]  = SUM( PeriodsToDate( [Year].Generations(1),
        [Year].CurrentMember ), [View].[Per] )
```

Figure 1.7 demonstrates the calculated values

	A	B	C	D	E	F
1		Sales	Actual	Scale	Product	Market
2		Periodic	Quarter To Date	Year To Date		
3	Jan	31,538	31,538	31,538		
4	Feb	32,069	63,607	63,607		
5	Mar	32,213	95,820	95,820		
6	Qtr1	95,820	95,820	95,820		
7	Apr	32,917	32,917	128,737		
8	May	33,674	66,591	162,411		
9	Jun	35,088	101,679	197,499		
10	Qtr2	101,679	101,679	197,499		
11	Qtr3	72,142	72,142	269,641		
12	Qtr4	-	-	269,641		
13	Year	269,641	-	269,641		

Figure 1.7

The calculation for Time Balancing is a bit more complicated and you will see once we add Time Balancing to the model, it also impacts our [QTD] and [YTD] formulas.

Time Balancing

As demonstrated in figure 1.4, there are cases when you do not want members to add over time. The solution to this problem is called time balancing. When there are time balancing members in an analytic model, you have to consider the results you desire. Primarily you need to think about how you want to handle missing or zero values. You also need to decide if you want to time balance based on the first or earliest member or on the last or latest member that you have values. Another option is to average over time. For purposes of this paper we will not go into all the possible variations, rather we will focus on the most common requests.

Most often when utilizing time balancing, it is to do what is known as time balance last. Referring back to figure 1.4, time balance last would result in Qtr1 value as 28,929 or the last value for the quarter. To calculate this value is not too difficult. The MDX would look like this:

```
[TB] = CASE WHEN IsUDA([Measures].CurrentMember,
     "TB_Last") THEN
IIF(IsLeaf([Year].CurrentMember), [View].[Per],
     (ClosingPeriod ([Year].Levels(0),
     [Year].CurrentMember), [View].[Per])
                          ELSE [View].[Per] END
```

Figure 1.8 shows the results.

	A	B	C	D	E	F
1		Time Balance	Colas	Market	Actual	Whole Units
2		Opening Inventory				
3	Jan	29,448				
4	Feb	29,124				
5	Mar	28,929				
6	Qtr1	28,929				

Figure 1.8

You can see the value for Qtr1 is now 28,929.

Where it gets more complicated is when you have to deal with time periods that do not have any data. Figure 1.9 shows there is no data for Sep therefore, Qtr3 is null. This might be acceptable based on end user requirements, but in some cases, users will require that Qtr3, reflect the Aug (last known) value.

	A	B	C	D	E	F
1		Time Balance	Colas	Market	Actual	Whole Units
2		Opening Inventory				
3	Jul	36,461				
4	Aug	36,267				
5	Sep	-				
6	Qtr3					

Figure 1.9

In order to work around this, you have to write your code to cycle through the time dimension and search for the last member with a non-missing value. There are a number of pitfalls you have to code for when doing this. If you search across the time dimension and get to the beginning of the dimension without encountering a value, you will get an error. To avoid these errors, you have to add conditional testing to your code to handle these situations. Ultimately, the finalized code looks like this:

```
[TB] =
CASE WHEN IsUDA([Measures].CurrentMember, "TB_Last") THEN
IIF(
  IsLeaf([Year].CurrentMember),
  [View].[Per],
  IIF (
    NonEmptyCount (
      [Year].CurrentMember.Children,
      [View].[Per]
    ) > 0,
    (
      [View].[Per],
      Tail (
        Filter (
                          Leaves([Year].CurrentMember), Not
      IsEmpty ([View].[Per])
        )
      ).Item(0).Item(0)
    ),
    MISSING
  )
)
ELSE
[View].[Per]
END
```

Figure 1.10 shows the correct results.

	A	B	C	D	E	F
1		Time Balance	Colas	Market	Actual	Whole Units
2		Opening Inventory				
3	Jan	29,448				
4	Feb	29,124				
5	Mar	28,929				
6	Qtr1	28,929				
7	Apr	29,860				
8	May	31,728				
9	Jun	34,483				
10	Qtr2	34,483				
11	Jul	36,461				
12	Aug	36,267				
13	Sep	-				
14	Qtr3	36,267				
15	Oct	-				
16	Nov	-				
17	Dec	-				
18	Qtr4	-				
19	Year	36,267				

Figure 1.10

Now that we have the time balance calculation working, we need to go back and update our QTD and YTD formulas to handle accounts that are tagged as time balance.

```
[QTD]
CASE WHEN IsUDA([Measures].CurrentMember, "TB_Last") THEN
IIF(
  IsLeaf([Year].CurrentMember),
  [View].[Per],
  IIF (
    NonEmptyCount (
      [Year].CurrentMember.Children,
      [View].[Per]
    ) > 0,
    (
      [View].[Per],
      Tail (
        Filter (
                            Leaves([Year].CurrentMember), Not
      IsEmpty ([View].[Per])
        )
      ).Item(0).Item(0)
    ),
    MISSING
  )
)
ELSE SUM(PeriodsToDate([Year].Generations(1),
      [Year].CurrentMember), [View].[Per] ) END
```

```
[YTD]
CASE WHEN IsUDA([Measures].CurrentMember, "TB_Last") THEN
IIF(
  IsLeaf([Year].CurrentMember),
  [View].[Per],
  IIF (
    NonEmptyCount (
      [Year].CurrentMember.Children,
      [View].[Per]
    ) > 0,
    (
      [View].[Per],
      Tail (
        Filter (
                          Leaves([Year].CurrentMember), Not
        IsEmpty ([View].[Per])
        )
      ).Item(0).Item(0)
    ),
    MISSING
  )
)
ELSE SUM(PeriodsToDate([Year].Generations(1),
         [Year].CurrentMember), [View].[Per] ) END
```

Figure 1.11 shows the full retrieve with correct values. Take note however that Periodic values for Opening Inventory will always be inaccurate because Periodic is the stored value. Users need to be properly trained on how to pull the correct values in the analytic dimensions. Thanks to George Spofford for his help on the Time Balance piece of code.

	A	B	C	D	E	F	G	H	I
1			Colas	Market	Actual	Whole Units	Metrics	Analytics	
2			Sales				Opening Inventory		
3		Periodic	Time Balance	Quarter To Date	Year To Date	Periodic	Time Balance	Quarter To Date	Year To Date
4	Jan	8,314	8,314	8,314	8,314	29,448	29,448	29,448	29,448
5	Feb	8,327	8,327	16,641	16,641	29,124	29,124	29,124	29,124
6	Mar	8,407	8,407	25,048	25,048	28,929	28,929	28,929	28,929
7	Qtr1	25,048	25,048	25,048	25,048	28,929	28,929	28,929	28,929
8	Apr	8,685	8,685	8,685	33,733	29,860	29,860	29,860	29,860
9	May	8,945	8,945	17,630	42,678	31,728	31,728	31,728	31,728
10	Jun	9,557	9,557	27,187	52,235	34,483	34,483	34,483	34,483
11	Qtr2	27,187	27,187	27,187	52,235	34,483	34,483	34,483	34,483
12	Jul	9,913	9,913	9,913	62,148	36,461	36,461	36,461	36,461
13	Aug	9,787	9,787	19,700	71,935	36,267	36,267	36,267	36,267
14	Sep	-	-	19,700	71,935		-	-	-
15	Qtr3	19,700	19,700	19,700	71,935	36,267	36,267	36,267	36,267
16	Oct	-	-	-	71,935		-	-	-
17	Nov	-	-	-	71,935		-	-	-
18	Dec	-	-	-	71,935		-	-	-
19	Qtr4	-	-	-	71,935		-	-	-
20	Year	71,935	71,935	-	71,935	36,267	36,267	36,267	

Figure 1.11

STATISTICAL ACCOUNTS

Another useful way to utilize analytic dimensions is to create built in statistical accounts to your model. Figure 1.12 shows what an analytic dimension with statistical calculations might look like.

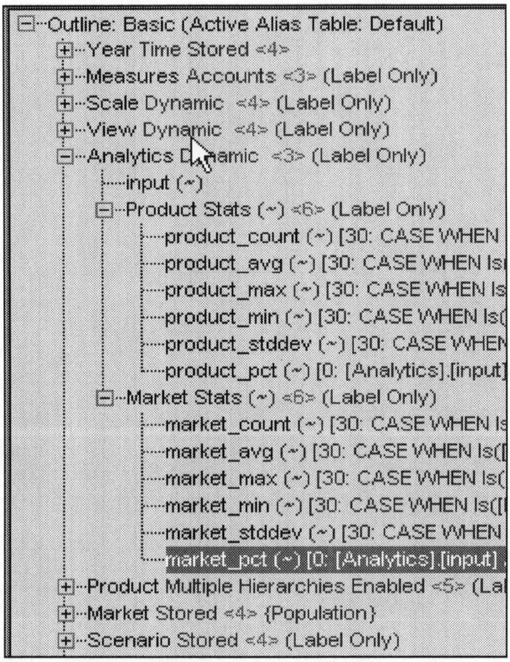

Figure 1.12

The formulas for these members would look like this:

```
[product_count] = CASE WHEN Is([Product].CurrentMember,
       [Total Product]) THEN
              NonEmptyCount(Leaves([Product]),
       [Analytics].[input])
       END

[product_avg] = CASE WHEN Is([Product].CurrentMember,
       [Total Product]) THEN
              Avg(Leaves([Product]), [Analytics].[input])
       END

[product_max] = CASE WHEN Is([Product].CurrentMember,
       [Total Product]) THEN
              Max(Leaves([Product]), [Analytics].[input])
       END

[product_min] = CASE WHEN Is([Product].CurrentMember,
       [Total Product]) THEN
              Min(Leaves([Product]), [Analytics].[input])
       END

[product_stddev] = CASE WHEN Is([Product].CurrentMember,
       [Total Product]) THEN
              Stddev(Leaves([Product]), Analytics].[input])
       END

[product_pct] = [Analytics].[input] / ([Product],
       [Analytics].[input])
```

(The formulas for Market would be the same, just substitute Product with Market.)

Figure 1.13 shows some of the results of these calculations.

	A	B	C	D	E	F	G
1			Sales	Product	Actual	Year	Scale
2		input	product_count	product_avg	product_max	product_min	product_stddev
3	East	58,921	12	4,910	15,888	839	4,267
4	West	89,420	12	7,452	10,335	3,033	2,444
5	South	33,804	7	4,829	6,836	3,393	1,082
6	Central	87,496	11	7,954	11,840	1,486	3,497
7	Market	269,641	13	20,742	42,606	7,554	10,323

Figure 1.13

Looking at the calculation results, an analyst could quickly determine that for the East region total sales was $58,921. The company currently sells 12 different products in the East region, the average sale for each product is 4,910, the maximum sales for a product in the East was 15,888, and the minimum was 839.

Figure 1.14 demonstrates the percentage of the total sales each product made up in the East region.

	A	B	C	D	E	F	G
1		East	Periodic	Sales	Actual	Year	Scale
2		input	product_pct				
3	Cola	15,888	27.0%				
4	Diet Cola	2,055	3.5%				
5	Caffeine Free Cola	987	1.7%				
6	Colas	18,930	32.1%				
7	Old Fashioned	5,511	9.4%				
8	Diet Root Beer	2,539	4.3%				
9	Birch Beer	7,554	12.8%				
10	Root Beer	15,604	26.5%				
11	Dark Cream	8,941	15.2%				
12	Vanilla Cream	4,018	6.8%				
13	Diet Cream	839	1.4%				
14	Cream Soda	13,798	23.4%				
15	Grape	4,704	8.0%				
16	Orange	1,987	3.4%				
17	Strawberry	3,898	6.6%				
18	Fruit Soda	10,589	18.0%				
19	Total Product	58,921	100.0%				

Figure 1.14

METRICS

The last analytic dimension we will discuss looks at how metrics and key performance indicators (KPI's) are calculated.

Almost all analytic models have calculated members beyond the basic roll up that consolidates the outline based on hierarchical relationships. In a financial application these might be members like EBIT, EBIT % , Margin %, etc. In a human resources application you might have full time equivalent or utilization calculations. Using the finance model as an example, a calculation like Margin % is simple to implement. You would simply create the member [Margin %] as a member of the Measures dimension with the formula:

```
[Margin %] = [Margin] / [Sales]
```

This is perfectly acceptable and the common practice among most developers. The problem with this approach is if you create [Margin %] chances are, someone is going to ask you to give them [EBIT %]. Then someone will probably ask for [COGS %] and while we're at it, we should probably create [G&A %] and [Selling %] and [SG&A %] and if we are going to create those, then we better create [Travel %], [Entertainment %], [T&E %], etc, etc, etc. You can see how this can quickly turn into a lot of work and many different calculations with different formulas. If you have a chart of accounts with thousands of members, users can come up with many requests, and those are for the individuals that ask. Many will not find the metric they are looking for and instead they will calculate it themselves in their spreadsheets. A better design approach might be to create a single member and write one formula to calculate every member in the chart of accounts as a percentage of Sales. Figure 1.15 demonstrates how we can do this with an analytic dimension. Figure 1.16 shows the results.

```
[% of Sales] = [Metrics].[Loaded] / [Measures].[Sales]
```

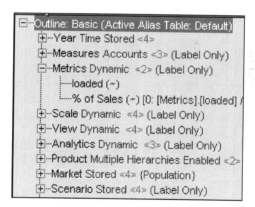

Figure 1.15

	A	B	C	D	E	F	G	H
1		Actual	Year	Scale	View	Analytics	Product	Market
2		loaded	% of Sales					
3	Sales	269,641	100.0%					
4	COGS	120,633	44.7%					
5	Margin	149,008	55.3%					
6	Marketing	44,586	16.5%					
7	Payroll	32,523	12.1%					
8	Misc	666	0.2%					
9	Total Expenses	77,775	28.8%					
10	Profit	71,233	26.4%					

Figure 1.16

The example demonstrates that with a single member we were able to provide end users with many reportable metrics. This order of magnitude demonstrates why analytic dimensions are a powerful design technique for developers to leverage.

CONSIDERATIONS FOR ANALYTIC DIMENSIONS

There are a number of things to consider when adding analytic dimensions to your data model. The first is that they can be slightly complicated and less intuitive to end users, especially those with limited multi-dimensional experience. Novice or casual users will generally not utilize analytic dimensions beyond scaling or perhaps time functionality. Statistical and metrics are something a power user would generally utilize.

Another very important thing to consider when using analytic dimensions is solve order. Solve order is something we did not get into, but it is crucial when implementing analytic dimensions to ensure calculation accuracy. Solve order, when tuned properly, will also yield much better performance from an MDX calculation. The general rule with solve order is to test, test, test.

MDX formulas can range from the simple, such as scaling a value, to extremely complex, as demonstrated with time balancing. It is a robust language, which when used properly can leverage advanced analytic results. When you use MDX with analytic dimensions you can increase the scope of your calculations and build more efficient models.

In summary, analytic dimensions are yet another design technique to augment analytic models. Test with new and existing models to see how you can leverage this methodology in your environment.

Gary Crisci is a Business Intelligence Professional with over thirteen years of finance experience, specializing in Oracle's Hyperion Performance Management software. He has comprehensive financial systems implementation experience with Oracle's Hyperion Business Intelligence (BI) Platform and Enterprise Performance Management (EPM) software; including Oracle Essbase Analytic Server, Hyperion

Planning, Hyperion Financial Management, Hyperion Analyzer/Web Analysis, Essbase Integration Server, Essbase Excel Add-in, Hyperion SmartView, and Hyperion Financial Reports.   Gary is one of only six individuals recognized worldwide as an Oracle Ace in the Oracle Business Intelligence space, specializing in Hyperion products.   Currently Gary is a Vice President for Financial Systems Development at a large international bank holding company.

The End. Really? Yes, go forth, Essbase *master* administrators. Find the meaning of life, show us the way to world peace, revolutionize your business with Essbase, and be sure to tell all your friends that you learned the path to enlightenment from this book.

INDEX

NO WOLVERINES WERE HARMED DURING THE MAKING OF THIS BOOK.

Made in the USA
Lexington, KY
18 July 2014